The Psychology of Risk

D0086828

Risk surrounds and envelops us. Without understanding it, we risk everything and without capitalising on it, we gain nothing. This accessible new book from Glynis M. Breakwell comprehensively explores the psychology of risk, examining how individuals think, feel and act, as well as considering the institutional and societal assessments, rhetorics and reactions about risk. Featuring chapters on all the major issues in the psychology of risk including risk assessment, hazard perception, decision-making, risk and crisis management, risk and emotion, risk communication, safety cultures, the social amplification and social representation of risk, and mechanisms for changing risk responses, Breakwell uses illustrations and examples to bring to life the significance of her research findings. She provides an innovative overview of current knowledge on the subject but also suggests that there are many fascinating questions still to be answered.

GLYNIS M. BREAKWELL is Vice Chancellor of the University of Bath. She is a psychologist specialising in leadership, identity processes, risk communication and military cultures, and her research has resulted in her acting as an advisor to a number of government departments including the Department of Health, the Department of Trade and Industry and the Ministry of Defence. Professor Breakwell has published over twenty books and hundreds of journal articles.

The Psychology of Risk

Glynis M. Breakwell

CAMBRIDGE
UNIVERSITY PRESS

CAMBRIDGE UNIVERSITY PRESS
Cambridge, New York, Melbourne, Madrid, Cape Town, Singapore, São Paulo

Cambridge University Press
The Edinburgh Building, Cambridge CB2 8RU, UK

Published in the United States of America by Cambridge University Press, New York

www.cambridge.org
Information on this title: www.cambridge.org/9780521004459

First published 2007

Printed in the United Kingdom at the University Press, Cambridge

A catalogue record for this publication is available from the British Library

ISBN 978-0-521-80296-3 hardback
ISBN 978-0-521-00445-9 paperback

This book is dedicated with love and respect to my father, Harold Breakwell, whose approach to risk is unpredictable and inspirational.

Contents

Boxes

Figures

Preface

Risk surrounds us, it envelops us. It is our personal and societal preoccupation and our salvation. Without understanding it we risk everything, and without capitalising upon it we gain nothing. This book comprehensively explores the psychology of risk. This entails examining how individuals think, feel and act about risks but, as importantly, it includes analysis of institutional and societal assessments, rhetorics and reactions to risks.

The object of this book is to provide a detailed overview of the empirical research that has been conducted on the psychology of risk and to piece together the theoretical and practical implications of the data. It is not representing a single theoretical model or standpoint. It is designed to be critically inclusive – that is, to offer a review of the full variety of explanations that have been developed and to present their respective pros and cons. There is no theoretical monolith that can currently encompass all of the interesting questions concerning the psychology of risk. Perhaps there never will be since risk and its corollaries are so multi-faceted. However, there are many medium-range explanatory models and these are all considered here.

While no single analytical model is privileged in the book, it does have a metatheoretical perspective that underlies it. This is an approach to the development of psychological theory which is described in Chapter 1. It essentially calls for an approach to the creation of explanatory models in psychology that provides an integrated analysis at a variety of levels from the individual (in terms of cognition, emotion and action) through the interpersonal and institutional (in terms of structural and processual determinants of influence and control) to the societal (through physical and ideological contexts). This approach to the evaluation and development of psychological theory informs the evaluation offered of each of the medium-range models presented in the account of the psychology of risk contained in the book.

The book is organised into chapters that reflect major issues in the psychology of risk: hazard perception, individual and group differences in risk perceptions, decision-making about risks, risk and emotion, risk communication, errors, accidents and emergencies, risk and complex organisations, the social amplification and social representation of risk and, finally, changing risk responses. In some senses, the presentation is linear and cumulative (each chapter builds upon its predecessors) in that, for instance, it is easier to understand issues concerning decision-making regarding risk if the groundwork on hazard perception is established. However, each chapter should provide a coherent analysis of its topic and be capable of standing alone, and it is possible to dip into the book selectively for specific topics. This is relevant because the book should be useful to different audiences, ranging from the student who wishes to understand the latest methods of risk analysis to the professional who wishes to know how better to manage risk or communicate about it. In order to help readers navigate selectively through the book, each chapter has a succinct preview that summarises its contents. Taken together, these previews offer a conceptual map of the book. Since models of the psychology of risk can sometimes be highly complex and formulated in abstract ways, the book uses illustrations and examples wherever possible to bring to life the significance of the research findings. Boxed information is presented to highlight important or interesting aspects of the arguments and illustrations.

Examination of the research on the psychology of risk proves that we are still very far from understanding all that we need to know about this topic. This book presents much of what is known. In doing so, it becomes only too clear that there are many fascinating questions still to be answered.

Acknowledgements

Over the years, I have had many co-researchers who have contributed massively to my understanding of the psychology of risk and I would like to thank them all. Most particularly, I thank Chris Fife-Schaw for his collaboration in the early studies that were transformed by his analytical rigour and organisational abilities. However, I owe my greatest debt of thanks to Julie Barnett, my long-term partner in risk research. Her ability to ask the questions that make you think more deeply is unparalleled.

I would also like to thank Dr Nicky Kemp for her diligence and kindness in the final stages of the preparation of the manuscript.

Last and most, I want to acknowledge the enormous support I have, always and in everything, from Colin Rowett.

1 A psychological framework for analysing risk

Chapter preview

This chapter introduces the definitions of hazard and risk, detailing how they are often confused. It goes on the describe the great debates of the last twenty years between science and social science that have called into question the existence of objective risk. The perspectives of Douglas, Giddens and Beck are briefly outlined. The role of fundamental uncertainty in undermining scientific bases for estimating risk and the difficulties of the precautionary principle as a regulatory tool are considered. The basis for producing a psychological framework for analysing risk is presented. This is a framework which requires data at levels of analysis that encompass all from the intra-psychic to the societal. A series of key questions that an integrative social psychological analysis of risk must address is listed.

1 Risk and hazard

Risk has been the arena for some of the most interesting debates in the social sciences of recent years. In effect, risk has been released from the sole ownership of the physical sciences, where it was treated as something that should be assessed and estimated quantitatively – if only the right tools could be developed. Instead, it has been captured by philosophers, political scientists, sociologists, geographers, social anthropologists and psychologists, who have all brought their own critical lenses to the conceptualisation of risk. However, the prisoner is not reconciled to its fate, ever and again manifesting in some new guise to evade captivity.

It is the fact that risk is simultaneously capable of very narrow, if contested, definition and yet is substantiated in myriad forms that makes it so fascinating. It may be boring to start with definitions but we need to know what we are talking about, we need to share an understanding of what we are talking about and, without definitions, words, especially in this domain of risk, can mean very different things to different people. Commonly, risk is defined in terms of two dimensions – usually simultaneously, though not necessarily. The first concerns probabilities. The second concerns effects. Risk is the probability of a particular adverse event occurring during a stated period of time. In terms of probability, risk refers to the likelihood of some specific negative event (delineated as closely as possible in terms of amount, intensity and duration) as a result of an exposure to a hazard. A hazard is defined as anything (animate or inanimate; natural or human product) that could lead to harm (to people or their environment). In terms of effects, risk refers to the extent of the detriment (the numerical estimate of the harm) associated with the adverse event. Risk used to refer to detriment focuses upon the severity or scale of consequences. So, for instance, it can be measured in number of fatalities expected to be associated with the event, the loss of property that would occur or the length of time it would persist.

It is clear that these two dimensions of risk (probability and effect) are conceptually quite distinct. There is no reason to muddy the distinction. It would be sensible to use two different words to refer to these two dimensions. However, in fact, custom over many years has resulted in risk being used to refer to both. It can result in confusion and it is often only through looking at the context in which the word 'risk' is used that it is possible to divine which dimension is actually involved. A very simple sentence may serve to illustrate the ambiguity of the word 'risk' and the significance of its context in determining its interpretation. Take the phrase 'There is a risk of rain today'. It could be associated with an interpretation of how likely the occurrence of rain was, or it could be associated with the negative consequences of rain today (for example, flooding or, perhaps worse still, the abandonment of a cricket match).

In practice, the two dimensions (probability and effect) tend to be examined in tandem. People do not wish simply to know how likely an adverse outcome is; they also want to know how bad that outcome will be. To be influential in directing decisions, a statement of risk optimally tells about both probability and effect.

This set of definitions clearly articulate the difference between risks and hazards. However, common parlance does not. A hazard is often referred to as a risk. So, for instance, we sometimes talk about smoking as a risk or drinking alcohol as a risk. Smoking is a hazard. Consuming alcohol is a hazard. The extent and the probability of either having negative consequences – that is, the risk associated with each – can be estimated.

2   The great debates

Since a hazard is defined as anything with the capacity to do harm and risk is defined as an amalgam of the likelihood and extent of harm, the great debates have focused upon who determines what is deemed harmful.

There has been a challenge to the so-called commonsense approach that harm is self-evident or a manifest quality of an outcome. It is argued that harm is not objective; it essentially entails an evaluation of an outcome and a conclusion that the outcome is unacceptable. At one extreme, there might be total consensus that an outcome was harmful. For instance, a landslide that deluges a village and kills almost all inhabitants would be likely to be consensually accepted as harmful. At the other extreme, there might be significant disagreement about whether an outcome was harmful. For instance, nuclear power generation arouses quite diverse estimates of harm. Even where there is relative consensus in the perception of harm, there will be dissenters. For instance, the result of terrorist bombing may be regarded as harmful by the majority, but not by all. The assessment of harm depends upon the extent to which the outcome is acceptable (or even desirable) and this will vary between individuals and across societal institutions, according minimally to who is its victim and who is its beneficiary.

The very existence of harm, and subsequently any estimate of harm, is thus deemed a product of social analysis and negotiation. Consequently, since they are both defined in relation to harm, the existence of a hazard and the estimate of risk is also a product of social analysis and negotiation. None of this requires us to dismiss the physical reality of the outcome itself (i.e. the dead bodies beneath the mud, the nuclear waste or energy production, or the bomb-riven mangled Underground stations). It simply requires us to recognise that the meaning attributed to these physical manifestations is achieved through a complex process of interpretation that is both social and psychological, occurring within and between institutions and within and between individuals.

The social science concern with this social construction of harm, hazard and risk has sensitised us to the way some institutions, some organisations and, indeed, some individuals have greater sway over the process than others.

In retrospect, the impact of the social science debate about risk over the last two decades is difficult to gauge. It is hard to step back in time and describe the initial effects of critiques that were published just over twenty years ago when they have so transformed the current platform for risk analysis. Propositions concerning the social construction of risk, that now seem obvious, were originally outrageously radical, challenges to the power of the scientific establishment to define and remedy hazards. Douglas (1986) argued that public perceptions of risk were not simply the sum of individual reactions to specific events but were shaped by social and cultural influences. She identified that all institutions are not equal in shaping risk perception or acceptance and challenged whether risk should be assessed without consideration of issues of morality and social justice. Highlighting the inadequacies of cognitive psychological models of risk estimation and choice, she called for the broader analysis of the impact of culture. From the vantage point of the twenty-first century, it seems almost incredible that it was necessary to demand this – why was it not already being done? The question is rhetorical, of course. In some senses it was being done – perhaps not as Douglas would have wished it done, but done nonetheless. Certainly, the psychologists involved in the early empirical work on risk did not ignore or reject the role of social factors in determining individual perception or judgement. However, their tools of analysis were not those used by philosophers, sociologists or social anthropologists. Their findings were centred on processes residing within individuals, not institutions. Their work was definitely not a form of social or political commentary and did not signal that the position of risk in societal discourse should be transformed.

Beck (1992) published *Risk Society* in German in 1986. He certainly did set out to shift the position of risk in societal discourse. The book has two interrelated theses: one concerns reflexive modernisation, the other the issue of risk. For Beck, modernisation is constituted of scientific and technological developments that create risks and hazards never before encountered; unlimited in time (affecting future generations) and space (spanning across national borders) and socially (impacting on many types of people). This is the 'risk society' where no one can be held accountable for its hazards, which are incalculable and beyond remediation or compensation. The way forward, according to Beck, was to promote reflexive modernisation; embodied in radicalisation and the rejection of the culture of scientism, together with its overblown and false claims. The passage from tradition to modernity has been supposed to instigate individualism and liberal democracy, based on enlightened self-interest. However, the postmodern critique already suggested that modernity itself imposes constraints through culture, particularly around the icon of science (and its cultural form – scientism). Scientism was said to impose identity upon social actors by demanding their identification with particular social institutions and their ideologies – notably their construction of risk but also their many other rationalisations for social control (for example, in the definition of insanity or appropriate sexual behaviour). Beck was arguing that reflexive modernity is the next phase in this development, where, through freedoms originating in the decline of the class structure and the renovation of hierarchies in the workplace, individuals can reflect upon and flexibly restructure the rules that they accept. The risk society is essentially an individualised society, structured around the distribution of ills (the harm hazards create); the fractures within it precipitate criticism of scientific orthodoxies and generate risk discourses that allow the status quo to be challenged. In parallel with Beck, but independently, Giddens (1990, 1991) examined the distinctive form reflexivity takes in modernity, particularly with respect to risk, trust and the creation of identity through managing one's biographical narrative. This work on the dynamics of risk discourses has served to highlight the conflicts that pervade this arena.

Capturing the definition of the hazard and its risk may be easier for technical or scientific experts, but their control is no longer complete. The social science analysis has exposed that these conflicts exist and demanded that they be given attention. More recently, Beck (2006) has extended his analysis. He now speaks of the 'world risk society', recognising that with globalisation come risks that are global. He argues that this state of global risk was unanticipated and the only possible reactions to risk that is experienced as omnipresent are denial, apathy or transformation. His interest is in transformation. Since 'risks exist in a permanent state of virtuality' – the moment they become real they cease being a risk and become a catastrophe – risks are events that are always threatening. The threat is open to transformation through social action and influence. Beck states that, since this transformation is a socially constructed phenomenon, some people will have greater capacity to influence it than others. He acknowledges that not all actors benefit from the reflexivity of risk, only those with real scope to define their own risks. The inequalities in the control of definitions allow powerful actors to maximise risks for others and minimise risks for themselves. Definitional control may not inevitably determine physical exposure to harm but it can do so. For instance, a company that diminishes the risk defined to be associated with some industrial process, and consequently is allowed to put workers in danger, is not just engaged in semiotics – it is engaged in social and economic control.

Although Beck does not say this, it could be argued that the uncertainty that surrounds many global hazards heightens the certainty of definitional turf wars. This is not uncertainty that can be expressed in terms of probability estimates because it is founded upon a deeper problem: we do not know what we do not know. This is more than acknowledged ignorance or limits to information. It is an awareness that there may be something more to understand but we just do not know what. The anticipation of the inevitability of the unknown, and thus unexpected, is now recognised in risk discourses. It opens avenues for contesting risk definitions, for undermining definitions originating with authorities of one sort or another. For, if there are such uncertainties, how can any risk estimate be believed? Risk can become a component in the rhetoric of dissent, a tool of minorities for initiating change, in ways that mirror its use by power elites in directing economic and political decision-making.

The great debate initiated by the social sciences has had the effect of nourishing across broad swaths of society globally – not least through its involvement of and impact upon the mass media – an abiding scepticism about hazard and risk pronouncements made by authorities (whether scientific or otherwise). Equally importantly, together with many other political and economic developments, it has stimulated new orientations to risk management by those responsible. The acknowledgement of uncertainty and the recognition of other contested risk definitions have led to the introduction of the precautionary principle in hazard regulation and management.

Precaution requires that protection is introduced against a hazard as yet undefined but suspected. Doubt and fear are allowed a part in dictating regulatory action in such contexts. There is a perfectly good rationale for doing this because, when the possibility exists of disaster if action is not taken, precaution seems defensible. There are, of course, new debates about the appropriateness, extent and justification of precaution. Precaution has given ammunition to some conspiracy theorists because it is a rationale for intervention and regulation that knows no bounds. Even those charged with executing the precautionary principle sometimes claim that they do not understand how it should be applied (Wilson *et al.*, 2006).

It seems almost inevitable that the philosophy of precaution will come under increasing scrutiny. Our society is formed of hazards and we know them through the fact that we label them. Implicit in the process of labelling is the desire to avoid or the determination to control them. Precaution can be accused of denying us the opportunity to take advantage of what might be a worthwhile risk. Cries that precaution stifles innovation and blunts the competitive edge are easily imagined. The next rhetorical battlefield is likely to concern the limits of precaution and the resurrection of positive risk. Already, there are attempts to defend precaution (Hanekamp, 2006).

During these great debates over the last two decades that have at times challenged the very epistemological bases of scientific fact, the psychology of risk has often been a target of attack. It has been accused of being solely concerned with the individual's perceptions and of ignoring their origins in social processes. Yet it is notable that during this period psychologists, particularly social psychologists, have been working to produce a substantial body of empirical evidence not just about how individuals think, feel and behave about risks but also about the social factors that shape cognitions, affect and action. They have been at the forefront of research on the way hazards come into being through the errors and decisions of individuals, institutions and governments, and how they are managed successfully and unsuccessfully. The analysis of the role of groups and intergroup dynamics in the evolution of risks has been ongoing. The examination of communications processes, including those associated with the mass media, has been extensive. Processes of social amplification and social representation of risk have been studied. It seems that the research from the psychological perspective has been piecing together a rather complex model of risk. Far from being situated at the level of intra-psychic processes in the decontextualised individual, this is a truly social model. The old attacks on psychological analyses that speak as if psychology is only concerned with cognitions of individuals seem now completely redundant and anachronistic.

3   A social psychological framework for risk analysis

Breakwell (1994) proposed a generic framework for the development of social psychological theory. Figure 1.1 presents a version of that framework. It is not itself a theory or model; it is a framework that suggests what might be considered when building theory or explanatory models within social psychology. The model is not intended to encompass all of the constructs that might be needed in a specific social psychological analysis; rather it is intended to suggest what should minimally be considered for inclusion. Notably the lines have no arrowheads indicating the direction of influence. At the level of a generic framework for theorising, such specificity is not appropriate. In practice, in certain theoretical formulations the lines of influence will go one way; in others they will go in the opposite direction; and in some there will be mutual and multiple influence. The purpose of the theorist in each case would be to determine the nature of the rules or principles that govern the relationship between each of the constructs in the framework. This flexibility within the framework is important, because different theories will have the object which they ultimately wish to explain located at different places. For instance, for some, the object will be the prediction of individual action; for others, it will be the prediction of social representations (that is, shared understandings).

The elements within the framework are briefly explained in Box 1.1. It is clear that they are designed to span the spectrum of factors that interact from the intra-psychic individual level to the societal structural level. Moreover, they traverse the objective–constructionist dimension. This is a framework that directs theorists to be interested not just in structure but also in process. It demands a variety of levels of analysis or explanation to be adopted (Doise, 1982). These range from the physiological, through the

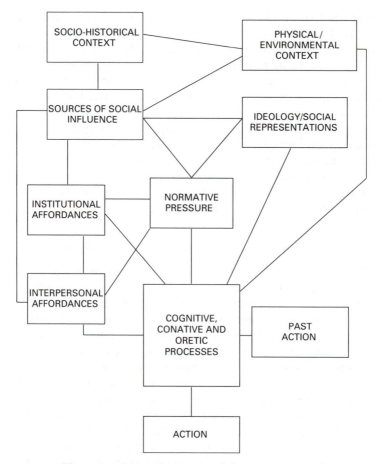

Figure 1.1 A generic framework for social psychological analysis

intra-psychic, into the interpersonal, and then on to the intra-group and intergroup, and beyond to the institutional and societal. It means that the methods that need to be used to elicit and analyse data will be diverse.

This framework offers a way to systematise the complex data that psychologists, and others, have collected concerning risk phenomena over recent years. To achieve an adequate social psychological theory of risk, risk researchers would need to have answered a series of key questions:

- What do individuals believe about hazards and risks
- How do individuals differ in their beliefs about hazards and risks – what personal and social factors predict these differences

---

Box 1.1 Elements in the analytic framework

Socio-historical context: reflects what has happened in the past that is relevant to object of analysis. Lyons (1996) has argued that this is a different order construct to the rest. Since the socio-historical context could be conceived of as nothing more than the sum of the movement of the other constructs through time, it could be signified in the framework by iterating the other boxes (presenting echoes of themselves diminishing in size to a vanishing point). Nevertheless, the socio-historical construct box is included here for diagrammatic clarity and also because it is a construct so frequently omitted by social psychology theories, which treat it as outside their remit. Consider the box present as at least a reminder. Of course, recent historical social psychology studies show how the socio-historical context is itself a product of active reconstruction driven by known social psychological processes. Such processes of social memory are increasingly a target for research in their own right and, again, make the presence of this box in the generic framework reasonable.

Physical/environmental context: reflects what is happening in the material universe. The line linking it to sources of influence and thence to ideology and social representations is meant to indicate that this physical reality takes on meaning through social construal and action.

Sources of social influence: reflects the wide array of social agents that may actively, both deliberately and unintentionally, influence events. This recognises the importance of structural differences in influence power. It acknowledges that sources of influence interact with each other in effecting an outcome.

Ideology/social representations: reflects systems of widespread or shared belief and values.

Normative pressure: reflects the processes and acts of communication that act as the channels of influence.

Institutional affordances: reflects the constraints and provisions, enacted in actions, offered by institutions relevant to the object of analysis. These will include the effects of intergroup relationships. They will include economic, legal, fiscal and religious facilitation and barriers.

Interpersonal affordances: reflects the constraints and provisions, enacted in actions, offered by other individuals relevant to the object of analysis. These include intra-group dynamics.

Past action: reflects the individual's past behaviour relevant to the object of analysis.

Box 1.1 (cont.)

Cognitive, conative and oretic processes: reflects the processes at the intra-psychic level that result in the thoughts, feelings and intentions of the individual relevant to the object of analysis. In conceiving of the intra-psychic processes in this tripartite way, the framework follows McDougall (who used the terms to refer respectively to thinking, emotion and will). In practice, this entails careful analysis of emotional states as they relate to decision-making and intention besides the more usual analyses of action-relevant schema (that is, information matrices) and goal-relevant evaluation (that is, the strength of purpose and its associated cost–benefits analysis). There is no assumption that these processes are necessarily rational or conscious.

Action: reflects the action of the individual relevant to the object of analysis. It should be noted that the individual's action can feed back into other elements in the framework. It is not deemed to be the ultimate outcome that the model seeks to explain.

- What factors, social and psychological, influence decision-making about hazards and risks at either the individual or institutional levels
- What role does affect or emotion play in individual reactions to hazards and risks
- How do actions with respect to hazards and risks reflect the beliefs, emotions or intentions of individuals
- How is risk communicated within the matrix of sources of social influence and prevailing interpersonal and institutional affordances – what normative pressures operate
- How does human action, at the levels of individuals or institutions, create hazards unintentionally and what socio-historical or physical-environmental factors influence the effects of such action
- How do institutions or complex organisations deal with hazards and risks
- What are the sequences of processes that transform a material object that has potentially harmful consequences into a socially recognised, if contested, hazard with its associated risk?

Interestingly, there are significant, empirically based, answers to these questions already – even though the researchers who have generated the data may not have formulated the questions in quite the same way. The next eight chapters of this book describe the evidence that is available and its interpretations.

Conclusion

Hazards and risks are socially constructed, though founded upon material objects. The debates that have surrounded hazard and risk over recent years have both stimulated and been enhanced by significant global societal changes in the tolerance and rhetorics of risk. Society now manifestly defines itself in terms of risk. The task of the psychological analysis of risk is to be comprehensive: to examine the processes of risk at not just the individual, but the institutional and societal levels. This is by no means an impossible goal, since there have been many studies that address the key questions it entails.

2 Hazard perception

Chapter preview

In Chapter 2 the distinction between risk assessment and risk perception is described, and the reasons why both should be understood are considered. In risk assessment, the relationship between risk estimation and risk evaluation is examined. The principles that underlie techniques for risk assessment are outlined and the way they are used in relation to different sorts of hazards are illustrated. It is emphasised that good risk assessment is dependent upon having good information about the hazard, its potential impacts, and the measures that could be used to control both the hazard and its effects. The chapter describes how risk can be expressed (for example, in terms of various measures of fatality, in terms of frequency of occurrence and in terms of tolerability). The psychometric paradigm for the analysis of risk perception is presented and the dimensions along which risks can be characterised are outlined. Research on the tolerability and acceptability of risk is described. The difficulties of comparing risks are explored in the context of methods used to determine the appropriateness of different regimes for allocating limited resources to remediate the hazards. The concept of synergistic risks is introduced. The various criticisms of the psychometric paradigm are summarised.

1 Distinguishing between risk assessment and risk perception

Complexities emerge when asking people to adopt a shared definition of risk, because in relation to many of the most important hazards there is great uncertainty about how risk can be assessed (the appropriateness and reliability of methods) and how it might be recorded (the language of risk, the measurements of risk). Risk assessment is something that we all do, a lot of the time. When we turn right on to a major road, as the driver of the vehicle we are assessing the risk of another car hitting ours before we join the stream of traffic. When we choose whether to go out on an autumn day without an umbrella, we are assessing the risk of rain. Everyday choices have risk assessment associated with them. It may not be something we do in a self-reflective manner. We may not be aware that we are doing it. It is unlikely to be something that we do systematically on the basis of detailed information. Even so, we do it.

Some of the most interesting social science research on risk explores these processes of risk assessment that people use habitually. Typically, however, risk assessment is the label used to refer to the systematic analysis of risk that is undertaken in formal studies or by professionals (for example, scientists, engineers, actuaries). What people without professional expertise in the area (often called 'lay people') do is not called risk assessment. It tends to be labelled in more subjective terms. Traditionally, it is called risk perception. See Box 2.1 for further details of the distinction and the importance of the distinction. We return to risk perception later in this chapter.

2   Approaches to risk assessment

Risk assessment can be subdivided into risk estimation and risk evaluation. Risk estimation entails the identification of possible outcomes of an adverse event, the estimation of their likely size and severity, and the estimation of the probability that these will occur if the adverse event does occur. It should be obvious from this that a second level of probability estimate has now been introduced. The first is the probability of the adverse event occurring at all. The second is the probability that the adverse event, once it has occurred, will have specific effects. Risk evaluation is even more complex. It is the process of identifying the significance or value of the hazard in the context of the risk estimate. It is an exercise in trading possible benefits off against possible costs. Since, in relation to most significant hazards, the estimates of benefits and costs are both open to challenge and may be intrinsically uncertain, risk evaluation is fascinating and surrounded by controversy. The way risk evaluation works is a theme – implicit and explicit – throughout this book.

In some disciplines, the need to engage in risk assessment in a comprehensive, consensual manner has resulted in more specialised definitions of risk and hazard. The existence of narrower definitions of risk or hazard means that conversations across discipline boundaries can be fraught with difficulty. An engineer might want to talk about hazard only in terms of age-related specific failure rate (for a piece of equipment). A psychologist might want to define hazard always with its subjective interpretation. This leads to quite different methods for estimating

---

Box 2.1 Risk assessment and risk perception

HOW DOES RISK ASSESSMENT DIFFER FROM
ANALYSIS OF RISK PERCEPTION?

Risk perception is used in the literature to refer to various types of
attitudes about risks and hazards and judgements about them.
Analysis of risk perception deals with explicitly subjective responses
to hazard and risk. Risk perception cannot be reduced to any simple
subjective correlate of an estimate of risk based on the product of
probability and consequences. Formal risk assessment attempts to
systematise the estimation and evaluation of risk such that subjectivity
is excluded as far as possible. It should be acknowledged that the
possibility of the complete exclusion of subjectivity, even in the most
rigorously controlled risk assessments, has been challenged by some
philosophers of science. Nevertheless, the distinction between the
objectives of risk-perception and risk-assessment research should be
noted. It should also be noted that risk assessment may incorporate
study of risk perceptions in drawing conclusions about the likely outcomes of an adverse event.

WHY IS IT IMPORTANT TO UNDERSTAND BOTH
RISK ASSESSMENT AND RISK PERCEPTION?

Doing risk assessment is important because it is a necessary precursor
to risk management. Understanding risk perception is important in its
own right, since it can explain why people choose to act in particular
ways. However, it is also important because it can contribute to
effective risk assessment since the human factor is often an ingredient
in determining the likelihood of an adverse event occurring and in
influencing its consequences. Risk assessment and analysing risk perception are both necessary.

Both risk assessment and risk perception are often linked to risk
management. Risk management is essentially the process of making
decisions about risks and implementing them.

---

risk. This lack of consensual definition and common measurement has
resulted in a lot of acrimony in debates between the physical sciences
and the social sciences. More importantly, it has been tied in to questions about the value of risk assessment made by professionals. The lay
public have become sometimes disillusioned with the capacity of professionals to provide certain and accurate risk assessments in part

because they know that there is controversy and dispute between different professionals in the conclusions they draw, based on disparate methodologies. The issue of trust (or, rather, lack of trust) in experts is dealt with in later chapters.

3   Principles of risk assessment

3.1   *The approach to assessment*

When it comes to the methods for examining risk perception, it is relatively easy to provide a catalogue of the qualitative and quantitative techniques used. Some are described later in this chapter. At one level, the methods used in risk assessment are so diverse they would defy taxonomy. Each discipline within the social, physical and biological sciences has specific techniques for measuring the particular outcomes of those adverse events that fall within their purview. However, there are underlying commonalities of methodological principle that cut across disciplines. These can be best framed in terms of the tasks facing the risk assessor:

- to specify the hazard very precisely
- to estimate the likelihood of the adverse event
- to specify the domain of possible event-outcomes precisely
- to estimate the likelihood of each outcome
- to estimate the severity of each possible outcome.

To expose the methodological principles, it may be easiest to start with an illustration in a physical system. Let us say that the hazard we are concerned about is the malfunction of an aircraft engine, the adverse event is a failure of the engine in flight, and the event-outcomes are possibly a forced landing, a crash landing or engine shutdown. Steps in assessment might be:

- to refine the hazard specification: this is a malfunction of a specified form that occurs in an engine that is in a particular type of aircraft, this engine has no history of malfunction, it has been operational for five years, it is regularly serviced, it is maintained expertly – important here to recognise that the hazard specification may be further refined after work on the steps below, dependent on the data available
- to estimate the likelihood that there will be a failure of this engine in flight: this might require several approaches – detailed examination of the engine for any evident weakness or fault; experimental studies to test the reliability of the engine 'on the bench' (outside of the aircraft), which could be graded in difficulty and longevity and might ultimately test the engine to failure or 'destruction'; the examination of the flight

performance record of engines of the same type; the examination of the flight performance record of engines of similar types

- to identify possible consequences of malfunction – this could be done through computer simulation of the specified malfunction in a mock-up of the aircraft (the computer simulation itself would have to have been generated by a systems analysis of the role of the part in the engine that malfunctions); it could be done through analysing any records of engines of the same or similar type that have experienced the precise malfunction in flight in the past
- to estimate the likelihood of each potential consequence of the mal-function and estimate the severity of each – this would require that each consequence is examined separately. It would also be possible that the co-occurrence of two (or more) consequences would alter their severity and this would need to be examined. Decisions would need to be taken about the measure of severity to be used. It could be life lost, injury incurred, time delays in flight, cost of repair, and so on. The incidence and severity of such consequences attached to similar mal-functions in past cases could be assessed. Experimental and simulation studies could test the likelihood and severity of impact of some out-comes. Another common device is to ask 'experts' to give their view about the probability and severity of particular outcomes. Such experts are assumed to be using their experience to synthesise information and draw conclusions.

This is a relatively simple hazard to consider. Nevertheless, it is apparent that the analysis is complex. The methodological principles revolve around:

- experimentation (or diagnostic testing) and the use of data from earlier experimentation
- simulation that relies on prior systems analysis
- modelling that replicates or imitates the system to be tested but on a smaller scale or with a limited range of elements
- analysis of databases that reflect patterns of previous incidence
- using expert opinion – this can be conceived of as another sort of database and/or another way to get data analysed.

The analyses allow risk to be specified in terms of probability of event and severity of effect. Box 2.2 illustrates how risk assessment methods are used in one aspect of clinical and forensic psychology. This emphasises that, alongside experimentation and modelling, epidemiological methods are vital for most areas of risk assessment. By relating the number of cases of harm (illness, accident, etc.) to the population exposed and to the periods and levels of exposure, epidemiologists estimate the probabilities for particular events.

Box 2.2 Risk of violence

Typically, a clinical or forensic psychologist wants to estimate the risk that an individual will be violent in the future. Often this will be because the individual is currently incarcerated and may be released or because the individual is in the community and may need to be restrained. In such contexts the practitioner will rely in part at least upon 'clinical judgement' that has developed as a result of experience in treating cases in the past. Increasingly, the assessment will also be informed by empirical studies of the predictors of violence in specified populations.

For instance, Harris *et al.* (1993) conducted a retrospective file study. They looked at the files of 332 men admitted to a maximum security hospital (i.e. serving criminals) for treatment and compared them with the files from 286 men admitted to the same hospital for brief assessment only. The two groups were matched on the basis of criminal charge, age, past violent and non-violent criminality, and time of occurrence of the index (initial) offence. Overall, the men had high levels of violence. The men were classified into two groups: violent after initial release (resulting in return to hospital or criminal charge) or non-violent (31 per cent were violent). Discriminant function analysis showed that twelve variables that had been indexed differentiated between the two groups. Positively predictive of violence were psychopathy (Hare's 1991 checklist), elementary school maladjustment, DSM-III personality disorder, separation from parents under the age of 16, failure on prior conditional release, property offence history, never married, and alcohol abuse history. Negatively correlated with violence were age at time of index offence, schizophrenia diagnosis, victim injury in the index offence, and female victim in the index offence. The correlation for all 618 subjects using the twelve variables (and weighted to take into account their relative power in the discriminant analysis) against violent outcome was 0.46.

Notionally, the practitioner wishing to estimate the risk of violent recidivism in a client from a similar population would be guided by this research to explore the twelve variables listed. Interestingly, several of these variables are themselves dependent upon clinical judgement (e.g. the psychopathy checklist) rather than independent measures. If these are removed, the seven remaining, more actuarial measures, are still good predictors of violence.

The empirical research work provides the framework for investigating the specific case in detail. It is a way to determine what evidence

Box 2.2 (cont.)

should be given priority. Heilbrun (1999) recommends a systematic collection of data in order to ensure that you have the relevant information: a social history, a criminal history, a prison history, psychological tests and an interview. However, the practitioner is still left to pull all the evidence together for the individual and come to a conclusion. There is no set of categorical standards against which the individual profile can be compared and then a firm prediction of violence can be made. Most practitioners would now resist the idea that a checklist approach to risk assessment should be used. The checklist at best guides one's attention to ensure details are not ignored. Thus the statement of risk is itself hedged around with uncertainty.

In this sort of risk assessment, the task is very much an amalgam of both risk estimation and risk evaluation. The risk estimate may be wrapped in uncertainty, but the decision about the client requires that estimate to be used in the context of a broader risk evaluation. This may include the practitioner's assessment of the possible victims for any violence and their likely resilience; the capacity of environmental support to restrain violence; the political intolerance for practitioner error; and so on.

It is an important part of the role of practitioners to be able to incorporate the findings of research into their clinical decision-making. The growing tendency for clinicians to be trained as practitioner-researchers is useful in this regard. It improves the chances of accurate use of research findings and it encourages practitioners to contribute systematically to the research data banks. As more actuarial data are made available, tied to better statistical techniques for modelling them, it should be possible to reduce uncertainty and idiosyncrasy that is associated with clinical integration of data (Bull and Carson, 2001; Hess and Weiner, 1999).

3.2   Limitations of risk assessment

The estimates of risk are only as good as the experiments, simulations and databases used. Ansell (1992) provides a useful analysis of some of the weaknesses in the assessment of reliability in industrial assessment that has more general applicability when criticising the approaches used in risk assessment. He points out that most hazards reside within systems of interacting hazards. He suggests that there are two approaches to systems analysis: the top–down and the bottom–up. The former relies on considering holistically the dangers to which a system might be subject. The latter entails analysis of each of the basic components of the system in isolation. This first approach is typified by event tree or fault tree analysis in which possible failures within a system are depicted relative to each other (using simple diagrams of logical and functional relationships). Figure 2.1 provides an example of an event tree.

The use of 'trees' to represent elements in a complex system is common. In organisational theory we see the use of 'decision trees'. In system design we come across the use of 'logic trees'. The basic steps in the construction of these trees are:

- definition of the elements
- specification of their logical relationship
- qualitative evaluation of their properties
- quantification of the tree.

Crossland *et al.* (1992) summarised the five common problems that emerge when constructing fault trees:

- the question of how to treat multiple failures that arise from a single event (called common-cause failures)
- the problem of allowing for the propagation of uncertainties in the primary inputs (i.e. unreliability in the performance of these elements in the system)
- the difficulty of ensuring a sufficient degree of comprehensiveness of the systems definition
- the issue of specifying bounds to the fault tree so that the problem is tractable
- the task of determining the form and parameters of probability distributions to incorporate into failure-data inputs.

The last, of course, is the prime problem. Event/fault tree analysis is useful since it demands that the risk assessor is systematic and logical.

Using Boolean mathematical expressions, it is possible to specify the nature of the system represented by an event/fault tree. The problem in using this method with complex systems is that it is unlikely that a single mathematical model can be found to represent the whole system. This means that it is often necessary to translate the complex system into a series of discrete components. In turn, this then results in the use of assumptions that may tend to simplify the system. The sensitivity of the results to variations in these simplifying assumptions must then be examined. If the conclusions differ substantially because an assumption is varied slightly, the robustness of the conclusions must be in doubt. This emphasises that building an understanding of risk in complex systems is an iterative business. The logical models are refined through empirical exploration. Testing the model will normally rely upon statistical analyses rather than any direct diagnostic test.

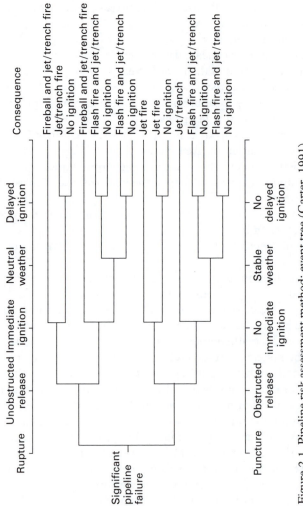

Figure 2.1 Pipeline risk assessment method: event tree (Carter, 1991)

It is not the purpose of this book to introduce the various mathematical techniques that currently underpin much of risk assessment. The statistical techniques are not intrinsically complex, and the same ones (such as the Markovian model) are used in many different hazard domains (from financial risk to environmental risk, from engineering risk to microbiological risk). Perhaps the most important thing to remember is that all of these techniques are valuable only in so far as the data to which they are applied are valid. Ansell (1992), in presenting some of the popular mathematical approaches, emphasises how important it is to the development of effective risk assessment that good databases providing information on hazards and the consequences of adverse events are created, maintained, accessible and properly understood by their users. Even good data in the hands of someone who does not understand them will tend to mislead.

The creation of good data banks is an essential requirement for future development of risk assessment. In some domains, notably in some engineering areas and in some biochemical areas, data banks have been established with international standards of recording and verification. There is still a long way to go in many hazard domains. Some data are recorded but are not structured intelligibly. Some data will not be made available because they are commercially sensitive or valuable. Some will not be collected because there is no profit motive for doing so. The list of reasons why data banks are limited is long. There is an imperative for researchers and practitioners interested in risk assessment and management to bring pressure to bear in order to improve these data resources.

The role of experts in risk assessment is one that deserves further consideration (see later chapters). If there is agreement between sources of evidence, the assessor may be more confident. When there are differences, the difficulty lies in determining what might be more accurate. The role of experts, who may be respected within an established community and consequently may be difficult to ignore, then becomes particularly significant.

Many hazards do not permit any relatively simple application of the methodological principles outlined above. Essentially, the hazard itself may be so complex that it defies coherent specification. Alternatively, the consequences are so multitudinous that they resist full articulation or measurement. Sometimes a partial risk assessment may be produced via limited hazard-definition and constrained consequence-definition. But under such circumstances the problem remains that such an assessment may be compromised by factors within the elements of the hazard that are inadequately specified or by unanticipated outcomes. Having to live with such incomplete risk assessments is often unavoidable. See Box 2.3 for an illustration of a complex hazard: avian and pandemic influenza.

Box 2.3 A complex hazard: avian and pandemic flu

The possibility of a global epidemic of 'bird flu' provides a good illustration of how complex a hazard can actually be. It is a useful illustration because it is this sort of hazard that is societally important. Flu pandemics are known to strike every few decades. The most serious on record was the 'Spanish flu' in 1918–19 that killed 20,000,000–50,000,000 people worldwide. The most recent was the 'Hong Kong flu' in 1968 that killed about 1,000,000 people. The 'avian flu' first broke out in Hong Kong in 1997, infecting 18 people and killing 6. The same virus (H5N1) reappeared in Thailand in January 2004. By August 2005, there were 109 human infections and 55 deaths in Thailand, Vietnam, China and Indonesia. By that time, the virus was widespread among birds, including domesticated poultry, in Asia and had spread to Siberia. Mass slaughter of birds failed to contain the disease. As flocks migrate, the disease spreads geographically. Humans are known to have contracted the virus from birds. At the time of writing this book, there is no evidence that the virus has evolved the ability to pass easily from one human to another. The major concern is that it may do so. There is an experimental vaccine available for H5N1, but the virus that transmits human-to-human is likely to have mutated and may be unaffected by this vaccine. It is not known how lethal the mutated virus would be.

A potential pandemic of 'bird flu' has initiated massive effort at risk assessment linked to proposals for risk management (Royal Society, 2006). One approach has been to model the spread of the virus. Neil Ferguson et al. (2005) proposed a model of the spread of the mutated virus from a single individual in a rural village in Thailand. Making explicit assumptions about the rate of transmission, incubation period before visibility of the disease or resultant incapacity, demographic characteristics of the area, travel and social patterns of those initially and subsequently infected, they showed that if nothing was done to contain the outbreak, a year after the first case 50 per cent of Thailand's 85,000,000 population had been infected. The team compared this model with one, using the same assumptions, but where action to control the outbreak was taken (first, involving giving everyone within a five- or ten-kilometre radius of the outbreak anti-viral drugs and, second, by reducing contact between people by closing schools and workplaces). The model suggested that spread could be controlled but only if anti-viral drugs were administered to at least 90 per cent of those at risk of initial contact before 30–40 people had contracted the virus.

Box 2.3 (cont.)

The study resulted in a call for the appropriate anti-viral drugs to be made available for immediate deployment anywhere in the world within three days. Whether there would be adequate supplies of the anti-viral drug was immediately questioned. The corollary requirement of quick intervention is the need for comprehensive surveillance and immediate reportage of any outbreak. Public compliance with attempts to limit movement and social contact would also be crucial.

The Ferguson *et al.* (2005, 2006) type of model is technically sophisticated but it is one of the least complex ways of approaching the risk assessment of this hazard. Their model deals with risk estimated in terms of percentage of people infected. The next stage in risk estimation would be to look at the other potential consequences of the disease. They might be medical (e.g. the failure of the health-care system). They might be in the economic domain (e.g. loss of industrial productivity, slump in consumption). They might be in the political domain (e.g. regime destabilisation, international power rebalancing). They may be social (e.g. crime, religious upheaval). The nature and severity of these adverse consequences will depend on the scale of the epidemic. For further consideration of these issues refer to the report of the Royal Society (2006).

When we start to look at the hazard in this broader context, the real scale of the complexity is evident. Many hazards can be subjected to risk assessment at a number of different levels of analysis. One looks at direct or immediate consequences. Others look at the indirect or distal consequences. The approach that encourages a multi-level analysis is known as the 'social amplification of risk framework'. This approach is examined in detail in later chapters.

This example of a complex hazard will be used elsewhere in this book to illustrate theoretical and practical arguments that are presented.

In the technical assessment of risk, the risk estimate should be accompanied by a statement of the uncertainty that is associated with it in a fashion that is as clear as possible (Barlow *et al.*, 1992). This means the expression of risk should be accompanied by an expression of the limitations in the data, model specification and analysis that led to it. The quantification of uncertainty in risk estimates is usually poor. Measuring what you do not know that you have ignored is not possible. There is nevertheless a responsibility that sits upon the risk assessor to be honest about the limitations as far as they are known.

4   The expression of risk

Description of the methods for assessing risk still leaves this question: Do we have commonly used summative expressions of risk levels? Another way of asking this question would be to say: Do we have any commonly accepted measurement scale on which levels of risk are represented?

In fact, we have not one but quite a few. Several revolve around the loss of life associated with an adverse event:

- mortality rate – the fraction of the population at risk that suffer death per unit time (e.g. per annum)
- death per unit measure of activity – the fraction of the population at risk that suffer death within a defined amount of exposure (e.g. number of deaths per passenger mile on the railway or number of deaths per 100 million person hours of exposure to a work environment)
- loss of life expectancy – the years lost that those affected might realistically have expected to have.

This preoccupation with death as an index of risk may originate in the assumption that death is the worst possible consequence and can be the ultimate common denominator for any type of hazard event. There are those who would argue that living with terrible injury or the eradication of fertility (since those who are not born cannot die) can be worse than death. While this may be true, the simplicity of the definition of death (and its absolute nature) seems to keep it a popular index.

The other major expression of risk focuses additionally upon the potential variability of consequences. This looks at the relationship between the frequency of a particular type of adverse event and the consequences it has (usually still expressed in terms of fatalities or more regularly cumulative fatalities over each instance). These calculations generate what are called fc curves (frequency multiplied by consequences). While these may be useful where there are large numbers of data points available for the construction of the plot, where there are not the assumed linearity of the trade-off between frequency and consequence size may be misleading.

Another representation of risk often used relies on plotting cumulative frequency of n or more fatalities against number of fatalities (Fn). See Figure 2.2 for an illustration of such a plot.

This figure is interesting, because it shows what can be done with these representations of risk estimates. The UK Health and Safety Commission was trying to determine what would be a level of risk that was societally intolerable. The space above the top line represents values of fatality that would be intolerable. The lowest line reflects risk that would be considered negligible socially. The middle line represents the

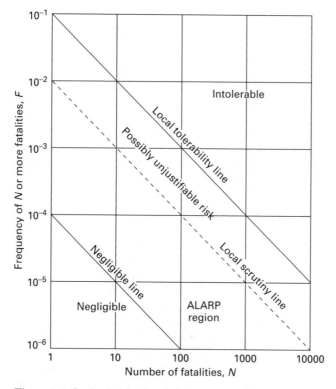

Figure 2.2 Societal risk tolerability
(Source: Health and Safety Committee Report, 1991)

risk level that a particular local community would wish scrutinised. The measures of tolerance or acceptability are always open to question, but they will be considered in a later chapter and need not trouble us here. The important part of this approach developed by safety experts is to focus upon the margin between the local scrutiny line and the tolerability line – in this area, risk levels might be unjustifiable. In the space between the scrutiny line and the negligible line, risk levels might be subject to improvement. But the improvement would be subject to what is called the 'as low as reasonably practical' (ALARP) principle. This requires those managing the risk to balance the costs and practicality of reducing the risk against the improvement in tolerance. It is worth bearing in mind that this sort of approach to determining whether a hazard and the risk associated with it merits governmental attention or intervention has been suggested because it emphasises the significance of 'tolerance' in risk decisions.

5   Risk perception: the psychometric paradigm and the characteristics of hazards

5.1   The origins of the psychometric paradigm of risk perception

The psychometric paradigm is a methodological approach to exploring risk perception (see Box 2.4). It is not a theory that explains risk perceptions, though it does give rise to models that attempt to do so. The distinguishing feature of this approach is that it uses a variety of psychometric scaling methods (including magnitude estimation techniques, numerical rating scales and attitude indices) to produce quantitative measures of perceived risk and perceived benefit.

At its most basic, the perception of risk is about risk estimation: how big is the risk? Many times already in this book, it has been emphasised that the two components of the extent of the risk are probability and effect. This can be couched in terms of likelihood of occurrence or of severity of impact if it occurs (or some amalgam of the two – common now in risk management regimes in complex organisations; see Chapter 8). As discussed above in relation to risk assessment methods, risk estimates can be quantified in a number of ways (for several, see Slovic *et al.*, 1979). For instance, Lichtenstein *et al.* (1978) asked lay participants to judge the annual frequency of death in the US from forty hazards. They did this against the anchor reference point of annual motor vehicle accident death for which a known rate was supplied. Providing such a reference point when asking for magnitude estimates is an established psychometric technique that allows standardisation and comparison across individual respondents. In the Lichenstein *et al.* (1978) study, subjective estimates of fatalities were compared with public health statistics. They found that lay people were reasonably good at estimating relative fatality levels for the hazards. Essentially they knew how risky hazards are in comparison to each other. However, there was systematic distortion in their estimates when compared with the absolute actual risk levels. The hazards whose risk is most overestimated are homicide, venomous bite or sting, fire or flames, cancers overall, botulism, flood, tornadoes, pregnancy, childbirth and abortion, motor vehicle accidents and all accidents. Most underestimated were smallpox vaccination, diabetes, stomach cancer, lightning, stroke, tuberculosis, asthma and emphysema.

In his 2000 book, which is a tour de force in presenting research on risk perception from within the psychometric tradition, Slovic describes how his work stems from an initial study of gambling decisions in the late 1950s. In the 1960s he worked with Edwards, Lichtenstein and Tversky on boredom-induced changes in bet preferences (Slovic *et al.*, 1965). In 1970, Slovic was moved by Gilbert White to query whether studies on

Box 2.4 The psychometric paradigm

WHAT IS A PARADIGM ANYWAY?

'[A] worldview underlying the theories and methodology of a particular scientific subject' (*Oxford English Dictionary*) – and a paradigm shift is a fundamental change in approach or underlying assumptions (after Thomas S. Kuhn). Most frequently, now it is used to refer to a typical example or pattern of something.

WHAT IS PSYCHOMETRICS?

'The science of measuring mental capacities and processes'. Typically, these are characteristics of the individual that do not lend themselves to direct physical measurement. As a result, the discipline of psychometrics has developed a series of measurement procedures and models of statistical estimation. There are many types of psychometric test. They broadly fall into three categories (Hammond, 2000):

- *projective tests* – require testee to offer an unstructured response to a set of stimuli or tasks
- *self-report inventories* – testee articulates verbally or in writing responses to a fixed series of questions found to be valid and reliable indicators of the psychological characteristic under consideration
- *objective tests* – testees are asked to prove knowledge or competencies by display.

Psychometric tests can be founded upon three interpretive approaches:

- *normative* – assumes data exist that tell us what range of scores can be expected from the population under investigation and that the distribution of scores is statistically normal, and it is against these that the researcher interprets individual scores
- *criterion referenced* – assumes that external performance criteria are established in advance and the testee competence is judged in relation to these
- *idiographic* – assumes that the focus is on a single individual and performance is assessed over time relative to past personal performance; the idiographic approach allows for completely idiosyncratic data to be collected for each individual.

The psychometric paradigm of risk perception originates primarily in the work of Paul Slovic and various collaborators (primarily Sarah Lichtenstein and Baruch Fischhoff). Slovic (2000) states that 'risk is subjectively defined by individuals who may be influenced by a wide array of psychological, social, institutional and cultural factors' (p. xxiii).

decision-making under risk could provide an insight into behaviour in response to natural hazards. Slovic, in 2000, reflected that the question had highlighted the inadequacies of the experimental methods that he had deployed previously. The simple decision-structures incorporated in the experiments did not reflect the complexity associated with decisions concerning natural or technological hazards.

He began to broaden the definition of his research programme to explore cognitive processes and societal risk-taking. He reports finding the work of Tversky and Kahneman (1974) on heuristics and biases in probabilistic thinking and decision-making particularly valuable in explaining responses to the threats posed by natural and technological hazards. Key tenets of the Tversky and Kahneman findings on heuristics and biases are presented in Box 2.5, and are considered further in Chapter 4. The broad range of work stemming from them is also reviewed there. Interestingly, Lichtenstein *et al.* (1978), in their study of fatality estimates mentioned above, showed that participants overestimated the likelihood that hazards that were vivid or easily imaginable causes of death would result in fatalities (compared to the actual statistics available nationally), illustrating the availability heuristic.

Box 2.5 Heuristics and biases in judgement under uncertainty

Tversky and Kahneman argued that we often need to make judgements under conditions of uncertainty. They found that people rely on a limited number of heuristic principles, which reduce the complexity of the task of assessing the probabilities of uncertain events and predicting the values of uncertain quantities. Tversky and Kahneman describe three heuristics that are used:

- *Representativeness*: where asked what is the probability that object A belongs to class B, typically people assume that the probability is greater if A resembles B
- *Availability*: where asked to estimate the frequency of an event or probability of an event, typically people assume that the probability is greater if they can easily remember an instance of the event
- *Adjustment from an anchor*: where asked to make an estimate of the value of some object, typically people will start with an initial guess (the 'anchor'), which may be based on the formulation of the problem or on some partial computation, and will then adjust the estimate based on further data or analysis but rarely are these adjustments adequate.

These heuristics are usually economical and effective, but they also lead to systematic and predictable biases and errors.

5.2   Characterising hazards

Measurement of risk estimates, and the biases of inference they might reflect, represents only one component of the psychometric approach. People's perceptions of hazards do not simply revolve around estimates of fatalities. Lay discussions of risk reveal quite complex interconnected layers of understanding of what constitutes a hazard. Ordinary talk about hazards often entails lots of references to different features that characterise them. To enrich their exploration of perceptions of natural and technological hazards, Lichtenstein, Fischhoff and Slovic decided to borrow an approach from personality theory. They decided that they would get people to rate hazards on a variety of qualities or characteristics. Box 2.6 lists the nine characteristics on which they were rated in an early study (Fischhoff *et al.*, 1978c). These characteristics were originally chosen because they were believed to be influential in risk acceptability (Starr, 1969; Lowrance, 1976).

Typically, ratings were done on a seven-point scale with every hazard (referred to as risk in these studies) being rated on every characteristic. In the Fischhoff *et al.* (1978c) study the hazards included were activities or technologies. They included smoking, alcoholic beverages, vaccinations, X-rays, swimming, mountain climbing, pesticides, prescription antibiotics, fire fighting, police work, bicycles and railroads.

Box 2.6 Risk characteristics

Voluntariness of risk – do people get into the risky situation voluntarily?

Immediacy of effect – to what extent is the risk of death immediate?

Knowledge about the risk – to what extent are the risks known precisely to the person exposed to the risk?

Knowledge about the risk – to what extent are the risks known to science?

Control over risk – if you are exposed to the risk, to what extent can you, by personal skill or diligence, avoid death?

Newness – are the risks new and novel, or old and familiar?

Chronic-catastrophic – is the risk one that kills people one at a time (chronic) or one that kills large numbers simultaneously (catastrophic)?

Common-dread – is the risk one that people have learned to live with and can think about reasonably calmly, or is it one that people have great dread about?

Severity of consequences – how likely is the risk, once realised, to have fatal consequences?

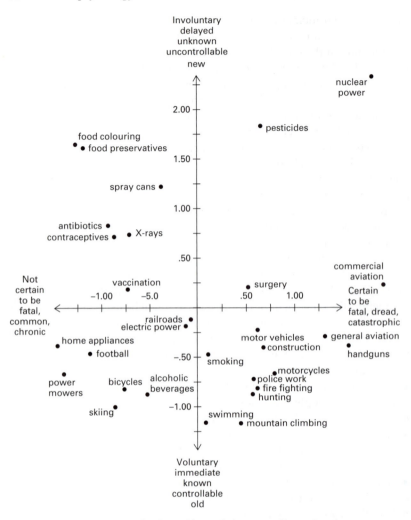

Figure 2.4 Distribution of hazards in a two-dimensional space
(Figure reproduced from Fischhoff *et al.* 1978c – Slovic, 2000: Fig. 5.5)

It is obvious that having additional hazards and characteristics in this study was associated with a different dimensional structure for the risk perception space (see Figure 2.5). Besides the appearance of the third factor being consequent upon including the additional characteristics concerning number exposed, the big difference is that control and involuntariness are no longer linked to lack of novelty and knowledge. Such differences in factor structure can be a product of differences in the

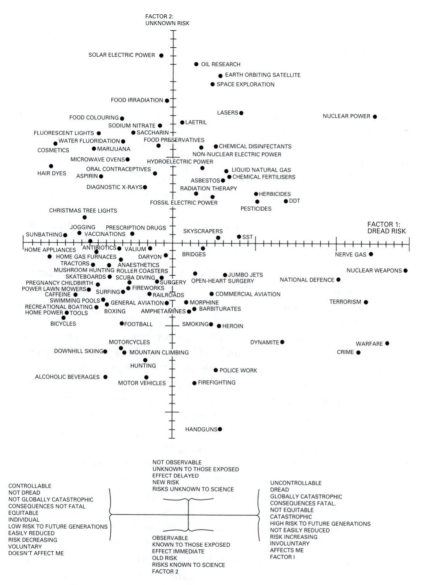

Note: Factor 3 (not shown) reflects the number of people exposed to the hazard.

Factors 1 and 2 of the three-dimensional structure derived from
interrelationships among 18 risk characteristics in the extended study

Figure 2.5 Factors 1 and 2 of a three-dimensional factor structure
(Taken from Slovic *et al.*, 1980, reproduced in Slovic, 2000: Chapter 8)

sample, in the range of objects assessed (hazards) and in the range of characteristics rated – or in any combination of differences in these three. Where differences across studies in factor structure occur, it is always difficult to establish why.

This second study, and the two prime dimensions in risk perception that it postulated, has become the benchmark for much of the subsequent research. Of course, there have been no genuine full replications of the original 1980 study. This would be logically impossible, because any replication would have to be done at a later date (even if it were done with matched samples and matched data collection). The fact that the study would be conducted at a different time is important. Time, in this instance, would be a cipher for the real world changes that may have taken place in the nature of the hazards and their riskiness since the original study. However, those studies that have most closely followed the original Slovic et al. (1980) procedures and samples have typically found a similar pattern of two or three factors (the third normally tied to the number of people exposed) (Pidgeon et al., 1992). In fact, Slovic and Krause have argued that broadly comparable factor structures emerge when different sets of hazards are examined (Krause and Slovic, 1988, on railway transport hazards; Slovic et al., 1989, on medical hazards).

Nevertheless, there have been some studies that have found somewhat different factor structures. Brun (1992) showed that a different factor structure emerged for natural as opposed to man-made hazards. Fife-Schaw and Rowe (1996) examined perceptions of food-related hazards and found two key dimensions that they labelled 'severity' and 'awareness of the hazard'. Their work is interesting, particularly because they included some hazards about which the public knew very little (e.g. Campylobacter bacteria) and they found that these were perceived as both serious and in need of regulation. They suggest that this may represent the normal starting position for the public when faced with 'new' hazards. In their discussion, they introduce the concept of the 'lifecycle of the public perception of a hazard'. As the hazard first enters public awareness, it will have certain perceived characteristics but these will change as information about the hazard becomes available to the public. Fife-Schaw and Rowe consider it appropriate that the way hazards traverse the perceptual risk space is eminently worthy of research. It is rather sad that there have been few studies that have seriously attempted to map these movements over time.

The existence of the third dimension on which hazards are differentiated in the Slovic model – the number exposed – is intriguing. At first sight, it might be supposed that this would sit alongside catastrophic potential but it is not viewed by the public in that way. Upon reflection, this is perhaps understandable. The number habitually exposed need not be inevitably linked to the number that would be affected if something went wrong. Take a rather obvious example: hundreds of thousands of people may cross a major bridge in any one day, but if that bridge collapses relatively few will be hurt. For a hazard to have catastrophic potential many must be exposed, but just because many are exposed it does not mean that the hazard has catastrophic potential. The third dimension of hazard characterisation merits consideration in its own right. After all, when it comes to policy-making, the perceived number exposed is often a vital ingredient in decision-making.

Many of the subsequent studies within the psychometric paradigm explored differences between different groups of people in their perceptions of risk. The quantitative approach to examining risk perception is said to be particularly useful in identifying similarities and differences among groups or categories of people. The data regularly suggest that different groups perceive hazards differently. These findings are discussed in Chapter 3 of this book.

The upshot of this welter of research looking at socio-demographic differences in risk perception has been to shift the emphasis away from thinking that the psychometric paradigm might provide a single normative description of the perception of the characteristics of hazards towards accepting that it is a tool for exploring group differences.

6   Risk perception and risk acceptability

6.1   Acceptability and benefit

The two-dimensional representation of the characteristics of hazards derived from Slovic et al. (1980) tends to be used as the icon for the psychometric approach to risk perception. However, it is actually only one product of the broad battery of quantitative data elicitation and analytic techniques that are used in this tradition. Risk estimation was mentioned earlier. Most notable as an additional product is the assessment of risk acceptability. Participants in these studies are regularly asked to rate the extent to which a risk is acceptable to them. Sometimes this is done by asking them to order hazards relative to each other in terms of their personal acceptability (and subsequently, often, then assigning an acceptance score to each ranging from 1 to 100). At other times, the task merely requires each hazard to be rated independently on a three-point scale: 'could be riskier and it would still be acceptable', 'just acceptable', 'too risky and would only be acceptable if it were less risky'. The point about this method is that it allows the researcher to ask how many times

required. This is primarily done in order to determine priorities for the deployment of limited resources available for risk management. It may be done in order to determine where a newly identified hazard (e.g. a new form of disease, like BSE in the 1990s, or a new type of technology, like cloned animals in the 2000s) sits within the overall picture of people's concerns. In the commercial context, risk comparison can be part of selling. For instance, in the UK there is a National Lottery system that has several different types of lottery game. In one (Lotto), the task is to choose which seven numbers (out of forty-nine) will be chosen at random by a machine. In another (Thunderball), the task is to choose which six numbers will be chosen at random by a machine. Thunderball has been promoted with an advertisement that has a young man being telephoned by his girlfriend, who invites him over to her place immediately for passionate sex. He dashes out to his car in order to drive over to her, only to find that his car will not start. The punch line is that even *he* is more likely to win if he plays Thunderball. In voiceover, the basis of this assertion is explained: he is more likely to win Thunderball in comparison to his chances of winning Lotto.

Florig *et al.* (2001) and Morgan *et al.* (2001) proposed and validated a method for ranking risks. In this method, they first have experts define and categorise the risks to be ranked, identify the relevant risk attributes and characterise the risks in a set of standardised risk summary sheets. Then these summary sheets are used by lay (or other) groups in a structured ranking exercise. Participants are instructed to do the ranking first by sorting all of the summary sheets according to how concerned they are about the risks, without regard to the availability or cost of risk-management options. Second, they can be asked to rank the risk attributes in terms of their relative importance. Individual or group rankings can be requested. The method is a mechanism for risk communication (through providing the expert views on definition and characterisation of risk), but also a means of gaining feedback on that communication through the rankings. This is regarded as archetypically a deliberative method for producing risk rankings and is most valuable as an input to public risk-management decision-making. The method is thought to be valuable because it alerts the public to the perspective of the experts and allows experts to structure the feedback that is gained from the public and to facilitate informed decision-making. Willis *et al.* (2004) used the method and reported that their participants indicated support for using it in real-world decision-making.

Within the social sciences, and particularly within economics, there is a tradition of research that compares the perception of risks by asking people what they would pay in order either to remove the hazard from themselves or alternatively to remove it from society. It is assumed that people would pay more to remove those hazards that they find most concerning. This 'willingness-to-pay' approach is widely used to estimate how people value changes in risk and is regularly built into benefit–cost analysis. Two variants of the approach are used: willingness to pay for a reduction in risk, or willingness to accept compensation for an increase in risk. Both measures can be used to compare risk responses. There is also a growing tendency to use them to compare concern levels over the way the same hazard affects different types of people. For instance, Dockins *et al.* (2002) consider differences in willingness to pay for health and safety risk reductions for children and for adults. This approach is not without its critics. The method that uses expressed preferences to evaluate willingness to pay is known as contingent valuation (CVM). Bateman *et al.* (1995) present a good summary of the weaknesses of CVM. These revolve around the biases in responses introduced by the way willingness to pay questions are formatted. The main message is that apparent willingness to pay is seriously influenced by how the question is asked. Anyone thinking about using the CVM should ensure that they take this into account, but it is beyond the remit of this book to review these issues in detail.

Johnson (2004a, 2004b) has described how risk comparisons are used in some risk communication programmes in order to situate or frame the level of the risk associated with a hazard. These risk comparison approaches include reference comparison (e.g. where the hazard sits in relation to an established public health standard) and risk ladders. Risk ladders have been used in various formats but essentially rely on ordering hazards in terms of some common index. It might be the impact they have to increase lifetime risk of death. So smoking might be highest on the ladder (a smoker has an increased lifetime risk of death of 88,000 per million), saccharin in soft drinks (170) next, chest X-rays (41) after that, aflatoxin in peanut butter (11), and then radiation from living in a brick house (4). Ordering could use other metrics: a probability format (e.g. 0.0006 deaths per average year from accidental injuries) or a frequency format (e.g. 14 in a million chance of death per year on average from accidental injuries) or the average time interval between deaths (e.g. one death per thousand years). Johnson argues that the way the risk comparison is expressed may well influence the subsequent relative concern expressed about the hazards compared. However, from his own research, Johnson concludes that risk comparison information has little impact on the absolute risk estimates for individual hazards. So it seems that risk comparison has the effect of changing levels of concern but not in association with changing the assessment of absolute levels of risk. This is fascinating. The comparative information fails to shift simple risk ratings of the individual hazard but does have the capacity to raise a hazard into an individual's list of things to be concerned about.

There is another stream of work that uses qualitative methods to build a picture of how people construe different hazards. Confusingly, this is also known as laddering but is based on quite different assumptions. Miles and Rowe (2004) describe the laddering technique for the exploration of data derived from interviews. This technique basically allows the researcher to pick out themes in statements about hazards that are common across a set of interviewees and then to show how they are linked in the way the interviewees talk about the hazard. It also encourages the interviewees themselves to explain the linkages between the attitudes, values, beliefs and decisions that they present in the interview. Laddering entails three stages: the elicitation of attributes (associated with the hazard); the interviewees produce attribute–consequence–value chains; and these chains are then compared across interviewees to establish commonality of theme. Software is now available to aid the production of the 'ladder map'. The method has been used to establish the hierarchical structure of attributes attributable to hazards as well as to determine the relationships between the perceived consequences they have and the values that are used in assessing them. Miles and Frewer (2001) used the method to explore perceptions of food hazards. Grunert *et al.* (2001) used it to examine cross-cultural perception of genetically modified food products. The laddering technique is presented here to emphasise the importance of looking beyond simple rating methods when examining the perception of hazards. The data generated may be difficult to analyse but they can offer a rare richness of insight into the way a hazard is construed and the way it fits into the universe of hazard perception available to an individual.

6.5   Synergistic risks

It may be worth a brief mention of synergic risks. 'Synergistic' is used to refer to hazards that combine to produce risks that are greater than the risks attached to each singly. For instance, the risk of contracting cancer is greater for the person who both regularly smokes tobacco and drinks alcohol than for the person who only smokes or only drinks. These synergies between hazards are clearly important. Being able to estimate them and enabling people to understand them can be crucial.

Measuring how people estimate synergistic risk is not simple (French *et al.*, 2002). Hampson *et al.* (2003), in an insightful description of methods in this area, suggest that anchored, relative scales should be used. These entail having the participant rate risks of the hazards singly and combined relative to a familiar risky activity. For instance, if smoking a pack of cigarettes a day is the familiar risk, a seven-point scale might range from '1 = many times less risky than smoking a pack of cigarettes a day' to '7 = many more times risky than smoking a pack of cigarettes a day'. Since ratings are likely to be subject to order effects, the collection of data must be counterbalanced to ensure that they are controlled. Methodological rigour in this area is rewarded. There is enormous scope for developing a further understanding of how people perceive synergistic risks. Work in this area is in its infancy. The finding that combined hazards tend to be habitually seen as more risky is a very preliminary assertion. Hampson *et al.* (1998) looked at the lay understanding of the combination of smoking and radon exposure in producing a synergistic lung cancer. They found that, while people had extensive mental models of the risks of smoking, 32 per cent knew little or nothing about radon. Despite reading an informational brochure, their risk-perception ratings showed no perception of the synergy between smoking and radon risk. In this study, participants appeared to be combining the single-hazard risks sub-additively to arrive at their combined-hazard risk perceptions and consequently underestimating the synergistic risk.

7   Criticisms of the psychometric paradigm

Many empirical studies described elsewhere in this book use psychometric methods. Some of these are conducted by researchers who would not identify themselves as working within the 'psychometric paradigm of risk'. In addition, much research on risk is eclectic in its epistemological roots. This means that it would be very difficult to isolate or draw a clear boundary around that research which lies within the psychometric paradigm of risk. Nevertheless, one thing can be clearly said: those researchers, like Slovic, Fischhoff and Lichtenstein, who do acknowledge that much of their early work relied upon psychometric quantitative methods, established a framework for the conceptualisation of risk perception and risk acceptance that has impacted upon all subsequent work on the topic – even if that impact has been because researchers from other traditions have vehemently rejected it.

Adherents of the approach would claim that it was adopted with no naivety. The researchers were fully aware that their conclusions were dependent upon the hazards studied, the specificity of the nature of the hazard, the questions they asked about these hazards, the participants who were studied and the form of data analysis used. Subsequently, the research has been criticised for ignoring the significance of these factors in determining the findings. However, such criticisms are themselves overly simplistic. The early studies were conducted in a full appreciation of their methodological limitations. Reports of those studies make this clear. Most especially, the intrinsic difficulty of questions that asked lay people to rate the risks associated with various unfamiliar high technologies was understood.

It is inevitable that the status (in the sense of reliability or validity) of the data generated from ordinary people in risk-perception studies will be a matter of debate. Researchers are asking them to comment on issues that they do not fully understand (and, in many cases, no one fully understands). We capture an appreciation of the risk that they have at the moment of the study and in a way that they can articulate at that time (often constrained deliberately by us). The potential transience of the picture of the perception of risk must be acknowledged. Yet against this must be placed the extraordinary richness of data over time that the psychometric paradigm has generated.

Despite the evident sophistication of the researchers associated with the psychometric paradigm and despite their (often vehement) acknowledgement of the limitations of their approach, their critics have tended to be unremitting. There may be several reasons for the rejection of the psychometric paradigm. Some reject it simply because it is seen to be based on a positivist or realist model of psychological functioning. Some reject it because it privileges aggregated data on individual attitudes, judgements and beliefs over the societal or cultural levels of analysis. Some challenge it because it uses aggregated data and neglects individual differences in risk perception. Some reject it because it seeks to quantify what they believe to be unquantifiable. Often these criticisms come from outside of psychology (notably from sociologists and anthropologists), yet sometimes they come from within (see Sjöberg, 1999b; Siegrist et al., 2005a). Chapter 3 looks at individual and group differences in risk perception and will further unpack the implications of some of these criticisms for development of a coherent model of risk perception.

The critiques often merely represent clashes of world-views, battles between paradigms. The position adopted in this book is one of advanced relativism: that any new student of the psychology of risk should acquire a deep understanding of each of these world-views and be able to take advantage of the insight that each has to offer. The important thing is to evaluate the products of a paradigm in terms of the system of basic assumptions that guide work in that tradition. Opting for one paradigm rather than another might be what the student will ultimately wish to do, but this should be based on a genuine understanding of what each has to offer.

Conclusion

This chapter has attempted to present an overview of the classic approaches to risk assessment and to relate them to the perception of hazards. It has to some extent acted as an introduction to the dominant methods in the study of risk. The limitations of those methods have emerged and in those weaknesses lie the origins of many of the more interesting debates that pervade the risk literature. The uncertainty that surrounds many aspects of risk assessment is at the heart of much of the societal distrust in pronouncements made about risk levels and risk management measures. Hazards are normally complex. The potential consequences of an adverse event are normally more complex. Uncertainty in risk estimates is probably the only certainty to expect. What then becomes most interesting is the social psychology that can explain how uncertainty in risk assessment is managed socially. The next chapter looks at the variation that there is in risk perception (across individuals and groups). It also looks at how risk perception links to risk-taking. It is, however, always worth bearing in mind that, when they develop their perception of risk, people have available to them many sources of information. One source may be the technical risk assessments that have been done. Another most important source is each other. The social psychology that explains the way hazards are perceived will locate the perceiver in a context that offers close to inexhaustible, and often conflicting, information.

3   Individual and group differences
in risk perception

Chapter preview

Chapter 3 presents studies that explore the factors that predict variation
in risk perception. Among the individual difference factors examined
are personality, cognitive style, beliefs and experience. From the studies
examined, it is concluded that risk-taking is better predicted than risk
perception by personality differences. However, neuroticism-anxiety
and impulsivity are related to risk perception. There is also evidence of
a complex link between self-efficacy levels and locus of control orientation and perceived risk. The chapter also examines the relationship
between the personal exposure to or experience of hazards and the
perceived risk associated with them. The group factors that may influence risk perception that are reviewed in the chapter include nationality,
socio-demographic characteristics (like gender or race) and belonging
to an expert profession. The contribution of Cultural Theory to the
understanding of hazard perceptions and judgements is also reviewed.
Throughout, the chapter examines the methods of both data elicitation
and data analysis that are used in the studies described and explains how
in a variety of ways methods tend to determine the nature of the results
that are reported.

1   The need for methodological rigour

When examining the conclusions drawn from studies of individual and
group differences in risk perception, it is important always to evaluate
the quality of the data provided. This means it is necessary to look at the
samples chosen, the methods employed to collect information and the
forms of analysis undertaken. Box 3.1 summarises some of the questions
that should be asked before deciding that a quantitative study is offering
valuable insights. Surprisingly often, reports do not provide all of the
information needed to make these evaluations. Studies using qualitative
methods require other criteria to be employed but the principles are

---

Box 3.1 Assessing the value of quantitative empirical studies

- *What is the nature of the sample?*
  How large is it? How representative of the population is it? What was the response rate (relevant for survey research particularly)? What information is collected?
- *How are variables defined?*
  What measures are used to index these variables? Are the measures valid and reliable? When were the data collected, in what sequence, by whom, and on what pretext? In experimental or quasi-experimental studies, are the conditions and controls sufficiently well specified?
- *What analyses are performed?*
  Are they appropriate? Do the analyses reported actually address the hypotheses to be tested? Is the statistical significance of findings adequate? Is the power of one variable to account for variance in another reported?

---

similar – who they are basing their conclusions on; what evidence they have got; and how they are making sense of that information. The National Centre for Social Research, on behalf of the Strategy Unit of the UK Government Cabinet Office, has developed a framework to guide assessments of the quality of qualitative research that is worth examining for further details on the issues relevant to evaluating qualitative data (Spencer *et al.*, 2003).

2 An individual difference approach to data analysis

It is notable after the original psychometric research on the characteristics of hazards that there has been a growing momentum to examine individual differences in risk perception. Gardner and Gould (1989) published an important study that was the first to obtain probability (rather than convenience) samples from populations in some US states. They limited their data collection to six technologies and three characteristics (catastrophic potential, dread and known to science). More importantly, they introduced a different way of dealing with the data. They performed individual differences analyses rather than mean score analyses on relationships between perceived risk and risk acceptability on the one hand, and risk characteristics on the other. Sjöberg (1995) emphasises the differences between this and the Slovic approach. Slovic analysed mean ratings and estimated models of variation between technologies. Gardner and Gould analysed each technology separately and estimated models of individual differences. The two approaches answer different questions:

- The Slovic approach analyses why people on average judge technologies differently.
- The Gardner and Gould approach analyses why different people judge the same technology differently.

It was the start of a flood of research that examines the differences between people and the factors that explain those differences.

Siegrist et al. (2005a) revisited this issue of the way data should be analysed. Typically, the data in risk studies can be conceived as comprising a cube (hazards × rating scales × participants). They say most researchers use aggregated data, which means that they reduce the matrix to a two-dimensional space (hazards × rating scales). See Figure 3.1 for a summary of the possible combinations of data type that can be analysed given the ratings collected in the standard study of perception of hazard characteristics. The factor loadings are computed for the rating scales and factor scores computed for the hazards. The factor scores are the basis for the two-dimensional 'cognitive map' of hazard perception (see Figure 2.4). Siegrist et al. point out that, because aggregate data are used, it is not known whether the model neglects individual differences in risk perception. Multi-level modelling procedures do allow the simultaneous analyses of individual responses and those aggregated for hazards (Langford et al., 1999). Siegrist et al. used a statistical method appropriate for the 'data cube' (called three-way principal component analysis – PCA) to test how far the 'cognitive map' commonly described represents individual risk perception. Their sample was 302 randomly selected Swiss nationals over 18 years of age, reflecting a response rate of 34 per cent. Participants rated 26 possible hazards (selected to represent each of the 4 quadrants of the cognitive map) on 9 five-point scales (adapted from Fischhoff et al., 1978b). Two analyses were conducted. To replicate the original cognitive map structure, a two-way PCA was conducted; then a three-way PCA was used. The first analysis revealed roughly the same component structure as Fischhoff et al. reported. The 'unknown risk' and 'dread risk' components explain 80 per cent of the variance. The study effectively replicated the cognitive map found in other studies that have used the psychometric paradigm. The second analysis showed that individuals differ in terms of their risk perception of different hazards. There appeared to be three core dimensions on which individuals differed:

- the extent to which they perceive unobservable hazards as unknowable and unpredictable

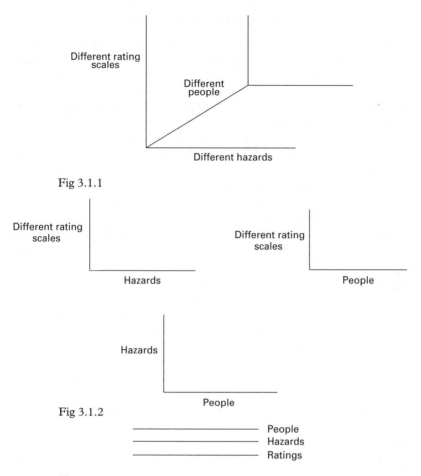

Fig 3.1.1

Fig 3.1.2

Fig 3.1.3

Figure 3.1 Analysing perception of hazard characteristics
(Series of three-, two-, and one-dimensional drawings)

- the extent to which they perceive old hazards as unknowable and unpredictable
- the extent to which they perceive unobservable hazards or old hazards as dread risks.

These three components explain a small absolute amount of variance between people (13 per cent). The precise nature of these individual differences is perhaps of less importance than the mere fact that they can be systematically catalogued. Their existence pushes us to explore further what differences between individuals do exist and how they might be explained.

3   Personality, risk-taking and risk perception

The psychometric paradigm of risk perception has concentrated on validating the dimensions of risk perception across countries (Englander et al., 1986; Teigen et al., 1988; Keown, 1989; Goszczynska et al., 1991; Kleinhesselink and Rosa, 1991; Jianguang, 1993; Nyland, 1993), comparing the composition of the dimensions of risk, the positions of hazards on these dimensions and the perceived magnitude of risks. Such studies have attempted to account for variance in perceived *magnitude* of risk (Teigen et al., 1988), rather than examining variables, such as individual differences in personality, that may determine the focus of risk perception. However, research on health risk perception has shown that personality dimensions affect both the perception of risk and risk-taking behaviour (Breakwell et al., 1994; Horvath and Zuckerman, 1993), suggesting that it may be fruitful to examine their role with respect to a wider range of hazards. Box 3.2 provides a definition of personality traits and introduces the concept of the Big Five.

The majority of studies concerned with individual differences have concentrated on voluntary risks taken in the areas of general health (Nagy and Nix, 1989; Wong and Reading, 1989), alcohol consumption (Cherpitel, 1993; Zuckerman, 1987), drinking and drunk driving (Stacy et al., 1991), smoking (Breakwell et al., 1994; Zuckerman et al., 1990), sexual activity (Breakwell et al., 1994; Cliff et al., 1993; Hendrick and Hendrick, 1987; Zuckerman et al., 1976), illegal drug-taking (Zuckerman, 1987), driving behaviour (Dorn and Matthews, 1995) and adolescent risk-taking (Lavery et al., 1993). Individual differences in appraisal of technological or involuntary risks are less frequently examined (notable exceptions are: nuclear waste, Sjöberg, 1995; general risk perception, Weigman and Gutteling, 1995; nuclear disaster, Mehta and Simpson-Housley, 1994).

The individual differences in personality profile investigated in relation to risk-taking include: sensation seeking (see Box 3.2), hardiness (Nagy and Nix, 1989), extraversion, neuroticism and psychoticism (Eysenck, 1967), impulsivity (Eysenck and Eysenck, 1978; Breakwell, 1996; Abbey et al., 2005), venturesomeness (Eysenck and Eysenck, 1978; Breakwell et al., 1994), egocentrism (Lavery et al., 1993), anxiety (Sjöberg, 1995) and self-efficacy (Wiegman and Gutteling, 1995; and see Box 3.2). Bromiley and Curley (1992) also summarise some of the findings on individual differences in risk-taking.

Eysenck suggested that there are three main dimensions to personality: extraversion, neuroticism and psychoticism. It can be seen these could be argued to map on to the Big Five described in Box 3.2. General

Box 3.2 Personality traits and the Big Five

Personality refers to those relatively stable and enduring aspects of an individual which distinguish that person from others. A personality trait is one attribute of personality and can be manifested in consistent patterns of thought, feeling or action. All traits are unique to the individual, although some are much more like those of other individuals and may be called general traits. Psychological research has attempted to identify and measure these general traits.

Goldberg (1993) proposed the 'lexical hypothesis', which states that the most meaningful personality attributes tend to become encoded in language as single-word descriptors and he examined the factor structure of adjectival descriptors extracted from dictionaries to identify the major dimensions of personality. Based on American English, he discovered five. These, the Big Five, are usually labelled:

> extraversion (vs introversion)
> agreeableness (vs disagreeableness)
> conscientiousness (vs undependability)
> emotional stability (vs neuroticism)
> openness to experience (sometimes called intellect or imagination).

Over the decade after 1990, a broad consensus emerged among trait psychologists concerning these basic dimensions of personality. Costa and McCrae (1992) refer to it as the five-factor model. They have argued that the five-factor model of personality is found in all cultures and that there are pan-cultural gender differences in the five (McCrae and Terracino, 2005). Inevitably, such claims to generalisability have been challenged (e.g. Saucier *et al.*, 2005). The suggestion that personality on these five traits is basically stable after the age of 30 has also been questioned (Ardelt, 2000). Nevertheless, the significance of the Big Five for describing and potentially predicting large areas of human activity cannot be denied. Miller *et al.* (2004) showed evidence that risk-taking is related to the Big Five. For instance, they report that low agreeableness, low openness to experience and high extraversion were significantly related to engaging in multiple high-risk sexual behaviours.

Interestingly, the personality theorist who has generated most research relevant to risk appraisal and risk-taking is a man who has proposed an alternative five-factor model of personality. He is Marvin Zuckerman. The dimensions identified by Zuckerman (see Zuckerman, 1991; Zuckerman, 1992, 2002, 2004, 2005a, 2005b) are: impulsive sensation seeking, neuroticism-anxiety, aggression-hostility, sociability-extraversion and activity. This alternative approach emerged from a

Box 3.2 (cont.)

concern with the psychobiological basis of personality (Barratt *et al.*, 2004; Schmitz, 2004; Donohew *et al.*, 2004). Zuckerman (1996, 2003), for instance, argues that sensation seeking is associated with low mono-amine oxidase, norepinephrine (noradrenalin) and serotonin levels but high dopaminergic activity. Impulsive sensation seeking has been linked to risk-taking. Sensation seeking has been shown to be positively related to heavy drinking (Zuckerman, 1987), smoking and accepting their health risks (Zuckerman *et al.*, 1990), and increased sexual activity (Hendrick and Hendrick, 1987). Horvath and Zuckerman (1993) evaluated the relationship between sensation seeking and risk appraisal in several areas (e.g. crime, financial, social violations, sports, risk of HIV infection from sexual activity) and risky behaviour in the same areas. Sensation seeking was a strong predictor of risky behaviour (especially with regard to criminality and social violations), but not of risk appraisal. Zuckerman and Kuhlman (2000) found that risk-taking (with regard to drinking, drugs, sex, driving, smoking and gambling) was related to impulsive sensation seeking, aggression and sociability, but not to neuroticism or activity. Rosenbloom (2003) found that high sensation seekers would take greater risks while driving. In studies of gamblers, sensation seeking is linked to high frequency of gambling, size of bets, expenditure on gambling, reported loss of control and the pattern of 'chasing good money after bad' (Zuckerman, 2005). The nature of the impact of impulsive sensation seeking upon risk-taking may be complex. Goma-i-Freixanet (2004) also found higher levels of sensation seeking to characterise athletes compared to controls, no matter whether the sport they follow is high or low risk. Risk-taking may be a by-product of the impulsive sensation seeking rather than an objective. Nevertheless, it is an important dimension of individual differences in personality that seems to be predictive of risk-taking proclivity. The data linking sensation seeking to risk perception are not as numerous. However, Henderson *et al.* (2005) did find that higher sensation seeking was associated with lower estimates of risk associated with new sexual partners.

'impulsivity', together with sociability and liveliness (Eysenck and Eysenck, 1963), is considered to be a part of extraversion. Further work (Eysenck and Eysenck, 1978, 1980; Eysenck *et al.*, 1985) showed two distinct components of impulsivity, one correlating with extraversion (venturesomeness) and one correlating with psychoticism (impulsivity). These constructs are measured by the I_7 Impulsiveness questionnaire, which measures impulsivity, venturesomeness and empathy. This measure has been validated and its reliability tested on a number of occasions with English samples (Eysenck *et al.*, 1985; Breakwell *et al.*, 1994) as well as non-English samples (in Egypt by Eysenck and Abdel-Khalek, 1992; in Germany, Eysenck *et al.*, 1990; in Australia, Heaven, 1991). Impulsivity has been found to be related to age of first intercourse and number of sexual partners (Breakwell, 1996). Venturesomeness has been positively correlated with sexual risk-taking (Horvath and Zuckerman, 1993; Hendrick and Hendrick, 1987), alcohol consumption and cigarette smoking (Breakwell *et al.*, 1994) and general risky behaviours (Moore and Rosenthal, 1993). Taken together, these studies and those focused on sensation seeking show a relationship between personality variables and risky behaviours, but not risk perception. In fact, Zuckerman *et al.* (1990) found that there was no relationship between sensation seeking and risk estimates. Breakwell (1996: 5) emphasised this point, suggesting that, with respect to sexual behaviour, 'personality effects on risk taking are not mediated by some cognitive mechanism which reduces the perceived risk involved'.

This separation between the level of risk perceived and the willingness to take the risk is something which should be clearly recognised and not lost in our subsequent discussions. Repeatedly, it has been found across many domains of behaviour that risk estimates do not predict willingness to take a risk. For instance, McKenna and Horswill (2006) studied risk-taking by automobile drivers and found that it was unrelated to self-estimates of accident concern but was related to self-ratings of their driving skill and the perceived thrill of driving. The significance of affect in risk-taking will be considered further in Chapter 5. Here the point to be made is that the relationship between risk estimates and risk-taking is not at all simple.

Venturesomeness is an aspect of personality that reflects general willingness to take risks. Twigger-Ross and Breakwell (1999) examined the relationship between this aspect of personality (measured using a subset of the Eysenck and Eysenck, 1978, impulsiveness questionnaire), and the perceived risk characteristics (using the nine dimensions from Fischhoff *et al.*, 1978c) of certain voluntary and involuntary hazardous activities. It should be noted that in this study all hazards were presented in the form of hazardous activities. So, for instance, X-rays became having an X-ray, and food colouring became eating food colouring. In the traditional set of hazard stimuli-using within the psychometric paradigm, hazards and hazardous activities are mixed. By translating all those used into activities, the hazards were personalised and were made clearly open to being construed as either voluntary or involuntary. A random sample of 102 people from the UK, aged between 18 and 44 years, roughly half of whom were female, took part in the study. No significant correlation between venturesomeness and perceptions of any of the voluntary hazardous activities was found. However, venturesomeness was positively correlated with perceiving involuntary risks as having delayed effects and being familiar.

These data clearly do not support any simplistic notion that venture-someness is tied to generic differences in the perception of hazards. In the main, the personality trait is unrelated to the structure of risk per-ception. Nevertheless, the fact that there is a significant correlation between venturesomeness and perceiving the effects of involuntary hazardous activities to be delayed and familiar cannot be dismissed. Venturesomeness may be characterised by underestimating the immedi-acy and the uncertainty of the risks attached to involuntary hazards. This suggests that a much more differentiated model of the relationship between stable personality tendencies towards taking risks and construal of the characteristics of hazards and hazardous behaviour is required.

Anxiety as a personality factor has also been studied in relation to risk perception. Results have been inconclusive. Some studies have shown a link between enduring anxiety level and risk evaluation. Simpson-Housley *et al.* (1986) found it correlated with anticipation of flood damage. Larrain and Simpson-Housley (1990) found it associated with anticipation of earthquake damage. Mehta and Simpson-Housley (1994) linked it to belief in the possibility of nuclear power disaster. However, de Man *et al.* (1984) found it unrelated to expectations of future nuclear waste disaster. De Man *et al.* (1984) even found a negative association with expectation of flooding. Not only are these findings contradictory; they are actually focused upon the relationship between anxiety and the anticipation of a negative event rather than upon its relationship to the characteristics of hazards.

Bouyer *et al.* (2001) took a rather broader perspective. They examined both enduring anxiety dispositions and transitional anxiety states in relation to the perception of a very large number of hazards. Unusually, they used factor analysis to determine which hazards were perceived similarly, and on that basis created categories of hazards. The analysis entailed a two-way analysis: hazard × participants. This means again that anxiety cannot be related to the perception of the characteristics of hazards. Instead, it is only possible to aggregate the ratings of character-istics of the hazards in a particular category to generate a score. The score is impossible to interpret sensibly. It cannot be assumed to represent some recognisable higher-order characteristic of the category of hazards. This illustrates how confused thinking about the analysis of data can result in meaningless assertions. Bouyer *et al.* show that higher transitional state anxiety was associated with higher scores on three types of hazard category (common individual hazards; pollutants; and outdoor activities) and lower on one (public transportation and energy). Enduring anxiety was associated with a lower score on the psychotropic drugs category. All that can be said from this is that state anxiety and enduring anxiety appear to be associated with a different pattern of responses to the perception of certain hazards. We do not know what those differences are. Bouyer *et al.* might have benefited from using the three-way analysis used by Siegrist *et al.* (2005a) described earlier (see Fig. 3.1).

In a rather more useful study, Kallmen (2000) studied manifest anxiety, general self-efficacy and locus of control as determinants of general and personal risk perception. Kallmen found that individuals low in anxiety, having an internal locus of control and high in self-efficacy perceived both general risks and personal risks to be lower than did individuals high in anxiety, having an external locus of control and low in self-efficacy. This finding supports the general theoretical analysis provided in Box 3.3 below.

Sjöberg and Wåhlberg (2002) in a study described further below also looked at Eysenck's MPI measures (extraversion, psychoticism and neuroticism), plus paranoia and schizoid thinking in relation to risk perception. They found that only neuroticism had any consistent correlations with risk perception data. Neuroticism was positively correlated with perceived level of risk. Myers *et al.* (1997) found that the degree to which people worry about hazards was positively linked to their desire to be in control of events in their lives and their intolerance of ambiguity in situations that are equivocal or complex. They did not find simple relationships between these two personality traits and perception of the level of risk.

Bringing together this work on personality, the conclusion that probably has to be drawn is that risk-taking is better predicted than risk perception. Neuroticism-anxiety and impulsivity (sensation seeking or venturesomeness) are the personality variables that have been shown to relate to risk perception. These factors could logically be expected to be directly relevant to risk perception, since neuroticism is a reflection of tendency to anxiety, and impulsivity (and especially venturesomeness) is a reflection of the tendency to seek out or at least not avoid novelty. Other general dimensions of personality would seem not to be determining risk perception and perhaps there is no logical reason why they should. Of course, there have been no large-scale studies of the Big Five personality traits in relation to risk perception. While not ruling out the possibility that personality variables might have a significant role in predicting individual differences in risk perception, the evidence to date suggests

Box 3.3 Self-efficacy, locus of control and risk perception

Perceived self-efficacy is an index of a person's belief in their capacity to perform in ways that give them control over events that affect their lives (Bandura, 1997). Efficacy beliefs are considered a foundation of human agency – unless they feel they can produce the results they want, there is little incentive for people to take action.

Efficacy has many correlates. High efficacy is associated with greater cognitive resourcefulness, strategic flexibility, and effectiveness in managing one's social and physical environment. Belief in efficacy affects how much stress, anxiety and depression people experience in threatening or demanding situations. Those who think they can manage threats find them less aversive. Beliefs in efficacy also facilitate control over perturbing and dejecting thoughts. When faced with difficult tasks or problems, those low in efficacy focus on the difficulties they face, not on the possible solutions to them. Low efficacy is associated with lower motivation to succeed and greater willingness to attribute failure to personal inadequacies.

The locus of control construct emerged in the 1970s and 1980s, originating with Rotter (1966) and developed by Lefcourt (1982). It refers to a generalised expectancy that pertains to the perception of causal relationships between behaviours and experiences. Internal locus of control is associated with believing that experiences are a result of personal characteristics and actions. External locus of control is tied to believing that experiences are a product of forces outside of one's control. Internal locus of control has been said to characterise individuals who try to deal with problems actively in the hope of overcoming them. External locus of control is regarded as being linked with fatalism and failure to act in the face of obstacles. It is also associated with persuadability and conformity. 'Internals' exhibit less emotional reactions and more problem-solving approaches to stressful events. External locus of control has been said to characterise groups that have historically suffered subjugation and limited opportunity to exercise power.

Is self-efficacy a general orientation, or is it specific to certain areas of activity? Should we talk about a self-efficacious person or self-efficacy levels linked to particular situations? Similarly, are people 'internals' generically or are they internal in locus of control only when it comes to a fixed range of issues? There has been considerable debate about the stability and generalisability of efficacy or locus of control. The jury is still out, however. It is the case that measures of efficacy or locus of control that are specific about the behaviour that is to be predicted are better predictors than measures of more general

Box 3.3 (cont.)

efficacy or locus of control. So, for instance, if we wanted to know whether someone would be willing to follow a particular regime of health protection (e.g. stopping smoking), it would be better to measure their perception of their self-efficacy in relation to that change in behaviour than to measure their overall sense of self-efficacy.

Given the overlap in the nature of these two constructs, one might expect that self-efficacy and locus of control would relate to risk-taking and risk perception in similar ways. For the sake of clarity, they are dealt with separately here.

There is no simple relationship between self-efficacy and risk-taking. It depends on whether the risk is taken voluntarily or imposed:

- In relation to voluntary risk-taking, the link to self-efficacy appears to depend upon the desirability of the outcome of taking the risk. If taking a risk satisfies some desire or need, those high in self-efficacy are more likely to take the risk. For instance, with regard to high-risk sports, Schumacher and Roth (2004) found that those higher in self-efficacy took greater risks. However, if not taking a risk serves some objective, then the highly efficacious are less likely to take the risk. For example, Siero et al. (2004) found those higher in self-efficacy were more likely to be able to quit smoking, and Houlding and Davidson (2003) found drug users with higher self-efficacy were more likely to be able to insist on the use of condoms in contexts were HIV infection was possible.
- In relation to imposed risk, the effect of self-efficacy is to motivate attempts to escape, avoid, neutralise or eradicate the hazard. Floyd et al. (2000) showed that, faced with a range of natural hazards, the self-efficacious would attempt adaptive self-protection.

Self-efficacy should also be linked to risk perception. It might be expected that lower self-efficacy would be associated with higher perceived personal risk, since low efficacy suggests an inability to take action to protect oneself. This seems to be supported. For example, Macintyre et al. (2004) found that males who feel self-efficacious with regard to the use of condoms perceive their personal risk of HIV infection to be lower. Other evidence suggests that efficacy may also be important in determining estimates of risk that are not directed at the individual. For example, Kuttschreuter and Gutteling (2004) showed that computer users with lower levels of self-efficacy were more likely to rate higher the risks of the millennium bug (i.e. the danger that on 1 January 2000 computers all over the world would crash). The question as to how self-efficacy might influence risk perception is interesting but not satisfactorily answered. Trumbo (1999) suggested that self-efficacy

Box 3.3 (cont.)

affects the way people seek and use information relevant to the hazard and consequently will influence their risk perceptions. This idea that self-efficacy might be associated with certain cognitive styles is as yet unproven.

There are fewer studies in the recent past that have explored the connection of locus of control to risk-taking or perception. However, the pattern is predictable given the summary above. Internal locus of control is associated with lower levels of risk-taking in contexts where danger is salient (Miller and Mulligan, 2002). Internal locus of control is correlated with more adaptive precautions when the individual is at risk. For instance, McMath and Prentice-Dunn (2005) found that externals were less likely to take appropriate precautions against skin cancer from exposure to the sun. However, internal locus of control can result in greater risk-taking under some conditions. For instance, Franco et al. (2000) found that internals were less compliant with medical instructions to undergo health screening. It seems that reliance on external locus of control can result in lower risk-taking if the external force is pushing in a low-risk direction.

Locus of control is related to risk perception. Richard and Peterson (1998) found that those higher in internal locus of control were more likely to rate environmental hazards as more risky. It seems that those who seek greater control in their lives are more worried by those hazards over which they think they have less control. This connection between desire for control and perceived risk has been catalogued (Myers et al., 1997). There is some evidence that, where the hazard is subject to some degree of personal control, those with greater internal locus of control appear to be more accurate in their personal risk estimates (Crisp and Barber, 1995).

It is evident that self-efficacy and locus of control are constructs that are strongly conceptually related. Wallston (2005) suggests that measures of both may be needed if prediction of behaviour is to be enhanced, but if only one construct can be measured it would appear self-efficacy may be more powerful.

Rimal and Real (2003) argue that, where self-efficacy is high and perceived risk is high, self-protection will occur. The same effect could be expected where internality is high and risk high. This has led many risk communicators who want to trigger self-protective behaviour change to focus on attempts to manipulate self-efficacy and/or locus of control as part of their programme. We return to that approach briefly in Chapter 6.

that, beyond those factors that might be expected stereotypically to relate to risk judgements (like neuroticism, anxiety and venturesomeness), personality does not account for much variability.

4   Cognitive style and risk perception

This suggests that perhaps the focus should shift to other characteristics that differentiate between individuals. Ulleberg and Rundmo (2003) suggest that personality traits are related to risk-taking but the relationship is mediated through attitudes. Cognitive style and processing capacity would seem a promising area to explore. After all, there is a batch of studies that looks at self-efficacy and locus of control in relation to risk estimation. The studies show consistent patterns. Box 3.3 presents a summary of findings on self-efficacy and locus of control. Estimates of self-efficacy and locus of control are primarily self-evaluations. They represent how much control individuals believe they have over what they do or what happens to them. Intuitively, it seems likely that this should relate to risk perception. The link of such self-evaluation to personality traits is not established, so there would not seem to be an indirect connection between personality and risk perception through efficacy or locus of control. Cognitive style and processing capacity is also relevant to the 'mental models' that individuals evolve to account for hazards. Research on mental models of risk is described in Chapter 4. People are also likely to differ in their experience of hazards and this might influence their risk perceptions. The section below addresses this possibility.

5   Experience of risk and perception of risk

There has been relatively little research on the relationship between having experience of a number of risks and general risk perception. One interesting study suggested that societies that have greater levels of exposure to technological hazards, because they are more experienced with the hazards, are less sensitive to the risks. Lima et al. (2005) used data from the 2000 International Social Survey Programme on environmental issues to examine this proposition. This study used data from twenty-five countries on the perceived threat to the environment associated with a series of technologies and activities. They found that risk perception was related to economic indicators of the diffusion of each of the technologies or activities in each country. Their results indicate a negative association of risk perception with the level of technological prevalence (what they call the 'societal normalization effect') and a positive association with the rate of growth of the technology ('the societal sensitivity effect'). The greatest perceived risk is found in countries where the level of technological prevalence is still low but where there has been substantial recent technological development. While the researchers did not interpret their analysis in this way, it could be argued that, at a societal level, habitual experience of the hazard reduces risk perception whereas recent experience of the hazard enhances risk perception. It seems that the extent to which the experience is a deviation from the norm and the expected is the driver for the perception of risk.

At the individual level, Richardson *et al.* (1987) found that experience determines future sensitivity. Repeated exposure to a hazard may lead to desensitisation to the threat and a redefinition of what is acceptable. Increased experience of hazards might then be related to a lowered estimation of risk. In fact, Zuckerman (1979) showed that increased experience of an activity was related to judging that activity as less risky. Benthin *et al.* (1993) found that adolescents who participated in an activity perceived its risks to be smaller, better known and more controllable than non-participants. However, in a longitudinal study, Breakwell (1996) found with respect to sexual activity that over time subsequent risk estimates were not influenced by participating in risk behaviours. Siegrist and Gutscher (2006) found that people are aware of expert estimates of risk (in relation to flood) and tend to echo their assessments, but even so personal experience does modify the acceptance of expert opinions. If people had experience of floods, they enhanced the assessed risk of flooding – irrespective of expert opinion.

Twigger-Ross and Breakwell (1999) examined the relationship between levels of risk experience and the perception of risks in terms of the dimensions of risk perception as defined by Slovic *et al.* (1997). Since there is some evidence to suggest that voluntary and involuntary hazards are perceived in systematically different ways, they examined how experience of risk related to both types of hazard. Overall experience correlated negatively with the perceived controllability of hazards. However, when hazards were broken down into the voluntary and involuntary, it proved that experience is actually primarily correlated with perceiving involuntary hazards to be uncontrollable. Experience is correlated with considering voluntary risks to be better known to science and to be taken voluntarily. The need to distinguish between the perception of voluntary and involuntary hazardous activities is evident. Richardson *et al.* (1987) argue that experience of risk results in desensitisation. There is some evidence to support this with regard to voluntary hazardous activities. Those who had greater experience of risk were more likely to perceive the risks associated with voluntary hazards as understood. However, the desensitisation hypothesis does not apply to involuntary hazardous activities. In this case, greater experience of risk was associated with a greater tendency to consider the risks attached to involuntary activities to be unknown, uncontrollable and unfamiliar. Of course, it seems reasonable to suppose that desensitisation effects may be highly specific. This study employed a relatively crude measure of experience which did not index intensity or frequency or outcomes. It would be useful for research to explore further how the quality of risk experiences influences patterns of risk perception. This study indicated that risk experiences do have some bearing on risk perception but that the relationship is complex.

Experience of a hazard may in some way be tied to risk perception through the information that exposure offers. Exposure provides data about the hazard. In some cases it may not be new information; in others it will be. If exposure is habitual or serial, then the information offered may be cumulative but it might also be provided in a single-step change at some point in the exposure (with no subsequent accretion). The information derived from the exposure can have different objects: it could be about the person exposed (e.g. how they react), it could be about the hazard itself and it could be about the broader situation in which the exposure occurs (for instance, about the people/institutions that managed the hazard). The information can be actively or passively acquired: the individual can seek it out or can have it provided. The information can vary in its intelligibility. The characteristics of the source of information can vary (e.g. in trustworthiness, expertise). The role of information (as distinct from knowledge) in shaping risk perceptions is very complex. The role of hazard exposure in providing information is easily as complex. Many of these issues are examined in detail in Chapter 6. Here it is sufficient to say that individual differences in profile of exposure should affect individual differences in hazard information and might be expected to correlate with differences in risk perception. The direction of the relationship between information and risk perception really must be said to depend on the substance of the information. However, Wildavsky (1993) proposes that being given new information about a hazard increases the risk it is perceived to pose. This has to be an overgeneralisation. Some types of information about a hazard will reduce risk estimates. For example, showing that there is a new vaccine available for bird flu would reduce the risk estimates associated with it, whereas reporting that there are insufficient supplies of anti-viral drugs in production would increase risk estimates.

Wildavsky also points out that people are remarkably resistant to changing their prior risk estimates when given new information. Resilience to revision of risk estimates would suggest that individual differences in experience or exposure would have limited capacity to explain them. It should perhaps depend on the significance of the exposure to the individual (perhaps in terms of personal relevance or in terms of social impact). An example of the impact of a significant experience comes from the work of

Katsuya (2001), who studied the influence of the 30 September 1999 nuclear accident in Tokai village (Japan) upon the public's estimates of nuclear risk. Katsuya was able to compare risk estimates made by large samples before the nuclear accident and after it. Note, however, that this was not a longitudinal study and the samples at the two times may not have been perfectly matched. Perceived accident likelihood increased and acceptability of nuclear power operation decreased. Most interestingly, Katsuya was able to show that increase in risk estimates was not related to any change in knowledge about nuclear power generation and that the increase in risk estimates was primarily produced by those who were previously opposed to nuclear power anyway. Such a study elegantly illustrates that exposure has multi-dimensional impacts. The relationship between risk perceptions, exposure (or experience) and information (or knowledge) deserves greater empirical investigation. Thus far, there is evidence that contact with a threat is associated with becoming habituated to its presence. The association between a hazard and its negative consequences becomes 'normalised' (Halpern-Felsher et al., 2001); that is, expected or part of the furniture of living. This is particularly true for voluntary risks (Twigger-Ross and Breakwell, 1999) or those with less visible consequences (Barnett and Breakwell, 2001). Halpern-Felsher et al. (2001) showed that, for a number of voluntary and involuntary health risks, people who have experienced a threat tend to underestimate its negative consequences, compared to those that have not had that experience. A more persuasive illustration of risk normalisation is given by Lima (2004). Using a longitudinal design to look at residents' perceptions of the risk associated with an incinerator, it is clear that residents living near the facility gradually reduce their estimation of the risk associated with it over time. This is a much stronger effect than for those living further away. This normalisation of the risk has been explained in terms of desensitisation to danger (Richardson et al., 1987), as the result of the lack of immediate negative consequences of risk exposure (Taylor and Brown, 1988; Keller et al., 2006) and through the development of positive illusions (MacGregor et al., 1994; Lindell and Earle, 1983). The significance of the nature of the experience of the hazard in determining the perceived risk is something which we return to later in this book when we consider the role of affect in risk estimation (Chapter 5).

6   Beliefs and risk perception

When it comes to their perception of risks, other beliefs and attitudes that are held by an individual matter. This should be uncontentious. The more difficult task is to identify what sorts of beliefs and attitudes influence risk perception. In general, it would seem sensible to start with the proposition that the perception of a particular hazard will be influenced by those beliefs and attitudes that are immediately relevant to it. So, for instance, the perception of smoking tobacco might be influenced by beliefs about the importance of maintaining a healthy lifestyle and by attitudes towards people who smoke. It would be less obvious why beliefs about, say, traffic congestion or attitudes towards, say, insurgents might be relevant. However, intuitive assertions about what is relevant lead nowhere and the empirical investigation of the link between beliefs and risk perception has tended to look at more general systems of belief.

Sjöberg and Wåhlberg (2002), in a ground-breaking paper, examined the relationship between risk perception and new age beliefs (including traditional folk superstition and belief in paranormal phenomena, as well as alternative healing practices). It might be expected that the perception of technological, medical and environmental hazards would be related in some way to new age beliefs, since these beliefs guide the explanations that are used to interpret events. New age beliefs are associated with scepticism about modern science and its way of explaining the world. Sjöberg and Wåhlberg hypothesised that people who hold new age beliefs and those who hold traditional religious beliefs would regard technology risks as larger than those who did not. The sample, with a 60 per cent return rate, numbered 151 Swedes drawn randomly from the population, roughly half were women, and their median age was 44 years. From ratings on a large number of individual items measuring new age and superstitious beliefs, four factors were found to emerge: belief in the existence of a higher consciousness, belief in the physical reality of the soul, denial of analytic knowledge, and traditional folk superstition. Beliefs in paranormal phenomena and the use of alternative therapy forms were separately indexed. The hazards that they asked people to rate were: genetic engineering, nuclear waste and climate change. Three scales were constructed from the hazard characteristic ratings: dreaded, new and tampering with nature. Hazards were also rated in terms of personal risk, general risk, seriousness and demand for risk mitigation. They found that only beliefs in the existence of a higher consciousness and denial of analytical knowledge had a consistent and moderately strong relationship with ratings of the three hazards. They were positively associated with regarding the hazards as dreaded, new and tampering with nature. These two aspects of new age beliefs were also found to be positively correlated when nuclear waste was considered with perceptions of the level of risk, the seriousness of the risk and the demand for mitigation of the risk. When a regression analysis was conducted that took into account all six types of belief, it was belief in a higher consciousness that was clearly the most powerful dimension in predicting perceived level and seriousness of risk and in demands for mitigation.

Caution is required, as usual, in interpreting these findings. Just 13 per cent of variance in level of perceived risk and in seriousness was accounted for by the six beliefs, and only 6 per cent of variance in demand for risk mitigation. Not overly impressive figures in themselves but they become more so when Sjöberg and Wåhlberg show that this effect of beliefs cannot be accounted for by socio-demographic factors (like age, education or gender). It seems that we are genuinely seeing the impact of beliefs per se upon risk perception. However, emphasis upon the significance of belief in a higher consciousness (what might be taken to be God or some other guiding essence) should not be overstated. The interesting thing about the four belief scales is that three of them were relatively highly correlated with one another (i.e. all except the denial of analytic knowledge). This suggests that it might be worth thinking about new age beliefs as a single constellation and acknowledging that adherence to this system can account for some individual differences in risk perception.

Cotgrove (1982) also proposed that adherence to a belief system explained individual differences in risk perception. He divided worldviews into the 'cornucopian' and the 'catastrophist'. Cornucopians believe that innovation in technology provides access to a world of plenty. Catastrophists believe it opens the door to disaster. These are general frames of reference, orientations to the evaluation of new information. The direct empirical evidence for Cotgrove's proposition is limited, but again it ties in to work on cognitive styles. Cotgrove's catastrophists seem to believe the consequences of technological change are not only bad but also uncontrollable. In this context it might seem sensible to review some of the work on what has come to be called 'optimistic bias'. However, that is reviewed in Chapter 4, in relation to decision-making about risk.

Another major differentiator between people is their belief in the trustworthiness of experts or regulatory regimes. For example, not surprisingly, Williams and Hammitt (2001) found that distrust in regulatory agencies and the safety of the food supply were linked to greater perceived risk. The role of trust in risk perception and responses to risk communication will be examined in Chapter 6. There is some evidence that people generally are more distrusting of some sources (e.g. politicians) and trusting of others (e.g. medical practitioners) and this also is discussed in Chapter 6. There is evidence that some groups of people are more distrusting of particular sources than others. For instance, environmentalists are less likely to trust industry or government scientists. However, there is a question as to whether an individual's trust levels are specific to the particular source and/or to the particular hazard or, indeed, whether some people are generally more 'trusting' when it comes to risk. Nevertheless, belief in the trustworthiness of information about a hazard will normally differ across people and the extent to which it does can be expected to affect risk perceptions.

So far this section has focused on the possibility that general belief systems may influence risk perceptions. There is also a wealth of research that examines the relationship between specific attitudes to a hazard or values applicable to the hazard and the risks perceived to be associated with that hazard. For instance, van der Pligt (1992) reports a programme of research on attitudes towards nuclear power. He found that negative attitudes towards the siting of a nuclear power plant locally were highly correlated with estimates of its risk. Establishing that this sort of association of attitude and risk estimate exists may seem trivial at one level, but it begs further analysis. The origin and precise role of the negative attitude then become a target for research. Does the attitude account for variability in risk estimates independent of differences in knowledge or independent of differences in potential personal gain from having the nuclear plant located locally? Is the attitude dependent upon knowledge in any way? Is the attitude open to change? Is the attitude self-serving (i.e. justifying decisions already taken or prior actions)? Is the attitude an attribute of group membership (e.g. of a pressure group or a political party)? The list of questions is virtually infinite. Van der Pligt (1992) addresses many of these questions admirably. His approach is one that shows how intimately the study of risk perception can and should be linked into the broader methods and theories of social psychology. He treats the topic of the risk of nuclear power as a target of social psychological analysis. In doing so, it is inevitable that individual differences in attitudes will be carefully explored and related to risk perceptions.

7   Group differences in risk perception

7.1   International comparisons

There have been numerous studies that have looked at whether the Slovic et al. (1980) pattern of hazard perception would be replicated in samples from different populations. Cvetkovich and Earle (1991) emphasise the importance of cross-cultural comparisons in potentially identifying explanations for differences in risk perception. International studies contrasted perceptions of people in the United States, Hungary (Englander et al., 1986), Norway (Teigen et al., 1988), Hong Kong (Keown, 1989), Japan (Hinman et al., 1993; Kleinhesselink and Rosa, 1991; Kleinhesselink, 1992), Poland (Goszczynska et al., 1991), China

(Jianguang, 1993), Sweden and Brazil (Nyland, 1993) and the erstwhile Soviet Union (Mechitov and Rebrik, 1990). While Brun (1992) reported that the classic factor structure had been shown to be stable across different populations in the USA (for instance, by Gould et al., 1988; and by Kunreather et al., 1990), some of the international studies (Englander et al., 1986; Teigen et al., 1988) have shown cultural differences in the factor loadings for some of the dimensions. For instance, in US samples, involuntary and uncontrollable characteristics loaded on the 'Unknown' risk dimension, whereas in the Hungarian sample (Englander et al., 1986) they loaded on the 'dread' risk dimension. Moreover, the Hungarians estimated the risk associated with most of the hazards to be lower than did those in the USA. In a Norwegian study (Teigen et al., 1988), though the two dimensions emerged with the same characteristics loading on them as for the US samples, they were reversed – that is, the first factor to emerge (with the biggest percentage of variance) had the characteristics that loaded on the Dread dimension. Within each country the relative ordering of concerns was also different. For instance, Hungarians saw relatively greater risk from common hazards (e.g. railroads, home appliances), whereas those in the USA were more concerned with high technology hazards (e.g. radiation, chemicals). Kleinhesselink and Rosa (1991), studying Japanese, replicated the original factor structure but also found difference between the United States and Japanese. For instance, the Japanese were more likely to rate nuclear power generation and AIDS risks as 'known'. Bronfman and Cifuentes (2003) studied a large sample in Chile. They found the expected dimensions of 'dread' and 'unknown' risk and additionally a factor which they labelled 'personal effect' (a composite of number of exposed people and the attribute 'personal effect'). Slovic has also engaged in international studies: for instance, in Sweden (Slovic et al., 1989), in Canada (Slovic et al., 1991; Krewski et al., 1995a, 1995b) and in France (Slovic et al., 1996). He and his collaborators have generally found support for the original model.

However, Rohrmann (1991), reviewing the evidence to that time, concluded that it was unproven that there are cross-cultural universals in the structure of hazard perception. There are clearly some differences between countries. It is not possible to say whether these are a function of culture in the broadest sense or a product of some complex interaction between other factors (e.g. differences in direct exposure to the hazard, differences in political or economic context in which the hazard is generated and controlled, or differences in the availability of information about the hazard).

In any case, Sjöberg (1995) has advised caution in using the studies quoted above as the basis for making assertions about national differences. Researchers have seldom carried out large surveys of random samples of a national population. Often they take a convenience sample of students. Mechitov and Rebrik (1990) offer the only pre-Glasnost study of risk perception in the USSR, but their sample comprises members of the Moscow academy of sciences. While the demand for fully representative samples may be unrealistic given the resource implications, Sjöberg offers an alternative that researchers should consider. Several of his studies involve diverse samples of widely different key groups (e.g. unskilled workers, teachers, engineers, medical workers, and so on). He cannot claim representativeness, but he aims to sample from groups that might highlight weaknesses in his hypotheses.

7.2   Gender and socio-demographic differences

Gender differences in risk perception have been thoroughly explored, even though no comprehensive review of the literature in this regard has been published. Several studies have shown that women perceive more threat to the environment than men (Schmidt and Gifford, 1989; Pillisuk et al., 1987). Savage (1993) claimed women, blacks, less well-educated and the young are more likely to dread aviation accidents, house fires, auto accidents and stomach cancer. Gustafson (1998) found greater perceived risk of crime among women. Davidson and Frendenburg (1996) found women rated the risk of nuclear waste and power higher. Barke and Jenkins-Smith (1997) showed even women scientists report higher risk assessments for nuclear technologies. Bord and O'Connor (1997) report women show greater concern about hazardous waste and global warming. Dosman et al. (2001) found that women rate food safety risks higher. Such gender differences are apparent in childhood: girls have a higher estimate of the risks associated with play than do boys (Hillier and Morrongiello, 1998).

Slovic (1997) argued that sex is strongly related to risk judgements and attitudes. He quotes several studies that report that men tend to judge risks as smaller and less problematic than do women (Brody, 1984; Carney, 1971; Dejoy, 1992; Gutteling and Wiegman, 1993; Gwartney-Gibbs and Lach, 1991; Pillisuk and Acredolo, 1988; Sjöberg and Drotz-Sjöberg, 1993; Slovic et al., 1993; Spigner et al., 1993; Steger and Witte, 1989; Stern et al., 1993). Flynn et al. (1994) offer a suggested reason for this apparent difference between men and women. In their sample of 1,512 Americans the difference between white males and females actually arose because a subset of about 30 per cent the men rated the risks particularly low. The rest of the men performed like the women. The men who rated risk low were more likely to be better educated, had higher household incomes and were politically more conservative. They showed greater trust in authorities and institutions, were anti-egalitarian and did not want power to make decisions on risks devolved to the public. This study also showed no difference between non-white males and females. The study suggests that the sex difference that is proclaimed to exist may occur because those males and females who are chosen for risk research studies have different socio-demographical and attitudinal characteristics. This would explain why many studies do not report sex differences in risk perceptions. They may have better-matched male and female samples. If Flynn *et al.* are right, it would suggest that before claiming any sex differences in risk perceptions, in the future researchers should partial out the effects of other socio-demographic and attitudinal variables. It would also suggest that any differences between the sexes that are found in this arena are unlikely to be traceable to biological origins.

Hakes and Viscusi (2004) explored demographic differences in the overestimation and underestimation of mortality risks in a sample of 493 US adults. They found the expected pattern overall: people overestimate the small risks of death, such as botulism or fireworks, and underestimate the larger risks, such as diabetes and heart disease. They used regression methods to determine the separate effects of gender, race and education upon mortality risk perceptions. If people had been to college, there were no differences by race or gender. If they had not been to college, females and non-whites were found to have a less accurate perception of mortality rates. Age was positively correlated with accuracy of estimates, especially for women concerning frequent causes of death. Non-white men were less accurate than white men, but there was no difference by race among females. Non-whites tended to exhibit less improvement of accuracy with age.

Race and gender are often examined in parallel (Finucane *et al.*, 2000). Satterfield *et al.* (2004) set out to explore whether the finding that a subset of white males (as identified by Flynn *et al.*, 1994) stand out for their uniformly low perceptions of environmental health risks in comparison to most non-whites and most females should be simply attributed to the advantageous social position that sub-group occupies in the USA. Satterfield *et al.* suggested that the effect of material social advantage might be paralleled by differences in the subjective experience of vulnerability and by socio-political evaluations pertaining to environmental injustice. This thesis would suggest the gender and race differences that are regularly found in risk perception originate not just because of substantive differences in power to control risk but also because people with less power over risks feel more likely to be at risk and feel risk to be inequitably distributed. Using the US National Risk Survey ($n = 1192$, stratified random household sample of over-18-year-olds contacted by telephone, reflecting a 47 per cent response rate), Satterfield *et al.* explored 'the white male effect'. Bord and Connor (1997) had already argued that women perceive risk to be higher because they feel more vulnerable. Satterfield *et al.* found that white males rated themselves as significantly less vulnerable (operationalised primarily in terms of their control over risks to their health and whether they felt discriminated against) than did females or non-whites. They then examined the relationship between subjective vulnerability and perception of a broad range of hazards. They found vulnerability most positively related to environmental health hazards. The relationship was weaker with natural hazards, those that were extremely familiar or those risks over which individuals have personal control. It seems that subjective vulnerability is linked to raised risk estimates in precisely those areas where social inequalities might result in the less powerful being more subject to risk. Satterfield *et al.* also measured beliefs about environmental injustice. The measure revolved around beliefs about whether minority communities had a disproportionate share of hazardous facilities, whether they were forced to accept them for economic reasons, whether they lacked the political power to prevent their imposition, and whether government should have intervened to restrict their placement. The major division on this measure was between whites and non-whites, though white females did perceive greater environmental injustice than white males. Risk estimates were positively correlated with perceived environmental injustice. Satterfield *et al.* note that, taken together, perceived vulnerability and environmental injustice are good predictors of risk estimates. They suggest that the 'white male effect' is in part at least a product of white males feeling less vulnerable and perceiving less injustice. Those white males who had higher vulnerability and injustice scores also produced higher risk estimates. Satterfield *et al.* do not argue that these two beliefs completely explain differences in risk perception attributable to race and gender. Even when age, education, income, political orientation and religious commitment were added alongside vulnerability and injustice in a regression attempting to explain variability in risk estimates, race and gender still accounted additionally for risk ratings. It turns out, then, that gender, and to a lesser extent race, remains a robust predictor of risk perception.

Johnson (2002a) also explored gender and race differences in risk perception. Using a convenience sample of 1,100 found in Philadelphia courthouses while awaiting the call to jury service, he examined perceptions of air pollution. While he found few statistically significant differences between the sexes or by race, he did find that non-whites (and particularly non-white women) reported more concern about and sensitivity to air pollution. They also reported more outdoor activity and exposure to air pollution. This seems to fit the Satterfield *et al.* pattern: greater perceived exposure, hence vulnerability, and higher risk estimates. In relation to perceptions of air quality, Howel *et al.* (2002) also showed that concern was greater in those living proximate to industry and who had health problems. Again, vulnerability might be seen to be relevant in explained risk perception. Dosman *et al.* (2001), in examining the socio-economic correlates of risk perception concerning health and food safety, found that women rate such risk greater, but also that more risk is perceived by those who have more young children and who have lower household incomes. This may provide further support for the suggestion that material or subjective vulnerability plays a role in explaining socio-demographic differences in risk perception.

It is important in examining socio-demographic effects upon risk perception not to become too focused upon data from the USA, particularly because the significance of ethnicity is quite different in some other cultures. Frewer (1999a) conducted a national survey sampling 1,000 adults in the UK to examine perceptions of the person risk or the risk to the general public engendered by a broad range of hazards. The demographic effects considered were: gender, ethnicity, responsibility for young children, age, occupation, income and region. She found that women perceived more risk from a given hazard than did men. Comparing Europeans, Asians and Afro-Caribbeans in the sample, she found that personal and general risks were perceived to be greater by Afro-Caribbeans, whose ratings were similar to those overall of women. Members of occupational groups A and B tended to perceive less personal risk from the hazards. Perceptions of both personal and general risk were highest for those earning least and lowest for those earning most. Responsibility for young children was not associated with increased perceptions of risk or increased demands for risk mitigation. Older people perceived greater personal risk but not general risk. There appeared to be greater concern for both personal and general risk in the Midlands and south of the UK than in the north and Scotland.

In China, Xie *et al.* (2003) conducted two surveys (in 1996 and 1998) in urban areas. Overall, they found greater concern for risks that threaten national stability and economic development than for those associated with technological developments. Women tended to perceive higher risks than men. However, there were smaller and fewer differences between men and women in the more educated and more influential occupational groups. Workers who had lost their jobs or who were employed by companies that were in difficulty were more likely to be concerned about risks in their daily lives. Employees in high-profit firms were more likely to be concerned about macroscopic catastrophic hazards. Interestingly, other work in China (Schmidt and Wei, 2006) has shown that the Chinese are more likely than Western counterparts to perceive that they have control over a broad range of risk topics. The researchers accounted for this by proposing that the Chinese are less critical of scientific innovation and the controls that surround it than those in Europe or the USA.

This brief review of socio-demographic differences in risk perception will be supplemented elsewhere in this book, because in reporting the findings of most studies of risk decision-making, communication or management it is necessary to refer to the impact of background factors. However, the review gives a flavour of where theorising about the established socio-demographic differences is going. Theories that explain gender or race or age differences in terms of, on the one hand, subjective vulnerability and control and, on the other, material inequities in exposure and social beliefs about injustice are gaining momentum. This is essentially a move to explain risk perception in terms of a social psychological analysis. In some ways, this is related to the assertions that emerge from the cultural biases theory of Douglas (1986) that is described below. There are also important differences between this social psychological theorising and that of the cultural biases theorists. The social psychological models will incorporate explanatory constructs at a number of levels of analysis: the intra-psychic (cognitive, conative and oretic), the interpersonal, the institutional and intergroup, as well as the socio-historical and material. The social psychological models are designed to analyse change. In considering how data about risk perception can be interpreted, it is useful to assess the relevance of each of these salient levels of analysis.

The existence of individual and group differences in risk perception needs to be taken into account in the context of efforts at risk communication and risk management. It might be sensible to use these findings to sharpen the focus of interventions to educate about risk. However, in deciding how to use these findings, particularly those concerning group differences (like race or gender), it is important to remember the caveats about methodological rigour with which this chapter began. The jury must still be out on the viability of significant generalisations about socio-demographic differences.

The research that systematically examines cross-cultural differences in risk-taking is more limited. There are some examples – for instance, Hsee and Weber (1999) reported Chinese to be more risk seeking than Americans, even though both sets of nationals predicted the opposite. It is possible that this finding ties in to the finding mentioned above from

Schmidt and Wei (2006) that suggested that Chinese believe they have greater control over risks.

Clearly, the methodological difficulties of conducting robust research in this area are significant, but it would be worth attempting. The globalisation of hazards means that cross-cultural relativities in the willingness to seek and take risks become of vital importance. Johnson (2004a, 2004b) acknowledges that progress in this area will probably require work that focuses upon ethnic identity and the processes of acculturation rather than simple indicators of ethnicity. The reasons that groups differ in their responses to risks lie in their systems of beliefs and their positions in power hierarchies. Individuals within groups will differ according to the extent to which they identify with the group and the extent to which they are fully acculturated into its norms and beliefs. We return to the significance of social identity processes in Chapter 9.

7.3   Expert and lay differences

The significance of the differences between experts and lay people in risk perceptions is recognised. To these differences are attributed many of the problems that arise when decisions have to be taken about controversial hazards. Garvin (2001) said that scientists, policy-makers and the lay public employ different, though equally legitimate, forms of rationality when evaluating evidence and generating knowledge about hazards. She opines that scientists use scientific rationality, policy-makers use political rationality and the public use social rationality. This may sound glib but it is shorthand for a proposition that the three work with different analytical paradigms. Scientists look for legitimate evidence from studies that adhere to the scientific method and base dismissal of conflicting evidence also on this method. Estimates of the certainty of conclusions are given in probabilistic terms. Complex issues are analysed by compartmentalisation of their elements, and knowledge is recognised as specific and limited. Knowledge is achieved in the scientific paradigm through incremental accumulation of evidence. Policy-makers look for evidence that is readily available and from any source. Its legitimacy is perceived in terms of its political, economic and social implications. Evidence is dismissed if it is not politically expedient to acknowledge it. Conceptualisation of certainty is thus context-specific. For complex issues, only those elements that are immediately known to need to be understood are examined. The knowledge that results is instrumental and contextualised. It is applied to the current situation only. The public use popular sources. Evidence is legitimated through 'received wisdom' and dismissed if it fails to be considered 'common sense'. Degrees of uncertainty are not easily recognised: a thing is, or it is not. Understanding of complex issues is constrained by the access to limited sources. Knowledge is tacit, experiential and individualised. Knowledge accumulation is not systematic but focuses upon personal history.

Garvin would be the first to note that these descriptions present oversimplified notions of stereotyped or caricatured differences. It certainly ignores the complexity of the concept of the 'lay public'. Yet it serves to raise the question about the way identifiable groupings do differ in their ways of collecting and interpreting information. Unfortunately, there is no comprehensive review of the empirical relationship between differences in analytical paradigm adopted and risk estimation.

Of course, there are many empirical studies of the differences between experts and lay people in their estimates of risk. Kraus et al. (1992) and Slovic et al. (1985, 1995) explored differences regarding toxicological hazards. Barke and Jenkins-Smith (1993) and Flynn et al. (1993) looked at the nuclear industry. McDaniels et al. (1997a) and Lazo et al. (2000) examined ecological risks. Gutteling and Kuttschreuter (1999, 2002) studied computing hazards. The conclusion that emerges is that there are substantial differences between lay and expert views of risk (Wright et al., 2000). Experts generally rate risk as lower. There is also some, weaker, evidence that they are more likely to produce risk estimates that more closely approximate the empirical data available. So, for instance, if the risk estimate required is the number of fatalities associated with a particular hazard, experts are more likely to be able to provide an estimate close to that on the records. In one sense this is unremarkable: expertise is defined in terms of knowledge and it would be surprising if experts were not more accurate on the estimate of risks pertaining to their own area of expertise. The more interesting differences between the lay public and experts emerge where there are no record-book right or wrong answers, where the level of risk is still uncertain. Even in these areas, where experts cannot be assumed to have preferential knowledge, there are differences between them and the public. For instance, Krause et al. (1992) showed that, while experts perceive similar risks to be associated with chemicals and prescription drugs, lay people attribute greater risk to chemicals than prescription drugs. This may be because experts are not factoring in potential benefits when they evaluate the risk of prescription drugs and lay people are. Unfortunately, this study, like a lot of those that examine differences between experts and lay people, provides no integral test of possible reasons for the differences that are found. It would be of tremendous value if researchers did start to examine the substantive correlates of these differences between experts and lay people. This would parallel the effort now to explain the social psychological bases for gender and race differences.

Thomson *et al.* (2004) is illustrative of another type of study. They compared risk perceptions of experts and novices in relation to helicopter operations. Matching for demographic characteristics, gender and background factors, they still found that experts were more veridical in their estimates of risk. Interestingly, experts were also more willing to undertake activities that they knew to be risky. This study clearly does not deal with the lay/expert dichotomy; novices even though not expert are not lay. It is presented here because it is one of the few studies that takes seriously the need to match for socio-demographical variables before making comparisons between experts and others.

Rowe and Wright (2001), after reviewing nine studies of the expert–lay differences, argued that they were not so clear-cut as had been previously suggested. The failure of studies to match expert and non-expert samples on the basis of age, socio-economic status, culture and gender (all factors established to affect risk perception) undermines their prime conclusion. Often studies fail to provide details of the socio-demographics of the two groups. Where they do, they often show that the experts include more white males and are more highly educated than the non-experts.

Understanding properly the nature of disparities between expert and lay views of risks is undoubtedly important (Wright *et al.*, 2002). Some of the early research was used in policy-making to suggest that, since lay risk estimates were more inaccurate, their concerns were to be taken less seriously. Doubtless, it was not the researchers' intention that their findings should be used in this way. Lay perceptions cannot be discounted just because they may be more inaccurate when judged against limited objective criteria. If lay perceptions account for lay decisions and actions, it is those perceptions that will matter to practitioners in risk management.

8   Cultural Theory

Any examination of differences in risk perception must include Cultural Theory. This theory has been important in asserting that what societies choose to call risky is determined not by nature but by social and cultural factors. Therefore, inevitably there will be systematic differences in risk judgements between people from different cultural backgrounds irrespective of the objective evidence and thus there can be no simple generally acceptable metric for risk assessment.

Wildavsky (1993) argued that the literature on risk perception generally assumes that individuals pursue preferences or interests that they already have. These inform their perception of risk. Indeed, this has been amply evidenced above in the work on individual differences. However,

Wildavsky goes further than this; he wanted to explain why individuals have these prior preferences and interests. He postulated that culture explains the pattern of risk perceptions. Essentially, Wildavsky says that culture explains the preferences people have for different ways of life and the way they justify their actions, and these in turn determine their priorities in choosing what to fear.

Wildavsky claims that there is no systematic relationship between what people know about a hazard and their perception of the risk associated with it. This claim would seem overstated given some of the evidence described above, but it is then allied to a further claim. Wildavsky also wishes to propose that no one has related individual differences in personality to risk perception or risk-taking. This is clearly open to challenge. Having made these assertions, Wildavsky proceeds to acknowledge that the most powerful predictor of variability in risk perception is 'trust in institutions'. Evidence of this relationship has been presented above. The implication that Wildavsky takes from this finding is that individuals make their decisions about what to fear after determining whether they believe the source that provides the risk assessment. This leads to the more basic question: How do people know whom to trust?

Wildavsky believes that the Cultural Theory first developed by Mary Douglas (Douglas, 1986; Douglas and Wildavsky, 1982; Thompson *et al.*, 1990; Dake and Wildavsky; 1991) provides the answer. According to Cultural Theory, people choose what to fear to defend their way of life (or culture). The hazards that people will be concerned about are those that threaten locally valued social and institutional arrangements. So, risk perception will vary systematically according to the preoccupations of the culture (its biases). Douglas (1982) defines cultural biases in terms of the attitudes and beliefs shared by a group. Cultural biases prioritise the risks to which a group will attend. These differences between groups cannot be explained in terms of individual cognitive processes or by the technical assessment of risk levels.

Cultural Theory suggests that there is a finite number of mutually contradictory cultural biases. In this theory, cultural biases are not assumed to be totally predetermined for the individual by societal constraints. The individual is seen to have some choice in the cultural bias they adopt. People vary in the extent to which they are part of bounded groups (a dimension labelled 'group') and the extent to which their social interactions are rule-bound or negotiated (a dimension labelled 'grid'). 'Group' and 'grid' position have been linked to identify four types of cultural bias: hierarchists (high grid/high group), sectarians or egalitarians (low grid/high group), fatalists (high grid/low group) and individualists (low grid/low group).

The theory predicts that members of a hierarchical culture will approve of technology, providing it is certified safe by experts and they will expect their experts normally to pronounce technology as safe. Individualists are predicted to view risk as an opportunity and will therefore be optimistic about technology. Fatalists do not knowingly take risks but accept that they will be subjected to risk and accept it. Egalitarians will suspect technology, considering it as part of the machinery that maintains inequalities that harm society and the environment. The problem posed for any policy-maker managing a hazard is that people from within these different cultural biases will inevitably not achieve a consensus upon the acceptability or desirability of the risk (Schwarz and Thompson, 1990).

Dake and Wildavsky (1991) provided empirical support for the theory by comparing how individuals rate the risks of technology compared to social deviance, war and economic decline. Egalitarians feared technology a lot, but social deviance less. Hierarchists thought technology benign, as long as it was approved by experts, but feared social deviance. Individualists thought technology was an opportunity, deviance an irrelevance if it did not affect them personally, but considered war fearful because it disrupts economic activity. Fatalists were not considered in the study.

Douglas and Calvez (1990) use cultural theory to explain the way communities react to the existence of HIV infection. In their paper, rather confusingly, the four types of culture are labelled 'isolate', 'individualist', 'central community' and 'dissenting enclave'. Differences between the four types in attitudes towards the body and infection are highlighted. Effectively, four viewpoints are identified: the established medical community, the community at large, the enclaves and the gay community. Need for protection of the wider community at the expense of certain individuals is seen to emerge as a prime concern and determiner of attitudes towards, and beliefs about, the risks of AIDS/HIV.

Central to the cultural approach to risk is the assumption that there is nothing 'hard-wired' in cognitive processes that requires certain biases in perception. This is something that cultural theorists accuse those cognitive psychologists who study heuristics and biases in risk judgements of introducing implicitly. Cultural theorists, in contrast, would have us focus upon the social determinants of what individuals choose to pay attention to. They would emphasise that risk judgements only have meaning because they exist within a social frame of meaning construction.

It is not clear from the theory how people come to adopt a particular cultural perspective. Why are some people egalitarians and others not? For the theory to be more than just another illustration that certain attitude patterns are related to risk perceptions in a systematic fashion, it would need to provide a model of how people acquire their cultural stance. It is also not clear whether people are thought to inhabit these ideal cultural personas (the egalitarian, the hierarchist, the individualist) in a transient fashion or to reside in these categories for long periods. A good social psychological model would need to explain change in cultural perspective that characterises an individual.

Cultural Theory has also been criticised because its two-by-two classification of cultural diversity is seen as overly simplistic. Not all ways of life can be fitted into this neat framework. It might be considered ironic that it posits two orthogonal dimensions upon which all cultural biases can be encapsulated. Cultural theorists would certainly castigate the psychometric paradigm for such dimensional paucity.

Boholm (1996), in an unremitting critique of Cultural Theory, dismisses it as conceptually confused and inconsistent. To mention but a few of the problems Boholm identifies: the nature of the interaction between cultural bias and social relations to produce 'way of life' is poorly defined; the group-grid constructs are both open to various interpretations; the typology of four 'ways of life' (with a fifth – the hermit – sometimes acknowledged) is treated as exhaustive; there is assumed to be a one-to-one correspondence between the individual and a 'way of life'; and, the model cannot explain change. Boholm is attacking the epistemological base of Cultural Theory: it is a functionalist theory and is thus argued to be tautological. Essentially, the theory says that people fear those things that threaten their way of life, but their way of life is defined by the very things they say they fear. The failure to adequately, independently, define 'way of life' or cultural bias is a great problem for Cultural Theory.

In fact, in Cultural Theory empirical work, it is the self-reported belief systems of individuals that are the basis for classification rather than any independent allocation of people to the four types on the basis of verifiable social or cultural parameters. It also turns out that, in several studies (e.g. Dake, 1991), measures of hierarchism and individualism are highly positively correlated, suggesting that it may not be sensible to assume they are separate cultural biases. In reality, Dake's data suggest that the main distinction is between the egalitarians and everyone else. This ties back to Cotgrove's (1982) separation of cornucopians and catastrophists described earlier.

Sjöberg (1997) presents a thoughtful review of empirical work on Cultural Theory and risk perception. He concludes that there is little quantitative evidence (e.g. Brenot and Bonnefous, 1995; Grendstad and Selle, 1994) that shows cultural biases are strongly predictive of risk perception. While acknowledging that a quantitative approach to the test of Cultural Theory may offer only a limited evaluation of what it has to offer, he goes on to present a telling critique. In the article, Sjöberg presents new data sets that explore the relationship between cultural biases (using the scales developed by Dake) and risk judgements. He found that the reliabilities of the scales were weak and that the correlations between biases and risk judgement were low (suggesting that cultural bias explains little variability in risk judgements). Interestingly, cultural bias indices were found to add very little to the explanatory power that the psychometric paradigm hazard characteristics provide for risk estimates. The samples he used were drawn from Sweden, Brazil, Romania and Bulgaria. They included people from very different social backgrounds: teachers, students, blue-collar workers, slum dwellers and homeless people. Contrary to the expectations of Cultural Theory, risk judgements followed similar rank orders in these very different categories of people. Sjöberg concludes that cultural biases are not major factors in risk perception but make a very minor contribution to its explanation.

As a postscript, it should be noted that Marris *et al.* (1998) did present data that they argued provided support for the cultural bias explanation of variability in risk perception. Sjöberg (2002) provides an informative critique of that work. It is useful to reflect upon this, in that he exposes areas of common weakness in the empirical risk research. Sjöberg points out:

- the low response rate (30 per cent) on which the sample is based
- the prime variable was poorly measured – only one third of the sample could be assigned to one of the four types suggested by the theory, and the rest could not be classified using the self-report data collected
- the weakness of the absolute level of the reported relationship between cultural biases and risk perception (the former explained on average 3 per cent of variability in the latter) was not treated as critical; for practical purposes, the failure to explain major amounts of variability undermines the value of finding a statistically significant correlation.

The cautions inherent in this critique are worth bearing in mind when looking at the conclusions drawn from any of the survey research presented in this chapter.

Conclusion

Individuals and groups do differ in their perception of risks. This much is clear from the empirical evidence. However, no one would pretend that such differences have been fully catalogued. The data appear in many different types of study and often the exploration of individual or group (particularly socio-demographic) differences is not the main object of the research. Such differences are reported merely as additional findings.

Sometimes they are treated as 'noise' in the data. Consequently, there is actually a lot of evidence that these differences exist, but their existence has not been subjected to any coherent systematic analysis. The attempts to describe them tend to pose more questions than they answer.

It is important – when the body of evidence is still relatively slender or, more accurately, incoherent – not to draw grand or overgeneralised conclusions. Yet it is tempting to suggest that, when there is more systematic evidence, the significance of differential vulnerability in predisposing differences in risk perception will emerge. Vulnerability would need to comprise two major components: the psychological and the material. Psychological vulnerability would include enduring anxiety levels, cognitive style biases and proclivity to seek novelty. Material vulnerability would include limitations in control over exposure to the hazard as a consequence of social position. This proposition is supported by recent research on the effects of perceived power upon the willingness to take risks. Anderson and Galinsky (2006) found that individuals with a higher sense of their own power were willing to take greater risks and to seek greater risk. They found that the effects of power were mediated by optimistic risk perceptions rather than by self-efficacy beliefs.

Vulnerability would not in itself explain risk-perception differentials. But it could be a vital ingredient in determining the mental model of a hazard that an individual or group would accept as appropriate or, indeed, help to create. The less vulnerable might be more likely to accept a model of the hazard that posits that it can and will be controllable. This type of explanation for differences in risk perception relies upon the assumption that people are actively engaged in the interpretation of hazards but they are constrained in how they do this by the psychological, interpersonal, societal and material resources that they have available. The interpersonal and societal resources that are differentially available will include access to particular mental models of risk or specific social belief systems that evaluate the hazard.

4   Decision-making about risks

Chapter preview

All decisions involve risk at some level – minimally they involve the risk that they will be the wrong decision to have made. Consequently, it is necessary to be selective about the work on decision-making that is reported here. This chapter focuses upon three domains of research relevant to decision-making and risk. It looks first at heuristics, biases and risk framing; including optimistic bias and hindsight bias. Second, it describes the role of naive theories, schemas and mental models of risk in decision-making. Finally, it summarises some of the literature on risk in group decision-making, focusing upon group dynamics that influence individual risk estimates.

1   Decisions in uncertainty

There has been considerable research that has examined how people make decisions under conditions of uncertainty. Some of this work explores how people make decisions when they have incomplete or contradictory information. For instance, how will I decide where to go to meet a friend in a large train station when I do not know where exactly in the station she will be? Alternatively, how do I decide what to do if I have two sets of instructions and one says my friend will be at one train station, the other says she will be at a different station? Such studies are not examining decisions about what would commonly be called hazards. Yet they are investigating decisions where risk is involved. Failing to find my friend is the risk I run in the example given. Other work focuses specifically on how people make decisions about established hazards or known risks. For example, there is a volume of research on how gamblers determine on what, when and how much to bet. Similarly there are studies of how communities decide how to respond to the prospect of having a dangerous industrial facility sited in their midst. Such studies are clearly concerned with how decisions about a hazard are taken. The distinction between decision-making under uncertainty and decision-making about known hazards may seem fuzzy, since uncertainty engenders risk and even known hazards are normally surrounded by uncertainty. However, the notion of the distinction is worth bearing in mind when considering the various studies described here, because much of the work on heuristics used in decision-making under uncertainty is not primarily aimed at understanding risk-taking; it is aimed at achieving a fundamental understanding of the cognitive processes that underlie the use of information.

2 Heuristics, biases and risk framing

Humans appear to fail miserably when it comes to rational decision-making (Haselton and Buss, 2001). They ignore base rates when estimating probabilities; commit the 'sunk cost fallacy' (continuing to invest in failure because they have done so before), are naively optimistic, take undue credit for their achievements and do not recognise self-inflicted failures. In addition, they overestimate the number of others who share their beliefs, demonstrate 'hindsight bias', have limited understanding of chance, perceive illusory relationships between non-contingent events and overestimate their own ability to impose control. The list could be extended: they are overconfident in their judgements; they engage in spurious hyperprecision when making predictions; they ignore the limits of the data available to them, and so on. Some of these apparently non-rational aspects of human decision-making are explored below. Not all can be covered. The selection here is based on the particular relevance of the bias to risk-related decisions.

2.1 Heuristics and biases

Chapter 2 briefly introduced the work of Tversky and Kahneman (1974) on heuristics and biases that influence decision-making under conditions of uncertainty. It is appropriate here to examine that work in greater detail. They started from the fact that we frequently have to make judgements about the probability of something with incomplete information. They noted that a limited number of heuristic principles are used when we assess the probability of an event or the probability that an object will possess certain characteristics. These heuristics revolve around representativeness, availability and anchoring (Nisbett and Ross, 1980; Kahneman et al., 1982).

2.1.1 Representativeness If asked what is the probability that object A belongs to class B, people typically assume that the probability is greater if A resembles B in some fashion. This approach to probability assessment leads to serious errors, because it ignores several factors that should be considered when estimating probability:

- It is insensitive to the prior probability of the association between A and B – the probability estimate should be influenced by any data on the frequency with which A and B have been associated in the past, but the representativeness heuristic tends to block attributing importance to these baseline data.
- It is insensitive to information on the size of the sample to be used in assessing the association between A and B – the probability estimate should take into account whether information on the past association between A and B was based on a large or small sample of instances, but the role of a larger sample offering a more robust platform for assuming association is ignored.
- The nature of chance is misconceived – people tend to assume that patterns will occur in what are in reality truly random events (for instance, after a series of heads appearing when a coin is tossed, they believe a tail is 'due' even if the number of tosses is relatively small).
- It is insensitive to the amount of information provided that is actually predictive – people are willing to make estimates of probability even when they lack any predictive data.
- It is not subjected to appropriate tests of validity – the greater the apparent representativeness, the greater the assumed validity of the inference.
- It is not sensitive to established statistical phenomena (such as regression to the mean where in successive measurements the parameter will return from any outlying value to the mean value) – the representativeness heuristic tends to lead to the assumption that the observed association between A and B will not vary over time or circumstances.

2.1.2   Availability Where asked to estimate the frequency of an event or the probability of an event, typically people assume that the probability is greater if they can easily remember an instance of the event. This leads to predictable biases:

- If the event is associated with more retrieval instances, its probability will be overestimated. Many factors influence retrievability – including familiarity and salience (i.e. personal significance). The cognitive approach adopted for searching for instances will also influence retrievability. For instance, if asked to evaluate the probability of flooding in London, the retrieval from memory of relevant information or images might be organised by a preoccupation with climate change or by concern for property prices. The images retrieved will be dependent upon the frame of search and these in turn will influence the perceived probability of flooding. It might be imagined that the climate change frame would result in a greater probability estimate.

- Sometimes the event is not associated with retrieval memories. In such cases it seems that estimates of probability can be affected by the ease with which it is possible to imagine that something, or things like it, might occur – the ease of imaginability is positively associated with perceived probability. For instance, where someone can easily imagine a variety of disasters associated with a possible course of action, they are more likely to consider that action will lead to disaster.

- It is associated with persevering in believing in 'illusory correlations' – assumptions of the association between two objects that have been based in systems of social belief (for example, that all people with red hair have fiery tempers). The availability heuristic would support illusory correlations because the predominant social belief would prioritise retrieval of instances that support the claim.

2.1.3   Adjustment and anchoring Where people are asked to make an estimate of the value of some object, typically people will start with an initial guess (the 'anchor'), which may be based on the original way in which the question is formulated or on some partial computation, and will then adjust the estimate as they acquire further data or conduct more analysis. However, the adjustments made to the initial estimate are rarely adequate, as they tend to be too small.

2.1.4   Heuristics and risk It is not difficult to see that these heuristics that drive probability estimates will have significance for risk perception and for decisions that have to be made about risks. It is easy to imagine how probability estimates associated with a new hazard that resembles some earlier hazard could be affected by the representativeness heuristic. For instance, the public's estimate of the likelihood of a new food contaminant affecting human health might be driven by the perceived similarity between it and some earlier contaminant. The fact that the two are very different at the microbiological level might be dismissed. Evidence of much smaller health impacts in the later contaminant might be ignored. The greater viability of medical interventions for it could be underestimated. The role of the representativeness heuristic in distorting risk estimates on a daily basis cannot be ignored.

Similarly, the availability heuristic is used all the time. It is worth remembering that increased availability increases perceived probability, but availability is driven not just by the frequency with which the thing (for example, the hazardous event) is seen to occur. It is also driven by retrieval from memory of other psychologically (not necessarily logically) relevant things. For instance, probability estimates of specific disasters can be associated with images from films or books lodged in the memory. Since disaster movies are not infrequent, the question becomes: Do people learn to discount the retrieved film or TV image when coming to their estimates of risk in their daily lives? Rather more intriguing is the issue of whether, by discussing a low-probability hazard, the perceived probability of its occurrence increases because availability has been increased. There does seem to be evidence of this from the debates concerning genetically modified organisms, where in the UK perceived risk increased as the media coverage of the issues surrounding GM crops increased. At a more mundane level, general estimates of street crime are linked to press reports of incidents.

Anchoring also affects risk estimates. This is most noticeable when people are given a baseline risk estimate for one hazard and then asked to generate risk estimates for other hazards. Their estimates are skewed towards the baseline figure. For instance, Lichtenstein *et al.* (1978) found that when subjects were asked to estimate the number of deaths per annum from 40 different causes, if they were given an illustrative figure that 1,000 people died from electrocution their estimates for deaths from other causes was significantly lower than if the illustrative figure they were given was 50,000 deaths from motor vehicle accidents. It should be noted that this may not be the perfect illustration of the effect, since in this experiment two factors were simultaneously changed (the death estimate figure and the hazard to which it referred). It is possible that by focusing the respondents upon electrocution in one case and on motor accidents in the other, it is not just the differences in the evidence on the scale of the fatalities that is shifting the risk estimates for other hazards. In effect, the hazard to which the baseline risk estimate is attached should be held constant for such a conclusion to be drawn.

2.1.5   Optimistic bias It is rare that people are given detailed personal information about their own risk from a hazard. Typically, they are given information about the risk to people on average. Yet people have been found to believe that they are personally less likely to experience negative events, and more likely to experience positive events, than other people. The phenomenon has become known as 'optimistic bias' or 'unrealistic optimism' (Weinstein, 1980). In the context of threats, this is sometimes known as 'perceived invulnerability' (Klein and Helweg-Larsen, 2002) and others have called it 'subjective immunity'.

Weinstein asked students to tell him how likely they were to experience forty-two life events and how likely their classmates were to experience the same events. They saw themselves as more likely than their peers to experience good events and less likely to experience bad events. In a less hypothetical study, Middleton *et al.* (1996) found that bungee jumpers felt they were less likely to be at risk than their fellow jumpers. The same pattern has been found for many health and safety problems, such as being a victim of mugging, being in a car accident, becoming overweight, committing suicide, having an unwanted pregnancy, suffering a smoking-related disease, getting cancer, suffering food poisoning, becoming alcoholic, having a car accident while using a mobile phone, and getting skin cancer or tooth decay (e.g. Boney-McCoy *et al.*, 1992; Burger and Burns, 1988; Dejoy, 1989; Eiser and Arnold, 1999; Fontaine and Snyder, 1995; Frewer *et al.*, 1994; Lek and Bishop, 1995; Raats *et al.*, 1999; van der Velde *et al.*, 1992; Weinstein, 1980, 1982, 1984, 1987; Whalen *et al.*, 1994; White *et al.*, 2004; Redmond and Griffith, 2004). The phenomenon is present in children (Whalen *et al.*, 1994). Parents have been shown to evince optimistic bias on behalf of their children (Gordon *et al.*, 2002). Salmon *et al.* (2003) presented evidence that, in relation to their assessment of their risk from bio-terrorism, corporations show similar optimistic bias. The phenomenon is not the preserve of individuals alone.

Of course, an individual may be correct in estimating his or her own risk to be smaller than that of others. It is the fact that it is a majority effect – most members of a sample will say that they are less at risk than the average person – that makes it a noteworthy phenomenon. In reality, in purely statistical terms, a majority cannot be less at risk than the average because if they were then the average itself would reduce. This is the paradox of optimistic bias.

Weinstein (1989) proposed that optimistic bias has two types of source:
- Motivational – this may involve two routes:
  o defensive denial – a form of defensive avoidance against the threat of harm (Schwarzer, 1994) – proving that this is occurring is obviously difficult but it is a notion that should be considered
  o maintaining or enhancing self-esteem – the exercise of comparing one's own risk levels with those of others is seen as an opportunity to achieve positive distinctiveness; to show one is better than others.
- Cognitive – this entails three elements:
  o *Egocentrism* (inability to adopt the perspective of the other and thus inability to understand that the same factors that affect others will affect oneself)
  o *Availability of information about the risk* (lack of information is associated with seeing oneself to be less at risk, though increasing knowledge does not necessarily eliminate optimism; Weinstein *et al.*, 1998) – the origin of the information seems of paramount importance, that drawn from personal experience of any threat

seems influential in reducing bias (Janoff-Bulman and Frieze, 1983), as does the vicarious observance of the experiences of friends and family (de-Wit *et al.*, 1994)

o *Stereotype salience* (making a comparison with the stereotype that they hold of a high-risk individual). Riskiness of behaviours associated with one's own groups is usually underestimated and that associated with other groups is overestimated. Campbell and Stewart (1992) propose that this is a result of the desire to achieve a positive social identity for the group and oneself through the comparison. Where the outgroup is already negatively stereotyped, this tendency is heightened. Weinstein suggested that, typically, when asked to compare oneself with some unspecified 'other', people conjure up a 'fuzzy stereotype' – not an image rich in detail – which is a loose amalgam of risky features. Of course, the use of a fuzzy stereotype can also serve motivational ends. Comparing oneself with the riskier stereotypical other allows self-enhancement and the maintenance of self-esteem. Individuals who conjure strong negative stereotypes for comparators also seem to perceive themselves as more in control of their relationship with the risk (Weinstein, 1980).

The phenomenon, if general and robust, is of major concern since it may significantly influence decision-making. It might be at the root of the unwillingness of individuals to take precautions to look after their own health or safety. If they believe themselves to be less at risk than others, they may not see the need to defend themselves. This has been seen in respect to young people's unwillingness to adopt safer sexual practices in the face of the risk of HIV (Abrams *et al.*, 1990). It has also been seen elsewhere (Burger and Burns, 1988; Rothman *et al.*, 1996; Weinstein and Lyon, 1999). However, it is worth noting that Weinstein (1982) showed that the predicted relationship between optimism and future behaviour can disappear if one also takes into account the extent to which people are worrying about the risk. Furthermore, we know from other studies that there is often no significant relationship between perceived risk and interest in taking self-protective precautions (e.g. Weinstein *et al.*, 1991). The link between optimistic bias and decision-making is not clear-cut.

Moreover, optimistic bias is not found for all hazards or for all people. For instance, even schoolchildren realise that they are as likely as their peers to catch the flu or experience the bad effects of air pollution (Whalen *et al.*, 1994). The task now for risk theorists is to model the conditions under which it does occur and when it does not.

There has been research on this question. It appears that optimistic bias is more likely when the risk is thought to be in the control of the individual. For instance, Lima (2004) argued that optimistic bias was a product of believing oneself more capable or likely than others of taking measures to protect oneself against the risk. She found that when people were allowed to include the effects of self-protection measures within their risk estimates the optimistic bias was reduced. Generally, optimistic bias seems to be enhanced when the risk is seen to be under personal control (e.g. Heine and Lehman, 1995; Sparks *et al.*, 1994). Indeed, Dolinski *et al.* (1987) found that the absence of control leads to unrealistic pessimism. Van der Velde *et al.* (1992) suggest that if control is perceived to be insufficient to surmount obstacles to preventive behaviour, then people will become pessimistic rather than realistic or optimistic.

In keeping with this, optimistic bias is less likely when the individual has had direct personal experience of the hazardous outcome. For instance, Helweg-Larsen (1999) showed that people showed less optimistic bias with respect to earthquakes just after they had lived through one, even though they displayed optimistic bias with respect to other hazards. Parry *et al.* (2004) similarly showed that people who had experienced salmonella food poisoning were less likely to show optimistic bias about contracting it again than those who had not had it. Perhaps not surprisingly, Facione (2002) showed women who had experienced breast cancer estimated their risks of further cancer as higher than those of the average. However, McKenna and Albery (2001) showed how complex the effects of experience might be. They examined several groups that had been exposed to varying degrees of threat, associated with accidents during driving in their motor vehicles, and found that only those who had experienced the most severe threat (being hospitalised after an accident) showed a reduction in the optimistic bias. Furthermore, they found that the debiasing effect of severe threat was domain-specific and did not generalise to reductions in optimistic bias concerning other types of hazard.

Other factors seem to influence the manifestation of the bias. For instance, Perloff and Fetzer (1986) found that when people compare their risk with that of close friends or family, the bias is reduced. Simply being specific about the comparator, rather than talking about 'average' people, also reduces the bias (Alicke *et al.*, 1995). Also, McKenna and Myers (1997) found that if participants expected that their judgements could be independently verified the bias disappeared. This may suggest that people are aware that they are illegitimately favouring themselves.

The comparison target is also important in determining whether optimistic bias appears. Harris *et al.* (2000) also showed the extent of optimistic bias could be reduced if the perceived social distance of the person used as a comparator for the self was diminished. Similarly, McKenna *et al.* (1993) found that smokers, although thinking themselves to have a lower risk to their health than the average smoker, unequivocally rated themselves as being far more at risk than the average non-smoker.

There may also be some cultural differences in the prevalence of optimistic bias. Most of the studies have been conducted in Western industrialised communities. Where parallel studies are done elsewhere, the effect is sometimes not found. For instance, Heine and Lehman (1995) found the bias virtually absent among Japanese respondents.

The variety of findings suggests that the process of optimistic bias may be seriously sensitive to the precise circumstances under which it is elicited. Fife-Schaw and Barnett (2003) suggested that the visibility of optimistic bias might also be a function of the methods used to measure it. There are two main ways it has been measured:

- *Direct comparison*: the participants are asked to rate on one scale whether their own risk is smaller, greater or the same as the risk of another person. The main disadvantage with this is that, when changes in the level of bias occur following an experimental manipulation, there is no way of knowing whether it is the assessment of the 'self' or the 'other' that has changed.
- *Indirect comparison*: the participants are asked to rate themselves on one scale and the comparator upon another so the assessment is no longer directly relative.

Otten and van der Pligt (1996) state that the direct procedure provides a stronger comparative frame and Schwarzer (1994) noted that the direct procedure tends to elicit social comparisons with abstract stereotypes of victims rather than with an existing reference person or group. The indirect method also introduces the possibility that there may be order effects from whether the self is presented for assessment first or second. Otten and van der Pligt postulate that, if the self is assessed first, it is treated as the standard (anchor point), but if the other is assessed first, then it becomes the standard. They argue that there is a larger discrepancy between self–other assessments when the other is established as the standard by being rated first. There are many potential explanations for this finding. However, none has been tested. A third method is also used – dissociated ratings (Spitzenstetter, 2003) – which appears to further reduce the bias phenomenon.

Perhaps the most important point to take from this work on the effects of method of measurement is that the phenomenon of optimistic bias is so sensitive to small contextual changes. Under such circumstances, it is difficult to predict how it might work over time in directing an individual's decisions about risk activities in very complex environments where many comparisons between the self and others can be made iteratively and are often based on rich information.

It might also be worth mentioning that there are studies that examine 'comparative optimism' – that is, the degree to which two or more hazards elicit different levels of optimistic bias. This area is even more fraught with methodological complexities (Klar and Ayal, 2004).

Inevitably, the discovery of optimistic bias, despite the complexity of its manifestations, has given rise to various attempts to find ways to reduce it. These include:

- Providing information designed to heighten understanding of the relevance of the risk factors to the self – this has not proven effective in most contexts.
- Challenging egocentrism by giving more information about the comparators – this has also not proven effective.
- Making the unpredictability and uncontrollability of the risk salient – this tends to reduce optimistic bias.
- Inducing a negative mood – making people feel sad or anxious reduced the bias (at least in one study, Abele and Herner, 1993).

The bias seems to show a certain resilience to attempts to ameliorate it – except where modification in expectations of risk control is involved. Perceived controllability does seem to be important. This echoes the significance of self-efficacy in risk perception that was described in Chapter 3.

2.1.6   Hindsight bias Hindsight bias (Fischhoff, 1975) is the label given to the tendency that people have to say, 'I knew that all along.' Another way of encapsulating it is to say that it is foresight after the event. Typically, people given information about an event after it occurs will say (and think) that they could have (or did) predict it. Fischhoff *et al.* (2005) present a clear example of the phenomenon. They examined the evolution of cognitive and emotional responses to terror risks for a nationally representative sample of Americans between late 2001 (post-9/11) and late 2002. Respondents displayed hindsight bias, changing their memories of their earlier risk judgements to fit the changing data available to them. Hindsight bias was also found with respect to the Y2Y (or Millennium Bug) fears; Pease *et al.* (2003) found that respondents claimed that they had predicted that there would be little disruption to computer networks as the 2000 date was reached.

Interestingly, when people are not allowed to recreate their memories because the evidence of what they thought earlier is still before them, they will modify the significance of their previous predictions by re-estimating the degree of certainty that they attributed to the predictions (Bradfield and Wells, 2005). Therefore, they admit that their estimates were inaccurate but make it clear that they had never been very certain that the estimate was correct anyway – a form of discounting the error.

There have been many hypotheses to account for hindsight bias. There have been motivational explanations. For instance, Dekker (2004) argued that hindsight bias creates a greater sense of control over the future by making us feel we predicted the past – a form of meta-self-delusion. Indeed, there does seem to be some association between the strength of the bias and the level of field dependency or need for favourable self-presentation evinced by the individual (e.g. Campbell and Tesser, 1983; Davies, 1993; Musch, 2003). Tykocinski et al. (2002) suggested that hindsight bias is a part of retroactive pessimism that people introduce in an attempt to regulate disappointments – in retrospect, predictions of the undesirable outcome are changed to make it appear more inevitable and, of course, if it was inevitable, self-blame and disappointment are not appropriate. Retroactive pessimism becomes a form of self-defence.

There have also been cognitive explanations. For instance, Villejoubert (2005) explains how it could be a product of memory encoding and retrieval processes. It is suggested that, after an event, memory is probed in a detailed and selective way for evidence of what one thought about the event prospectively. This selectivity then supports the conclusion that one had expected the ultimate outcome (e.g. Appleton-Knapp, 2003; Pohl et al., 2003). Effectively, the prior judgement is reconstructed as knowledge is updated (Hoffrage et al., 2000). Stalhberg and Maass (1998), after reviewing many studies, concluded that the hindsight bias seemed to be largely associated with some form of biased reconstruction of the prior judgement rather than some impairment of memory, though that could not be ruled out completely.

Hindsight bias is not a simple process. Holzl and Kirchler (2005) found that hindsight bias occurred selectively for events that were attitude-consistent. So, for instance, they had their respondents rate the likelihood of several economic developments six months before and six months after the introduction of the Euro in 2002 as the currency for most of the EU. Euro-supporters showed stronger hindsight bias for positive developments that occurred after its introduction than for negative ones. Euro-opponents showed the opposite pattern. Holzl and Kirchler argued as a consequence that hindsight bias is a means of stabilising subjective representations of events.

Furthermore, the amount of hindsight bias changes over time (e.g. Bryant and Guilbault, 2002). Renner (2003) showed that people given feedback that they had unexpectedly high cholesterol levels would display the bias immediately after being given the feedback, but that if they were retested several weeks later the bias was eroded (a reversal of hindsight bias). It is not at all clear why this should happen. Pezzo (2003) suggested that bias increases with the 'surprisingness' of the outcome. Perhaps as surprise fades over time or as it is explained or rationalised, so does the bias. This fits with other findings that the greater the original knowledge of the predicted event, the smaller the hindsight bias (Hertwig *et al.*, 2003).

As usual, there are claimed to be cultural differences in the expression of this bias. Pohl *et al.* (2002) report that Koreans exhibit more hindsight bias than North Americans, Japanese show marginally less than Canadians on occasion, while Germans and Dutch showed no hindsight bias. However, evidence of cultural differences is limited and should be further investigated.

2.2   Risk framing and prospect theory

Prospect theory (Kahneman and Tversky, 1979; Tversky and Kahneman, 1981) describes the decision processes involved when people make comparisons between options. There are two important components in this theory: frame of reference and subjective value function. Figure 4.1 presents a typical subjective value function with a neutral reference point that prospect theory postulates.

2.2.1   Frame of reference 'Frame of reference', when used in prospect theory, refers to the introduction of a reference point that makes a frame

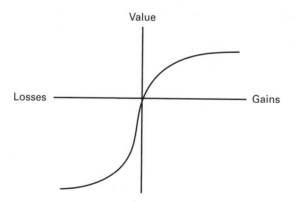

Figure 4.1 Prospect theory value function
The subjective value function of prospect theory
Kahneman and Tversky, 1979: 279. Copyright 1979 by The Econometric Society.

casting 'the same critical information in either a *positive* or *negative* light' (Levin *et al.*, 1998: 150). Prospect theory is interested in the shifts of the internal reference point as a result of the ways in which the same information is presented (positive vs negative frames).

Prospect theory posits that the selection of a reference point is crucial to option evaluation. A reference point is the point (an internal standard) with which people compare the objective value of an option so as to classify the option as something positive (i.e. when the option's value is larger than the reference point) or as something negative (i.e. when the option's value is smaller than the reference point). Objectively identical options can be framed positively or negatively, such that an option perceived as a gain in one frame will be perceived as a loss in another frame. A positively framed option is thought to decrease one's evoked reference point, whereas the same information framed negatively is thought to increase the evoked reference point (Abelson and Levi, 1985; Highhouse and Paese, 1996).

A common example used to illustrate the effects of framing would be in a scenario describing that 400 people are infected by an unusual disease; the effectiveness of a medical programme could be framed in a positive way (e.g. 100 people will be saved). This framing would lead people to presuppose all lives might be lost had the medical intervention not occurred, and this would evoke a relatively low reference point (i.e. 0 people will be saved). However, framing the same programme negatively (i.e. 300 people will die) would lead people to presuppose that no lives may have been lost if the intervention had not been made, which would evoke a relatively high reference point (i.e. 400 people will be saved or 0 people will die). This shift in the reference point across the two frames leads to a perception that the medical programme is more attractive (i.e. it has a higher subjective value) when it is positively framed than when it is negatively framed. The programme in the positive frame will lead to a sense of saving 100 lives when compared with the loss-of-all-lives reference point. Conversely, the negative frame will lead to a sense of losing 300 lives when compared with the no-lives-lost reference point. A treatment that will save 100 lives is more desirable than one that will cause 300 deaths. Thus, the medical programme is more attractive when it is presented in a positive frame than when it is presented in a negative frame. Of course this scenario relies upon the assumption that people, given the information, will themselves make assumptions about what would have happened without the intervention and this is somewhat speculative.

However, framing effects like this have been shown to be empirically very robust. Similar findings that the perceived favourability of an option depends on framing have been demonstrated in a wide variety of social and personal settings (for a review, see Levin *et al.*, 1998a), including layoffs (Brockner *et al.*, 1995), purchase of products (Levin and Gaeth, 1988), escalation situations (Davis and Bobko, 1986), project funding allocation (Dunegan, 1993), medical treatments (Levin *et al.*, 1988b), and condom use (Linville *et al.*, 1993).

2.2.2 Subjective value function Under the framework of prospect theory, an option is associated with a subjective value expressed as positive or negative deviations (i.e. gains or losses) from a neutral reference point (i.e. with a subjective value of zero). The hypothesised value function follows the non-linear perception and judgement function in many sensory and perceptual dimensions (Stevens, 1962), such as loudness (Stevens, 1936), brightness (Stevens, 1961) and weight perception (Engen, 1972; Gescheider, 1976). The value function is S-shaped (see Figure 4.1): concave in the positive domain (i.e. above the reference point) and convex in the negative domain (i.e. below the reference point). Specifically, as the gain increases in the objective value, the increase in the subjective value (or the slope in the graph) decreases.

For example, the difference in the subjective value between gains of £5 and £10 appears to be greater than that between gains of £50 and £55. As the loss increases in the objective value, the drop in the subjective value (or the slope in the graph) decreases. For example, the difference in subjective value between losses of £5 and £10 appears to be greater than that between losses of £50 and £55. Consistent with the S-shaped value function, previous studies have shown that the marginal subjective values of money, non-monetary events (e.g. stepping on chewing gum), and objects (e.g. the Irish Sweepstakes) with both gains or losses decrease as their sizes increase (Bernoulli, 1954; Galanter, 1990; Galanter and Pliner, 1974).

Despite the robustness of this S-shaped value function, the evidence that might explain this pattern is rather sketchy. One explanation offered by Arkes (1991) is that the value function evolved to be non-linear because of its superior adaptive merit over a linear system. From the perspective of evolution, a physiological system that translates external stimuli on to psychological responses in a way that follows non-linear functions is more economical than a linear transduction system. In explaining the S-shaped value function of prospect theory and other psychological power functions, Arkes (1991) noted that a system that translated physical intensity in a linear manner on to psychological responses would impose an immense cost on any transduction system. Extreme stimuli, which occur relatively infrequently, would have to be coded with as great a level of discriminability as the more frequent middle-range stimuli. Any non-linear system with an asymptote at the extreme end (or ends) would have the benefit of eliminating the structures and processes needed to discriminate small changes in rare events, such as very intense sounds or extremely heavy weights. Of course, besides offering information-processing gains, sacrificing discriminability at the ends of the continuum has a cost.

In terms of its relevance to risk judgements, according to 'prospect theory' (Kahneman and Tversky, 1979), outcomes that are merely probable are given less consideration than outcomes that are deemed certain. Thus, for instance, any protective action that reduces the probability of harm from, say, 0.01 to 0 will be more valued than an action that reduces the probability of the same harm from .02 to .01. You will note than in both cases the absolute probability reduction is the same, but one results in the certain elimination of the harm and the other does not.

Slovic *et al.* (1982) report a study where this proposal was tested. They presented two different messages about a vaccine. In the first case (probabilistic protection), participants were told that a vaccination for a disease that was expected to infect 20 per cent of the population would be effective in 50 per cent of cases. In the second case (pseudocertainty), participants were told that there were two strains of the disease, mutually exclusive and equally probable, each likely to afflict 10 per cent of the population and the vaccine was said to give complete protection against one strain but none against the other. Participants were asked how likely it was that they would seek to be vaccinated. While in both cases vaccination reduced the chances of contracting the disease from 20 per cent to 10 per cent, the researchers predicted that those participants who received the pseudocertainty message would be more likely to accept vaccination. This proved to be what happened.

The pseudocertainty effect highlights the limited nature of people's understanding of probability information and the impact that the apparent elimination of risk has – even when it is in effect only partial. Prospect theory should be borne in mind in the context of formulating risk-communication messages. The message that promises the elimination of risk has a very different effect from the message that promises an equivalent percentage reduction but not the elimination.

2.2.3   Framing risk issues The concept of 'frame of reference' as used in prospect theory is rather narrow. Many other theories would also suggest the nature of the decision that is reached about the significance of a risk, and the way it should be addressed is influenced by the way that risk is 'framed'. This is essentially not a complex idea and flows from much of the earlier discussion of the perception of risk. At one level, it is a simple statement like that in prospect theory that choices are sensitive to the formulation of the question, to its context and the procedure used to introduce it (Kahneman and Tversky, 2000). At another level, basically, it is argued that the risk is seen in terms of broader frames of reference. So, for instance, Vaughan and Seifert (1992) describe the way in which, in many controversies, groups have differed systematically in framing risk issues. They suggest three dimensions of differences in framing that are particularly salient in generating conflict between groups over risk decisions:

- whether the risk is treated as a question of science or economics; or, alternatively, as a question of fairness and equity
- whether the risk is treated as relevant for one at-risk population or another
- whether the focus is upon what is gained from the risk or what might be lost as a result of it.

These dimensions in the frames of reference will determine what evidence is seen as relevant for coming to decisions about the risk, and they will determine also what courses of action are seen as appropriate. Of course, it is not only groups that differ in their frames of reference for risk – individuals can adopt very different frames of reference, too. Hornig Priest (1999) found evidence that the pre-existing frames of reference that people held about various hazards moderated the way they interpreted and used information from the media about those risks. Her work suggested that the media present their audience with various ways of framing a risk, but that the audience is by no means passive in its reception of that offered frame.

It has been suggested that by encouraging groups or individuals who are in conflict over a risk issue to make their risk framing explicit, it is possible to reduce or eliminate the conflict. The work on mental models of risk takes the framing argument several steps further.

3   Theories, schemas and mental models of risk

3.1   Theories and scripts

The decisions that individuals make about a hazard will at least in part depend on what 'mental model' they have of it. Nisbett and Ross (1980) described how people's understanding of the rapidly changing world around them depends less on formal rational judgemental procedures than upon a pre-existing store of beliefs or theories that they hold. These theories can be characterised as, in some cases, fairly explicit propositions (e.g. medical doctors can be trusted, or rivers are polluted because of the effluent released into them from factories). In other cases, the understanding is not organised in a propositional way but in a more holistic schematic (e.g. knowing what happens in a hospital or knowing what environmental conservation entails). The labels for such knowledge structures that psychologists have used are varied, including 'scripts' (Schank and Abelson, 1977), 'frames' (Minsky, 1975), 'prototypes' (Cantor and Mischel, 1977) and, of course, 'schema' (Bartlett, 1932; Piaget, 1936). In the domain of risk, the term used now is 'mental model'.

Theories, whether propositional or schematic, can influence the way people utilise information and bring into play their heuristic biases. Particularly significant are what Kelley (1972) labelled 'causal schemata'. These are highly abstract content-free notions of the relations among causes and effects. People appear to possess very general notions of the sufficiency and necessity of causal relations. These general causal schemata are brought to bear when explanations or predictions of events are required. The fact that the causal schemata themselves may be subject to various biases (well documented in the attribution theory literature) means that they militate against the creation of systematic information-driven explanations or predictions.

Consequently, individuals will often build a 'script' about a hazard. The script is a sort of story that will describe the components of the hazard; it may explain how it changes over time, or indicate who is implicated in the hazard, or indicate how it can be controlled. The script, and the dramatis personae it contains, need have no relationship to the factual circumstances of the hazard. See Box 4.1 for an illustration of such a hazard script. There is no standard format and no predictable longevity for a script. They appear and evolve according to the individual's need to make sense of something. They are sometimes shared with others (we return to this later in Chapter 9). They are often partly communal and partly idiosyncratic. There is no requirement for them to be internally consistent.

The script is not necessarily bounded by the specifics of the hazard. The hurricane script introduces broader belief systems about religion.

Box 4.1 Hazard script: hurricanes

A script (or theory) about hurricanes from a young woman living on an island where hurricanes hit every year: 'The hurricanes come to us because it is God's will. They are a punishment for the wicked ways of the people. They will not come to my house. They have never hit here before. There is no escape if they are meant to hit your house. I pray to protect my house from them. There is no point in sheltering or moving somewhere else to live. Only the weak go to live in the north.'

They are not theories or explanatory models in the sense that these concepts are used in science. However, they are explanatory in a psychological sense. They account for the hazard, and often provide the basis for predicting the occurrence of the hazard, in ways that the individual can understand. They also frequently provide a reason for the decision that the individual has taken in relation to the hazard. In the case of the hurricane script, the young woman is not moving to a region on her island that is less affected by the storms because there is no point, since it is a divine decision as to whether you are harmed by the hurricane or not. What is more, she takes pride in her decision and emphasises her strength when she says 'only the weak' seek to escape. Interestingly, the script itself also shows signs of the heuristic biases described earlier. She is sure her house will not be hit and this smacks of optimistic bias (though not couched in the classic comparative rating).

The growing appreciation of the role of 'scripts' in reactions to hazards has resulted in considerable research aimed at developing methods for identifying and then correcting scripts. As this work has developed, it is now more common to refer to 'mental models' rather than scripts or any of the other terms previously used.

3.2   Mental models

Considerable work has now been done to develop methods which allow examination of the 'mental models' which individuals use in their appreciation of hazards (Fischhoff *et al.*, 1997). Figure 4.2 depicts a stylised

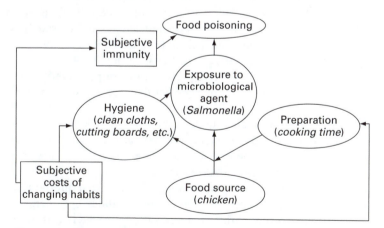

Figure 4.2 Stylised mental model of food poisoning

and simplified mental model of food poisoning that might be held by a lay person (reproduced from Breakwell, 2000).

The approach is possibly one of the most productive bases for developing risk communication interventions (Morgan et al., 2002) and this is considered further in Chapter 6. The mental models approach seeks to identify for a particular hazard both accurate and inaccurate beliefs that are held by a target population. These are then used as the basis for developing risk communication material that will correct misunderstandings. In this approach, the object is to bridge the gap between lay and expert models of the risk by adding missing concepts, correcting mistakes, strengthening correct beliefs and minimising peripheral ones (Fischhoff, 1994).

The approach generally adheres to three tenets:
- the audience needs to be offered a basic understanding of the exposure, effects and mitigation processes relevant to making decisions about the hazard
- the existing beliefs of the audience are assumed to affect reception and interpretation of any new information
- new information must be presented in a such a way as to be consistent with the levels of understanding (textual or other) that is manifest in the audience.

Essentially, the mental models approach argues that people have an 'intuitive understanding' of risks and that they can be helped to a better appreciation and consequently be placed in a position to make more informed decisions if they are given new information in a format that is consistent with their initial belief system. The mapping of the initial belief system about the hazard that is the target for risk communication is thus crucial (Bostrom et al., 1992; Jungermann et al., 1988). Bostrom et al. (1994b) describe the variety of techniques that can be used. They must ensure that the method of data elicitation does not overly bias the mental model that is exposed. Therefore, they include:
- *think-aloud protocols* – where participants are presented with material on the hazard and asked to say what they are thinking about it as they read
- *recall* – where participants are asked to say what they remember of material that they have seen about the hazard
- *problem-solving* – where participants are asked to say how they would react to scenarios that involve the hazard
- *knowledge tests* – where participants answer factual questions.

Each data elicitation approach has its own weaknesses but effectively the more structured the method becomes the more likely it is to introduce biases originating in the participant reacting to information about the

---

Box 4.2 Mental models of global climate change

Bostrom *et al.* (1994b) used the techniques to establish what people know about global climate change. They found that in general people regarded global warming as both bad and likely; many believed that it had already occurred. They tended to confuse stratospheric ozone depletion with the greenhouse effect and the concept of climate with weather. Additionally, 'the greenhouse effect' was often interpreted literally as the cause of a hot and steamy climate. Causes of climate change were thought to be automobile use, heat and emissions from industrial processes, aerosol spray cans, and pollution in general. The effects of climate change included skin cancer and changed agricultural yields. The mitigation and control strategies proposed by interviewees typically focused upon general population control, with few links to carbon dioxide or energy use. Respondents in the early 1990s were unfamiliar with the regulations such as those banning CFCs for non-essential uses.

---

hazard that is embedded in the very questioning itself. Also, the greater the emphasis upon testing knowledge, the less opportunity there is to catalogue inaccurate or idiosyncratic beliefs. As a consequence, a multi-method approach is often used. Box 4.2 provides information on a study of the mental model of climate change conducted in the early 1990s. In the years since that study was conducted, there has been extensive scientific debate and research on climate change. There has been enormous media coverage of the phenomenon and the scientific controversies and political manoeuvring that have surrounded it. The lay mental models have undoubtedly changed. Nevertheless, Leiserowitz (2005), reporting data collected in 2003, found that Americans perceived climate change as a moderate risk that would predominantly impact geographically and temporally distant people and places. This research also illustrated that there is no one mental model of climate change. It identified several distinct 'interpretative' communities, including naysayers and alarmists, with widely divergent perceptions of climate change.

There are now also several publications which describe in detail how mental models may be corrected (Atman *et al.*, 1994). These techniques will be considered further in Chapter 6.

The particular value of the mental models approach is that it requires one to think in terms of a complex interacting system of beliefs which underpins risk appreciation and decision-making. In order to have its desired impact, any information provided by a risk communication must be designed so as to take account of the way in which the entire system of beliefs will respond. Successfully shifting one belief in the system may not ultimately bring about the desired outcome because other elements in the system dampen any impact of movement in one. Figure 4.2 depicts a very basic lay individual's mental model of the risk of food poisoning associated with eating chicken. It should be noted that this is not a simple causal model that links the food source to exposure to illness. It recognises that exposure can be controlled by certain hygienic and preparative precautions. It also recognises that failure in hygiene precautions can result in exposure without direct consumption of the food source (e.g. through transmission via dishcloths). Most importantly, it has, as an integral part of the model, subjective assessments of the costs of taking precautions and assumptions about personal immunity from illness caused in this fashion. Assessments of subjective immunity may even result in reinterpretation of apparent symptoms of food poisoning. If the person harbours expectations of immunity, symptoms can be reinterpreted as the product of overeating or drinking too much. Any effort at risk communication directed at the person who held a mental model of high subjective immunity would need to take account of the motivational as well as the informational elements it entails.

3.3   Shared mental models

The discussion of mental models above may have suggested that they are the product and preserve of the individual. In fact, mental models are often shared. Organisations often encourage shared modelling in order to establish strong team work (Levine and Moreland, 1999; Cannon-Bowers et al., 1993). Mental models are particularly shared within expert communities. Experts are in fact educated to use the same mental models when conceptualising a hazard. Expert knowledge is founded upon shared understandings of 'established' facts and theories. This is not to say that established theories should be confused with mental models. The point is that shared mental models that prevail in a particular expert community may represent a pre-theoretical set of assumptions or expectations about a new problem area.

This can be significant when examining how expert teams or communities react to the need to analyse the implications of a new hazard. They may tend to transpose shared mental models (for example, of causation or impact) that are not relevant to the problem. The fact that the models are shared makes it that much more difficult to take another perspective and address the problem in a novel way. Perseverance with employing a model that is ineffective is not just the preserve of the lay person. Several of the examples in Chapter 8, where safety culture is explored, illustrate how experts within organisations, having achieved a shared understanding of a hazard, then resist any attempt to shift their model and this results in significant errors. It is possible that the fact that the model is shared makes it more difficult to relinquish in the face of countervailing evidence.

4   Risk and decision-making in groups: the risky shift or shift to increased risk or group polarisation

One area of research on group decision-making is particularly worthy of description because it illustrates how dangerous it is to make generalisations about the way in which groups will deal with risk.

4.1   The risky shift

Stoner (1961) reported that group decisions following discussion are consistently riskier than decisions that members of the group make individually. This effect was initially labelled 'the risky shift'. Stoner elicited this effect when he asked groups to consider a series of twelve problems, each of which describes a situation where the central character is faced with a choice between two actions whose outcomes differ in their attractiveness and probability. Respondents have to indicate the minimum probability of success that they would require before adopting the alternative that has the more desirable outcome.

An example of the situation might be: a man is offered a new job with higher pay but with a company that has the prospect of failure, or he can stay in a secure, low-paid job. The choice put before respondents is: What is the lowest probability of the company remaining sound that you would require before recommending the man to take the job (e.g. 1 in 10, 3 in 10, 5 in 10, 7 in 10, 9 in 10)? Or do you think he should not take the job? The decision was taken to be riskier if the probability chosen as acceptable was lower (i.e. 1 in 10 is riskier than 9 in 10). So, for the purposes of this research, risk was not gauged in terms of the size of the prize to be won or lost (i.e. severity) but purely in terms of the likelihood of gaining it (i.e. probability).

Stoner first had his respondents give their recommendations individually, and then required them to discuss the problem with five other similar people and arrive at a unanimous recommendation. He found that for most of the groups he created there was a significant shift between the means of the individual decisions and the later group decisions toward greater risk. In a control condition, respondents who made choices a second time individually showed no systematic shift.

Stoner also asked his respondents in the experimental condition to record their private judgements after the group discussion, acknowledging that the individual choice might be different from that of the group. He found 39 per cent of his respondents changed their private recommendation towards greater risk and 16 per cent changed towards greater caution. It would appear that, not only was the group recommendation riskier than the individual ones, but the group discussion precipitated more individuals to accept greater risk. However, detailed examination of the findings reveal that what typically happens is that the range of individual choices is narrower after the group discussion – people move away from the extreme choices (either risky or cautious).

Researchers during the 1960s repeatedly found the risky shift phenomenon when people made choices in experiments about hypothetical scenarios (Wallach et al., 1962; Marquis, 1962). It was also found in studies where the decisions would have real, though relatively trivial (i.e. small financial) consequences for those participating (Wallach et al., 1964).

4.2   Why shift?

Assuming for a moment that the phenomenon does occur, why would it occur? Wallach et al. (1962, 1964) postulated that it is a result of the diffusion of responsibility that occurs in groups. In the group, the individual can discount responsibility for the consequences of a high-risk decision because the responsibility for the decision can be attributed to the other members of the group completely or in part.

While this may seem reasonable and is on the surface a simple proposition, there are other explanations that have been offered. One of these focuses upon the extra information that is made available to all participants through the discussion that occurs in the groups. Where the group has members whose initial choices are different, the discussions usually encourage people to defend their own position. These defences provide new information or alternative interpretations of already available information. This explanation assumes the burden of additional information would support the riskier conclusion. This is open to empirical test and Nordhøy (1962) found that discussion tended to contain more information that favours risk than favouring caution. It does not seem that the phenomenon is simply a function of having more information; the arguments are biased to risk.

The mere presence of the arguments may be one factor, but the reason they have an impact upon participants may lie in other processes. It may be more to do with conformity processes that occur within the group. This would account for the convergence of individual choices after the group discussion. The discussion allowed participants to cite evidence but also to give each other explicit signs of approval or disapproval. They attempted to persuade each other. The requirement that they reach unanimity would also emphasise the significance of having to shift.

The problem with the conformity explanation is that it will only explain the shift to risk (rather than the convergence) if it is assumed that conforming to a riskier choice is more likely than conforming to a more cautious choice. Conformity processes that operate within groups should not result in the shift to risk unless there is some prior value attributed to risk. It does seem that there may have been some added value to risk in so far as more arguments in favour of risk were generated than arguments in favour of caution. If this value-led conformity were at the root of the risky shift, it might be expected that the societal value or subcultural norms associated with risk-taking would shape the willingness of group participants to focus on risk arguments. In some cultures, where risk is less valued, this would suggest that the risky shift would not occur and would perhaps be replaced with a shift to caution. It may also be the case that for some types of problem risk is valued, but for others it is not – even within the same society or subculture.

Perhaps leadership within the group has a role to play in shaping this emphasis upon arguments that support riskier choices. It could be that the individuals that emerge in these experimentally contrived groups as influential are more likely to have made risky choices. Indeed, Wallach et al. (1962) and Marquis (1962) found that respondents believed that those who were initially riskier in their choices were more influential in the group.

Obviously, there is circularity in this suggestion: respondents are simply describing post hoc a factual relationship since the group decision was riskier; those whose initial individual position was riskier were apparently more influential. This really does not prove they actually exerted influence, nor does it explain why they might be influential. Is it to do with the content of their arguments or style of argument? Is it to do with personal characteristics – attractiveness, charisma, etc.? Another question also remains: If an individual with great capacity to influence were to try to lead a group to greater caution, would that be effective? It could be argued that leaders emerge in these groups because of the extent of their feeling about an issue. They feel strongly and argue forcefully and persuade others. In other contexts, people with extreme views have been found to be more likely to feel strongly about the issue. This proposition is known as the leadership and extremity hypothesis. It has the advantage of being able to explain both risky shift and shift to caution, since extreme views can be held in either direction.

Needless to say, the description of the risky shift phenomenon and the complexity of the possible explanations for it gave rise to many studies. Kogan and Wallach (1967) even found that they could generate the shift to risk when the only information exchanged iteratively concerned what probability each participant would accept, with no additional information or discussion among group members. This suggests that the elaborated explanations in terms of information and persuasion might be flawed.

Some problems produce more shift to risk than others. Essentially, those with a greater stake (i.e. severity of risk) induce less shift to risk (Ridley et al., 1981). Those problems associated with initially riskier individual choices show greater shift to risk. The first of these findings seems to undermine an explanation of the shift to risk solely in terms of diffusion of responsibility. If that were the main motivator for shift to risk, it would presumably occur most in the high-risk severity scenarios. Nordhøy (1962) found that he could construct problems that would consistently result in a shift to caution after group discussion. Again, it is difficult to see how the diffusion of responsibility approach would explain this effect.

Some types of problem seem to trigger groups to value caution. The people that participants saw as influential in such groups were those who had espoused initially more cautious choices, suggesting that perceived influence is dependent upon holding views that are congruent with the dominant value relevant to the problem. The difficulty lies in predicting in advance which problems will result in a shift to risk and which in a shift to caution. Without this capacity, the most one appears to be able to say is that group decisions on risk acceptability will be different from individual decisions – sometimes! However, this would be a little harsh. There have been some very sophisticated developments of the original idea.

4.3   Who shifts?

Some research has sought to show that the group effect is dependent upon the characteristics of those in the group. For instance, Begum and Ahmed (1986) showed that the amount of the shift to risk was related to the extent to which participants were competitive. The groups with the more competitive participants displayed greater shift to risk. El-Hajje and Ahmed (1997) showed that participants in a sad mood show greater shift to risk. Supporting the diffusion of responsibility argument,

Hashiguchi (1974) in Japan found that the larger the number of decision-makers in a group, the greater the risk in the decision. This echoed an earlier finding by Vidmar and Burdeny (1971). Tullar and Johnson (1973), in a large multinational study, showed that the shift to risk either disappears or tends towards the exercise of caution as the problem area becomes more important to the individual. Higbee (1972) challenged the proposition that the shift to risk would occur in significant decisions involving professional competence, using military decision-making as an example.

4.4.   Group polarisation

The research on the shift to risk really does illustrate many of the range of issues that must be taken into account when trying to understand how a group behaves when faced with decisions about risks. The nature of the risk problem is important. The characteristics of group members are important. The structure of the group is important and its norm or value systems are vital. The purpose and goals of the group should never be ignored. The position of the group vis-à-vis other groups is fundamental. The general processes of membership (like conformity or diffusion of responsibility or identification) are key. Thus, while the risky shift phenomenon may be specific to certain conditions and cannot be used as a substratum for large predictive models, the fact that it has been systematically examined opens a whole panoply of new ways to think about what groups are doing when they deal with risk.

Instead of talking about the risky shift or the cautious shift, more recently the concept of 'group polarisation' has been introduced. This treats the risky shift as part of a much broader phenomenon. Group polarisation simply refers to the tendency for group discussion to produce more extreme group decisions than the mean of the individual members' pre-discussion opinions but in the direction already favoured by the mean (Moscovici and Zavalloni, 1969; Isenberg, 1986; Myers and Lamm, 1976: Wetherell, 1987).

The explanations for this more general phenomenon fall into three clusters, echoing those proposed initially to explain the risky shift but with one novel addition. The 'persuasive argument' theory suggests that people in groups are persuaded by novel information generated during the discussion but only in so far as it supports their initial position and they consequently become more extreme in their endorsement of their initial decision (Burnstein and Vinokur, 1977; Gigone and Hastie, 1993; Larson et al., 1994). The theory is supported by the fact that the process of thinking about an issue (i.e. generating novel arguments for yourself) strengthens one's opinions (Tesser *et al.*, 1995). Public repetition of one's own and other's arguments has the same effect (Brauer *et al.*, 1995), though it may not unearth novel arguments.

The second theory is the 'interpersonal comparison' theory (or 'cultural values' theory). It posits that people seek social approval, the group discussion shows what is socially desirable, so the individuals shift in the direction of the majority to achieve acceptance. These two approaches have received mixed support, rather like the original attempts to specifically explain the risky shift. Isenberg (1986) suggested that both may be right but under different circumstances.

The third explanation uses social identification theories. Self-categorisation theory proposed by Turner (1985; Turner *et al.*, 1987) suggests that group polarisation is a product of normal conformity processes. The argument runs like this: people in a group during discussions will come to create a representation for themselves of the norm that the group is applying to the problem as distinct from the norms that might be applied by people not in that group (outgroup members). In order to belong fully to the group and to gain identity from it, individuals will shift their decision toward the perceived group norm. Such processes result in the narrowing of variability within the group. They also result in attempts to differentiate the ingroup from the implicit or explicit outgroup by shifting the norm away from that presumed or known to be characteristic of the outgroup. Self-categorisation, the process responsible for identification with the group, induces conformity with the assumed ingroup norm and, if the group norm has been polarised through attempts at differentiation, group polarisation. Interestingly, this theory predicts that, if the group norm has not been polarised as a consequence of the intergroup dynamic, self-categorisation will simply induce convergence on the mean group position.

Hogg *et al.* (1990) examined the phenomena of shift to risk and to caution from a self-categorisation theory perspective. They proposed that an ingroup confronted by a risky outgroup would polarise to caution, and an ingroup confronted by a cautious outgroup will polarise to risk, but an ingroup confronted with both risky and cautious outgroups will converge on its pre-test individual choice mean. They showed evidence of these effects. They also showed that participants' post-test choices converged on their estimate of the consensual ingroup position. Turner *et al.* (1989) showed that groups could be moved to polarise either toward risk or toward caution by emphasising the comparative salience of ingroup norms of either risk or caution.

As an explanation for the variety of phenomena associated with group polarisation, self-categorisation theory seems to have considerable

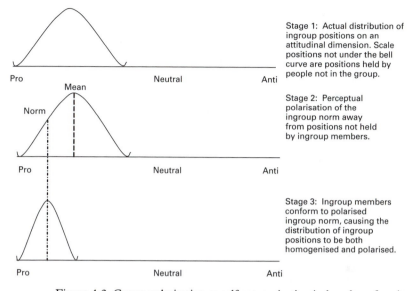

Stage 1: Actual distribution of ingroup positions on an attitudinal dimension. Scale positions not under the bell curve are positions held by people not in the group.

Stage 2: Perceptual polarisation of the ingroup norm away from positions not held by ingroup members.

Stage 3: Ingroup members conform to polarised ingroup norm, causing the distribution of ingroup positions to be both homogenised and polarised.

Figure 4.3 Group polarisation as self-categorisation induced conformity to a polarised norm (after Hogg and Vaughan, 1998)

strength since it incorporates the need to specify the precise nature of the group context before predicting in which direction decisions will shift in the group.

Figure 4.3, taken from Hogg and Vaughan (1998), illustrates the self-categorisation processes. The figure is useful because it shows that the theory assumes that the initial individual positions are normally distributed (i.e. the inverted bell-shaped curve). It is not clear how the theory would work in a group where the initial arguments were distributed in a bipolar fashion (see Figure 4.4). Would two putative norms emerge? Would that be more likely where the outgroup was known to be 'moderate' in view? This is a non-trivial question because very often in discussions about real world risks participants do hold initial views that are on either pole of the decision-spectrum. Very often in those debates, the discussion is a process of erecting group boundaries on the basis of information given concerning views held. The self-categorisation approach seems to explain the dynamics that may occur once the group boundary is established; other perspectives may be needed to explain the array of processes that lead up to the group boundaries being drawn in the context of meaningful hazard-related decisions. Some of these are addressed in Chapters 6, 7 and 9.

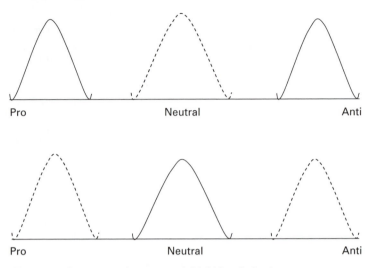

Pro   Neutral   Anti

Pro   Neutral   Anti

Figure 4.4 Ingroup and outgroup initial bi-polarisation

Conclusion

This chapter has not explored formal decision-making processes about risk that occur in complex organisations or in the context of public debate and controversy. Those processes are considered in other chapters (notably Chapters 6, 8 and 9). Consequently some of the significant factors that constrain and direct individual and small group decision-making about risk are not covered here. The focus instead has been upon what is known about the way individuals and small groups make inferences about risk on the basis of limited information.

The overwhelming conclusion that emerges from all the research described here is that human inference processes in conditions of uncertainty are riddled with biases – that is, systematic deviations from what would be expected if the inferences were based on mathematical or formal propositional rules for probability estimation. Moreover, the catalogue of biases presented here (availability, representativeness, anchoring, optimism, hindsight, prospect) is unlikely to capture all that exist.

The intriguing question is: Why do these biases encroach upon inference processes? There are two types of answer. The first argues that the biases are based in cognitive factors – limitations in computational capacity, mostly derived from the weaknesses of memory or the inadequacies of information available. The second suggests that these biases serve motivational ends – primarily enhancing self-esteem in one way or another. The problem with coming to any firm conclusion about the reasons these biases appear lies in the relative unpredictability of their occurrence. Optimistic and hindsight biases seem particularly susceptible to variation according to circumstance. However, overall, the attempts to explain the manifestations of bias solely in terms of cognitive factors, especially memory effects, do seem to have been unsuccessful. Motivations explanations, perhaps because they are less specific and are open to post-hoc rationalisation, seem more popular. Chapter 5 will examine further some of the motivational and affective factors that influence risk perceptions and decisions.

The role of naive theories, schema and mental models in directing inferences about hazards and risk is well established. Again the origins of these explanatory systems are open to debate. In later chapters, some of the processes whereby individuals acquire their own mental models are examined. The significance of the existence of shared mental models is considered here but will be revisited later.

The discussion here of 'shift to risk' or group polarisation phenomena inevitably leads to questions about the significance of group membership (as opposed to social category membership like nationality or gender) and, indeed, intergroup relationships in risk perception and reactions. The phenomena described here may be the tip of the iceberg in terms of group dynamic effects upon responses to risk. Further elements of these effects are discussed in Chapters 6 and 9. It is, however, clear that explanations of the impact of group dynamics upon individual risk reactions will need to encompass both cognitive and motivational components.

One final point is necessary here. Since most of the studies that examine decision-making in uncertainty are concerned with the ways in which heuristics, biases and mental models, and so on, affect risk estimations rather than choices, it would be reasonable to ask whether they address decision-making at all. Not all studies ignore actual choices (e.g. the work on prospect theory), but most do. It is an important issue to address because there is a substantial body of literature that shows that risk estimation is not related in any simple fashion to the decision to take a risk. There is another complexity that must also be considered: intentions concerning risk-taking are not related to actual risk-taking in any simple fashion. This suggests that there is a very real need for studies that follow the decision-making process from risk estimation (linked to biases, etc.) to risk-taking. Risk-taking in such research would need to be broadly conceptualised – being concerned not just with individual choices regarding risk but also with societal decisions about the tolerability of particular risks.

The research on decision-making in the context of risk emphasises the importance of building psychological theories that span the intra-psychic, interpersonal, intragroup and intergroup levels of analysis and explana-tion. The findings demand analyses that focus on the interplay of cogni-tive, conative and oretic processes with social processes of influence and conformity. It is interesting to note how many of the models that appear to be based in cognitive level analyses, initially concerned with informa-tion processing and inference, develop a concern first for emotional and motivation influences and then for contextual – including institutional and ideological – affordances upon decision-making. Often it seems that the models acknowledge the broader factors that must be determining decision-making but choose to set them aside as not core to their imme-diate purpose. It is as if the complexities of including them in the analysis would be too great. Indeed this may be true. However, as long as they remain outside of the models, these models fail to be predictive and are not comprehensive.

5   Risk and emotion

Chapter preview

This chapter examines the role of emotions in risk perception and decision-making. The traditional dominance of cognitive models in explaining risk estimates and risk-taking is challenged. Instead, the possibility that there are dual processes at work is explored – one of which is embedded in an intuitive, experiential, affective base, while the other is embedded in formal propositional information processing. This proposition has led to research on the affect heuristic. The affect heuristic states that representations of objects and events are tagged to varying degrees with affect, and people refer to this when they make risk judgements. In addition, the evidence that the emotional state of the individual directly influences risk perceptions and actions is examined. The role of worry in risk estimations and the significance of the 'worried well' is described. Anticipated regret is also shown to have an impact in risk decisions. The relationship of fear, anger and outrage with risk judgements is considered. The way terror and panic may operate with regard to behaviour in disasters is outlined. It is concluded that an analysis of risk perception and decision-making that fails to consider the affect attached to a hazard or the emotional state of the individual is inevitably flawed. It is not appropriate to talk about the global primacy of either cognitive or affective components in the determination of risk reactions. A model of risk appreciation that incorporates both streams of influence and which details how they interact is necessary – if not yet available.

1   Feelings and the affect heuristic

Traditionally, emotions have been ignored when theories of risk perception or risk-taking have been developed. The cognitive approach has dominated. Yet we have reviewed in an earlier chapter the significance of self-concept factors, like efficacy, which tend to suggest the role of motivational factors in risk appreciation and response. We have also already seen that if people are sad or depressed, they are less likely to exhibit the optimistic bias. So there does seem to be a role for motivational and emotional state in determining how memory and other cognitive functions operate in relation to risk perceptions.

It could be even argued that emotions have primacy in the evaluation of risk in a variety of situations. In some, the emotional response to the hazard could be more immediate and influential than any rational computation of likelihood of harm or relative gain. In certain cases, the truth of this proposition is obvious. For instance, you are faced with a man that you recognise is a criminal on the run. He has a gun, and is threatening that he will shoot you, first in the arm, then in the leg, and then in each bit of your body if you do not obey him. In such a situation, it would be likely that you would feel fear and that the fear would drive your decisions immediately. The idea that you would engage in a self-conscious matrix of calculations that resulted in an estimation of risk and plotted the optimal behavioural responses is somewhat surreal. Fear in such a situation would drive reaction at the time.

The timescale then becomes important. The appreciation of the subtleties of the risk might be achieved in retrospect rather than prospect. In the extreme, the emotional reaction might even be said to block the cognitive reaction to the hazard, not just to modify it. The block may be temporary, but it is important to understand. It may determine the initial response to the hazard and it may condition the subsequent manipulation and use of information in the processes of either rationalising decisions concerning the hazard or choosing subsequent action about the hazard. As the incident unfurls, the initial emotional reaction may take on a variety of influential roles:

- imposing filters on what information is selectively attended to (e.g. 'I saw the other gun that he had on the bureau; the very first thing that I saw was that he was equipped with several weapons')
- justifying the discounting, or accentuating the importance, of information (e.g. 'He told me that I was safe as long as I co-operated, but I knew no one who could scare me that much was going to let me go')
- providing an affective tinge to a fragment of information that imbues it with positivity or negativity (e.g. 'I was afraid and when he shook the gun at me I was certain that he was about to fire' – i.e. the action was threatening and heightened fear further)
- providing explanations or rationalisations for decisions retrospectively (e.g. 'I was so afraid I hit out') – such reasoning reduces the relevance or indeed necessity for a rational evaluation of the situation.

Whether all of these clear rationalisations went through the mind of the victim consciously in real time is irrelevant. The point is that the existence of the emotional reaction makes these interpretations, whether post hoc or in situ acceptable – personally and socially.

In fact, the importance of affect is now being acknowledged more broadly in the research on decision-making processes and risk perception (Slovic *et al.*, 2004). On the basis of the analysis above, it could be argued that intuitive emotional reactions are the predominant method by which human beings evaluate risk. In fact, the early research on the characteristics of hazards should have signalled the significance of the emotional response. One of the prime dimensions in the characterisation of risk was the 'dread' dimension. Feelings of dread were a major determiner of the public acceptance of risk for a wide range of hazards.

Slovic and his co-workers consequently refer to 'risk as feelings' – the fast, intuitive, perhaps instinctive, reaction to danger. Yet they are talking about more than just a raw emotional reaction of fear to danger. They are talking about the subtle hints of affect that form a veneer around all our perceptions (Peters *et al.*, 2006b). They are not just talking about the reaction to the man with the gun.

Zajonc (1980) was an early proponent of the significance of affect in decision-making. He argued that affective reactions to stimuli are often the very first reactions, occurring automatically and subsequently guiding information processing and judgements. In fact, he suggested that all perceptions contain some affect – all objects have some emotional valence associated with them: liking, distaste, fear, attraction, and so on. This may seem far-fetched and somewhat simplified. It would be easy to imagine that some previously unknown novel object (for example, a new type of plant seed) should have no affective resonance for some particular individual (for example, a 5-year-old child) at a specific moment in time (for example, the first time she sees it). However, as a general rule of thumb the assertion can probably be seen to hold. Even the novel object will be attributed with meaning by association with other objects that are known (for example, the seed may be categorised with other horticultural products) and within moments it will be linked into a series of associations and memories that themselves have some emotional connotations. Escaping that web of meaning-making is impossible and, within it, emotional associations are inevitable at some level. They may not be immediately obvious and they may not be equally salient in all cases, but this is not necessary for Zajonc's argument to be important.

Finucane *et al.* (2000) propose that people use an 'affect heuristic' in making decisions and as a guide to judgements. They argue that representations of objects and events that people hold are imbued to varying degrees with affect. People consult or refer to an 'affective pool' (containing all the positive and negative tags associated with the representation, whether consciously or unconsciously) in the process of making judgements. Just as imaginability, memorability and similarity serve as cues for probability judgement (via the availability and representativeness heuristics), affect may serve as a cue to judgement. Effectively, the proposition is that attention to the affective tone of the object makes it less necessary to engage in a long-winded evaluation of the object's pros and cons when coming to a judgement. This can be advantageous when a speedy judgement is needed or when relevant information is sparse.

Even when a short cut is not required, the impact of affect may still be important in making some information more salient in the assessment of the pros and cons. Nisbett and Ross (1980) showed that emotional interest, positive or negative, increased the vividness of information and increased its salience in directing judgement relative to information that lacked such emotional connotations. Vividness is also, of course, likely to enhance memorability and availability and additionally achieve biased impact on judgement also through those routes.

Finucane et al. (2000) used the affect heuristic to explain the often observed inverse relationship between perceptions of risk and benefit. Risk and benefit should, obviously, be treated as distinct entities. The nature of the gains to be got from the pursuit of a hazardous activity or technology is analytically separable from the nature of the risks. For instance, the benefits from having aeroplane transport available (e.g. speedy international travel) are different from the risk (e.g. environmental pollution). Generally, there is no logical reason for risks and benefits to be related in any systematic way. It should depend entirely upon the nature of the hazard. Yet there are many studies that show that they are popularly thought to be negatively correlated (e.g. Fischhoff et al., 1978a, 1978b; Slovic et al., 1991; McDaniels et al., 1999) – the greater the perceived benefit, the lower the perceived risk. For example, smoking is seen to be high in risk and low in benefit. It should be noted in this that risk is apparently being treated as some index of adverse consequences; it is not being treated in any simple sense as an estimate of probability.

Perhaps this inverse perceived relationship of risk and benefit can be explained in terms of the way affect influences judgements. Alhakami and Slovic (1994) observed that this relationship between perceived risk and benefits was linked to the individual's general affective evaluation of the hazard. If they 'liked' the hazard (i.e. the object, activity or technology), they tended to rate the risks as low and the benefits as high. Going back to the earlier example, this would suggest that if you like flying you should rate the benefits of commercial aeroplanes as high and the risks associated with them as low.

Finucane et al. (2000) in a series of ingenious experiments extended this exploration. Introducing time pressures upon a judgement task they enhanced the arousal level of participants and reduced the opportunity they had for analytical deliberation. They expected as a consequence that judgement would be more influenced by affect. Participants were asked to rate a list of things (e.g. pesticides, surfing, railroads, eating beef, etc.) in terms of their perceived risk and perceived benefit on seven-point scales. Those participants who rated the objects under the time-pressure condition produced higher negative correlations between risk and benefit than those who were under no time pressure. Heightening the likelihood that affect can play a role seemed to be linked to greater inverse risk–benefit associations. It should be noted that in this study it was assumed that affect was heightened; there was no independent test that it had been heightened.

A further study by Finucane *et al.* took a more indirect approach to assessing the impact of affect. In this case, they attempted to manipulate affect by altering the information that people had about either the risks or benefits of the hazard. They reasoned that if perceived risks and benefits are linked by general shifts in affect, then manipulating only one would result in a change in the other. This prediction would not be derived from cognitive analyses of the relationship between risk–benefit assessments. The cognitive analysis would predict that information that changed perceived risk should have no contingent effect upon perceived benefits and vice versa.

The results of this study are interesting for two reasons. First, they did find the effect they predicted: when they shifted the perceived benefits of a hazard, they more often than not shifted the perceived risks in the opposite direction. So, for instance, information that indicated that gas as an energy source was less risky resulted in its benefits being seen to be greater. The ratio of the risk/benefit changes was not similar for all hazards but the direction of movement was always as predicted (i.e. inverted). Second, they found it difficult to manipulate perceptions of risk and benefit. The changes that occurred did not always go in the direction they intended from the information provided, and in roughly one third of the trials no change occurred at all. This is in itself worth noting. Having an impact in an experimental context upon perceptions of risk and benefit associated with well-known hazards is not so easy. Of course, it may not be easy because those perceptions are actually strongly linked to affective associations. Alternatively, it could be that they are embedded in a strong system of reasoned argument. However, this second explanation is less attractive than the first because in two-thirds of the trials the manipulation did work and worked in the way the affect heuristic would have predicted.

The researchers who have posited the affect heuristic have merely just begun to push forward our understanding of one aspect of the role of emotion in risk judgements (Slovic, 2001; Slovic *et al.*, 2005). They have, however, nudged a door ajar and the glimpses through it are fascinating. They promise the possibility of further systematic exploration of the motivational infrastructure upon which decision-making relies (Slovic *et al.*, 2004).

Part of this analysis will inevitably conclude that the degree to which emotion will play a role is intimately connected to the availability of information on, or experience of, the risk. For instance, Ganzach (2001) found that financial analysts base their judgements of risk and return for unfamiliar stocks upon their global feelings about how good they are, but for stocks that they know well they do not assume risk and benefits are inversely correlated, suggesting that feelings play a more minor role.

Other work has a similar emphasis. For instance, Rottenstreich and Hsee (2001) investigated whether the acceptability of risk changed when outcomes had a positive or negative affect associated with them. Essentially, they found that people will gamble on greater uncertainty if the potential emotional gain is greater. In fact, Loewenstein *et al.* (2001) observe that when an outcome carries sharp and strong affective meaning, as would be the case with, say, winning the Lottery or contracting cancer, people become insensitive to probability estimates. Their decisions are driven by the significance of the possible outcome, not its probability. They also argue that responses to uncertain situations have an 'all or none' characteristic that is sensitive to the possibility rather than the probability of strong positive or negative consequences. This they use to explain why societal concerns about hazards, such as nuclear power generation or waste disposal, which are characterised by feared consequences with low probabilities of occurring, fail to recede in response to the provision of further information about the very small probabilities of their feared consequences.

The role of affect can also be heightened or dampened according to the context in which judgements are made. Gasper and Clore (2000) found that when, under experimental conditions, people were made to pay attention to their emotional state, their judgements were influenced by it, and otherwise they were not. They also showed that simply telling people to pay attention to their feelings – rather than to the facts – shifted the focus of judgements. It seems that in some circumstances, where they have both information on a hazard and knowledge of their emotional reaction to it, people can choose which aspect of this dual system of determinants they will use in coming to a judgement. Gasper and Clore (1998) even found that the impact of trait affect (e.g. anxiety) upon risk estimates could be moderated if the respondents were told not to pay attention to their feelings.

Peters *et al.* (2004) take the argument one step further to explore the way affective reactions and cognitive world-views (i.e. generalised attitudes towards the world and its social organisation) activate predispositions to appraise and experience events in systematic ways that result in the generation of negative emotion, risk perceptions and stigma responses. They studied reactions to radiation sources that scored high on a measure of stigma (i.e. nuclear power plants, radioactive waste from power plants, radiations from nuclear weapons testing). Stigma is considered further in Chapters 6 and 9. Stigma attached to an object is essentially an indication that it is considered flawed, deviant or undesirable/unacceptable.

Peters *et al.* found that individual differences in negative reactivity (i.e. the chronic emotional state of the individual) and world-views were associated with the strength of emotional appraisals and these were associated, in turn, with negative emotion towards stigmatised radiation sources. Through structural equation modelling of their data, the researchers showed that perceived risk was more a function of negative emotion than vice versa. Peters *et al.* used their study to support their proposal that there are both emotional and cognitive prerequisites for the generation of a stigma response to a technological hazard. At its most basic, this argument would claim that a hazard is considered unacceptable not simply because the risk associated with it and appreciated at a cognitive level is too great, but also because it gives rise to an emotional reaction, instigated by a world-view and precipitated by a chronic state of affective reactivity, that is negative – too negative to allow acceptance. This model is, of course, one which deals with individual differences in susceptibility to stigmatise a hazard. An explanation of the way whole communities come to agree on which hazards to stigmatise would need to consider additional factors. This issue is considered further in Chapter 9.

2   Emotional state

The affect heuristic is concerned with the emotion associated with the object of the judgement rather than with the emotional state of the subject engaged in the judgement.

It does, however, seem fair to ask whether the emotional state of the individual, irrespective of the affect directly associated with the hazard, might be important. This is not to ignore the possibility that the emotional state of the individual may be determined by the affect associated with the hazard or by the judgement process it requires. For instance, Loewenstein *et al.* (2001) highlighted the role of the affect experienced at the moment of decision-making. They found that in a wide range of contexts the emotional reaction at the moment is more influential in determining choice than the rational evaluation of the options that may have been conducted beforehand. Peters *et al.* (2004), echoing the work of Peters and Slovic (1996), also found that emotional reaction, and the strong affect-laden imagery associated with it, determines perceived risk rather than the reverse in their examination of reactions to nuclear power plants, radioactive waste and radiation from nuclear weapons.

There have been surprisingly few direct examinations of how emotional state influences risk perception or risk-taking. Townsend *et al.* (2004), who looked at the perceived risk associated with GM food, interestingly, found no effect for stress levels on risk perception. Pereira-Henriques and Lima (2003) showed that affect tended to be more important in driving risk perception in unfamiliar situations. This might be consistent with the assumption that affective state will be more important when the individual is more uncertain of the relevant facts. Williams *et al.* (2003) tested the effects of affect, as measured by the dispositional traits of positive affectivity (overall feeling good) and negative affectivity (overall feeling bad), on risk perceptions and risk intentions among managers from a variety of industries and companies. Positive affectivity was predictive of viewing risk-related uncertainty and personal involvement in risk more optimistically, but was not linked to greater willingness to seek risk. Negative affectivity was associated with thinking the gains associated with risk-taking would be less and was linked to greater avoidance of risk-taking. O'Connor *et al.* (2005) also concluded that 'feeling at risk' matters. They examined how managers of community water systems made use of weather and climate forecasts. They showed that water managers who expect to face problems from weather events in the next decade are much more likely to make use of forecasts than those who expect few problems. This may seem hardly surprising. The surprising fact is that those who expect to face problems may have no specific reason to anticipate a problem. Feeling at risk, regardless of the specific source of the weather-related risk, stimulates a decision to use weather and climate forecasts. Of course, the literature on personality differences cited in Chapter 3 indicates that trait anxiety levels play a part in risk judgements. We will not rehearse that again here. However, it is worth exploring the role of worry in shaping risk perception and choices.

2.1   Worry

Worry is difficult to define. To worry is to be uneasy, troubled or concerned. It can range from being highly targeted, focused on a particular object, to being very generalised and non-specific. Worry is a well-recognised emotional state that has acknowledged cognitive effects (Leventhal, 1984). It is used to explain both one's own behaviour and that of others. There are culturally sanctioned objects of worry and ways of expressing worry.

Hazards often engender worry. In fact, Baron *et al.* (2000) found that the greater the perceived probability of a risk, the greater was the level of worry expressed, especially by lay people. Worry is future-oriented in that it is a current emotional state that is stimulated by the anticipation of some negative outcome in the future or by some outcome that is uncertain and thus may be negative in the future. It is therefore an obvious accompaniment to risk. While not all hazards initiate worry, all worry is associated with risk (of some sort).

To the extent that it is future-oriented, worry may be seen as adaptive: anticipatory concern that will stimulate action that avoids harm. The future orientation of worry distinguishes it from regret (which may also have an adaptive function but which focuses upon past events and their lessons for subsequent action). Worry can be seen as a route to risk reduction in so far as it can change behaviour or decisions and thereby remove the individual from the path of risk. For instance, a woman might worry about the possibility of being raped after hearing that a serial rapist is operating in her neighbourhood and as a result she may refrain from going out alone at night in the area. In such circumstances, it might seem that worry is a rational response to the circumstances and the precautions taken are also rational. Worry may also allow us to prioritise risks. The more worry we experience, the greater the attention we need to pay to a particular risk.

Bergstrom and McCaul (2004) illustrated the role of worry in risk-taking decisions. They wanted to know whether worry would be predictive of willingness to fly after the terrorist attacks of 9 September 2001 (9/11). In a study conducted thirty-four days after 9/11, college students rated their willingness to fly to New York City or to Washington DC. They also recorded their beliefs about the likelihood that more attacks would occur, the severity of such attacks and how worried they were about flying. Finally, they also made these estimates for similar others. Worry was found to be the strongest predictor of one's own and similar others' willingness to fly.

Inevitably in this discussion of worry, the perennial question springs to mind: What comes first – the affect or the risk perception? Rundmo (2002) did a nice study that allowed him through the use of structural equation modelling to address the question. He used survey questionnaire data from a large sample of respondents to statistically test alternative structural models – one model posited that affect precedes risk estimate, another posited that risk estimate precedes affect. While he showed variation across different types of risk and dependent upon sex and education, he generally found that the overall affective 'image of the risk' predicted the risk estimate rather than the reverse. However, he also warned that we are too lax in the way we conceptualise affect when we ask this question about which comes first. He emphasised that it may be only one dimension of affect that is salient in deriving risk cognitions and behavioural responses. This facet of emotion that has greatest impact on risk perception and behaviour may be what is commonly called worry.

Peters *et al.* (2006a) also report a study that attempts to provide a model of the antecedents and consequences of worry. They found that risk characteristics such as dread and preventability, negative reactivity and vulnerability to medical errors appeared to motivate worry about medical errors. Worry about medical errors was a better predictor of intentions to take precautionary actions than were risk perceptions.

However, frequently worry is not linked rationally to objective indices of risk and sometimes worry engenders changes in behaviour that are irrelevant or even counterproductive in dealing with the risk. The 'worried well' phenomenon is a useful example of non-rational worry and its relationship to risk estimation. See Box 5.1 for a description. The 'worried well' are clearly ignoring medical advice on the probability of them having contracted the disease. It may be that they do not believe that medics actually know the true risk factors and so they should be ignored. It may be that they do not believe that the medics are being honest with the public and so personal self-protection is the only rational choice. It may be that their health worry is non-specific and they would present for treatment irrespective of the target disease. Sadly, we do not know what motivates the 'worried well'.

From the 'worried well' phenomenon, maybe the most important lesson to learn is that these people are not behaving irrationally, but in a non-rational manner. That is to say, they do not appear to be conducting the computation of costs and benefits and assessment of likelihoods and then dismissing their conclusions (as would be implied by tagging them irrational); instead, they seem never to make the computation. They are thus

---

Box 5.1 The worried well

The phenomenon known as 'the worried well' refers to people who, despite being told that they have no reason to seek medical assistance on the basis of known risk factors, choose to do so. These are people who believe themselves to be at risk of a disease even though they are characterised by none of the features that would mean they are likely to

Box 5.1 (cont.)

contract the disease. What is more, they are so worried about the prospect that they seek medical attention – sometimes repeatedly.

In relation to some diseases, the scale of the 'worried well' is significant. For instance, the numbers of 'worried well' for HIV infection has been notable. Figure 5.1 presents the numbers of people in the UK taking HIV tests in the period 1989 to 1997 (quarterly figures; from the PHLS, 2000). The numbers are broken down by category of exposure: no risk, many heterosexual partners, homosexual males, heterosexuals with a high-risk partner. Those who have the HIV test and who are in the no-risk exposure category could be labelled to be the equivalent of 'worried well'. Figure 5.1 illustrates the very high level of take-up of the testing facility by these 'no-risk' individuals. Throughout the period, even after the criteria for HIV risk had been well publicised, the numbers of 'worried well' are roughly twice those of all the other categories summed. It is also interesting to note that no clearly effective management techniques have been evolved to deal with the HIV 'worried well' (e.g. Hedge, 1989). There is remarkably little reduction in the number of tests sought by 'no-risk' individuals over the period.

The number of 'worried well' will doubtless depend to some extent upon the nature of the disease itself. Though there are no large-scale comparative empirical data sets that would allow rigorous testing of the propositions, it is intuitively attractive to suppose that the diseases that will stimulate more 'worried well':

• are new and thus publicly little understood
• have slow onset and thus could be thought to be present undetected
• have been dramatically publicised and thus are salient in popular imagery.

The implications of the 'worried well' phenomenon for agencies planning for any major disease outbreak or epidemic are important. One might be that people would not only seek medical assistance unnecessarily; they might also use or seek to acquire medical treatments unnecessarily. Looking at a side effect of 'worried well' behaviour, Navas (2002) considers the potential for the massive stockpiling and consumption of anti-microbial agents in the event of an epidemic due to pathogenic bacteria. He describes the massive increase in sales of ciprofloxacin, some for immediate use but more for home stockpiling, after the anthrax bioterrorist attack in the USA recently. Navas emphasises the potential for such use leading to the emergence of antibiotic-resistant strains and the appearance of undesirable side effects.

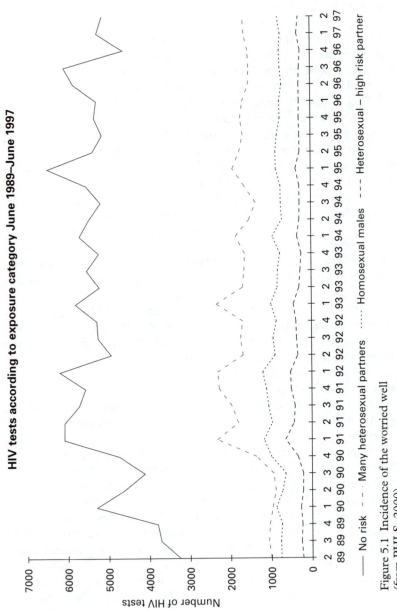

Figure 5.1 Incidence of the worried well
(from PHLS, 2000)

behaving non-rationally. Their emotional response to the hazard is such that the rational assessment of risk does not get triggered. Interestingly, HIV 'worried well', after they have been tested and proven negative, will often go back again for further tests – even though they know that they have not behaved in a way that would put them at risk afresh. For them, even the strong feedback of the negative test is not enough to assuage the worry and the perception that they are personally at risk. The risk estimates of the 'worried well' are driven by their emotional reaction to the hazard.

Another phenomenon sometimes associated with the existence of the 'worried well' is mass sociogenic illness. Bartholomew and Wessely (2002) suggest that one of the main dangers of a hazard, such as an epidemic, is the possibility of stimulating mass sociogenic illness. This may mean that large numbers of individuals exhibit symptoms, not because they have been infected but because they are afraid that they may be and see others behaving as if they were. There are illustrations from the USA where, for instance, fear of 'toxic gas' produced psychogenic symptoms in about 1,000 male military recruits in California in 1988. There are other examples from other communities in the USA. The process that results in sociogenic illness probably has nothing to do with any logical analysis of personal risk levels; it is one that focuses upon conformity – believing and behaving in the same way as others.

2.2   Anticipated regret

Another emotional driver for risk estimates and risk avoidance is regret. Regret is the emotion of feeling sorry for an event or for a loss. It is often associated with feeling repentant – wishing one had not done something or feeling sad that one has done something. Regret is typically an emotion that operates in retrospect: the thing that initiates the emotion has already happened. However, researchers who have studied risk perception and risk-taking have observed that regret can work prospectively. They talk about 'anticipated regret'. People are motivated to avoid certain risks because they anticipate that they will feel regret later if they do engage in them.

This pattern is illustrated in a series of studies by van der Pligt (e.g. van der Pligt and Richard, 1994; Richard et al., 1996), who found that adolescents' willingness to engage in risky sexual behaviours was significantly moderated by their anticipated regret. Similarly, Bakker et al. (1997) found that people were more likely to use condoms when they anticipated negative feelings as a result of not using condoms (particularly when they felt they had the power to exercise control over the sexual situation – i.e. high self-efficacy). In fact, Buunk et al. (1998) found that anticipated regret was an independent predictor of condom use even after other factors that might predict use (such as the known HIV risk factors) were taken into account. It seems that anticipated regret adds an additional modicum of behavioural prediction over and above anything that might be derived from a rational analysis of risk factors.

The phenomenon occurs in other domains, too. Zeelenberg and Beattie (1997) found that anticipated regret would predict levels of risk-taking in financial decisions. Zeelenberg (1999) also showed that it operates in choices concerning gambling, interpersonal relationships and consumption. He points out that the significance of anticipated regret is dependent upon the decision-maker expecting to receive post-decisional feedback. If there is no expectation that feedback will be given, anticipated regret is not engendered. While somewhat obvious once stated, this is important in predicting what types of risk-taking will be affected by anticipation of regret. In some risk-taking, feedback is either not provided – at least to the individual – or is provided only very much later and may be too distant to be salient in generating contemporary anticipation of regret. This may be why anticipated regret is only sometimes implicated in motivating self-protective health behaviours (Steptoe et al., 2000; Frost et al., 2001).

Anticipated regret may particularly deter risk-taking in areas where the individual has had no prior experience. Once experience is gained, the anticipated regret will be open to modification based on the actual feedback from doing the risky thing. So, for instance, Caffray and Schneider (2000) found that adolescents with no experience of certain risky behaviours (smoking cigarettes, using drugs, drinking alcohol, having unprotected sex and skipping school) were more focused on avoiding the negative affective consequences associated with regretting unfavourable outcomes of these behaviours. In contrast, adolescents with more experience of participating in risky behaviour held strong beliefs that doing these things could both enhance positive feelings and reduce negative ones. This suggests that the regret that is anticipated sometimes fails to materialise and then changes future anticipation of regret.

However, while it exists, anticipated regret does seem to be a strong motivator of risk decisions. Furthermore, this does not seem to have its effect on choice via changes in risk estimates. The individual who anticipates regret does not need to feel more at risk for the effect to occur. The avoidance of regret is the motivation. If one were to translate this into what the individual might be thinking, it might be: 'I may not be particularly at risk if I do this, but if I do it and something bad does happen to me, I will be very, very sorry and that is why I will not do it.'

To think of anticipated regret as simply a brake on behaviour would be an error. There is evidence that anticipated regret will also motivate behaviour. For instance, Chapman and Coups (2006) found that both anticipated worry and anticipated regret were stronger predictors of vaccination than perceived risk and mediated the effect of risk on influenza vaccination. Also, the anticipated level of emotions differed systematically from experienced emotions, such that vaccinated individuals anticipated more regret and less worry than they actually experienced. Additionally, anticipated and experienced emotions had implications for subsequent vaccination decisions. Those who did not vaccinate in the first year, but had high levels of worry and regret, were likely to be vaccinated the following year.

Manipulating anticipated regret has become a significant part of the risk communicator's armoury. If people are unresponsive to information that deals with probabilities, and we know that they frequently are, then explaining what people will feel like if they do succumb may be a viable alternative route to behaviour change.

2.3   Fear, anger and outrage

2.3.1   Fear and anger The significance of affect for theories of self-protective behaviours has been underestimated. Weinstein *et al.* (2000) looked at the role of fear in predicting self-protection. They studied the actions taken by individuals after natural disasters to prepare for future disasters. They questioned individuals who lived in three communities struck by severe tornadoes but who had not themselves been injured or incurred damage. They were questioned on two occasions – immediately after the tornado strike and around fourteen months later. Initial reactions to the tornadoes were used to predict precautionary measures reported at the initial and follow-up interviews. The extent to which individuals were preoccupied with tornadoes (i.e. thinking about them a lot) predicted action independent of affect, perceived risk and perceived personal control. However, recollections of fear felt during the tornado and negative affect when thinking about tornadoes were also related to action: both negative affect and high fear (if combined with preoccupation) were associated with less action following the tornado. This is not what might be expected from a rationalist interpretation of the impact of fear on action. Fear does not appear to be stimulating adaptive self-protection; it appears to be dampening efforts at risk minimisation.

Lerner and Keltner (2000) report findings that may contribute to an explanation of this effect. They found that fearful people make pessimistic judgements about a hazard, whereas angry people make more optimistic judgements. If fear does prime pessimism, this may account for an unwillingness of people who have high levels of fear to take self-protection measures. Perhaps fear at this high level is associated with perceptions of helplessness. In turn, this suggests that the actual level or degree of fear experienced will be important in determining responses to hazards. There is no reason to suppose that the curvilinear relationship that is often found between arousal levels and responsiveness should not apply here. Chapter 6 looks at how fear arousal is used in some risk messages in order to change behaviour, and returns to this question of the precise relationship between degree of fear and reactions to hazards.

Fischhoff *et al.* (2005) conducted a complex and elegant study which also explored the effects of fear and anger upon risk estimates. In this case, fear or anger was induced through experimental manipulation. The researchers examined the evolution of cognitive and emotional responses to terror risks for a nationally representative sample of Americans between late 2001 and late 2002. Respondents' risk judgements changed in ways consistent with their reported personal experiences concerning terrorist events. However, they did not recognise these changes, producing hindsight bias in memories for their judgements. An intensive debiasing procedure failed to restore a foresightful perspective. A fear-inducing manipulation increased risk estimates, whereas an anger-inducing manipulation reduced them – both in predictions (as previously observed) and in memories and judgements of past risks. Thus, priming emotions shaped not only perceptions of an abstract future but also perceptions of a concrete past. The manipulations in this study involved stimuli drawn from national news media (designed to provoke either fear or anger). It is noteworthy that such stimuli, supported by directed personal reflection, affected the respondents' emotional state enough to influence risk judgements – even one year after the tragic events of 11 September 2001. The study suggests people are at risk of manipulation. They can be made angry enough to accept policies they would otherwise not accept – because anger reduces the risk perceived. Equally, they can be made fearful enough to accept more precautionary policies than they would otherwise accept – because fear increases the perceived risk.

2.3.2   Outrage Sandman (1989), having noted that dread was associated with factors such as voluntariness, controllability, lethality and fairness, incorporated these into his 'outrage model'. Reliance on outrage was, in Sandman's view, the major reason why lay public and expert evaluations of risk differed. Essentially, if a noxious event was imposed involuntarily, but was controllable by those in power, caused grave harm, and that harm had effect in an inequitable way, then outrage would result.

Outrage and anger are not equivalent. Experience of a noxious event may cause anger, annoyance, irritation, distress, etc. but it will not become outrage until there is an attribution of blame and the explanation for the event abrogated various moral or ethical codes. Effectively, outrage occurs where someone or some group is seen to have failed to do what they morally were required to do to prevent the crisis.

In facing major hazards, the concern of those in power is always to curtail outrage. Anger is an unfortunate correlate of a noxious event, but outrage implies the event has not been managed effectively. The requirement to prevent outrage is now salient in the minds of those who plan crisis management. This issue is considered further in Chapter 9.

Outrage may be seen as the product of an event. However, it may also condition responses to that hazard in the future and may influence risk estimates. A useful example might be the outrage generated by hoax claims of terrorist action. It is notable that the real 2001 anthrax attack was preceded over a period of three years with a series of hoaxes in the USA threatening anthrax exposure. In 1998, there were thirty-seven incidents involving threat of anthrax exposure, and in the first two months of 1999 there were ten threats (Swanson and Fosnocht, 2000). The prior occurrence of empty threats may be important in influencing the public response to the real thing. Knowledge of previous hoax threats may prime 'worried well' behaviour because it may suggest the possibility of attack on several fronts simultaneously. It may also prime the population for immediate outrage when the actual attack occurs. The hoaxes provide the practice arena for defining an emotional reaction and, through the fear and outrage engendered, raising risk estimates.

2.4   Terror and panic

The effects of terror or panic upon risk perception and decision-making may be thought to be obviously important. Establishing exactly what they are, nevertheless, is rather difficult. One way would be artificially to induce terror, but this would be deeply unethical. Another way of looking at it would be to explore how people change their risk estimates and choices when they might be expected to be terrified as a result of being involved in some disaster.

Glass (2001) reports a study of ten disasters which took place between 1984 and 1994 in the USA and Mexico. These included an earthquake, a train derailment, a plane crash, a tornado, a bomb explosion and an underground gas explosion. Part of the study was designed to examine the role of victim response in the events. Glass derived five main lessons from the work:

- The disaster plans that were in place prior to the event rarely worked in practice.
- Rigid top–down planning often failed because communications systems were dysfunctional and the plans were targeted at the wrong things or failed to encompass the potential for changes in external context (e.g. weather or political priorities).
- Flexibility in planning is vital (it was the Duke of Wellington who said, 'My plans are made of string, and when they break I just tie the knots and go on again').
- Victims responded with 'collective resourcefulness' – responding effectively and creatively. Repeatedly, victims were seen to form spontaneous groups that developed roles, rules, leaders and a division of labour. In many of the disasters studied, the lay public worked to rescue more of those trapped or hurt than the emergency services. They were the first responders in contexts where the emergency services were disrupted, particularly with multi-site accidents.
- Panic was rare among those affected by the disaster. In fact, there was an absence of complaints and irrational behaviour. The exception was in the case of strangers caught in a fire. Even people caught in the World Trade Center bombing of 1993 reported little panic.

This analysis leads Glass and Schoch-Spana (2002) to argue that the public can and should be integrated into bioterrorism response planning. They should be treated as an ally, home-based patient care should be anticipated, and this means it is necessary to invest in public outreach and communications strategies, though these can only be expected to work if they acknowledge the cultural value systems of the at-risk populations.

Whether such cases generalise to all disasters – for example, bioterrorist attacks – is dubious. Unseen dangers are perhaps most frightening. However, the anthrax releases in the USA in 2001 did not result in mass panic, despite their apparent randomness. In the main, people took the precautions that they were instructed to take. The use of anti-microbial agents may have been excessive but was not disruptive.

Glass also quotes the historical example of the 1918 pandemic, when panic did not occur despite an enormous death toll. All the evidence appears to suggest that the better informed a population is about the hazard in advance, the less likely it is to panic when it happens. Glass emphasises that, where there is a dearth of genuine information, rumour will fill the gap.

At the end of his report, Glass extrapolates from his study to possible bioterrorist events. He argues that victims will self-transfer and seek treatment in places that they trust (not necessarily where they are told to go). He suggests that there will be 'emergent systems' of support and community alternatives to the command and control structure that authorities impose (so that rumouring and volunteerism will be vital determinants of the course of events). He predicts that hospitals will not be able to cope with a mass attack and home care will be needed.

Glass believes that prior to an attack the public must be provided with all suitable information. This is part of a philosophy he espouses that takes the public into partnership with the emergency services in dealing with the crisis. The measures to ensure the appropriateness of the public response during an epidemic (whether bioterrorist-induced or otherwise) must have been taken before the attack occurs. Not least, emergency service staff need to know how to mobilise and work with the public.

The extent of panic that would follow a bioterrorist attack probably cannot be extrapolated from behaviour patterns in other types of disaster (e.g. an accidental event). There are a number of factors that make the bioterrorist attack scenario different:

- the aftermath is likely to be long-lived
- the possibility of further attack is present (and the possibility of a further but different attack is also present)
- there is an enemy deliberately causing the hazard and can be held responsible
- controls imposed by the authorities (e.g. quarantine) may be seen to increase the risk to the individual.

Should we conclude from Glass's work that panic is not the upshot of disaster? That may be too bold a conclusion. Perhaps it is safer to assume that, when it occurs, it is fleeting. It happens in a fire because there are limited constructive responses, other than attempts at immediate escape. Possibly where constructive problem-solving responses are available, panic, if it occurs at all, subsides rapidly. Panic is, after all, defined as unreasoning and hasty action precipitated by terror.

This leaves the question of the relationship between terror, panic and risk perception unanswered. Perhaps terror and panic are too fleeting and too context-bound to be useful in making risk estimates and risk choices more intelligible or predictable. There certainly appear to be no good data that elucidate the relationship.

There is, of course, a big difference between being terrified and being terrorised. The conscious attempts to induce 'terror' that characterise terrorism can be clearly linked to resultant changes in risk estimates and choices. These are considered further in Chapter 9. However, it does seem pertinent here to say that terrorism, despite its label, does not seem to rely on terror per se for its effects. Instead, it relies upon inducing uncertainty into previous assumptions about safety and norms of behaviour and thereby inculcating greater ambient fear and anxiety levels.

Terrorism is less clearly tied to the acute sense of terror and more evidently linked to chronic and debilitating doubt and fear.

There is, of course, no doubt that terrorism attacks do affect risk estimates. For instance, Gigerenzer (2006) showed that, after the terrorist attacks of 9/11, Americans reduced their air travel. The attack raised the perceived risk of air travel. Ironically, more people used the roads during the year following the attack, suggesting a shift from air to car travel, yet in the same period the number of fatal highway crashes exceeded the baseline of the previous years. Gigerenzer postulates that 1,500 Americans died on the roads in an attempt to avoid being killed in an aeroplane terrorist incident. Perhaps the most chilling aspect of this study is the apparent failure of those who switched mode of transport to consider the significance of the relativities of risks.

Conclusion

From the evidence reviewed in this chapter, there must be absolutely no doubt that there is a significant role for emotion in the determination of risk perception and risk decision-making. This role can be exerted either through the affect attached to the hazard itself or through the emotional state of the individual reacting to the hazard. It is evident that it is not appropriate to talk about the universal primacy of either cognitive or affective components in the determination of risk reactions. A model of risk appreciation that incorporates both streams of influence and which details how they interact is necessary – even if it is not yet available.

At one level, this assertion should be unnecessary in an era when psychology has repeatedly acknowledged that affect and cognition are intimately connected (Forgas, 2000). However, it is still rare to see research that actually provides an integrative analysis of the cognitive and the affective factors that may be at work in determining risk reactions. Of course, the corpus of work generated by Slovic during his career represents a remarkable illustration that such integrative analyses can be done. It is interesting to note that Peters et al. (2006a, 2000b) summarise the four functions of affect in decision-making (affect as information, as a spotlight, as a motivator and as common currency). They emphasise that the role of affect in decisions and decision processes is quite nuanced and deserves careful empirical study in basic and applied research.

The work described in this chapter on worry, regret, fear, anger, outrage, terror and panic is all of immediate practical importance to practitioners and policy-makers. In many ways, it is of more obvious relevance than studies of the perceived characteristics of hazards or the impact of probability estimates on risk decisions, because it speaks directly about what the public feel and then how they will react to a hazard. It may be easier to see the link between this and the interventions that are needed in order to respond to a hazard. Work on emotions is itself often more graphic and attention-getting than research on cognitions. Obviously, good policy and effective interventions will be a product of learning the lessons that each sort of research has to offer.

6 Risk communication

Chapter preview

This chapter considers the difficulties associated with risk communication and summarises the social psychological findings concerning the factors that make communication persuasive. The use of the mental models approach to the design of risk communication strategies and messages is described. The impact of fear inducement on the efficacy of risk communication is assessed. The significance of trust in the process of developing the representation of the risk is examined. The effects of uncertainty upon the construction and efficacy of risk messages are outlined and the use of the precautionary principle as a determiner of risk management is critically assessed. The roles of the mass media as risk communicators are outlined. Pressure groups' activities in negotiating the status of a hazard are briefly considered. The changing model of risk communication that is signalled by the use of consultation and participation methods is introduced. The difficulties associated with involving a broad spectrum of the public in such methods are noted and some suggestions for overcoming them are presented.

1 Communication about hazards

It could be argued that communicating about hazards is just the same as any other sort of communication. Is there anything that sets risk communication apart – other than that it is about risk? One thing that makes it interesting, if not unique, is that it seems very difficult to do well. This may be because risk communication is seen basically to revolve around one party (A) trying to get another party (B) to accept a representation of a hazard that B finds any (or any combination) of the following:
- incomprehensible – i.e. meaningless or confusing
- unbelievable – i.e. inadequately substantiated
- irrelevant – i.e. of no personal import
- unacceptable – i.e. in conflict with other previously adopted systems of belief or value.

However, getting risk communication right is considered to be vitally important. It is necessary in order to ensure, first, that people and institutions behave in ways that improve their well-being and safety, and, second, that they accept the introduction of changes that others deem necessary (whether technological, political, legal, economic, or anything else). Protection and acceptance-rejection are twin themes of risk communication.

As a result, risk communication research has focused on what happens not simply when information is being transmitted but when that information is part of a message that is designed to persuade. The persuasion is aimed at making the recipients see the hazard in a different way and as a consequence change their attitude or behaviour towards it. In the main, the initiation of the risk communication process is seen as coming from some authority source (for example, the ubiquitous 'experts' or regulators). In the early days of risk communication research, the process was virtually always seen as one-way (from the authorities to the public). This has been replaced more recently by a focus upon the dynamic flow of risk communications across systems and networks over time, particularly as processes of deliberation and participation in risk decision-making are elaborated.

Fischhoff (1998: 134) produced an entertaining and illuminating speculative (i.e. unsubstantiated empirically) history of risk communication. He summarises the approaches underlying different eras of risk communication succinctly in terms of eight developmental stages characterised in the following way:

- All we have to do is get the numbers right
- All we have to do is tell them the numbers
- All we have to do is explain what we mean by the numbers
- All we have to do is show them that they've accepted similar risks in the past
- All we have to do is show them that it is a good deal for them
- All we have to do is treat them nice
- All we have to do is make them partners
- All of the above.

In this, Fischhoff is pointing to a move from an era of experts thinking no risk communication was necessary, if they could simply get the risk calculations right so that 'the public' was safe, to an era when risk decisions are made in partnership with those affected. His conclusion, however, is that risk communication is still not optimised.

2   What can social psychology contribute?

The vast bulk of social psychology has been aimed at understanding how beliefs and behaviour change under social influence. It should have something to say about the factors that will improve risk communication. The work on persuasion would seem to be most relevant. Some of those findings are briefly summarised in Box 6.1 (further details can be found in any standard social psychology textbook, including Breakwell and Rowett, 1982).

The issue of what the audience is doing with information during an attempt at persuasion has also been explored. Petty and Cacioppo (1986) first proposed that there are two routes to persuasion: the central and the

---

Box 6.1 Factors influencing the persuasiveness of a message

Traditionally, the factors influencing the persuasiveness of a message are broken down into:

- **Message structure and content**
  - *Order effects* – in complex or long messages the audience tend to remember what is presented first and what is presented last (known as primacy and recency effects), but lose the middle section. This suggests the elements that must be remembered should be presented at the start and again at the end of a message.
  - *One-sided versus two-sided presentations* – a one-sided presentation makes the argument only for the position adopted by the presenter; a two-sided presentation makes the case for and against the argument of the presenter but is weighted in favour of it. The latter has sometimes been shown to be more persuasive with audiences that are initially negative towards the presentation. The former has been shown more effective with an audience that is already inclined to be positive. The explanation given suggests that the two-sided argument can encourage an antipathetic audience to feel that the presenter really does understand the opposition viewpoint but has come to a considered opinion against it. The positive audience does not wish to feel the presenter has any residual doubts and this might be implied by recounting the opposition case even if only to dismiss it.
  - *Simplicity and repetition* – messages that are internally consistent, unambiguous and phrased in simple language are more persuasive (all other things being equal). Repetition of a message over time is also persuasive. The explanation for this seems to be in terms of growing familiarity with the message leading to reduced resistance to it.
  - Fear or anxiety arousal affects the reception and interpretation of the information in a message. The relevance of this complex phenomenon is elaborated further in the main body of the text.

Box 6.1 (cont.)

- **Medium of the message**
  - All other things being equal, messages delivered face-to-face are more persuasive than those delivered televisually, which in turn are more effective than those presented by audio media, and textual messages are least persuasive of all. The original explanation for this focused upon the extra cues available in the face-to-face situation as to the veracity of the source.
- **Characteristics of the message source**
  Other things being equal:
  - If the source of the message is attractive, according to the norms of the audience's culture, the message is more likely to be persuasive.
  - If the source is powerful (in terms of perceived position status or expertise), the message is more likely to be effective.
  - If the source is trustworthy, the message is more likely to be persuasive. This area is extensively studied in relations to risk communication.

Note: These simplistic generalisations must be treated with great care. The phrase 'all other things being equal' may mislead. In practice, all other things are not equal. The factors described co-vary and their interactions make it nigh on impossible to predict whether persuasion will be enhanced or not. For instance, it has been shown in one study that easy-to-understand messages are most persuasive when videotaped, and difficult messages are most persuasive when written. It is also quite clear that this summary of factors influencing persuasion ignores the very complex issue of the nature of the audience (both in terms of individual members and as social entity). The importance of the characteristics of the audience is addressed elsewhere in this chapter.

peripheral. The central route entails the audience being in an analytical and motivated state, ready to engage in a lot of effort with the arguments, willing to elaborate upon them and determine whether they agree or not. It requires cogent arguments from the persuaders and can evoke enduring change. The peripheral route relies on influencing the audience because it pays attention to incidental cues (such as the attractiveness of the source) rather than to the arguments. The audience does not need to engage with the information analytically and relies on heuristics to interpret it. The effects of such persuasion are likely to be only temporary. The two routes may be suited for different types of messages. The empirical evidence for the existence of two routes is not overwhelming, but the idea has intuitive appeal. Certainly, in the context of risk communication, both routes could be used. It is noteworthy that this model (sometimes called the elaboration likelihood theory) is not concerned with affect. It does not suggest that certain mood states are associated with the peripheral route or with the central route. In its original form, it is a cognitive model. However, it is not difficult to see that affective components could be added into it that might improve predictions as to whether the route chosen is peripheral or central. One hypothesis might be that fear would trigger the peripheral route. This will be further considered in discussing the effect of fear inducement on risk communication.

3   Mental models and risk communication

While one road to understanding how best to communicate risk is to start with the basic generic tenets of how persuasion works, another route is to focus upon what needs to be changed. In risk communication, what essentially needs to be changed is the mental model that is held about the risk. The notion of mental models was introduced in Chapter 4. A mental model of the hazard is basically the intuitive understanding that a person has of the risk. The mental model is a system of beliefs (which can include explanations) and attitudes, with their affective connotations, that the individual holds about the risk (Fischhoff *et al.*, 1997; Bostrom *et al.*, 1992, 1994a, 1994b; Jungermann *et al.*, 1988). It could be argued that, if risk communication is to be properly targeted, the mental model must be mapped and interventions designed specifically for it.

In this approach, the object is to renovate the mental model of the risk by adding missing concepts, correcting mistakes, strengthening correct beliefs and minimising peripheral ones (Fischhoff, 1994). The approach is sensitive to the way the extant mental model will influence the reception (interpretation and acceptability) of new information and suggestions or instructions. It is an approach to risk communication which inevitably acknowledges that there is no 'one size fits all' magic formula that could be developed for risk communication strategies. It is particularly useful because it treats the differences between the mental models of the hazard held by relevant experts and those held by the lay public as serious objects for research (Fischhoff *et al.*, 2000). The disparities between experts' and lay mental models are often the reason that risk communications produced by the experts for the public fail to have the desired effect. The risk communication structure that is predicated upon the experts' mental model rather than the lay mental model may easily fail to target the appropriate elements for change.

A large number of studies have used the mental models approach when constructing and then evaluating risk communication interventions. They illustrate that a very wide range of types of risk communication can be improved with this approach. This list includes a few examples of that range:

- Jungermann *et al.* (1988) applied the approach to informing people about pharmaceutical drugs with patient package inserts (the information people need about the drugs they are taking). Such inserts include extensive risk information about the drug that will need to be considered in using it, but often people misinterpret this information. The mental models approach offered a way to examine how people understand the inserts and a basis for improving their content and design.
- Kovacs *et al.* (2001) used the approach to explore the understanding that dry-cleaners and their customers had of the risks associated with the use in the cleaning process of perchloroethylene (PCE), which may be carcinogenic. The public showed virtually no awareness of the risk and the dry-cleaners mostly refused to give the risk credence, though they knew of it. These initial mental models were used as the basis for developing a revised risk communications strategy.
- Read and Morgan (1998) argued that the mental models approach should be used to develop risk communications to correct misperceptions about exposure to magnetic fields from high-voltage power lines.
- Cox *et al.* (2001) proved the approach useful in developing risk communications in the workplace in the chemical industry. This study particularly focused on establishing the gaps between expert and user mental models of the chemicals and then introduced new 'safety data sheets' to better communicate information on the safety of the chemicals.

Cox *et al.* (2001) articulate the stages in the method:

- Development of expert influence diagram – this is an amalgam of available expertise depicting the characteristics of the hazard and the behaviour it requires of users. This can be a very complex set of information and requires authoritative analysis. It is made more challenging when the hazard is multi-faceted. For instance, in the case of chemicals used in the workplace, there are organisational and personnel factors influencing safe use, there are technical factors in the processes that employ the chemical that influence safety, there are operational factors associated with the movement of substances that influence safety, the route whereby the chemical achieves its physical impact will affect safety, and the range and longevity of health effects may vary. The expert influence diagram is designed to capture all facets of the hazard as it applies to a particular user group.

- Development of user model – this is an amalgam of the individual mental models held by users, and there has to be sufficient consensus among users for this to be appropriate.
- Overlay the influence diagram and the user model – the object is to identify omissions in knowledge or misconceptions on the part of users, allowing the content and prioritisation of the risk communication to be determined in a form that is both meaningful and relevant to users and to their protection.
- Development of communication format – the acceptance and intelligibility of any message will depend upon its design characteristics and a fully evaluated design should be used.
- Communication evaluation – the object of evaluation is developmental, allowing revision of the content of the communication and its formatting if necessary. The evaluation phase can lead to iterations of the intervention. It may also modify the expert influence diagram by revealing some facet of the hazard that was not appreciated previously or by establishing that the intervention has changed but not sufficiently diminished the hazard to the users.

The studies used as examples above may lead to the conclusion that the mental models approach is most suited to risk communication requirements that derived from relatively closely defined hazard forms, where the expert influence diagram can be assembled and where the lay mental model is broadly consensually held. However, Morgan *et al.* (2002) tackled the very complex issue of HIV/AIDS. Recognising that the spread, control and consequences of HIV/AIDS involve processes still being studied by specialists from many disciplines, Morgan *et al.* sought, in creating their expert model, to identify the factors most relevant to predicting the probability of the virus transmission to uninfected individuals, the associated health (and other) consequences and the feedback mechanisms that affect the likelihood of infected individuals passing on the virus. The researchers thus circumscribed the domain to be included in the expert model. They also chose to create a single representation for all modes of HIV transmission (sex, mother to foetus, blood transfusion, intravenous needle sharing) arguing that they each pose the same challenges for people trying to understand the epidemic and their exposure to it. The expert model of the risk of contracting the disease which the researchers generated included:

- the prevalence of the disease in an area, which affects the likelihood that the individual will come into contact with a source of the virus that provides blood, needles or sex
- the extent to which the individual is vigilant in screening for sources of the virus and avoiding them

- the rigour with which the individual uses mitigation methods (i.e. forms of protection against transmission of the virus – e.g. condom use), recognised to be influenced by the perceived benefits and costs of these measures
- the incidence of alcohol use – which reduces vigilance (screening and mitigation) and may increase the frequency of risk behaviours (willingness to have sex, share needles)
- the willingness to take tests for HIV – impacts on likelihood of passing on the virus unintentionally
- the extent to which capacity to transmit the virus is curtailed as symptoms of the disease affect behaviour.

Morgan *et al.* showed, in semi-structured interviews, that a sample of 13- to 18-year-olds typically held mental models that in large part encompassed the expert model but tended to be unspecific and under-elaborated. However, when this age group was asked to respond to a structured survey that required them to indicate whether propositions derived from the expert model were true or false, it became clear that they did not understand the link between repeated exposure and increased risk. Having identified this and other systematic errors in the model that the sample was using of HIV risk, the researchers designed a risk communication brochure to correct their understanding. Participants provided with the brochure designed on the basis of the mental models data performed better on subsequent tests of knowledge of transmission routes than did individuals receiving no information or those receiving a standard AIDS/HIV information leaflet. The researchers acknowledge that this is not a very good test of the approach because it entails circularity: the mental models method was used to establish what had to be achieved on the test, an intervention based on this improved test scores more than an intervention blind to the purpose, but if the alternative brochure had been the basis for setting the test, perhaps it would have been more effective. It should also be noted that exposure to the mental models brochure produced relatively little absolute change in risk appreciation.

The meticulous work of Morgan *et al.* goes to show that the mental models people hold about complex hazards that have been subject to masses of public communication over long periods will have significant components of the expert model. However, a detailed appreciation of these components and their interrelationships may be missing. Moreover, the reinterpretations of these components (and the accretion of quite different elements) will be driven by the other social influences to which the individual is subject. Morgan *et al.* highlight that informational approaches to risk communication, such as the mental models approach, are based on the assumption that people are engaged in a sort of deliberative cost–benefit thinking when they deal with incoming information about hazards. In fact, Morgan *et al.* emphasise that stigma can override the deliberative thinking. The stigma associated with having (or even discussing) some disease states will sometimes prevent modification of the pertinent mental model and prevent that mental model influencing behaviour.

The mental models approach to designing risk communications has enormous value. Properly used, the methods of mental model elicitation, the identification of changes required, the design of the intervention, and evaluation of impact, can help to produce effective risk communications. Nevertheless, there are many additional factors that will influence the impact of the risk communication – even that so carefully designed by the mental models approach. Some of the key influences are considered below.

4   Fear and risk communications

Risk communication usually takes place in an arena that is highly emotionally charged. The audience for risk communication is typically either already afraid, or about to become afraid, to some degree. Even risk messages that are ostensibly purely factual, and are intended to be so, carry emotional connotations. This can be because they remind the audience of past events or experiences or tie in to strong social representations that have affective facets. One salient question consequentially emerges: What is the role of fear in risk communication? We have already considered the general role of emotions in risk perception in Chapter 5 and that will not be repeated. The task here is to specifically examine fear.

The classic research in this area has shown that fear arousal can be a potent aid to achieving behaviour change regarding a risk – even though there has been little agreement about why it works (Leventhal, 1970; Rogers, 1975; Witte, 1992; Maddux and Rogers, 1983; Janis, 1971). In trying to get people to cut down on smoking, brush their teeth more often, get a tetanus injection, or drive more carefully, a fear-arousing message can be effective (Muller and Johnson, 1990). How much fear is needed? Leventhal (1970) conducted experiments that showed that, often, the more frightened people are, the more they respond. This assertion is probably true only within limits. Very extreme levels of fear are likely to result in the individual either removing themselves from exposure to the message or failing to fully assimilate the message (since extreme arousal impairs cognitive processes).

Fear does not have to be a product of overt threat. Fear can be induced in the framing of the risk communication message (i.e. stating an outcome in terms of negative rather than positive effects; for instance, 'if you continue to smoke tobacco, you will die sooner' – negative – compared with 'if you stop smoking, you will live longer' – positive). Negative framing induces greater behaviour change (Wilson *et al.*, 1987, 1988). Levy-Leboyer (1988) showed that attitudes towards drinking alcohol were changed by fear-arousing images incorporated into TV campaigns.

However, things are not so simple. Fear does not always make a message more potent. For instance, health campaigns that have simply made people very fearful of AIDS/HIV have often not changed their sexual behaviour. Aronson (1997) has suggested that when the fear message is directed at a pleasurable activity, the result is often not behavioural change but denial. The same could be said when the fear message is targeted at something which is defining of the individual's sense of self (e.g. living in a particular neighbourhood). Denial may also occur because the message frightens without offering a way to deal with the threat, so the appropriate change in behaviour is not understood. Fear arousal seems to work best as a mechanism for changing behaviour if the required changes are an integral part of the message (Maddux and Rogers, 1983). For example, frightening people about the risks of cholesterol if tied to descriptions of what constitutes a low cholesterol diet can induce dietary changes (Millar and Millar, 1996). The position of the fear appeal within a message matters. It seems that presenting the consequences (i.e. the frightening part) before the recommendations works best in persuading people who are already inclined to follow the advice, but reversing the order (recommendations, then consequences) for those who are inclined to reject the advice works better (Keller, 1999). Keller argues that the rejecters who receive the recommendations first are more likely to perceive themselves as more susceptible to the hazard, regard the recommendations as more efficacious, feel they are capable of following the recommendations, and are less likely to refuse the message claims. It seems that receiving the consequences (threat) first encourages rejecters to discount the rest of the message.

There are other difficulties with using fear in risk communications. If the risk communication is public (not a one-to-one customised exchange with an individual), there are problems in making sure the fear is induced in the right people and that the right object of fear is delivered. This is best illustrated by a story concerning some pilot research done for a health education campaign. The campaign was directed at stopping pregnant women from smoking because of its effects on the foetus. The message comprised a poster picturing a naked, heavily pregnant woman with a cigarette protruding from her navel. The pilot study drew a sample of women, some of whom were pregnant, and asked them to say what the poster made them think. The virtual 100 per cent initial response from the non-pregnant women was that the poster made them think that they should never become pregnant if they were going to look like that. Among the pregnant women, few noticed the cigarette until prompted. Manipulating fear takes careful planning and a good understanding of the subcultural interpretations of cues for fear.

The significance of the heterogeneity within the audience for risk communications involving fear appeals has been repeatedly illustrated. For instance, de Hoog et al. (2005) showed that those who are more vulnerable to a health risk will be more likely to be threatened by a fear appeal and more likely to change their intentions concerning the hazardous behaviour. Das et al. (2003) had previously shown that the vulnerable are more likely to be persuaded by a fear appeal and are more likely to experience negative emotions as a consequence of the message. These studies may imply that those with low vulnerability are complacent when faced with a fear appeal. Given that people are actually poor at estimating their own vulnerability (evidenced by the subjective immunity and optimistic bias findings), this is likely to mean that fear appeals will 'miss' many of their key targets.

The empirical research on the impact of fear inducement in risk communication has to be treated with caution. It tends to be overreliant on forced exposure and short-term follow-ups. Hastings et al. (2004) point out that the general use of fear appeals in marketing provides examples that are fraught with unintended side effects (often deleterious). Girandola (2000) provides a useful review and re-analysis of the literature on fear and persuasion between 1953 and 1998. She suggests that the effects of fear appeals can only be predicted through understanding the complex interactions that occur between perceptions of self-efficacy and the availability of a viable self-protection plan that allows the control of both the danger and the fear.

5   Trust

Trust has been long understood to affect whether a risk is accepted. There is a dazzling array of data to illustrate this. It ranges from individual acceptance of personal risks (e.g. associated with medical procedures) to societal acceptance of risks with global or in-perpetuity implications (e.g. genetic modification or climate change). For instance, Motoyoshi et al. (2004) showed that residents living in the area affected by the Tokai flood disaster of 2000 were more likely to accept flood risks if they had trust in the public administrative authorities. In contrast, Grobe et al. (1999) found that consumers' risk perceptions toward the food-related biotechnology, recombinant bovine growth hormone, was significantly predicated upon lack of trust in governmental regulators' ability to protect consumers in the marketplace. Hiraba et al. (1998) also showed lack of trust in government to be correlated with increased estimates of the risk of crime. Summers and Hine (1997) reported that trust in government regulatory agencies accounted for substantial proportions of variation in willingness to accept hosting a nuclear waste repository or being along the transportation route to such a repository. This echoed the Kunreuther et al. (1990) findings from Nevada, where people were more likely to accept a nuclear waste repository at Yucca Mountain if they trusted the US Department of Energy to manage the repository safely. Siegrist et al. (2005b) showed that trust in authorities was positively correlated with perceived benefits and negatively with perceived risks of mobile phones and mobile base stations. In general, trust in the source of information about a hazard or in those responsible for managing the hazard is more likely to be an important predictor of risk estimates when the individual lacks personal knowledge of the hazard (Siegrist and Cvetkolich, 2000).

Distrust is commonly seen to be vital in creating controversy about whether a hazard should be tolerated and how it should be managed (e.g. Poortinga and Pidgeon, 2004; Tanaka, 2004; Hossain and Onyango, 2004; Slovic, 1993; Renn and Levine, 1991; Laird, 1989; Rayner and Cantor, 1987; Bord and O'Connor, 1990). Kasperson et al. (1992) proposed that it is necessary to understand trust as a multi-dimensional construct that includes cognitive, emotional and behavioural aspects which drive expectations about others, subjective perceptions of situations, and awareness of taking risks. They argue that four key dimensions of trust are perceptions of:

- commitment
- competence
- caring
- predictability.

Distrust is then said to arise when expectations of these four dimensions are violated. Frewer et al. (1996) showed empirical support for this approach when they found trust in sources of information about food risks to be determined by perceptions of their accuracy, knowledge and concern with public welfare. Interestingly, expertise and freedom (independence) did not lead to trustworthiness unless accompanied by the other characteristics.

Others (e.g. Earle and Cvetkovich, 1995; Siegrist and Cvetkovich, 2000; Earle, 2004) have suggested that trust is also founded upon the perception that salient values are held in common. More recently, however, Siegrist et al. (2003) have argued that it is counterproductive to collapse the distinction between trust that is based on value similarity and confidence that is based on performance. They found that both trust (defined in terms of value similarity) and confidence contribute independently to predictions of risk acceptance. Sjöberg (2001) reasonably suggests that in arenas where experts or officials are not believed to have knowledge or competence (e.g. concerning the long-term impact of radioactive waste) trust levels in those experts will have little power to explain risk perceptions. In this sense, trust and confidence are dependent. Fischhoff (1999) has commented that greater consistency in the theoretical definition and operational measures of trust in the risk arena would be valuable. Consensus and consistency have not yet arrived.

Within the social science literature there has been broad consensus that since the 1950s in Western industrialised societies there has been a ubiquitous increase in the distrust of major social institutions and their leaders (e.g. Cvetkovich and Löfstedt, 1999). Sometimes this is tied to arguments about the demise of respect in authority as old social orders have been disrupted by technological changes that have brought globalisation (e.g. Giddens, 1991). It is evident in these discussions that different researchers are employing quite different conceptualisations of trust.

We would say that it is necessary to distinguish at least three strata in the trust concept:

- *public trust* – the amalgamated feelings of trust towards all societal institutions and leaders – the diffuse communal sense of confidence in the system that makes decisions
- *institutional trust* – the general feeling of trust about a particular organisation or social category – this is, the overall assessment of confidence in the institution
- *specific trust* – the feeling of confidence in a particular institution as it deals with a specific issue at a single time.

All three strata are forms of 'social trust' – i.e. shared estimates of confidence. When considering how a hazard will be perceived, all three strata can come into play. Public trust levels set the background ambience for receipt of information about the hazard. For instance, in a country where there have been perceived to be two decades of political, economic and scientific calumny, the reception of declarations about the safety of a new hazard will be seen in the context of the past failure and deceit. For those organisations identified to be associated with the hazard, institutional trust levels will influence the interpretation of information about the hazard. It should be noted that institutional trust will have a role to play not just in focusing interpretation of information the organisation itself gives, but also it will affect information offered by others. For instance, if the company that is responsible for an oil spill is generally distrusted, the fact that a regulatory agency states the oil spill is minor may be less influential than if the company had previously had an excellent record of trustworthiness. Specific trust also has a role. The way an organisation deals with the particular hazard will elicit trust reactions that are peculiar to that risk at that time. For instance, the oil company that upon the discovery of a spill immediately spends billions in remedial action is affecting trust levels (even if only to prevent a decline in trust). Breakwell (2001b) proposed that institutional distrust is correlated with specific distrust but not perfectly. Specific distrust will depend upon a number of factors, including:

• what is actually done and said in this case by the institution
• perceived motive of the institution in this specific case
• perceived level of support for the institution from other more trusted (or distrusted) sources
• possible specific gain for the audience – distrust can be discounted if the audience anticipates some personal advantage will result.

Viklund (2003) explored the relationship between trust and risk perception in four European countries. He distinguished between general and specific trust and found significant variation in mean levels of both between countries. He also found that the correlation between general trust and risk perception was higher than that between specific trust and risk perception. Moreover, the risk perceived for some hazards was more predicted by trust levels than for other hazards (e.g. nuclear risk perception was more closely tied to trust levels).

Any exploration of the basis for specific trust raises the question of direction of causality. Do public trust, institutional trust and specific trust levels determine the reaction to a hazard or risk, or does the reaction originate elsewhere and then determine levels of trust? Cvetkovich (1999) analysed how social trust comes to be attributed. He argues that inferences about shared salient values are central to making attributions of trust: persons whom we perceive to share our important values are deemed more trustworthy. Attributions of trust are consequently seen to be a result of implicit not explicit reasoning. Once established, however, Cvetkovich suggests attributions of trust can influence the interpretation of actions. Poortinga and Pidgeon (2005) addressed the question of whether trust in risk regulation is a cause or the consequence of the acceptability of a hazard (in their study, GM food). They concluded that, rather than a determinant, trust in the regulator is an expression or indicator of a more general inclination to accept or reject GM food. Similarly, Frewer et al. (2003) concluded that, with regard to genetically modified food, trust in the source of information did not drive perceptions of the risk but rather these attitudes towards the risk informed perceptions of the motives of sources and thus affected their trustworthiness. Eiser *et al.* (2002), again concerning food risks, came to the same conclusion: trust and perceived risk are both reflections of prior attitudes towards the technology.

The difficulty with statements about the direction of causal influence between trust and risk acceptability is that they seem never to be based on data that allow the long-term exploration of the relationship between the two. Over time, it is easily conceivable that the direction of causality will shift: perhaps, initially prior trust in a source of risk information about a novel hazard will predispose the reaction to any message; later, established representations of the hazard will influence how any source that offers new information is regarded. Thus, whether the researcher sees that trust leads to acceptance or vice versa depends on what slice of the process is studied. This is not an uncommon problem in divining causality in social systems.

Maybe the question of ultimate origin is not one that needs to be answered. Perhaps it is best to focus on the relationships between social, institutional and specific trust with risk acceptability within defined time-scales and contexts. At least this may lead to predictive models within tightly specified limits and make the assessment of trust useful in designing risk communication strategies.

There have been some fascinating studies that have tried to describe further the operational links between specific trust and risk communication. It is evident from these that trust is a fragile flower. Slovic (1993) refers to the 'asymmetry principle' that states that it is difficult to create trust and very easy to destroy it, because people are more affected by bad events than good. This may not be difficult to understand from an evolutionary perspective: trusting too readily could result in enhanced chances of placing oneself in danger.

However, Cvetkovich *et al.* (2002) illustrated the effect of negative and positive events on trust and on risk perception was not so simple. In fact, they found that, with regard to the nuclear and the food industry,

- the perceived positivity of an event was less if, prior to the information presentation, trust levels in the industry were lower
- those people with initial low levels of trust in the industry judged negative events as more informative than positive events
- low trust levels prior to the presentation of information were associated with lowering of trust after the information – whether the event was positive or negative.

Cvetkovich *et al.* explain this in terms of the salient value similarity model of trust – the trust attributed to an institution perseveres despite good or bad events, as long as the value match between the institution and the perceiver is unchanged. White and Eiser (2005) pursued this further, suggesting that information specificity and hazard risk potential might affect the appearance of the asymmetry phenomenon. They showed that the effect is stronger where the new information is highly specific and that it is more evident where the hazard entails greater risk. They concluded that in low-risk industries positive events (i.e. policies) can be more influential in generating trust than negative events.

Yet trust has been shown to be highly sensitive to situational cues. For instance, the content of a risk message will affect the perceived trustworthiness of the source. For instance, Matsumoto *et al.* (2005) showed that messages that elaborate not only on the benefits but also on the risk involved in nuclear power were evaluated as being more fair, honest and reassuring than those which described only the benefits. Furthermore, two-sided messages were more likely to elicit sympathy and trust from the audience. Moreover, the same message will result in different estimates of trustworthiness of the source depending upon what motivation is attributed to the source for making the communication. Attributions of self-interest in comparison with attributions of selflessness will erode trustworthiness, even if the content of the message is identical.

The conditionality of specific trust really does mean that studies which seek to provide league tables of the trustworthiness of various risk communication sources are of limited value. It may be of only arcane interest to know that, at one moment, for one set of hazards, one sample rated medical sources more trustworthy than the government as a source of information they might hypothetically offer (e.g. Lang and Hallman, 2005). Nevertheless, Frewer and Miles (2003) do argue persuasively that within one hazard domain (food risks) the components of trust were robust over time. They showed that food industry sources were least trusted to convey information about food to consumers. It would be valuable to have similar longitudinal studies of trust regarding other hazards sets. Heath and Palenchar (2000) showed that institutional trust can be enhanced over time by ensuring that people have an understanding of what the organisation is doing to improve safety and reduce risk. They hypothesise that background, ongoing information encourages the public to feel a greater sense of control and this is translated into greater trust in the source that offers them control. Schutz and Wiedermann (2000) found a similar effect: chemical companies that offered more information about the risks associated with their operations and the management measures in place to deal with them were more trusted. Silence about your risks seems a reliable trigger of distrust. This appears to support the Peters *et al.* (1997) contention that perceptions of trust are dependent on perceptions of openness and honesty as well as perceived knowledge/expertise and concern/care.

The apparent inconsistencies in the evidence base between, on the one hand, studies that show perseverance of trust levels irrespective of new evidence and, on the other, studies which show that trust levels are responsive to minor manipulations of information content, are troubling. Perhaps they are actually a product of the variability between studies in the way trust is operationalised or defined. Fischhoff (1999) was probably right that greater consensus in the operational definition of the concept of trust would be helpful.

Despite the inconsistencies in findings across studies, it is clear that the relationship between trust in a risk communicator and the impact of a message is complex (irrespective of the definition of trust):

- Trustworthiness may be changed by engaging in risk communication (because of what is communicated, what context it is communicated in, when it is communicated, to whom it is communicated and with what purpose).
- Risk communication impact may be changed by levels of ambient public trust, relevant institutional trust, and specific trust in relation to the particular hazard at that time.

Sadly, our understanding of the nature of this relationship is rudimentary and does not provide the basis for predictive models or practical recommendations for the design of risk communications strategies.

6   Uncertainty

Calman (2002) suggests that three factors are relevant to the communication of medical risk to patients and the public: the certainty of the risk (the evidence base), the level of the risk (high or low) and the effect of the risk on the individual or population. He argues that risks can therefore range from hypothetical risk (possible, biologically plausible, but no evidence of its certain existence, its level or effect) to clearly identified (certainly established, level defined and effect assessed). Of course, even in the latter case, the risk to the individual remains only calculable as a probability. Calman uses Creutzfeldt-Jakob disease as an example of the former risk type and hepatitis B as an example of the latter. He goes on the say that communication is most difficult when the risk is 'hypothetical'.

The fundamental importance of the level of uncertainty about the risk to the effect of risk communication should not be ignored. Both actual uncertainty and assumed uncertainty have their effects on the way risk communications are interpreted and acted upon. In truth, there is often some degree of uncertainty about risk estimates or the viability of risk management strategies. Moreover, even when sources claim a particular degree of certainty, the public may perceive certainty to be at another level. This means that the significance of real (and perceived) uncertainty needs to be examined.

Frewer *et al.* (2003) studied whether scientific experts thought that the public could understand uncertainty associated with risk assessment. They found that there was a widespread belief among scientists that the general public were unable to conceptualise uncertainties associated with the management of risk. Many thought that providing the public with information about uncertainty would increase distrust in science and scientific institutions, besides causing confusion about the extent and impact of the particular hazard.

There have been some studies that have explored actual, rather than assumed, effects of uncertainty. Schapira *et al.* (2001) found that when participants were told about the amount of uncertainty that surrounded a medical risk estimate, some (but not all) would lose trust in the information. It should be noted that this effect of admitting uncertainty falls upon trust in the information itself, rather than the source. Johnson and Slovic (1994) tested whether discussing uncertainties in health risk assessments reduced perceived risk and increased the trust in the risk-assessing agency. They found that including details of uncertainty made some participants increase their estimate of the agency's honesty and trustworthiness, but others regarded it as a mark of incompetence.

Johnson (2004b) extended this research by examining how people interpret uncertainty in risk estimates by exploring their reactions when information was given in terms of ranges of risk estimates rather than a single risk estimate. Ranges of risk estimates from a hypothetical industry source elicited divergent evaluations of the risk assessor's honesty and competence from residents living close to the factories: some saw offering ranges of risk estimates as both honest and competent, but the majority judged the use of ranges as deficient on one or both dimensions. Johnson considers that these residents wanted definitive conclusions about safety, and tended to believe that the high end of the range was most likely to be an accurate estimate of the risk. Respondents believed that institutions only discuss risks when they are 'high'. They thought acknowledgement of scientific, as opposed to self-interested, reasons for uncertainty and disputes among experts was low. Attitude toward local industry seemed associated with attitudes about ranges of risk estimates. This last finding has echoes of the findings that suggest that trust in a risk communication source is dependent on prior attitudes towards the hazard.

The impact of uncertainty both upon risk perception and upon trust in the source of risk communication seems likely to depend on how it becomes known. There are a variety of ways in which uncertainty can become public:

- *Proactive explanation* – the institution managing the hazard chooses spontaneously, without duress or prompting, to explain the uncertainty associated with their risk estimates.
- *Reactive explanation* – the institution responsible for the hazard explains the uncertainty after some event or action on the part of others calls for further clarification of the risk estimate.
- *Revealed* – the uncertainty can be disclosed or proclaimed by sources other than the institution managing the hazard (e.g. the media can run stories of the 'hidden facts' or 'hidden ignorance').
- *Emergent* – the uncertainty may be inferred by the public rather than stated by any source (this can happen when there are conflicting expert sources offering different risk estimates to the public; the mere existence of alternative representations of the risk can suggest uncertainty).

While it may seem intuitively reasonable that proactive explanation of uncertainty could enhance trust both in the information and in the source of the information, it seems unlikely that the other routes for delivery of uncertainty caveats would do so. Further empirical work is needed in this area. Breakwell and Barnett (2003b) began the examination of emergent (what they called 'inferred') uncertainty in a series of experiments. Box 6.2 summarises this study. Emergent uncertainty, generated by conflicting messages from different sources, is shown to enhance risk estimates. It might have been expected to lower the credibility of the information in each of the conflicting messages but this only happened when a high-risk message was following by a low-risk message (and not vice versa) – maybe we expect routinely the supplanting of low-risk by high-risk estimates and this sequence has less power to erode credibility. Additionally, the positive impact on average upon its credibility of proactively acknowledging uncertainty associated with a high-risk message, even in a conflict situation, is very notable.

The research on uncertainty in recent years has led to advice to risk communicators that they should explain uncertainties associated with their risk estimates and risk-management processes. Thompson (2002) has rightly commented that this requires a much better understanding of how to express uncertainty and characterise variability in risk assessment. The actual content, as well as the timing, periodicity (e.g. rate of repetition) and vehicle (e.g. medium and source) for release, of information on uncertainty are inevitably going to be important. The simple mantra that being open about uncertainty is necessary in order to maintain (or retrieve) trust and risk acceptance or compliance with safety measures is misleading. The communication of uncertainty is rarely a matter of 'one shot'. The process is iterative and frequently contested. The actual dynamics that determine how uncertainty statements will be interpreted and affect behaviour are not yet understood. This is an area of enormous importance in which there should be much more research.

Box 6.2 Emergent uncertainty

Breakwell and Barnett (2003b) designed two experiments to highlight some of the ways in which the impact of risk communication can be affected by the presence of acknowledged (proactively explained) and inferred (emergent) uncertainty.

Experiment I compared responses to acknowledged uncertainty in a single-source risk communication with inferred (emergent) uncertainty generated by conflicting messages. The participants were fifty women aged 30–40 who were not using Hormone Replacement Therapy (HRT) and believed the risks of HRT to be low or negligible. Individuals were assigned to one of five groups.

- The *Control Group* received a risk communication message purporting to describe the results of a study of the possible health effects of HRT that showed users of this form of HRT had a tripled likelihood of developing breast cancer, that the effect was not limited to any particular sub-group of the users, and that the increased risk was present after two years of use.
- *Experimental Group 1* received the message with one modification: the negative effects of the HRT were likely to be specific to some subsets of women but it was uncertain who would be negatively affected.
- *Experimental Group 2* received the message with the modification: there was uncertainty about the onset time for any negative effects of HRT.
- *Experimental Group 3* received reports purporting to come from two different studies: the first contained the Control Group message and the second contained results from a similar study that had found no significant enhancement of risk (the high–low risk sequence).
- *Experimental Group 4* received the same message as Experimental Group 3 but with the order of the studies reported reversed (the low–high risk sequence).

The first two experimental groups thus faced proactively explained uncertainty, and the second two experimental groups faced emergent uncertainty (derived from the conflicting evidence of the two reports that they received).

Box 6.2 (cont.)

Participants each rated, on five-point scales, first the risk to users of HRT and then the credibility of the evidence that they had been given. The study tested a series of hypotheses:

- *Hypothesis 1*: proactive acknowledgement of uncertainty will increase the level of risk perceived by the audience and enhancement will be greater if the uncertainty concerns who will be affected by the hazard. Results showed that the Control Group message engendered significantly lower risk estimates than the message that acknowledged uncertainty about who might be affected (Group 1).

- *Hypothesis 2*: emergent uncertainty, generated by conflicting messages from different sources, will enhance risk estimates in comparison to those in the Control Group and Groups 1 and 2. Results showed this to be the case.

- *Hypothesis 3*: where uncertainty is proactively acknowledged in a message from a single source, in the absence of any conflicting message, the credibility of the evidence will be higher than if no uncertainty is indicated. This hypothesis was not supported.

- *Hypothesis 4*: where there are conflicting messages from two sources, the audience will rate the credibility of the evidence lower. This was shown to occur where the emergent uncertainty involved a high–low risk sequence but not where a low–high risk sequence message was used.

Experiment II examined whether acknowledged (emergent) uncertainty affected responses in conditions of conflict.

A similar experimental design and sample ($n = 60$) was used. After reading their messages, participants rated the risk associated with HRT on a five-point scale. They then rated separately on a five-point scale the credibility of the evidence presented in both of the two studies that they had read.

- The *Control Group* received conflicting reports purporting to come from two different studies. The first (the high-risk message) described the results of a study of the health effects of using HRT that showed users had a tripled likelihood of developing breast cancer, that the effect was not limited to any particular sub-group of the users, and that the increased risk was present after two years of use. The second study (the low-risk message) reported finding no significant enhancement of risk of breast cancer in women taking HRT.

- *Experimental Group 1* received the same reports as the Control Group; however, the high-risk message was modified to include a

Box 6.2 (cont.)

clear acknowledgement of uncertainty concerning the sub-groups of women who might be most affected by the risk.

• *Experimental Group 2* received the same reports as the Control Group, but, in this case, the low-risk message was modified to include a clear acknowledgement of uncertainty again concerning the sub-groups of women who might be affected by the risk.

After reading their messages, participants rated the risk associated with HRT on a five-point scale. They then rated separately on a five-point scale the credibility of the evidence presented in both of the two studies that they had read. Analyses gave support to each of these three hypotheses:

• *Hypothesis 1*: the source acknowledging uncertainty would enhance the credibility of the evidence it provided relative to the conflicting source.
• *Hypothesis 2*: the enhancement of credibility would be greatest where a high-risk message acknowledged uncertainty.
• *Hypothesis 3*: the perceived risk would be higher when uncertainty was acknowledged by a high-risk message

In sum, the impact of proactively acknowledging uncertainty by a source which is giving a high-risk message even in a conflict situation is very notable. It accentuates perceived risk and increases the perceived credibility differential between the high-risk message and the lower-risk message.

7   The precautionary principle

The communication of uncertainty becomes particularly salient in the context of 'the precautionary principle'. Despite claims that the precautionary principle is 'incoherent' (Peterson, 2006), it has been adopted by many governments – in Europe rather than in the USA (Wiener and Rogers, 2002; Hammitt *et al.*, 2005) – as their preferred approach to risk management. The precautionary principle is not easy to define (Sandin, 1999, lists nineteen different formulations of it). The precautionary principle was outlined by the United Nations Conference on the Environment and Development (UNCED, Rio) in 1992 as: 'where there are threats of serious or irreversible environmental damage, lack of full scientific certainty shall not be used as a reason for postponing cost effective measures to prevent degradation'. The precautionary principle essentially describes a philosophy that should be adopted for addressing hazards subject to high scientific uncertainty, and rules out lack of scientific certainty as a reason for not taking preventive action. Although originally formulated in the context of environmental protection, particularly in connection with 'global' environmental issues (e.g. ozone depletion), the precautionary principle has been more widely applied. Indeed, in the UK, it has been linked to formal government frameworks detailing the tolerability of a risk. A key feature of policy is that risks, which are not totally intolerable, should be regarded as tolerable as long as they have been reduced to levels that are 'as low as reasonably practicable' (known as ALARP). 'Reasonably practicable' is assessed by weighing the quantum of risk against the sacrifice (of whatever sort – financial, effort, time) associated with averting the risk. The process of determining whether a reduction in risk is worth the cost depends on judgements of 'proportionality'. Is the gain proportionate to the cost? Inevitably, this is open to dispute. However, the introduction of the precautionary principle exacerbates the problem, since it requires anticipatory action before risks are fully understood or their likely impacts quantified. Knowing what is 'proportionate' in such circumstances is difficult.

Decisions to embark upon precautionary interventions are thus open to criticism. Tickner and Gouveia-Vigeant (2005) illustrate the problems by analysing the 1991 cholera epidemic in Peru, which is often cited as an example of the pitfalls of the precautionary principle. It has been suggested that the application of the precautionary principle caused decision-makers to stop chlorinating the water supply due to the risks of disinfection by-products (DBPs), and this led to the epidemic. Tickner and Gouveia-Vigeant dismiss this analysis, showing that the epidemic was a product of inadequate public health infrastructure that was unable to control a known risk: the microbial contamination of water supplies. Nevertheless, the case points to the problems of the precautionary principle:

- It is seen as anti-science – because it does not wait for science 'to establish the facts' and because frequently the precautionary measure is taken against the products of science (e.g. the effects of the chlorination method).
- It is seen to have unintended side effects (often promoting other risks).
- It is seen to be subject to political or economic pressure.
- It is seen to be driven by the potential fear or outrage of the public.

Balzano and Sheppard (2002) emphasise that the precautionary principle lends itself to regulation based on the perception of a threat or fear itself. They illustrate this with the way the precautionary principle is applied to questions about radio-frequency electromagnetic fields of cellular telephones and cellular telephone base stations and claim that it has produced wasteful and misguided regulations and questionable advice to the public. In another thoughtful critique, Tait (2001) explored the adoption in Europe of the precautionary principle with regard to the regulation of genetically modified crops. She notes that the precautionary principle was used in order to avoid some of the adverse effects that had followed earlier reactive/preventive regulatory approaches developed for pesticides, and so as to encourage public acceptance of the new technology. She concludes that the precautionary approach has failed to achieve either of these aims. This is partly because the issue of GM food engenders both interest-based and ethical or value-based responses. These two stances are clearly distinguishable and engender conflicting positions on the appropriateness of precaution. Precaution is often caught in the crossfire between interest-based and value-based perspectives. As a result, it can become part of an escalating conflict about a risk. Tait argues this is no reason for abandoning the precautionary principle, but it calls for a more balanced approach to its introduction into risk regulation; one that acknowledges the varied motivations of different stakeholders. She might have added that these stakeholders will include governments and even the regulators themselves.

Hanekamp *et al.* (2005) point out that the precautionary principle should be seen as part of an ideological reaction to the self-confidence of scientific postwar materialism and the ecological dangers it conceived. This suggests that it will be technically and logically difficult to sustain: it cannot be applied in a systematic manner that can be justified without recourse to a value-laden rhetoric. Starr (2003) argues that a precautionary response does not provide 'an operational governing principle, although it makes publicly plausible an indefinite concealment of de facto political actions, or nonaction'. The EU, in a 'communication' from the Commission in 2002, attempted to establish criteria for the adoption of appropriate precautionary measures. Graham and Hsia (2002) acknowledge that the EC recommendations are useful, but also believe that they fall well short of robust rules for the application of precaution. The House of Lords Select Committee on Economic Affairs in June 2006 published a report on government policy on the management of risk, having looked at the use of the precautionary principle among other approaches, and concluded that 'the use of ill-defined and ambiguous terms in risk-management and regulatory documents is generally unhelpful'. They go on to say that the precautionary principle, ALARP and gross disproportion should be more clearly defined or replaced with more specific and unambiguous requirements and concepts. Sandin *et al.* (2002) did offer one way to achieve rigour in the use of the precautionary principle: the precautionary principle could be combined with a clear specification of the degree of scientific evidence required to trigger precaution and/or with some version of the de minimis rule. Graham (2001) offered further suggestions for refinement of the approach, suggesting that it needs to encompass decision rules applicable where the exposure to be reduced or prevented has beneficial as well as hazardous consequences; where the protective action itself creates potential hazards; and where delay in protective action might allow time for research that could produce better protective interventions. Some of the revisionist approaches to the precautionary principle appear to be converting into something which would be more recognisable as decision-making based on maximising expected utility. Basili and Franzini (2006) offer a definition of the precautionary principle based on the alpha-maximin expected utility approach, applying it to the possible outbreak of avian flu among humans. Moreover, they show that this approach indicates that the shortage and/or lack of effective drugs against the infection of the virus A(H5N1) – avian influenza – among humans can be considered a precautionary failure.

Against this backdrop of debate concerning the appropriateness and viability of the adoption of the precautionary principle, it is not surprising that risk communication when the principle is invoked can be very problematic. The message has to explain why action is being taken when there is no unambiguous scientific basis for doing so. It has to explain why the action that is being taken is the right action in the circumstances. It has to explain why the public should accept the recommendations introduced, even though there is no evidence of immediate threat. The chances are that the mere introduction of the precautions will represent to the public that the risk is real and imminent. After all, risk communication is an active process; those in receipt of the message tend to seek out second and third order reasons for its content. Gurmankin et al. (2004) describe how there can be a gap between the intended message and the received message because the audience is trying to explain to itself why the source is offering the information. For instance, in a medical consultation, the patient may inflate the doctor's original risk estimate associated with treating a disease because it is believed that the doctor is minimising the risk so that the patient will be less worried. When the precautionary principle is invoked, the public will make attributions of motives and concern levels to the authorities that are using it.

There is little empirical research specifically on the most effective way to communicate about the use of precaution. However, government agencies have developed guidelines on risk communication that incorporate how precaution should be handled. Box 6.3 summarises the approach developed by the Department of Health in the UK (1997). Even a quick perusal of the contents of the box shows how this government department has clearly distilled the lessons to be learnt from risk perception and communications research. Of course, the guidelines are generic and the difficulties emerge in practice when they are translated into specific risk communications. For instance, the guidelines say acknowledge uncertainty. They do not say how to do this. The nitty-gritty translation of uncertainty into a risk communication message is left to the practitioners dealing with the management of a particular hazard.

Box 6.3 Communicating risks to public health

Principles for risk communication:

- Planning communication should be an integral part of risk assessment and management.
- Anticipate that some hazards involve 'fright factors' – i.e. those that are poorly understood by science, involuntary, inequitably distributed, inescapable, unfamiliar, man-made, causing hidden and irreversible damage, endangering children or pregnant women (or future generations), arouse dread, involve identifiable victims, and are subject to contradictory statements from responsible sources (or even the same source). The fright factors stimulate greater anxiety and affect the response to risk communications.
- Recognise that the media will be more likely to become involved if certain triggers are present. These include: questions of blame, alleged secrets or cover-ups, human interest (villains or heroes), links to high-profile personalities, conflict (between experts or between experts and the public), signal value (the risk is a portent of worse to come), many people are exposed, visual impact, sex and/or crime, and other media have decided it is a big story (the 'snowball effect').
- Be aware of the secondary effects of the initial risk and how these are affected by the communication.
- Plan a communications strategy: clarify the aims it has, identify the full range of stakeholders affected, consider how they may perceive the issue (and differences between them), check for inconsistencies with previous messages (if unavoidable, explain them), and review all these facets as the situation develops.
- The process of communication should be planned: who needs to know, who needs to decide what is said, who needs to be the visible source of the message, when should it be released. External stakeholders will be involved; make sure choices are consistent and defensible, decisions against openness are both necessary and well explained, mechanisms for involvement are made clear to all. Know whatever else is being done to deal with the risk. Fragmentation in communication or the loss of the 'big picture' will undermine the efficacy of the process.

Box 6.3 (cont.)

- Content of the message should take cognisance of the audience's values and affective condition besides the need to provide information. The emotional tone of the message is important in success.
- Acknowledge uncertainties in scientific assessments.
- If relative risks are cited, the baseline risk must be clear. Any risk comparisons should be relevant to actual choices (not unrealistic or flippant).
- Be fair and complete in explaining both the benefits and the risks associated with the hazard. Bear in mind framing effects.
- Evaluate the impact of the communication through monitoring procedures throughout. Disseminate lessons learned, for future practice.

8   Mass media as risk communicators

The major channel of risk communication to the public is the mass media. They are authors of risk communication in their own right and they are also used by others as a conduit for their messages. Chapter 9 discusses the role that the media are said to have in the social amplification of risk and the development of social representations of hazards. The task here is to consider how the media make choices about how they handle risk stories. Box 6.4 presents a few headlines taken from two major daily newspapers in the UK over a two-day period. The fascinating feature of the list is that is covers so many different types of hazard: social (immigration, opium production), medical (diabetes, insect stings), technological (nuclear, laptop batteries) and environmental (floods, tsunami, wind farms). Hazard is the omnipresent topic of news stories.

Breakwell and Barnett (2001) studied the factors that are perceived by editors and journalists in the televisual, radio and print media to affect the way they report stories about hazards and risks. Twenty-four leading UK editors and journalists representing a wide range of different media were interviewed. Certain themes emerged from the interviews, and some practical implications – in particular, for government departments engaged in risk communication – can be summarised:

- *'Scare stories' are important* – many considered all stories to have a risk element because 'all life is risk-laden', but 'scare stories' are identifiably different. The best scare stories involve a threat to a lot of people, primarily to the most blameless and defenceless but valuable (e.g. children and pregnant women), are invisible until they strike and have major, preferably fatal, long-term consequences. Scare stories are considered to be good for audience figures or circulation. They

---

Box 6.4 Hazard headlines

'Millions flee worst storm for 50 years – Chinese officials use text messages and gongs to alert people to typhoon threat'
   'Inbreeding is behind rise in cases of diabetes, claims MP'
   'Nuclear firms fined £4 m for safety lapses that led to radioactive leaks'
   'Is this the price of clean fuel? A massive wind farm could make the Hebridean island of Lewis the renewable energy capital of Europe'
   'Earth shattering – our fragile planet is being ravaged by man's inhumanity to nature'
   'Swiss alarmed by threat of lake tsunamis ... rocks from crumbling mountains could fall into lakes and cause devastating tidal waves'
   'Numbers flooding in threaten our society' (immigration)
   'Hold back the migrant tide'
   'Giving British jobs to foreigners is a recipe for national suicide'
   'Beaches are closed as jellyfish invasion hits holiday resorts'
   'A plague of flies descends to make village life hell'
   'Exploding laptop fears bring recall of 4m batteries'
   'Poppy harvest at a record level' (opium)
   'Beware the killer wasps'
   'Wet alert ... mass floods coming'

---

are also sometimes just a by-product of having to simplify the issues in order to get the story across to audiences that do not understand risk concepts. From this, it would seem that the commercial pressures on the media will always promote scare stories. If the object of any government organisation is to avoid becoming the source of a scare, it may be possible if it provides relatively concise, simple but accurate information (alongside, if necessary, more detailed facts) to avoid the accidental creation of the scare that is based on media misunderstanding. It would not avoid misrepresentation, but it will minimise the scope for it.

- *The significance of 'infotainment'* – the interviewees argued that the media do not sensationalise; rather, they provide infotainment (which sometimes entails exaggeration). Infotainment basically means providing information in a manner that is entertaining. Even the highly specialist magazines were recognised to 'be in the entertainment business'. In relation to stories involving risk, this effort after infotainment will preclude pursuit of stories that say there is no risk or minimal risk. More importantly, those stories that involve a hazard that is applicable to a large number of the public are 'more newsworthy'. Of course, infotainment value declines with repetition. Consequently, even serious hazards involving large numbers will fail to gain coverage. There are many implications for organisations concerned with influencing media coverage of hazards in this focus upon infotainment:

○ The newsworthiness of a story will decline unless fed with new information (where 'information' is broadly defined, i.e. can include commentary or interpretation). If it is desirable to continue coverage of a hazard – to prevent attenuation of the perceived risk, for instance – drip-feeding information to the media will be important.

○ The entertainment value of a story is linked to the controversy it reports. Managing the representation of the controversy is important for an organisation concerned with the development of a risk story and this may mean actively participating in the controversy rather than remaining silent.

○ An organisation should have representatives who can tell the story in the media in an entertaining way. This means they tell it in a way which is attention-grabbing and appealing to a wide audience.

• *The media avoid 'real science'* – there was agreement amongst the interviewees that the media – generally – avoid 'real science' in their stories. The message has to be stripped down to be palatable to the journalist's particular audience. This avoidance of the scientific details may be tied to the fact that few journalists dealing with scientific or medical hazard stories would have been trained as scientists, engineers or health specialists. Interestingly, none of those interviewed considered this lack of specific expertise to be a disadvantage for them. Taken together these factors suggest that any organisation that wishes to have a story involving sophisticated scientific or technical information carried by the media accurately will need to provide that information structured very carefully. It would perhaps seem sensible to offer a story that was already stripped down to the essentials (perhaps alongside any more detailed exposition). Also it would make sense to have an expert in the field ready to respond to follow-up questions, but again in a way which was directed at the level of the educated lay audience. A further practical implication for an organisation handling these stories with the media is that it either needs to train or to select its own personnel in order that they can communicate in the format required, or it needs to use external reputable mediators through which it sources media information.

• *The importance of individual journalists and editors* – everyone interviewed made a point of acknowledging the importance of the individual editor or journalist in choosing a story and determining what line would be taken. There was a general recognition that journalists and editors can be campaigners and that they can be highly biased as a result, in the way they choose to handle particular stories. Interestingly, it was suggested that these biases are relatively well known and established and thus predictable. Since many of those interviewed had been in their jobs for many years (more than twenty-five, in one case), their personal preoccupations and perspectives would be open to analysis and their future proclivities in decisions open to prediction. Any organisation wishing to deal effectively with the national media should be concerned to understand the key media players at a personal professional level. The media should not be treated as an impersonal mass when developing a communications strategy. There is another implication of the longevity in their posts of these senior journalists: they acquire massive portfolios of examples of hazard stories. They naturally draw the parallels across stories and they draw lessons for the interpretation of newly breaking stories from all the past instances they recall. These journalists have their own implicit records of hazard sequences (see Chapter 9). Each new instance is seen and interpreted within the frame of the relevant hazard sequence. From the journalist or editor's point of view this is essential, since it allows for a very rapid assimilation of a new story and offers 'hazard templates' for reporting it and following it up. It would seem beneficial in such situations for any organisation dealing with the media to determine what template for reporting is being used and what hazard sequence is being assumed. This serves two purposes:

o It can be used to refine the manner in which any refutation is provided.
o It can be used to anticipate the likely course of subsequent coverage of the story and this in itself should alert the organisation to the ways in which it might be expected to react.

• *The significance of interactions between media* – interviewees emphasised that scoops were good, but a scoop that no one else followed up was not valuable. It was good to beat the competition to a story but not to be the only person to report it. There was perceived to be safety in numbers. It is noteworthy that this professional code operates, since it may account for several of the phenomena of amplification (with regard to both intensification and attenuation) described in Chapter 9. It is often notable that a risk story is intensified by a bandwagon effect of the media (one runs the story and others reiterate and expand it). Attenuation will occur where journalists do not believe that they will find that others report the story and thus are disinclined to do so themselves. The practical implications for an organisation wishing to work with the media on risk stories are:

- They should analyse how they interact with the media in controversies.
- They should develop a policy for media briefing during the life cycle of the controversy.

Surprisingly, perhaps, many of the interviewees said that they would not mind organisations trying to manage media briefing more actively. They would value timely and properly structured information on risk issues.

These interviewees, without exception, showed a remarkable degree of insight about their own activities as professionals and about the values and organisation of their profession as a whole. They had already analysed for themselves what were the important issues in relation to their interactions with government and other organisations and they knew what to expect from them. More importantly, in large part, they shared these understandings. Among themselves, they had common objectives and values. They were in competition with each other, but within a shared frame of reference, and were consequently predictable to each other. Given the diversity of the media, this creates an unexpected degree of coherence. From the point of view of any organisation wishing to deal with the media, this coherence, once appreciated in all its complexity, must be an important factor in shaping strategy.

The Breakwell and Barnett study is different from most research on the media and risk communication because it focuses upon what the media leaders say about their own practices. Most research on the media and risk communication deals with the volume of coverage offered to hazard stories (particularly when exploring the role of the media in social amplification of risk) and, to a lesser extent, the content of this coverage (e.g. Feigenson and Bailis, 2001, showed media depictions of the risks associated with airbags were riskier than warranted by objective data). The object in much of this work is to trace the effects of mass media reports on risk perception (e.g. Yamamoto, 2004; Agha, 2003; Romer et al., 2003; Frewer et al., 2002a, 2002b; Wessely, 2002). Typically, these studies show that mass media reports of risk stories heighten fear and raise risk estimates – but not inevitably, since the type of risk dictates the reportage; sometimes reassurance is the report's objective.

In any case, the effect of the media report is dependent upon other factors, not least the knowledge of the audience. For instance, Tulloch (1999) found that the media had a role in heightening fear of crime but that crime risk perceptions were also significantly affected by personal experience of crime. Some argue that personal experience is used as a form of verification of media assertions (Wiegman and Gutteling, 1995): if the media report does not equate with personal knowledge, it can be discounted. This may account for the short-lived effect of many media-stimulated rises in risk perception. Kalichman (1994) provides a memorable example of the way media effects subside: the announcement of HIV seropositivity and early professional retirement of basketball star Magic Johnson resulted in increases in public interest in and awareness of HIV/AIDS-related information, as well as changes in high-risk behaviours (also rates of antibody testing) but most of these effects were short-lived, subsiding within three weeks of the announcement.

Differences between media have also been explored (e.g. Lane and Meeker, 2003, examined the relative impact of television and the press on perceptions of the risk of becoming a victim of crime). Such studies generate no simple statements of the differences that might exist. Perhaps this is not surprising, since within any one branch of the media there are enormous variations in style and purpose (compare what used to be called tabloids and broadsheets in newspapers, or commercial versus public service broadcasters). Joffe and Haarhoff (2002) present a nice analysis of the social representations of ebola in Britain and show how tabloids and broadsheets differed in their reports of the disease. Essentially, the tabloid representations were more stripped down to the essentials and graphics, while the broadsheets were focused on structural features linked to ebola's escalation. Interestingly, the readers of these two types of newspaper tended to reproduce the representation presented in their preferred paper.

The media are also agents in the process that generates stigma associated with a hazard. Stigma is defined in Chapter 9, and Fischhoff (2001) analyses the concept in detail. Essentially, being linked to a hazard can attach a negative evaluation to anything or anybody. This happens not because the qualities of the stigmatised have materially changed, it happens because those qualities are re-evaluated in the context of the connection with the hazard. The research has been particularly focused on how products, places and technologies can be stigmatised. Flynn et al. (2001), in their edited volume on risk, media and stigma, bring together a significant body of data on the role that the media play in instigating and shaping hazard-related stigma. For instance, Flynn et al. (1998) examined the media coverage of an FBI raid upon a nuclear weapons production plant near Denver, in the USA, and found that the stories were consistently negative in their headline message. The researchers subsequently looked at whether knowledge of the raid and its aftermath affected attitudes towards home purchases in that area. Knowledge of the raid was good and there was considerable antipathy towards buying houses in nearby communities. Flynn et al. point to the creation of the heightened stigma associated with the neighbourhood and the pivotal risk communication role of the media. The mass media may be particularly capable of introducing stigma that perseveres because they provide dramatic, memorable visual images of the hazard or event. Given what editors say in the Breakwell and Barnett (2001) study reported above, it is also likely that the media are aware that they are creating stigma and see it as part of the process of encouraging controversy and infotainment. For instance, looking at the headlines in Box 6.4, it would be unlikely that editors reporting heightened concern about immigration levels and consequent unemployment threats would be blind to the possibility, indeed likelihood, of stigmatising immigrants, the neighbourhoods where they seek to live, or the authorities that establish immigration policy.

Establishing a stigma or a social representation of hazard is not a one-way process. It is not a 'hypodermic injection' from media to the public, but a 'tangled web' of influence (Smith, 2005). Carvalho and Burgess (2005) present a 'circuit of culture' model of the development of climate change risk perception. They suggest that the producers and consumers of media texts are jointly engaged in dynamic, meaning-making activities that are context-specific and that change over time. They conducted a critical discourse analysis of climate change on a database of newspaper reports from three UK broadsheet papers over the period 1985–2003. They report three phases of the discourse, occupying roughly five-year chunks in this period, which are characterised by different framings of the risks associated with climate change. The first phase moves from silence on the topic to the construction of an image of climate change as dangerous (with labels 'global warming' and 'greenhouse effect' appearing). The second phase sees climate change recede as a topic and there is a discernible shift from asking basic questions about the science of climate change to exposing the political and economic pressures that may shape the technological processes that create climate change. The third phase is characterised by coverage that describes a threat which is 'close to home' and imminent. Throughout the three phases, Carvalho and Burgess identify that coverage is shaped by the concerns of their audiences, who are becoming increasingly knowledgeable about the issues of climate change. It is also affected by the variety of interests held by the differentiated audiences for media. For instance, as insurance companies become aware of the significance of the impending climate changes for their business, their political action stimulates a new focus for media coverage in phase two. Similarly, in the third phase, coverage was driven by a series of interventions from senior scientists and politicians who sought to galvanise action in response to climate change. Interestingly, they followed the advice given in Box 6.3 on risk communication in that their interjections were highly quotable (for instance, one compared climate change to a weapon of mass destruction). Carvalho and Burgess conclude that the coverage of climate change has been strongly linked to the political agenda on the issue. Furthermore, the analysis appears to indicate that the factions in the media each build particular images of scientific knowledge and uncertainty on climate change, and emphasise or de-emphasise forecasts or impacts, in order to sustain their own preferences regarding the regulatory role of the state, individual freedom and the economic or social status quo. The sort of analysis offered by Carvalho and Burgess for climate change is much needed for other hazards. It allows a detailed understanding of the evolution of the social representation of significant hazards and can allow us to map the role of key agents in that process.

However, such examinations of the mass media are rapidly becoming a form of social archaeology of a fading era. As the electronic media come to the fore, there is a new force that will influence risk discourses. It is largely unanalysed as yet. Richardson (2001) looked at the way internet news-groups operated and suggested that, because they are interactive, interna-tional and intertextual, they will have enormous power to influence risk perceptions and reactions. The fascinating thing about these groups is that they are self-elected; it is a question of choice as to whether exposure occurs – quite different from the omnipresent TV. There is a real question about the ways the multiplicity of new vehicles for sharing risk informa-tion that are emerging will affect not only how people understand the hazard, but also how they form groups and identify with movements designed to respond to the hazard. For some time, pressure groups have been using the internet to proselytise much larger audiences (e.g. Laforet and Saunders, 2005) than they would ever have reached through the traditional mass media, and they can do so without the editorial control that characterised their previous access. The scale and speed of the development of so-called 'social media' based on web technology must change the way risk communication happens. The research community has to accelerate its study of these forms of risk communication and their implications.

9   Minorities and pressure in risk communication

It is worth considering the role of pressure groups in risk communication. Pressure groups can be defined as a minority that come together to influence others to change their opinions or behaviour. The targets for change can be a single issue (e.g. preventing the siting of a mobile tele-phone mast on a particular farm) or may involve complex systems of belief and practice (e.g. adoption of an eco-friendly lifestyle). The pressure group can be any size (while remaining a minority) and may be virtual (in the sense that it never physically meets). The longevity of pressure groups varies massively and they may die only to be resurrected when an issue reappears. They are a fascinating topic for research in their own right.

However, there is actually little research on pressure groups in the psychological literature. One approach to their analysis comes from Moscovici (1976). He has explored the activities of what he calls 'minority influence groups' (note: this should not be confused with the use of the word 'minority' to refer to ethnicity). Moscovici points out that one effect of minorities is to problematise issues and sensitise large portions of the rest of the public to them. They generate what Moscovici calls 'polemical social representations' in their effort to achieve change (see Chapter 9 for further discussion of social representations). There is now a considerable literature on how minorities achieve influence (Moscovici, 1976; Moscovici et al., 1985; Maass and Clark, 1984). Although some of the details are still open to debate, broad conclusions can be drawn. In addition to using the standard methods to achieve persuasiveness, to be influential minorities must:

• Propose a clear position on an issue – unambiguous and preferably simple.
• Hold consistently to that position – which involves two elements: stability over time (diachronic consistency) and consensus within the minority at one time (synchronic consistency).

The influence of minorities will also depend upon:

• The strength of the prior conviction of the target audience. Minorities have greater impact if the majority are ready to change (uncertain of their current position).
• How sure their target audience (perhaps an individual or sub-group) is about the majority or dominant stance on the issue. Greater change is associated with greater uncertainty – for example, when the issue is novel and no clear social representation has been promulgated by the majority or when the individual has to respond in isolation without the means to consult others.

It is not simply the case that the minority influences the majority. It is also influenced by it. This 'backwash' effect is obviously of crucial importance in shaping consistency over time, but it is virtually unresearched at the present time.

It is useful to remember that minorities exert influence when considering processes of acceptance of a novel risk because the conditions which pertain when a significant new hazard emerges are normally precisely those necessary for a minority that has some interest in it to be maximally influential: general uncertainty and potent self-interest (Breakwell and Barnett, 2000).

Communication about a hazard is often the prime concern for a minority (or pressure) group. It may even be its reason for existence. Pressure groups have a voice through the mass media, through the electronic media, and increasingly through formal deliberative processes set up to allow input from across communities into risk decision-making. The capacity for pressure groups to have an impact is growing. However, research on the effects they have is still limited. A study by Blume (2006) represents a valuable contribution. He explored the impact of the anti-vaccination 'movement' on the declining willingness of parents in the industrialised world to have their children vaccinated. He reviewed two sorts of empirical data, drawn from the UK and the Netherlands. These relate to the claims, actions and discourse of anti-vaccination groups on the one hand, and to the way parents of young children think about vaccines and vaccination on the other. Clear evidence of the formative influence of the anti-vaccination 'movement' emerged.

10   Consultation, participation and deliberation in risk communication

Consultation, participation and deliberation methods are now commonly used as part of the process of risk management. Inevitably these methods rely on some form of communication about the hazard. Rowe and Frewer (2000) provide a useful summary of the public participation-consultation methods currently in use and suggest an approach to evaluating their usefulness. They describe eight approaches:

- *Referenda*: involve potentially all members of a population, vote cast at a single point in time, usually involves choosing one of two options, all participants have equal influence, final outcome is binding.
- *Public hearings/inquiries*: involve interested citizens, limited in number by size of venue, true participants are the experts and politicians making presentations, may last weeks/months and usually held in working week, usually entails presentations by agencies regarding plans in open forum, public can voice opinion but it has no direct impact on the recommendation.
- *Public opinion surveys*: involve samples of varying sizes (sometimes representative of some segment of a population), usually entails a single event lasting a short time, operated mostly through written questionnaire or interview; used primarily for information gathering indirectly sometimes affecting decisions.

- *Negotiated rule-making*: involves small number of representatives of stakeholder groups, timescale is variable but a deadline is normally set, usually requires a consensus to be achieved among the representatives assembled from stakeholder groups.
- *Consensus conferences*: involve 10–16 members of the public (non-experts) selected by a steering committee as representative of the general public, these are offered preparatory demonstrations and lectures about the topic followed by a three-day conference, the panel thus constituted, with expert facilitator's help, questions expert witnesses chosen by the stakeholder panel often with a wider public audience present, conclusions on key questions are made via a report or press conference.
- *Citizens juries/panels*: involve 12–20 members of the public selected by stakeholder panel to be roughly representative of a local population, entail a series of meetings over several days, the lay panel with expert assistance questions other experts, meetings are not generally open to the public, conclusions are made via a report or through a press conference.
- *Citizen/public advisory committee*: involves a small group selected by the sponsor to represent the views of specific groups or communities, takes place over an extended period of time, convened by the sponsor to examine a significant issue with feedback to the sponsor.
- *Focus groups*: involve a small group (5–12 people) selected to be representative of some population or part of it (a series of groups may be used to achieve representativeness), meet usually once for a period of up to two hours, allowed free discussion of the target topic, sometimes recorded, views expressed noted.

Rowe and Frewer argue that the evaluation criteria that can be used to assess these participation methods can be divided into:

- *Acceptance criteria*: the method perceived by the public as satisfactory. This is likely to be perceived as satisfactory if:
  o public participants involved comprise a broadly representative sample of the population affected
  o participation process is conducted in an unbiased way
  o the public is involved as soon as it is clear that a need for a value-judgement exists
  o the outcome of the process has a genuine impact on decision-making
  o the process is transparent and the public can see what is going on and how decisions are being made.
- *Process criteria*: the method perceived by the sponsor to produce usable conclusions in an appropriate way. This is likely if:
  o the public participants are properly informed

- the task of participant is clearly defined
- the exercise displays clearly the decision-making process
- the process is cost-effective.

Rowe and Frewer suggest that the eight methods vary in their profile of scores on these criteria – some are good on each; some are poor on each. The trade-offs between criteria are difficult to make and no clear leader among the methods is identified. They suggest that it would be worth breeding hybrid methods of consultation, taking the best elements of each of the current approaches. An alternative, attractive approach for any organisation wishing to establish a system of consultation would be to develop a package of methods, used in sequence over a period of time. Routine involvement of the community in decision-making is most likely to avoid the worst disadvantages of most forms of consultation (Carson, 1999).

Renn *et al.* (1991) suggest that there are conditions that must be satisfied if consultation processes are to be effective. Prime amongst these is that there must be at least two serious alternatives to choose between and the sponsor must be seen to be willing to seriously consider the recommendation emerging from those consulted and evidence understanding of the public's concerns. Carnes *et al.* (1998) confirm this conclusion and emphasise that a consultation exercise should only be regarded as a success if it enhances or maintains the public's trust in the sponsor. Much of the work that evaluates consultation methods makes it clear that the organisation that consults must be ready to act on the output of the consultation. The process of consultation is not an end in itself. To use it as such is to court disaster – the public will lose faith in those sponsors that fail to act following consultation. Interestingly, Chess and Purcell (1999) argue that form of consultation does not determine level of success (in terms of either the process or its outputs). It is the context, content and specifics of the consultation that explain its efficacy.

There is no evidence available that indicates what specifics (whether characteristics of participants, context, subject matter or decision required) of an issue will affect the utility of a particular consultation method. Research is required that explores how particular forms of consultation might be optimally suited for some issues and whether their utility varies according to type of decision required.

Why do people agree to participate in consultations? The question has never been answered specifically. It is possible to infer why they do so from the factors that make a consultation exercise successful (Frewer, 1999b; Allen, 1998; Arnstein, 1969). Essentially, people participate for one of three main types of reason:

- *Self-interest* – they believe that by doing so they will improve the like-lihood of achieving a personal gain.
- *Public interest* – they believe that by doing so they will be able to improve the well-being of their communities.
- *Conformity* – they do it because they think it is the norm to do it.

Given the importance of consultation now as a tool in risk communication and risk management, many institutions are concerned to break down the barriers that prevent some groups of people from participating. This is particularly important when the hazard concerns health risks because the very people who need to be involved may find it most difficult to participate (e.g. groups disadvantaged by socio-economic status, family commitments, language difficulties, and so on). Various suggestions have been made to improve participation in such groups:

- Use 'phone ins' publicised through the TV.
- Access through the workplace is one option for some disadvantaged, or otherwise difficult to access, groups.
- Kathlene and Martin (1991) recommended the establishment of very long-term citizens' panels. These panels might last several years, meeting periodically, working closely with policy-makers. The object was to allow representative samples of the public to be fully briefed in the substantive issues about which decisions must be made, to insist that they take responsibility for the decisions that they proposed, and for them to disseminate information concerning the issues within their community. The approach is attractive: it may be capable of sustainability if the decisions proposed by the citizens' panel are acted upon. It has the advantage of allowing what might be called *cascading* of information down over a period of time as part of a two-step flow of information – from the experts and policy-makers to the panel members and from them to their community. It also has the possibility of what might be called *fountaining* of information up from the community mediated through the panel members over time. The proposal that there should be ongoing, long-term networks for consultation and systematic communication has received extensive support (Walker *et al.*, 1998; Wernstedt and Hersh, 1998).
- An alternative that targets disadvantaged groups specifically has been suggested by Breakwell and Petts (2000). This entails consultation through mediators. Mediated approaches entail the organisation that wishes to gain access doing so, either through or in collaboration with one or more other parties. Ever since the seminal work of Katz and Lazarsfeld (1955), it has been recognised that the public rarely gain information that then influences their behaviour direct from an official or public source. It is mediated through 'opinion leaders' (Brosius and Weimann, 1996; Weimann and Brosius, 1994; Weimann, 1991). This

is the so-called two-step flow of information where certain individuals, the opinion leaders, identify emerging issues in the mass media and elsewhere and then diffuse these to others via their personal networks. Nowadays, it is thought that opinion leaders operate to set the public agenda, to focus attention and legitimate concern (Burt, 1999; Shaw et al., 1999; Yin, 1999; Geller et al., 1996; Zhu et al., 1993). In order to access publics that are difficult to reach, it is valuable to use such opinion leaders: in local communities, in trade associations, in the media, and so on. The question is how to do this in a reliable and cost-effective way. There are two obvious ways to do this: using linked intermediaries and otherwise independent intermediaries.

Mediated approaches through independent intermediaries have been the generally preferred route for accessing disadvantaged or socially excluded groups. The typical mediator is some service provider or representative. So, for instance, the Scottish Poverty Information Unit (1999) showed how low-income families could be accessed through their primary health care team. Cowley and Billings (1999) proved that health visitors could be used. Imrie (1999) showed that disabled people could be accessed through pressure groups that had emerged to represent them. Humphrey (1998) argued that access could be achieved effectively by routing through sub-groups within large organisations, for instance through the 'self-organised groups' for women, black members, disabled members, and lesbian and gay members within the public sector unions NALGO and UNISON. Community groups, churches and voluntary associations can be used in similar ways. Women's groups, mother and toddler groups, etc. are frequently used when access specifically to women is required.

This approach essentially entails the 'cascading' of information. Cascading through mediators only works effectively if:

- they are willing to co-operate
- they pass on the message and return any response accurately.

There is evidence to suggest that these two conditions are met most readily when:

- the organisation trying to gain access has a good understanding of the cultural expectations of the mediator (Nevid and Maria, 1999)
- the organisation trying to gain access shows respect for the mediator organisation and its clientele (Crane and Carswell, 1992)
- the partnership between organisations is planned and is expected to be long-lived. Kitchin (2000), with reference to disabled people, suggests that the target group should be involved as consultants and partners in the development of the contact strategy. Rodgers (1999) suggested much the same with regard to people with learning difficulties.

This suggests that institutions should be examining how to establish networks that will cascade information and also collect feedback from them.

Risk communication that revolves around consultation and participation is now undoubtedly established as a preferred option. While it can be seen from the discussion here that it is not always easy to achieve, it has become something like a holy grail – to be pursued ardently.

Conclusion

Risk communication is a mammoth topic. This chapter is selective in its coverage, attempting to highlight key constructs and considerations in the literature. In moving from an examination of the classic literature on persuasion through to the discussion of consultative and participation methods, it echoes the journey made by risk communication philosophy over the last half-century. There has been a move from seeing the public as targets for influence to recognising them as partners in the process of risk management. Of course, not all institutions have made this move and not all risks are particularly amenable to it. Equally obviously, this partnership approach is still based upon enormous inequities between the parties in the power to control the hazards – to the extent that they are ever controlled.

The chapter also points to the significance of affect in the process of risk communication whether it is articulated in terms of fear, or feeling trust, or suffering stigma. Information-deficit models of risk communication are simply inadequate to deal with the accumulation of data that illustrates the significance of emotional state and affective imagery.

The complexity of the role and effects of the mass media at every point in risk communication is evident. It seems an inescapable conclusion that it is naive to think of the impact of the media as in any way linear. The impact is dynamic – an unceasing and ever-changing flow of output. The impact is interactive – across the media and between the media and its consumers. The impact is motivated – the media are seeking to deliver particular effects, even when they fail.

However, perhaps the most fascinating conclusion that emerges from this review is how little is understood about communicating uncertainty. Uncertainty and precaution are two faces of a problem that requires much more careful examination. Perhaps an analytic and explanatory approach that systematically explores the relationships between individual processes (whether cognitive, emotional or motivational) and social processes (including intergroup conflict, minority influences and the expression of socio-political and economic interests) will be capable of providing a different route to understanding the role of uncertainty and precaution.

7 Errors, accidents and emergencies

Chapter preview

This chapter examines how human errors can produce hazards. It summarises the variety of types of error that come into play. One typology of errors focuses upon their aetiology and this is considered. The more general factors that result in human error are also outlined. It is emphasised that individual error must be seen in the broader context – determined by organisational structures and intergroup relations. The Chernobyl nuclear reactor accident is used as an illustration of the many error factors that can be at work in producing a major accident. It points to the significance of violations rather than error in the genesis of accidents, and this is explored. The chapter goes on to explain how errors not only create hazards; they can also be the product of hazards. Examples of hazard perception, risk-taking and error incidence are provided from everyday activities, like driving an automobile. The theory of 'risk homeostasis' is outlined and it is suggested that there is little empirical support for it. Similarly, the notions of error proneness and motivated errors are discussed but their limitations as explanatory tools are highlighted. The significance of major accidents, like Chernobyl, for the subsequent perception of hazards and risk decisions is analysed. It is concluded that, while major accidents can have an impact on risk estimates and tolerance, their effect is time-limited. The definition of an emergency is examined. The possibility of emergency profiling, akin to hazard characterisation, is suggested. The significance of the anticipation of emergencies and planning for them in generating risk tolerance is considered. Some of the common psychological consequences of emergencies are enumerated and some of the factors that influence the efficacy of emergency warnings are presented.

1 Errors

1.1 Types of error

Some hazards are the product of human error. Several types of error create hazards:

- *failures in problem analysis* – e.g. missing the way peripheral elements in the problem can interact with each other to become major obstacles to its solution – for instance, in assessing the scale of the problem associated with evacuating refugees from a war zone failing to consider the role of the relationships between the health and the social services systems that will receive the émigré
- *failures in problem-solving* – e.g. believing that the solution is identified without adequately testing it – for instance, extrapolating from past experience that the reason the washing machine has stopped working is that the power supply has suffered some interruption, rather than examining the condition of the machine without preconception
- *failure in attention to information* – e.g. ignoring information that is available (or, sometimes, not recognising what information is not available) – for instance, when driving, not noticing the stop sign at an intersection
- *failure in interpretation of information* – e.g. misunderstanding the implications of the data that you have noted – for instance, noting that every time you eat onions you get stomach trouble, but not concluding the two events are causally linked
- *failure in the choice of action that a situation requires* – e.g. deciding that it is necessary to intervene when it is not – for instance, climbing a tree to rescue an apparently stranded cat that, later, you discover habitually sits there
- *failure in the appropriate execution of the chosen action* – either in when it is done or how it is done – for example, simply doing the thing inefficiently – for instance, in climbing the cat-ridden tree, finding your way on to the wrong branch and getting stuck yourself.

Each of these types of error may also cause accidents. In this context, the hazard is an accident waiting to happen.

There is a venerable history of psychological research on why errors occur. This work extends and refines the categorisation of error types (Reason, 1990). Reason proposes three basic error types:

- skill-based slips, lapses, trips and fumbles
- rule-based mistakes
- knowledge-based mistakes.

Error types are often said to be rooted in the cognitive stages involved in conceiving and then carrying out an action sequence: planning, storage and execution. The form the error takes is thought to be dependent upon what aspects of the universal processes of selection and retrieval of pre-packaged knowledge structures from long-term storage fail to function effectively.

Reason (2000b) suggests that errors occur often because a task is 'cognitively underspecified'. This seems to be a concise way of saying that people make errors in the execution of a task because they have failed to work through all the skills, knowledge and rule-adherence that it will require. Cognitive underspecification can come in a variety of forms – inattention, incomplete sense data or insufficient knowledge. Instead of dealing with the specifics of the task, the individual defaults to contextually appropriate, high-frequency patterns of behaviour.

Effectively, the existence of some locally appropriate response pattern that is strongly primed by its prior usage, recent activation or emotional charge, and by the immediate demands of the situation, cuts in to deliver the error. An error of this sort is sometimes called a product of being 'absent-minded'. This is a rather nice way of capturing the essence of this explanation – the action that is inappropriate, the error, occurs without necessary cognitive supervision. Such errors are a part of everyday life: we go to the fridge for water, but return from the kitchen with a cup of coffee and no water; we set off for work and take our habitual route, even though we know that the road is closed and we should have taken the diversion; and so on.

Takano and Reason (1997) analysed evidence of accidental events in US nuclear power plants and human errors in nuclear plant simulators in order to understand the types of error involved. They found that error production was associated with limitations in the situation assessment, weaknesses in response planning and inadequate knowledge bases. Those making the errors showed signs of the common heuristic biases in inference and judgement (described in Chapter 4) and were often characterised by inappropriately elevated arousal levels (the relevance of which is explained by the work on emotion in Chapter 5).

In a more general analysis, Williams (1988) mapped the factors that produce errors:

- high workload
- inadequate knowledge, ability or experience
- poor design of the technologies that have to be used
- inadequate supervision or training
- stressful environment
- mental state (i.e. fatigue, preoccupation, anxiety, distraction, etc.)
- change (i.e. departures from routine or changes in circumstances).

Cognitive models of the origins of error have been useful in predicting when errors are likely, the forms that they are likely to take and the remedial measures that they require. The tradition has given rise to some fascinating research. For instance, Hunton and Rose (2005) report the effects of using hands-free mobile telephones upon driving error rates.

They showed that conversations on the mobile phone result in more crash-related driver errors than either holding a similar conversation with a passenger or not being called upon to talk. They argue that mobile phone conversations consume more attention and interfere more with driving than passenger conversations, because they do not provide non-verbal cues and those taking part in them must expend greater cognitive resources on them in order to compensate. These researchers also showed that communications training may reduce the hazardous effects of mobile phone conversations on driving performance.

However, it should be noted that analysis at the level of the individual is probably inadequate when trying to understand many important hazard-inducing errors. Reason (1995) outlines a model of the aetiology of large-scale accidents in hazardous well-defended technologies. His model describes two interrelated causal sequences:

• an active failure pathway that originates in top-level decisions and proceeds by producing error-producing and violation-promoting conditions in the various workplaces, leading to unsafe acts committed by those at the immediate human–system interface
• a latent pathway that runs directly from organisational processes to deficiencies in the system's defences (i.e. in its design safeguards).

Reason's model is undoubtedly relevant to the work described in Chapter 8 on safety cultures in complex organisations. It also highlights the way the work environment and the task requirements embedded in it can work either to minimise error or not. Reason (1998) emphasised that errors are often associated with the omission of some step in a task. Reason (2000a) outlined how maintenance-related activities are the largest source of performance problems among the activities carried out by people in complex technologies. Within maintenance, calibration and testing, installation and reassembly are identified as the most likely tasks to be less than adequately performed. Within these tasks, the omission of necessary steps is shown to be the most likely error form. Reason found that organisational context could render certain steps in tasks more prone to be omitted. For example, organisational time constraints can result in short-cuts and the deliberate omission of steps in a task but, more importantly, in some organisations workforces come to believe that elements of the technology with which they deal are so safe, so stable and so secure that thorough maintenance may be formally required but is not in truth necessary, and then steps in the task are omitted, often not consciously, but through an form of oversight bred of confidence.

Reason used his model to interpret the Chernobyl nuclear power plant accident. See Box 7.1 for a summary of his commentary. One of the most interesting features of Reason's analysis is the distinction he introduces

Box 7.1 The Chernobyl errors

The worst accident in the history of commercial nuclear power generation occurred on 26 April 1986, when two explosions blew off the 1,000-tonne concrete cap sealing the Chernobyl-4 reactor, releasing molten core fragments into the immediate vicinity and fission products into the atmosphere. It cost innumerable lives, contaminated 400 square miles around the Ukrainian plant, and significantly increased the risk of cancer deaths over a wide area of Europe.

Reason (1987) published a thoughtful analysis of the Chernobyl disaster. He pointed out that the accident was totally the result of human error. How could this happen?

The technology: the reactor (the RBMK) was designed when computing facilities and automated safety devices were relatively primitive and, as a result, much of the emergency handling of the reactor fell upon the operators. One of the design features of the RBMK reactor is that it has the potential for instability at low power settings and consequently operation below 20 per cent maximum power was strictly forbidden.

The tests: at the time of the accident, the operators were running tests to establish whether a new device could be used to protect the reactor from core meltdown in the event of an off-site power failure. This entailed running the reactor at reduced power during the trials.

The time pressure: the tests had to be done within a very narrow window of opportunity, dictated by the routine demands for operation of the plant, or else they would have had to wait a further year. This window of opportunity was dramatically reduced unexpectedly and at the last minute, when the reactor was required to stay online producing power for longer than planned.

The errors:

- The operators allowed the power setting to dip to 1 per cent of maximum – having switched off the autopilot and assumed manual control.
- The operators managed to stabilise the reactor power at 7 per cent – still in the zone of the reactor's maximum instability – but chose to continue the tests.
- The operators exceeded regulation maxima in the number of water pumps in operation and the feedwater flow, and overrode the steam-drum automatic shutdown – these acts resulted in control rods being removed from the core in order to sustain even the low power level that was present, by this point a maximum of eight control rods remained and twelve was the lowest permitted number, yet the operators decided to continue with the tests. This was the

Box 7.1 (cont.)

fatal decision: the reactor thereafter was without a mechanism for safe shutdown.

- The operators closed steam line valves to one of the turbine generators, as a consequence disconnecting the automatic safety trips.
- The operators attempted to 'scram' the reactor by driving in emergency shut-off rods, but these jammed in the warped tubes and moments later two explosions occurred and blew off the reactor roof.

All of this happened in less than one hour. The graphite fire in the core of the reactor continued for several days.

The Russian inquiry after the disaster pointed up that the programme for the tests was poor and had not been approved by the Russian nuclear establishment. It appears that it had gone ahead with approval from only the Chernobyl senior management. Moreover, two groups were at work that night: the operators and the experimenters. The operators, probably all Ukrainians, were members of a high-prestige occupational group, had recently won an award for grid availability and, like other plant operators, ran their plant using 'process feel' rather than a knowledge of reactor physics. It is likely that they were motivated to get the tests finished quickly and expected to do it successfully. The Russian inquiry suggests that 'they had lost any feeling of the hazards involved'. The experimenters were electrical engineers from Moscow. Their task was to crack a stubborn technical problem, but they knew little about the actual operation of a nuclear power station. Each group may have assumed that the other knew more than it did about the reactor.

Reason proposes two discrete types of psychological explanation for the Chernobyl errors:

- The problems of coping with complexity – Dorner (1987) has mapped the types of error that people make when faced with complex problem-solving environments. He noted certain primary mistakes common to virtually all people: insufficient consideration of processes in time; difficulties in dealing with exponential developments; and thinking in causal series rather than in causal nets. Reason emphasises the significance of the last of these in Chernobyl. When dealing with complex systems, people most frequently resort to analysing them in linear sequences. They are aware of the main effects of their actions on their path to the proximate goal, but are unaware of the impact of the action on the rest of the system. According to Reason (1987:204), 'In a tightly coupled, complex system, the consequences of actions radiate

Box 7.1 (cont.)

outwards like ripples in a pool; but people can only "see" their current concern.' The Chernobyl operators lost track of the 'whole system' perspective.

- Elements of 'groupthink' – the operators may have been subject to some of the dynamics that Janis (1972) described in small, cohesive, elite groups. They may have inflated their sense of their own invulnerability and the correctness of their decisions, so possible adverse outcomes of their actions were therefore discounted. This type of social identity explanation may be useful, particularly in explaining why the operators were willing to violate well-established operating regulations. Such violations are less immediately explained by cognitive accounts that focus on limited problem-solving capacity. It seems unlikely that the violations occurred unintentionally, as a result of a slip or lapse; several entail active decisions to break the rule (e.g. switching off the steam-drum override).

Reason concludes that the Chernobyl accident was caused by a complex string of aberrant actions: mistakes on the part of the experimenters in their planning; a slip on the part of the operators in undershooting the required power level; and a series of safety code violations.

---

between errors (slips, lapses and mistakes) and violations. The accident is a product of the amalgamation of errors and violations over a short period of time. The violations may in formal terms constitute errors of judgement but they are substantively different from the other errors that occurred. They appear to be a product of social processes concerned with intra- and intergroup dynamics.

1.2   Violations

Violations can be seen as a form of risk-taking. One does something which one knows to be unacceptable. It is hazardous because typically breaking rules results in some form of punishment. Violations occur in many guises – some are deliberative (e.g. driving the wrong way up a one-way street because it is a useful short-cut); some are habitual (e.g. failing to indicate when overtaking another car); and some are situationally imposed or pragmatically unavoidable (e.g. veering down a one-way street in the wrong direction in order to avoid a serious traffic collision). Unavoidable violations are important because they may account for risk-taking that is associated with significant accidents. Organisations often place their employees in situations where they are expected to deliver results and where they are expected to comply with rules, and yet the only way that they can actually deliver is by breaking the rules. For instance, a driver may be required to deliver goods to a fixed number of venues, but the time it takes to do this exceeds the limits imposed by his company on the number of hours he can drive at a stretch. This is a recipe for unavoidable violations. One of the purposes of the work on safety culture in organisations is to curtail the demands for unavoidable violations (see Chapter 8).

The Zeebrugge disaster is a classic, high-profile case of an accident that resulted from 'unavoidable violations'. The *Herald of Free Enterprise* ferry sailed with both sets of bow doors open in violation of shipping regulations. The ferry capsized with great loss of life. The captain was not aware that the doors were open. He had no way of knowing, since the management had refused to install warning lights on the bridge to indicate the doors were open and there were no officers stationed at the doors to give the alert. The captain had to get the ferry under way but should not have done so with the bow doors open, yet he had no way of knowing whether they were or not – the violation was unavoidable unless the ferry stayed put.

Given the potential hazards associated with such violations, it is strange that they occur. One factor might be that the violation comes to be regarded as 'normative'. Once it is done the first time and nothing bad happens, it is easier to do subsequently.

Violations do not need to be unavoidable. They may be actively chosen. Such violations should not be assumed to be meant to cause harm. They are decisions not to abide by safe operating procedures. Reason et al. (1994) describe two forms of such violations – the routine and the optimising. The 'routine' are essentially the habitual violations mentioned earlier: taking the route of least resistance to the goal even though it entails breaking regulations. The 'optimising' violations are different in that they are done not to get the job done but to use the task as a means of achieving other goals. For instance, a driver might break the speed limit not because she needs to get to a destination in a hurry but because she gets a thrill from going fast or she enjoys exercising her driving skills.

Violations can be seen to be an appropriate response under certain circumstances; notably when the rules are poor (i.e. irrelevant to the circumstances or tending to increase the risk). Violations can also be seen to be justifiable under other circumstances, primarily where the benefit of rule-breaking substantially outweighs the possible cost. Many improvisations in emergency situations rely upon people taking the decision to ignore established rules in order to seek a solution to a problem.

The proclivity to violate safety rules must be of major significance in understanding the origin of hazards and accidents. However, the perception of risk is also clearly a major determiner of the willingness to commit violations in the first place.

1.3   Risk-related errors

So far the focus has been upon how errors may create hazards. Of course, the causation may be reversed. In a risky situation, people may make errors because the risk itself affects the way they perform. Error in risky situations has been examined. One way in which risk may engender error is through raising arousal levels (e.g. through inducing fear). For instance, research on errors in the use of medication in hospital – hardly surprisingly – suggests that such errors occur more frequently when staff are performing in high-stress and high-risk situations (e.g. Grasso *et al.*, 2005). Deitz and Thoms (1991) provide similar examples of risk-related stress as a cause of aeroplane mishaps and crashes.

Notably, the error generated by risk does not need to be directly related to the experience of the hazard itself. So, for instance, there is an infinite array of stories of emergency service personnel who, after successfully dealing with a major hazard, find themselves making 'stupid' errors in everyday tasks in the period immediately afterwards (e.g. failing to spot traffic signs, not remembering where they were meant to be going, being incapable of adding up a bill correctly, and so on). This sort of folklore evidence suggests that the experience of a hazard simply triggers a predictable negative emotional response and this disrupts skilled or attentive performance. This would mean that there is nothing special about risk – it is just acting like any other stimulant of emotional or cognitive disruption.

Yet the perception of the hazard does seem to make some difference to the error rate it might induce. There is the obvious assumption that the bigger the risk, the greater its potential for engendering error – both in anticipation of the hazardous event and after the event – though this does not seem to have been proven empirically. However, there is a more subtle effect of the way the risk is perceived. This centres around whether the risk is seen to be 'active' or 'passive'. For instance, Deery and Love (1996), in studying the reactions of young drivers to road hazards, found they made a distinction between active hazards (hazards arising from the driver's own actions) and passive hazards (hazards arising from the actions of other road users). Active hazards were perceived as less dangerous than passive hazards by all the drivers. Accidents were more likely to be perceived to be associated with passive hazards. Interestingly, drivers with a record of drink-driving rated both passive and active hazards as less dangerous than those who had no record of driving code violations. Others have found a link between perceived risk and driving accidents. For instance, one study found that drivers who thought they could drive safely after drinking were more likely to have an alcohol-related accident.

Underestimating the risk level seems to be associated with error and accident in these cases. Perhaps, this should not surprise us: if the risk of error is underestimated, the person is more likely to embark on the behaviour, and has more opportunities to make the error. Driver behaviour is a useful arena in which to plot the factors that affect risk-taking and the errors that follow risk decisions. Feeling in control induces greater willingness to take risks (e.g. Horswill and McKenna (1999b) found that if people were driving themselves they would go faster than if they were a passenger). Interference increases risk-taking in everyday dynamic judgements (for example, Horswill and McKenna (1999a) found that drivers who were distracted by having to do a second task while driving were more likely to take more risks during the drive – a finding akin to that relating to mobile phone use by Hunton and Rose (2005) described earlier).

Given the complex aetiology of errors, it is hardly surprising that the measures necessary to reduce them in any specific arena may need to be complex. Mok and Savage (2005) provide a nice example of how multi-faceted the approach may need to be. They looked at the number of collisions and fatalities at rail–highway intersections in the USA. These have declined significantly over the last thirty years, despite considerable increases in the volume of rail and road traffic. They were able to unpick the impact of the constituent causes for this improvement. Two-fifths of the decrease is due to reductions in drink-driving and improvements in the emergency medical response. The installation of gates or flashing lights accounts for one fifth of the reduction. The development of a national public education campaign on the safe use of intersections accounted for one seventh of the improvement and so did the introduction of additional lights on locomotives. One tenth of the reduction was due to crossing closures following line abandonments. This analysis illustrates the complex interaction of factors that can depress the occurrence of errors: the technological cues that improve hazard recognition; the generic changes in behaviour patterns (i.e. less driving when drunk); the specific education about the appropriate behaviour in this situation; and, of course, the removal of the hazardous situation. The Mok and Savage analysis is a good model for research that wishes to expose how errors can be reduced.

1.4   Risk homeostasis

The risk homeostasis theory suggests that people seek to maintain a certain level of risk in their activities. Thus, if changes occur that would reduce the risk associated with a behaviour, they will alter their behaviour to heighten the risk again. For example, if motor vehicle manufacturers improve their safety features such as to reduce the risks of driving (e.g. improving braking, visibility, stability, etc.), the driver will compensate by driving more dangerously (i.e. driving faster, braking later, etc.). The theory proposes that the level of risk people are willing to accept or seek is the prime determiner of accident involvement.

This theory has generated considerable debate and has been highly criticised. McKenna (1985) questions whether the assumptions on which the theory is built are actually sustainable. He points out that the theory must assume that people:

- have a simple representation of accident risk
- can detect all changes in this risk
- can compensate for changes in accident risk
- cannot be prevented from compensating for changes in accident risk.

These are difficult assumptions to sustain. As McKenna (1988) pointed out, people have difficulty processing data on low-probability events, such as accidents, and there is ample evidence that target level of risk does not seem to be the sole determiner of behaviour. Appetite for risk undoubtedly is a determiner of behaviour but it does seem far-fetched to base the prediction of accidents upon the proposition that individuals are engaged in calculating their current risk levels and adjusting their behaviour to achieve a steady state in risk.

1.5   Error proneness and motivated error

Popular culture has traditionally included the error-prone character – someone who is always making mistakes. Empirical studies have found such characters illusive. There is no body of evidence that proves the existence of an 'error-prone personality' or behavioural profile. There are, of course, lifestyles that are to a greater extent associated with error. For instance, alcohol and drug dependency is associated with higher and habitual error levels on both motor and cognitive tasks. Intellectual ability is also related to performance, but such deficits can be argued to be less to do with error and more to do with incapacity. The original idea that a person might be error-prone, across situations and over time, has failed to be substantiated.

The other popular assumption is that errors sometimes occur because they have a function in their own right and people at some unconscious level wish them to happen (i.e. they are motivated). Stein (1988) makes a good case for motivated errors in the political domain. She describes how threats in international relations can be erroneously interpreted and how these misperceptions can justify the course of action that the nation making the error wished to pursue anyway.

Motivated errors must be an interesting category when considering the role of error in hazard generation and interpretation. It is possible to imagine any number of scenarios where a hazard might motivate error. For instance, an operator who perceives a hazardous situation and wishes to be moved away from it might be subconsciously motivated to make errors that would result in his superiors removing him from that situation. Equally, there might be a case where an individual protesting the existence of a hazard would find herself involved in making errors, or being involved in accidents, that proved the dangerousness of the hazard. However, there is no consolidated body of evidence that allows any serious estimate of the incidence of motivated errors. In fact, it could be argued that this is inevitable, because it is very difficult to determine whether or not an error has been motivated. The attribution of motivation largely has to be post hoc. It could be envisaged that experimental studies could be conducted that set up the conditions that should induce motivated error and then would allow the observation of incidence. Yet this would be open to the criticism that no error was involved, but rather deliberate poor performance. For an error to be motivated, it needs both not to be deliberate and to deliver a result which the individual does not consciously realise is desirable. Achieving this in an experimental manipulation may be a bridge too far.

2   The significance of major accidents

Major accidents, like Chernobyl, have widespread effects that may subsequently alter the way a hazard is perceived and whether a risk is tolerated. This might be expected on the basis of the likely impact of the event upon the availability heuristic alone, but there are many other routes through which an accident changes risk estimates. Chapter 8 looks at some of the organisational practices and regulatory changes that have been motivated by significant accidents. The discussion here focuses more upon the way an accident changes the way a hazard class is perceived. We will use Chernobyl as the example because the nature of the accident itself was outlined above and because so much has been written about it.

2.1   Local effects

Lee (1995c) reviewed the consequences of Chernobyl. These were evident at a number of levels. In those people living in the immediate vicinity of the plant:

- There were psychiatric disorders – akin to post-traumatic stress disorder symptoms – i.e. 're-experiencing symptoms' (for example, through intrusive recollections or dreams), 'avoidant symptoms' (for example, being unable to recall important elements of the event or feelings of detachment or estrangement from others) or 'arousal symptoms' (for example, difficulty sleeping or angry outbursts).
- Apart from the acute and chronic radiation sickness, there was evidence of the effects of chronic, low level radiation in the majority, though these tended to be attributed to the effects of stress (e.g. high levels of fatigue, stomach upsets, loss of appetite, chest pains).
- Stress symptoms were widespread, exacerbated by the failure of authorities to provide early and effective advice on preventive measures – people felt that they discovered the truth too late, resentment compounded fear and mistrust was rife.
- A vast majority wished to be relocated away from the area – it is important to remember that the vast majority were rural communities dependent upon agriculture and they perceived their land to be poisoned.
- There was a dominant belief that they were suffering from conditions caused by radiation exposure.

In those people living in Kiev, 90 kilometres south of the site, which avoided any significant contamination due to the direction of the prevailing wind, who were studied six years after the event:

- Public concern remained high, not mitigated by the fact that the city was used to host large numbers of evacuees.
- The authorities were seen as covering up the facts of the accident.
- Half believed themselves to be suffering ill health as a consequence of the accident.
- Half believed that the risk from the accident would never disappear.
- The vast majority are characterised by a deep sense of uncertainty and unease – they feel the scale of the accident is unknown and believe that a similar accident could happen in the future.
- Almost all were dissatisfied with the way the disaster was managed – with the rescue work, with the advice, information and warnings issued, and with reconstruction.

People living in Novozybkov were also interviewed six years later. The town is 160 kilometres away from Chernobyl but did experience contamination. Its residents did not hear of the accident until several days after the event:

- Lack of realisation of the severity of the situation until many months later, when the protection measures then urged upon them must have seemed outrageously belated.
- Some had relocated voluntarily after the accident, but many returned – disillusioned with their experiences elsewhere, often having received hostility where they went because victims were seen as potentially contagious.
- The majority reported feeling uncertain and hopeless, resigned to having to eat local produce that was probably contaminated.
- Reported stress levels increased post-accident and one in eight claimed to have received a dangerous dose of radiation.

The Chernobyl accident emphasised that disaster planning for an event of this scale at the time was primitive. A particular weakness was the provision of information: official sources following the accident said little about sheltering, relocation, food control, the use of iodine tablets, or other countermeasures. It is notable that later government and local information sources were highly distrusted. Foreign sources were significantly more trusted by the communities affected. The absence of reliable information led in some cases to the symptoms of stress being misinterpreted as the symptoms of radiation exposure. This, in turn, has led to an abiding belief that symptoms are untreatable. It is important to remember in this regard that stress is itself not just manifest in psychological changes and interpretations of the physical state but is also manifest in significant, sometimes chronic, changes in physiological functioning (for example, cardiovascular, neural and biochemical activity levels) implicated in modification of the functioning of the immune system.

Chernobyl also emphasised the peculiarities of a radiation accident: the consequences extend over a lifetime and may even affect later generations; the need for legislation that defines victim status over many years; and the role of lack of trustworthiness of information in fuelling social disintegration. This type of accident in one sense has no end-point.

Relocation of evacuees proved problematic. Not only did the receiving communities find the absorption a problem; the evacuees themselves found the upheaval traumatic. Relocation did not in fact appear to reduce stress levels as compared with those who stayed in contaminated areas. From both sides, this led to the conclusion that the relocation had been very badly handled. The problems of relocation may be a manifestation of well-established social psychological processes. The refugees represented a stigmatised minority (e.g. labelled 'glow worms' by host communities). They were not relocated en bloc and so scattered families had to face the task of integrating into new communities without adequate support.

From a social psychological analysis, Lee (1995c) concludes that the deep sense of being without personal control and absence of personal efficacy that victims felt meant that they did not benefit as much as they might have done from the countermeasures that were instituted after the accident. Many did not act effectively to help themselves (e.g. following advice on the consumption of certain food) because they did not believe that they could do anything that would work. Interestingly, it was found that fatalism, measured through a set of questions in a survey, was predictive of the level of radiation absorbed. Lee is possibly implying that there should be greater attention paid to the psychological, especially the social psychological, factors that will mediate the impact of practical measures. Over the intervening decade between Lee's analysis and the writing of this book, the validity of his point has been accepted. Most disaster planning or business continuity management has an analysis of the social psychological factors built in as an integral part.

2.2   Global effects

Lee's analysis of the psychological consequences of the accident for those in the Ukraine and Russia is fascinating. However, the significance of Chernobyl was much wider. Of course, the contamination was itself much wider, affecting many different communities, including those in the USA, Lapland and in Wales. But the really important repercussions were those that it had upon the overall perception of nuclear power generation.

People who know next to nothing about nuclear power know the name of Chernobyl and recognise it as the icon for nuclear disaster. The objective estimates of the risks it entailed are not the important determiners of the role it has in the perception of nuclear power hazards. Wilson et al. (1987) estimated the risk for each of the two million people living downwind of the reactor as an increased lifetime dose of .7 röntgoen equivalent man (rem). He put this into perspective by explaining that this is considerably less than the difference in the lifetime external dose a person would receive if they moved from New York to live in Denver because of the difference in natural radiation levels present in the two cities. Slovic (1996) states that it was also less than the difference in dose a person receives from inhaled radon if he or she moves from an average New England house to an average Pennsylvania house.

These sorts of attempts to create a proportionate image of the severity of the accident may have been effective in the USA (Lindell and Perry,

1990), where minuscule amounts of radiation from Chernobyl arrived, but not in Europe, where there were higher levels and 'hot spots'. Across Europe, the information provided to the public is regarded to have been extremely poor (Drottz-Sjöberg and Sjöberg, 1990; Drottz-Sjöberg, 1990; Gadomska, 1994; Hohenemser and Renn, 1988; Otway et al., 1988; Wynne, 1989). The technical language explaining exposure levels was not used consistently and not explained effectively in lay terms. The timing of the release of information was inappropriate – long silences were followed by partial information that was perceived as censored. The spokespeople used to provide information were not familiar and had no accumulation of trust associated with them. Advice was inconsistent over time (for example, recommendations on the food that it was safe to consume changed in unpredictable ways).

Van der Pligt (1992) provides a good summary of the limitations of the risk communication after Chernobyl. That it was poor is unquestionable. Consequently, levels of anxiety, anger and fear rose over the weeks following the incident. Some groups – for example, sheep farmers in Cumbria, as reports of contamination of the grazing hills started to trickle in – anticipated their livelihoods being wiped out. To speak of outrage being engendered, except in a few groups like the sheep farmers whose economic interests were put at risk, would be inappropriate.

Interestingly, the process of blaming and its concomitant outrage did not operate in response to this accident – at least, not in communities outside of the Ukraine and Russia. While there was little outrage, there was the rather more insidious erosion of trust in governments to protect the public from radiation and, by extrapolation, from other hazards.

Anxiety and fear about nuclear power did increase. Interestingly, Slovic et al. (1979) had illustrated that nuclear power was perceived as a catastrophic technology and, following the Three Mile Island accident, despite the fact that it did not lead to a disaster of immense proportions, it was found that nuclear power was associated with even more extreme images of disaster. Similarly, after Chernobyl, the level of dread and the perceived likelihood of a nuclear power plant accident did increase. Surveys using the psychometric method for assessing the characteristics of hazards illustrated that the position of nuclear power plants shifted along the two prime dimensions towards being less controllable and more catastrophic. Of course, comparisons across surveys over time using such methods are somewhat problematic – samples differ in structure and the position of any one item in the factor space is a function of all of the positions of other items. Nevertheless, the existence of these data is suggestive of a genuine shift in hazard perception.

Perhaps more persuasive at a visceral level is the way the image and name of Chernobyl began to pervade popular cultural representations of nuclear issues. The penetration of this change was also extensive. It was not always predictable. Post-Chernobyl, a study (Brown *et al.*, 1987) that asked UK schoolchildren (11–15 years old) to draw a nuclear power station revealed images that were different from those collected one year before: the 1986 post-Chernobyl drawings were more likely to contain chimneys, smoke, pipes and cooling towers. They were less likely to show bombs or rockets, features of earlier drawings. This might be thought a reversal of what should be expected. However, it fits the idea that the children were made aware of the real structure of power stations from the images that pervaded the press and TV at the time. They were no longer confusing nuclear power with nuclear weapons. Of course, the images themselves would not reveal whether the children found the power stations more or less threatening now they knew better what they looked like.

Adult opposition to nuclear power was strengthened across Europe and the USA. Renn (1990) reports attitudes survey results from pre-Chernobyl, immediately post-Chernobyl and one year after Chernobyl. He showed that support for nuclear energy declined immediately in all of the countries sampled (Austria, Finland, France, Greece, Italy, the Netherlands, Sweden, the UK, the USA, West Germany and Yugoslavia). However, a year later there was some recovery in support but in no case did it reach the pre-Chernobyl level. The incomplete bounce-back seems characteristic of reassessment of a hazard following a major accident.

Verplanken (1989) showed further that in the Netherlands citizens were not only more anti-nuclear after Chernobyl; they also believed that the probability of catastrophic accidents in Dutch nuclear power plants was greater. The perceived benefits of nuclear power did not change immediately after the accident, but were perceived to decline at nineteen months after it. This possibly coincided with the growing lobby that claimed that other energy sources could replace nuclear.

In the longer term, it has been evident that the subjective and political significance of the accident has been eroded. The arguments that energy needs cannot be met from renewable sources and that carbon emissions from other more traditional sources are unacceptable have been growing in significance in the UK and elsewhere in Europe (e.g. Broers, 2005). The implications of political changes in the Middle East and in Russia for the security of oil supplies have possibly re-emphasised the need for re-examining nuclear power sources.

The inevitable process of re-contextualising and reinterpreting past events will mean that any accident – no matter how appalling in its immediate aftermath – will lose its capacity to drive risk perceptions and decisions eventually. There may be some residual effect of its occurrence, especially if it completely shifted the baseline of the debate about a hazard. For instance, Chernobyl shifted the nuclear industry assumptions about the operating safety precautions that were acceptable on an international scale, so all subsequent debate about the industry has had to encompass the implications of those changes. Nevertheless, the direct significance of an accident to risk perceptions and management will have a limited shelf-life.

3   Emergencies

An emergency is defined as 'a sudden state of danger' or, alternatively, 'as a condition needing immediate treatment' (*Oxford English Dictionary*). Both forms of the definition focus upon speed and threat. An emergency is a product of a risk that becomes a reality. There might also be questions about whether an emergency is always short-lived – if handled appropriately, it subsides; if not handled appropriately, it becomes something else (such as a disaster or a war).

Accidents, of course, can precipitate emergencies. It is notable that accidents like Chernobyl create a sudden state of danger and a condition needing immediate treatment. However, some accidents do not. For instance, a car accident on a road unused by other motorists that causes immediate fatalities may not create a state of danger or the requirement for immediate treatment (after all, the victims are dead). Clearly, emergencies do not always have their origins in accidents. Often they can be the product of natural forces (e.g. floods or earthquakes). Sometimes, they can be the product of intentional acts (e.g. terrorism).

At one level, whether an emergency exists or not is also a subjective matter. One man's emergency is another's false alarm and still another's normal operating circumstances. It all depends on whether danger is perceived and/or upon whether remedial action is deemed urgent. While for some sets of circumstances there would be great consensus about the existence of an emergency, for others there would be little agreement. The extent to which an emergency can be in the eye of the beholder is perhaps best exemplified in cases where lay and expert assessments of a set of facts differ. An interesting example comes from the medical domain. During the last ten years in the UK there has been a debate about the safety of the MMR (mumps, measles and rubella) vaccination that has been given to infants. A significant proportion of the lay public have come to believe that the MMR is dangerous for infants – putting them at risk of becoming autistic. While a minority of scientific and medical sources initially made this suggestion, the vast majority of the medical and scientific establishment dismissed the claim. Over the years much research evidence has been accumulated to prove that the MMR cannot be implicated in the aetiology of autism and these findings have been massively publicised. However, a large percentage of parents have refused to have their babies vaccinated. The medical advice is clear: the baby should be vaccinated because otherwise it will be at risk of mumps, measles and/or rubella; and, importantly, if a large proportion of babies are not vaccinated, nationally there would be the risk of an epidemic of these diseases that would affect not just the young but the elderly, pregnant women, and so on. It is ironic that both 'sides' in this debate believe there is a serious hazard, but the hazard they perceive is different. The parents see the hazard to their child. The medical specialists see the hazard to the nation. As the numbers receiving vaccination have declined, doctors have begun to talk of a medical emergency (if not full formed, then brewing). Parents, who resist the vaccination and have been rejecting the extensive health information campaigns that have been designed to get them to agree to vaccinate their child, do not see the possibility of the epidemic as an emergency. They do see the possibility of any damage to their own child, brought about by their own decision, as the real emergency. Their child is placed in a sudden state of danger when the prospect of vaccination is raised.

MMR vaccination is only one example of the very important differences between lay and expert mental models of emergencies. There are many others. At a more local level, there might be the case of the mobile-home site, located on a flood-plain, whose occupants find one morning that they are being instructed to evacuate by the emergency services because heavy rain is forecast and their homes are at risk of serious flood damage. It is not uncommon in such circumstances to find that residents refuse to move out. The professionals regard the situation to be an emergency. The residents do not. The mismatch in emergency identification is not always between experts and others. Himiob-de-Marcano (2000) described how the floods that swept through Venezuela in 1999, taking tens of thousands of lives and destroying hundreds of thousands of homes in their path, were treated by some in the country as 'just bad weather'.

In some ways, emergencies are like hazards themselves: they are open to subjective characterisations. It is possible to imagine that the psychometric paradigm could be used to assess the dimensions on which a variety of emergencies could be mapped. One could even speculate upon the relevant parameters. They might include: solvable, containable, predictable, large-scale, etc.

The perception of the emergency may be affected by the extent to which it is anticipated. In Chapter 8, the process of business continuity planning is described. This is a reaction to the need to deal with the possibility of emergencies. It is an anticipatory framework. The organisation makes assumptions about the likely nature of an emergency and plans for how it will deal with those circumstances. It may test its effectiveness in emergencies through exercises, and some of these exercises are very elaborate and thorough. Notably, the emergency exercises that the nuclear power industry runs with the support of other agencies, and the input of the industry regulator, are designed to stretch the nuclear operators to the limit.

There is, however, an important implication of emergency planning that is sometimes ignored. Of course, it hopefully has the effect of making those who must react to an emergency think through what they have to do and to eliminate weaknesses in their systems before they have to face the real thing. But additionally, and perhaps as a corollary, it has the effect of 'normalising' the emergency. Emergencies that are planned for are perceived as more controllable and thus less dangerous, more within the normal bounds. There is repeated evidence that emergency services that have planned for a threat, that have exercised their response, do not appreciate the full magnitude or demands of the emergency when it arises (e.g. the flooding in New Orleans following Hurricane Katrin, in August 2005, which caused devastation along much of the North Central Gulf Coast of the USA, with the most severe loss of life and property occuring in New Orleans). While there is no question that emergency planning is of vital importance, there is the question of how far the very act of planning can become a suppressant of fear and estimates of risk. This is compounded, inevitably, when the plans are partial or based upon assumptions that turn out to be too optimistic.

While some emergencies are momentous (like Chernobyl), many are not of this sort. Emergencies can be the product of seemingly more mundane occurrences (e.g. the failure of a home computer system). Emergencies are actually omnipresent, but their scale varies, and this makes generalisations about the impact they have upon risk estimates and risk-taking rather difficult to sustain. Some consequences of larger-scale emergencies are evident:

• The Chernobyl accident analysis described in detail above showed the longer-term psychological effects of a major disaster. Post-traumatic stress disorder (PTSD) and depression were evident in victims. There is a wealth of data after other emergencies that proves Chernobyl was no exception. For instance, Boscarino et al. (2004) examined the evidence of mental health effects of the attack on 11 September 2001 and concluded that exposure was related to post-disaster PTSD and depression. Interestingly, Pulcino *et al.* (2003) showed that women were more likely than men to suffer PTSD after the attacks. Similarly, in the aftermath of the tsunami disaster that struck South Asia in December 2005, killing more than 300,000 people, reports of PTSD were rampant. Gorman (2005) claims that 33 per cent of people surviving a life-threatening traumatic event will develop PTSD within one month of the incident.

- Media portrayal of the emergency may mean that exposure to it extends considerably beyond those who are immediately involved in it. Some of the implications of this are further explored in Chapter 9. Here, however, it is worth saying that there is some evidence that if the event is big enough, even media exposure to it may be enough to precipitate PTSD. Ahern *et al.* (2004) showed in US citizens a link between the amount of TV viewing in the seven days after 11 September 2001 and the symptoms of PTSD.

- In Chapter 5, we showed that panic in situ is a rare response to emergencies or disasters (though more often found in fires, e.g. 't Hart and Pijnenburg, 1989). It is worth re-emphasising this here. Helsloot and Ruitenberg (2004), using an historical analysis, showed that most citizens act in a 'rather rational' way. This has led some to argue that emergency recovery plans should incorporate a role for the public (Durodie and Wessely, 2002). Despite the evidence that mass panic does not usually occur in emergencies, there is a persistent warning in the literature that it might. Pastel (2001) suggested that in a real or supposed attack from weapons of mass destruction, outbreaks of multiple unexplained symptoms (i.e. mass psychogenic illness, mass sociogenic illness, mass hysteria or epidemic hysteria) might be prevalent.

- While panic may be anticipated and yet rare, forms of antisocial behaviour may be unexpected but rather more frequent. There are repeated reports of individuals and groups taking advantage of emergency situations to loot and to harm others (e.g. Bernstein, 1990).

- People wish to establish reasons for the emergency after the event and they are quick to seek to attribute blame for failures either in anticipatory warnings or in remedial action. We will come back to this process in Chapter 9.

It should be added that reactions to warnings of an emergency have been studied. Silver and Braun (1999) showed that a range of personal factors influence response to warnings:

- familiarity with the hazard reduces responsiveness
- the lower the perceived risk, the less the response

- men respond less
- an internal locus of control is associated with responsiveness.

Three situational variables also have an impact on response:

- time pressure – if the warning requires immediate action, it is more likely to be effective
- cost of compliance – if responding has low cost, it is more likely
- modelling – if others are seen to respond, then the individual responds.

It is not enough to warning people that an emergency is imminent; they have to be warned in the right way if it is to have the desired effect.

Conclusions

A number of findings from the review offered in this chapter and their implications need highlighting:

- The importance of violations, rather than just errors, in bringing significant hazards into being is clear. However, the way risk perception and risk-taking relate to willingness to violate rules is still under-researched and requires further exploration. Doubtless, the nature of the relationship will depend upon a variety of personal and situational factors, but the significance of processes of violation would justify the effort. There does not seem to be a very commonsense assumption that can be made about the relationship of risk and violation. Low risk could motivate violation, but so could high risk; moderate risk could also encourage violation. It is interesting to speculate on what the model that specified this relationship between rule violation and risk-taking/perception would have to include. The capacity of the individual or group to break the rule (e.g. skill, power, intelligence, etc.), the likely costs of breaking the rule and being discovered, the likely rewards for violations, the regularity of past breaches, the presence of social conformity pressures for violation, the availability of risk information, the presence/effectiveness of hazard warnings – all may be intuitively obvious facets of any such model. Such a model would be an invaluable tool in complex organisations that were attempting to improve their safety culture (see Chapter 8).
- Errors not only produce risks; they can be the product of risks – the relationship of error rate and intensity of perceived risk is, however, not specified in the literature. One might envisage a curvilinear relationship: low and high risk being associated with more error, and mild risk with less error. Yet many factors would come into play to moderate this very simple prediction (for example, skill levels, reward levels or costs, difficulty of the task, etc.). Even a moment's consideration reveals that this could be a major research programme in itself.

- Major accidents affect the social representation of a hazard type – for an indeterminate period, but not for ever. There is a growing body of evidence from longitudinal studies of risk perception after disasters for this generalisation.
- Risk homeostasis, motivated error and error proneness are all concepts that have limited empirical support. Nevertheless, such ideas recur and are woven into explanations for accidents and emergencies. When they are used, it is useful to establish what evidence is offered from them.
- Emergencies are open to the same sort of 'characterisation' that has been done for hazards. It may be that the same two-factor model would emerge, but this is currently an open question. The effort to characterise emergencies might have considerable practical relevance. The approach could be used to identify conflicts between groups in the way emergencies are conceived, and consequently in the response they elicit. This could be used as the basis for developing emergency warning systems and emergency response plans.
- PTSD and depression are common psychological consequences of major accidents and emergencies. They are also associated with cognitive biases and emotional states that will tend to heighten perceived risk (see Chapter 5).

The analysis of errors, accidents and emergencies is no simple task. The work on the origins and nature of errors is very sophisticated and has resulted in some strong predictive models. The work on accidents has led to less theory and more detailed descriptions of the circumstances surrounding specific events. There is less work on emergencies and this is also often atheoretical. There is a real challenge here for psychologists to provide useful, valid models. The studies of the psychological consequences of accidents and emergencies are a good start. A comprehensive model that maps the relationships between, on the one side, risk perception and risk-taking and, on the other, error, accidents and emergencies, is long overdue.

8 Risk and complex organisations

Chapter preview

Chapter 8 analyses how risk is typically managed by complex organisations. The use of risk mapping and risk registers is explained and the limitations of both methods are examined. Business continuity management processes are described. The concept of safety culture is defined and the methods used to measure it are presented. The way safety culture relates to the occurrence of accidents is summarised and the ways safety culture may be improved are introduced. Aspects of the role of regulatory agencies in the process of risk management are considered. Organisational factors that inhibit effective risk management are considered. The significance of an organisation's 'risk reputation' is discussed.

1   Risk management

1.1   The framework for risk management

Risk management is now a major preoccupation of most large or complex organisations. This does not solely refer to the management of hazards that the organisation might create (for example, in the case of a chemical company, the possibility of toxic waste from an incinerator or, for a nuclear power generator, the potential of an off-site release of radiation). It refers also to the management of risks that might damage the organisation itself. These types of risk are diverse. For instance, they might be commercial or market-based, they might be structural and deal with human resources, or they might be financial or technological. It is worth briefly exploring this focus upon risk management in this broader sense.

The framework for risk management proposed in 1997 by the US Presidential/Congressional Commission on Risk Assessment and Risk Management is characteristic of the more traditional approach. It sees risk management as 'the process of identifying, evaluating, selecting and implementing actions to reduce risk to human health and ecosystems.

The goal of risk management is scientifically sound, cost-effective, integrated actions that reduce or prevent risks while taking into account social, cultural, ethical, political, and legal considerations.' This means that within this framework there are six stages: define the problem and put it into context; analyse the risks associated with the problem in context; examine the options for addressing the risks; make decisions about which options to implement; take actions to implement the decisions; and conduct an evaluation of the action's results. The framework is used in collaboration with stakeholders and is iterative if new information emerges that changes the need for, or nature of, risk management.

1.2   Risk management as quality management

This traditional approach sees risk management as *an* area of activity for managers. There has been an evolution of this approach and now the vogue in corporate circles is to see risk management as an approach to managing the whole organisation. The organisation is managed in terms of identifying and assessing the main risks that present opportunities or threats to meeting objectives, agreeing which are of highest priority and focusing continuing management attention on those priorities. This could be said to have been what good managers have always done. However, now there is a clear language for describing it. There is also a plethora of methods available for supporting the manager engaged in risk management.

The cornerstone of this approach is agreeing the key risks and this is predicated upon identifying priorities among objectives. Having to do this self-consciously can be revealing for some organisations and refocus the attention of managers and refine resource allocation. Numerous sectors of the economy have been moving to this approach, usually sparked by guidance from a central body or regulator. FTSE 100 companies have done so following Stock Exchange Turnbull Guidelines, so has central government in the UK with Treasury and National Audit Office support, and, prompted by the Higher Education Funding Councils, universities have followed suit.

1.3   Risk mapping

A common aid in the process of risk management of this type is the 'risk map' (see Figure 8.1).

A risk map is constructed by management, usually as a group exercise, supported sometimes by external facilitation. There are now several checklists of risks – often produced by accountancy or management consultancy firms – which organisations can use in order to ensure that

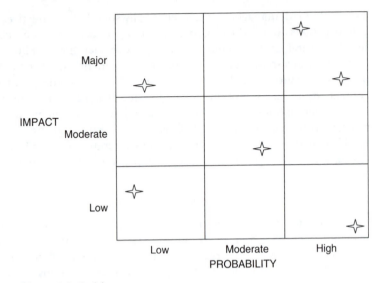

Figure 8.1 A risk map

they review all of the possible risks that might impinge on their success. The checklist will usually cover three broad categories of risk arising from:

- *External conditions* – including:
  - the nature of the competition
  - the requirements of customers
  - the political context
  - the legal or regulatory context
  - the technological context
  - relations with stakeholders
  - availability of capital
  - state of the sector or industry as a whole
  - the possibility of major physical disaster
  - financial market stability . . .
- *Internal conditions* – including:
  - characteristics of the operations of the organisation (such as capacity to attend to customer need, knowledge of staff, capacity to innovate, efficiency, capacity to grow, quality of performance, adequacy of availability of source materials, etc.)
  - capacity to manage cash (e.g. optimisation of cashflow, pricing policy, controlling credit)
  - leadership
  - quality (reliability and integrity) of IT systems used
  - the possibility of fraud or illegality.

- *Interactions of the internal and external conditions* – including:
  - ○ the adequacy of use of information about external conditions in the context of information about internal conditions (for instance, using information about customer need to determine price in the light of data about production efficiency)
  - ○ the adequacy of reports of business activity (for example, using inappropriate recording systems that fail to satisfy tax regulations or fail to take advantage of tax breaks)
  - ○ and the adequacy of strategic approach (for example, failure to adopt a suitable timescale for the analysis of budgetary impact given market conditions).

The examples are not meant to be exhaustive and the specific risks that need to be considered will depend upon the size and business of the organisation. However, the checklist needs to be reasonably comprehensive for the risk-mapping exercise to be valuable.

Having got the list together, management is generally asked to rate each of the risks on two dimensions: impact and probability. The rating is usually qualitative, with around three categories used. Impact can be low, moderate or major. Probability can be low, moderate or high. Sometimes more differentiated scales are employed. For the purposes of illustration in Figure 8.1, the three categories have been subdivided to create a nine-point scale. The risks, once rated, can then be located on a two-dimensional plot that becomes the risk map. The 'stars' in the grid in Figure 8.1 each represent the rated position of a different risk. It is evident that this approach to representing risks has been much influenced by the psychometric paradigm. Risks that are both high in likelihood and major in impact are obviously meant to be a focus of attention for management activity.

Impact is a difficult dimension to rate. For many risks, impact will actually be functionally dependent upon whether management takes appropriate action quickly. In coming to decisions about rating impact for any risk, it is necessary to acknowledge what is being assumed implicitly about management capacity to respond if the risk materialises. In many organisations the risk map is updated regularly throughout the year to allow progress to be plotted, with the most senior manager responsible for ensuring that risk mitigation is an omnipresent concern in decision-making.

1.4   The risk register

Some organisations use what is called a 'risk register' to record their risk estimates. Figure 8.2 gives an illustration of a risk register. Risks associated with each of the organisation's main objectives are indicated. It is notable that not only is each risk rated for impact and likelihood, but also the

Objective	Description of risk (2 to 4 aspects of the risk for each objective)	Impact (1–9)	Key controls or processes in place to mitigate risk	Likelihood	Net risk	Improvement actions	Timescale for improvement	Responsibility for improvement
High Reputation	Failure to manage the company's national and international profile: • Failure to actively manage positive and negative publicity • Failure to communicate distinct market niche, capitalise on unique selling points and publicise successes	9	• Regular monitoring of key performance indicators (e.g. quality of staff recruitment) • Improve approval procedures for all key promotional materials (e.g. advertisements) • Increased PR activity and proactive engagement with media	3	27	• Change institutional marketing strategy and action plan • Increase and co-ordinate marketing effort	Immediate	Director of Marketing and Communications Executive Team
High Reputation	Failure to manage health and safety: • Lack of investment • Risks to staff, students and visitors to campus • Litigation and negative publicity	9	• Departmental H and S audits • Standing item for Board	4	36	• Roll out H and S departmental audits to smaller support departments, as appropriate • Ensure closer liaison between Estates and Health and Safety	3 months	Safety Officer and Director of Estates

Objective	Risk		Controls		Actions		Timeframe	Responsibility
Strong Research and Development Arm	Failure of Research Strategy to focus activity • Failure to invest selectively • Insufficient critical mass of research groups • Poor satisfaction levels amongst research staff	8	• Greater central co-ordination of research investment • Increased use of competitor analysis and performance indicators	6	• New Procedures for pricing research • Acquisition of competitor research teams	48	12 months	Chief Operations Officer and Finance Director
Optimise Human Resources	Failure to deal effectively with poor performance • Reduced business efficiency • Poor staff morale • Wasted resources • Negative publicity	6	• Staff appraisals • Salary incentives	5	• Develop company strategy for handling poor performance • Provide training/development for line managers	30	Immediate	HR Department
Infrastructure Integrity	Disaster resulting in loss of business capacity: • Damage/loss of buildings through fire, flood etc. • Damage/loss of IT infrastructure	8	• Alarm and security systems • Insurance • Health and safety management • Disaster recovery plans	3	• Review span and viability of existing disaster recovery plans	24	2 months	CEO, Head of Security, Director of Finance
Financial Robustness	Capital project overspends: • Financial burden of arbitration/settlement • Reduction in quality if specification re-visited	7	• Regular reports to Board • Increased resilience of expenditure approvals • Appointment of Head of Capital Projects	4	• Seek means to improve the quality of initial estimates • Make greater contingency provision	28	Immediate	Director of Finance Director of Estates

Figure 8.2 Risk register

product of these two ratings is used to generate a 'net risk' figure. Improvement actions required are identified and deadlines for them specified. The individual or unit responsible for delivering the action is also identified. When the risk register is reviewed at regular intervals, changes in net risk can be monitored and the timeliness of action taken can be examined. Where responsibility for failure lies is also clearly visible.

The net risk measure is obviously statistically pretty meaningless. The two dimensions on which the risk (i.e. the hazard) is evaluated should be kept separate. Multiplying ratings on the two only produces figures that cannot be interpreted or compared with each other, since the same net risk score can be produced by a variety of combinations of figures on the two scales. This problem is compounded when it is recognised that the initial scales are merely categorical rather than interval or ratio measures. The message here to managers must be to keep the treatment of these ratings simple. They are not engaged in a statistical exercise. Risk mapping should be used as a tool for raising awareness and improving foresight.

1.5   Risk management and risk choices

The possibility that this approach makes managers risk averse has been mooted. Proponents of the approach claim that risk mapping, because it discourages denial of risk within a proactive management context, will encourage greater deliberative risk-taking. It also allows stakeholders in the organisation to better understand the nature of the risks that management might wish to take. Risk-taking is informed rather than blind or partially sighted. In fact, once risks are identified, the task of the managers has been said to be to decide whether to avoid, retain, reduce, transfer or exploit them. Some risks will be accepted and retained as simply inherent in the chosen business of the organisation. Normally such risks are predictable and can be offset by financial contingencies. Some risks should be exploited because they offer the prospect of great returns. Exploitation must be undertaken in the full knowledge of the possible costs. Some risks can be avoided. For instance, it is possible to cease certain activities and avoid the risk they entail. Choosing what to avoid depends critically upon knowing the implications of the activity that must cease for the organisation's overall priorities. Some risks can be transferred in the sense that they can be covered through insurance or shared through joint ventures. Outsourcing activities can be one classic example of attempting to transfer risk. Some risks can be effectively reduced, either by introducing controls that make better outcomes more likely or by charging a premium to compensate for their existence.

1.6   Organisational decision support systems: problem structuring methods

Risk mapping is a little static in its approach. It does not encourage managers to look at the dynamic relationships between complex networks of risk. Horlick-Jones *et al.* (2001) point out: first, that corporate risk management, especially at the strategic level, is becoming increasingly diverse and complex as it moves away from traditional insurance-based risk; second, that the political sensitivity of risk issues is leading to increased pressure from the operating environment to manage risks more effectively; and, third, a growing number of corporate decisions are being wound into an overall risk management strategy, so increasing the complexity and scale of the process. They suggest that organisations need decision support systems to help them under these circumstances.

There are many available. Horlick-Jones *et al.* describe problem structuring methods (PSMs) that are designed to assist management groups to agree the nature and boundaries of problems they must tackle and to secure shared commitments to action. There are a large number of variants of these methods. Their advantage is that they allow a problem to be multi-faceted and they admit that it may involve a number of uncertainties or ambiguities. Exposing the perceived relationships between the complex elements of the problem and elucidating the ambiguities are central to the task. Decisions are better informed as a consequence of laying bare the full details of the problem. The methods usually result in a diagrammatic representation of the elements in the problem or of the aspects of the action that must be taken to deal with the problem. Figure 8.3 provides an illustration of such a diagram, based on the way a university would respond if it discovered one of its students had contracted meningitis. The figure has two levels: the holistic and the segmental, the latter representing the detailed unpacking of an element of the former. The method is useful only in so far as the individuals or teams that address the problem are capable of identifying all its relevant facets and then can see the relationships between them. The method is merely a way of systematically interrogating the individual or team so that knowledge is exposed and used optimally. As an adjunct to the conventional risk-mapping systems, these methods are interesting.

1.7   Business continuity management

The illustration of the university that has to deal with a meningitis outbreak serves also to introduce a further central element of risk management nowadays: business continuity management. Introduced first in the 1990s, 'business continuity management is a label now commonly used

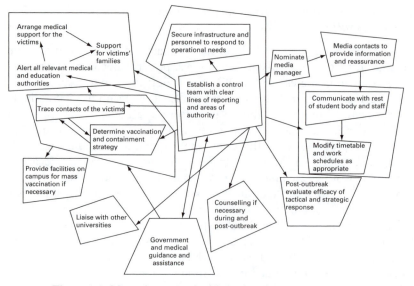

Figure 8.3 Managing a meningitis outbreak

for that process which follows a risk becoming a reality, often creating in its wake many more risks. Business continuity management is the process of ensuring that the organisation continues to function effectively after the disaster, crisis or other negative event has occurred. The phrase is also used to encompass the process of planning for the need for recovery after any event which threatens the life of the organisation. It is sometimes referred to as 'planning for all eventualities'.

Business continuity strategies are as varied as the events to which they are designed to respond. An example of one: just before Christmas 2005, a major UK fashion retailer lost half of its stock when one of its distribution centres burned down. It continued trading by chartering aircraft to fly backwards and forwards to China, bringing new stocks each day. This is an example of a discrete and contained disaster with an expensive but direct response. However, many disasters that occur impact upon complex organisations in much more multi-faceted ways. In an era when large organisations is interdependent across the globe, the nature of the threats they face is often the culmination of a long chain reaction of other failures somewhere in the network of institutions and environments in which they operate and upon which they depend. The need for focus upon disaster or emergency recovery has been brought home particularly following the series of terrorist attacks that have struck often at the heart of business centres. The list grows ever longer – the attacks on 11 September 2001, the bombs in London on 7 July 2005, the bombs in Mumbai on 11 July 2006 – and each is associated with appalling death and mayhem. Planning for all eventualities under such circumstances is an impossibility, but organisations are increasingly attempting to get as close to this ideal as possible. Obviously, government agencies have to plan for such events and there are elaborate, often internationally co-ordinated, plans for response. But other organisations must also have their own plans. For instance, they may need to know how they would ensure their staff got to work after a terrorist attack had disrupted transport, or they might need to know that they had backed up copies of data essential to their business and that these were held off-site just in case their major IT facility was damaged in an attack.

The ripple effects of other types of major incident, not associated with terrorism, also should not be underestimated. On 11 December 2005, explosions at the oil repository at Buncefield in Hemel Hempstead, UK, generated one of the biggest fires ever seen at such a facility. The governmental body responsible for business development in that region subsequently did a study of the effects of the fire. It claimed that 25 per cent of businesses in the area had been seriously affected by the fire and 1,422 jobs had been relocated as a result. Most of these businesses had no direct relationship with the oil depot – other than geographical contiguity. In the US, in 2005, Hurricane Katrina caused not only terrible flood damage in New Orleans and its environs; it also caused long-term electricity blackouts across a huge area of the South. Untold numbers of businesses were affected. Again, this emphasises the significance of understanding the wider interdependency of organisations when considering the viability of business continuity management and planning.

Much business continuity planning uses scenario planning as a method. Typically this entails creating a scenario for the organisation in which some disaster occurs, and then senior managers are asked to say what they would do in order to deal with the situation. Normally, the scenario would be managed, perhaps by a facilitator from outside the organisation, so that it was allowed to develop over a notional time period and in response to the initial responses that senior managers proposed. The essential ingredient in this type of exercise is that the scenario is dynamic and responsive. The object is to lead the managers into a virtual reality, partly responsive to their own actions and partly driven by the facilitator, whose job it is to ensure that the managers are made to think beyond their normal routines and habitual reactions. Consequently, it not unusual for the emergency or disaster in the scenario to be made to escalate as the exercise proceeds. The purpose is to stretch the capacity of the managers to their limits. Generating meaningful scenarios and managing the exercise is a very skilled activity. Scenario planning consultancy is now a business in its own right. Box 8.1 summarises

Box 8.1 Common lessons of scenario planning for business continuity

There are some lessons that commonly emerge from scenario planning exercises:

- To be effective in developing recovery plans, there is less need to focus upon the precise nature of the disaster/emergency and more need to focus on just what it will affect in the business. The question to ask is: How does it disrupt the business and how does it constrain any action that is designed to repair the disruption?
- Ensure that the managers of the recovery know where they should go to do it and how they should communicate with each other if they are not physically together.
- Ensure that information essential to the organisation is protected (the ways in which this can be done are myriad).
- Ensure that essential information is capable of being accessed in a timely and secure fashion.
- Know what needs to be communicated to all members of the organisation, all its stakeholders and all other interested parties (including the media).
- Know how messages will be communicated, when and by whom.
- Know the viability of all assumptions that are built into the recovery plan by testing them (including assumptions about the support available from third parties, such as government agencies or commercial organisations).
- Managers who are good under normal circumstances are not always effective managers of crisis recovery – scenario planning exercises can be used to test manager capacities.
- There are often ethical issues that emerge when recovery plans are considered (for instance, who among needy clients should be given priority in supply of goods or services). Being ready to deal with these and working through the organisation's stance in relation to them is an integral part of readiness.
- The significance of what is done in the immediate aftermath of the disaster (what some medical experts call the 'golden hour') must be emphasised. Speed and appropriateness of initial response in most cases is a vital determiner of success; hence the importance of anticipatory planning (the plans that may take months to formulate may have to be activated in minutes).

some of the generic lessons that the scenario planning approach has produced.

There is a final point that should be made concerning business continuity management. Much scenario planning will lead to the conclusion that resources must be used to create backup facilities (like data storage or telecommunications systems), to make available key staff, to train personnel, to line up alternative supply chains, to stockpile vital supplies, and so on. The decision that management faces is whether or not to invest in order to mitigate the potential consequences of a possible disaster. If it decides to invest, the question revolves around how much to invest. Management is in reality engaged in determining the acceptable ratio of risk to return. The scenario planning approach should merely highlight the complex nature of the risk and the full cost significance of both action and inaction.

2.   Safety culture

2.1   What is safety culture?

In examining the way hazards are managed in complex organisations, it is important to explore the role of what has come to be called safety culture. Psychologists have had a major impact upon the conceptualisation of risk management in organisations through the development of their work on safety culture. This work has transcended and incorporated the earlier work on 'human factors' or ergonomics in attempts to understand how large-scale accidents come about (Moray, 1994; Reason, 1990). The central idea is simple: an organisation can be characterised in terms of its safety culture and the culture of the organisation transcends those who work in it at any one time.

The concept of safety culture arose in the aftermath of the Chernobyl disaster as a different way of thinking about risk management in organisational contexts. Reason (1987) emphasised that the analysis of the 'Chernobyl errors' focused attention on the human and organisational elements that might contribute to the unsafe operation of technological systems. Lee (1995b) put it succinctly, having reviewed the inquiries that followed highly publicised accidents (i.e. the explosions at Flixborough and Bhopal, the fires at King's Cross and Piper Alpha, the capsize of the *Herald of Free Enterprise* ferry and the rail crash at Clapham Junction): despite the adoption of the full range of engineering and technical safeguards, complex systems broke down disastrously because the people running them failed to do what they were supposed to do. Moreover, these were not the result of a few errant individuals who made mistakes but a product of the underlying culture of their organisations.

Safety culture can be defined as that assembly of characteristics and attitudes in organisations and the individuals who work in them that establishes that, as an overriding priority, safety issues receive the attention warranted by their significance. This definition is derived from that of the International Nuclear Safety Advisory Group (1991). The definition emphasises that safety culture is attitudinal as well as structural, relates both to individuals and to organisations, and concerns the requirement to match all safety issues with appropriate actions. Pidgeon (1991: 129) offered a more detailed definition: 'safety culture is conceptualised as an ideational system of meanings concerned with the norms, beliefs, roles, and practices for handling hazards and risk'. Elements of a safety culture are: the norms and rules for dealing with risk, the attitudes towards safety and the reflexivity concerning safety practices that prevails. The Health and Safety Executive (1993) say that 'Organisations with a positive safety culture are characterised by communications founded on mutual trust, by shared perceptions of the importance of safety and by confidence in the efficiency of preventive measures.'

Safety culture may be comprised of intangibles, such as perceptions and attitudes, but it has eminently tangible and measurable consequences in terms of errors and accidents (Pidgeon and Turner, 1997). A poor safety culture is associated with higher error and accident levels. Traditionally, safety culture is said to be manifested in two major components: the framework determined by organisational policy and managerial action; and the response of individuals working within and benefiting from the framework. Hence improving a safety culture depends upon commitment and competence at the level of policy and management, and at the level of individual workers.

Box 8.2 summarises some of the characteristics of industrial plants that have been found to have low accident rates (HSE, 1993; Lee, 1993).

2.2   Safety culture and the regulator's role

In many industries, achieving the right safety culture is not simply a matter for an organisation's own management. Now, it is often a job for an official regulator set up by national government or sometimes by international treaty. Aviation, the rail industry, the offshore oil business, onshore petrochemical production and nuclear power generation – all have their regulators that prescribe their safety requirements. The governmental and regulator roles in establishing safety culture in an industry cannot be ignored. In the nuclear industry, the IAEA (International Atomic Energy Authority) has promulgated expectations with which both governments and specific national regulators are expected to

---

Box 8.2 Correlates of low accident rates in industrial facilities

- Safety matters are discussed and exchanges between managers and workers are both less formal and more frequent.
- Organisational learning is encouraged.
- Safety is a strong focus of the organisation and its workers.
- Senior management explicitly gives safety a high priority, devotes resources to it and actively promotes it personally.
- There is more and better training – not just on safety specifically, but with safety aspects emphasised in skills training.
- Working conditions are clean and comfortable (relative to the task) and good housekeeping is encouraged.
- Workers show high job satisfaction and approve the fairness of promotion, lay-off and employee benefits.
- Workforce includes employees recruited or retained because they work safely and have lower turnover and absenteeism, as distinct from higher productivity.

---

comply. Governments, or more accurately government departments, can be characterised in terms of their safety culture in a manner rather equivalent to the assessment of industrial or commercial organisations. For government, the objects of its safety-consciousness are the industries that it regulates. Different governments have different safety cultures when it comes to creating and implementing regulation. A large part of international negotiation and developmental work to improve safety is designed to achieve consensus across governments in the way in which their regulators will monitor and intervene in organisational safety. The task has been to ensure that governments legislate satisfactorily, fund regulatory agencies properly, conduct appropriate research, make public information on safety levels and refrain from interfering in technical arenas that have safety relevance.

The role of the regulatory agency in establishing organisational safety culture is much debated (e.g. Hutter (2001) in relation to the railways; HSE, 2001). In the UK, the Health and Safety Executive Nuclear Installations Inspectorate during the 1990s reviewed the role of their nuclear power plant inspectors to see whether they could be more actively engaged in promoting safety culture. They concluded that it was difficult for inspectors both to evaluate the safety of a nuclear plant and to act as an advocate for specific safety culture improvements. By becoming involved in the process of improving the safety of a site, it was argued that they could be accused of losing their independence and the objectivity of their site evaluations could be challenged. Separation of advisory and inspection activities was regarded as necessary. The resolution of this dilemma probably lies in ensuring that the regulatory agency establishes channels for educating and advising on the development of safety culture but the specific inspectors are kept away from delivering this input.

Regulatory agencies are likely to try to encourage the organisation to:

- establish a corporate level safety policy that is publicised and widely understood
- ensure that safety practices operate at the corporate level (e.g. board meetings have a formal item on safety, and a senior manager has prime responsibility for safety and is seen to monitor safety by visiting the industrial site)
- clearly assign safety responsibilities
- train well and often, and evaluate that training
- select and promote senior managers who recognise safety is important
- review safety performance regularly and have in place mechanisms for learning from the reviews
- have a system for identifying safety weaknesses and reward those who report them
- limit work practices likely to result in human error (e.g. excessive overtime)
- have management be open with regulators about problems they experience
- inculcate attitudes in managers at all levels that value safety
- explicitly examine the trade-offs that are made between safety demands and economic demands
- use the best independent research to inform safety judgements in a timely fashion
- make information on safety levels public.

This list is derived from the appendix of INSAG-4 (International Nuclear Safety Advisory Group, 1991) guidance for the nuclear industry, but can be seen emulated in other guidelines for other industries. It is notable that, when management follows these guidelines on their approach to safety, it tends to be correlated with greater employee satisfaction with safety and contingency measures (Rundmo, 1994).

Where safety culture has been weak, there have been some very dramatic incidents that have been of enormous economic significance to the organisation concerned. One example in the UK comes from the Sellafield nuclear reprocessing plant (see Box 8.3). The case illustrates how one violation of safety regulations can have enormous multi-faceted consequences.

Box 8.3 The case of Sellafield

MOX is a mixed oxide fuel, produced by mixing plutonium oxide, separated during the reprocessing of spent nuclear fuel, with uranium oxide. It is used in nuclear reactors as an alternative to conventional fuel made of uranium oxide. Sellafield Mox Demonstration Facility (MDF) manufactures mox pellets and incorporates them into fuel assemblies for use in nuclear reactors. Each pellet produced must be repeatedly checked to ensure it is the right diameter. In September 1999, the UK national newspaper, the *Independent*, alleged that British Nuclear Fuel (BNFL) employees had falsified measurement quality control data on mox pellets produced at its Sellafield MDF for a Japanese customer. The quality data from previous samples had been used instead of running the required checks. This allegation was accepted as correct by BNFL immediately. In fact, the falsification had been discovered by its own control team and had been reported to the Nuclear Installations Inspectorate (NII). The NII had initiated an inquiry.

BNFL was convinced that the pellets did meet the necessary quality standards because they had other supporting quality data. At this point, BNFL had mox assemblies aboard a transport vessel en route to Japan. BNFL then announced that initial investigations had revealed further falsified data – all relating to mox prepared for Japan but not yet despatched. BNFL took no dramatic action to emphasise protection of its customer. This contrasts with measures taken by other companies in other industries where quality control errors had occurred (e.g. Perrier withdrawing its bottled water from all shops after some evidence of contamination had been found). BNFL's stance was that this was not a safety problem but rather a procedural problem in quality assurance. None of the suspect mox assemblies had left Sellafield according to them. However, the Nuclear Installations Inspectorate had informed the Japanese government that there could be irregularities in two of the fuel assemblies that were on board ship. NII subsequently stated that four assemblies might be affected. Only at this point did BNFL publicly acknowledge the irregularities in the additional batch of fuel. The Japanese suspended all mox imports from BNFL and the Japanese industry minister stated that they 'were losing trust in BNFL'. The UK Energy minister demanded a full explanation from BNFL's chairman 'of this clearly unacceptable failure by management'. By this stage, the fault in BNFL is not seen as a difficulty lodged at the level of poor practice in the data-checking

Box 8.3 (cont.)

team of a small unit within the company; it has been expanded to be seen as a symptom of more widespread lack of control and honesty by management at the most senior level. The Chair and the Chief Executive of BNFL at separate times apologised to the Japanese. The fact that, in Japan, BNFL is dealing with a culture that has quite different expectations concerning blame and acknowledgement of guilt does not seem to have impacted sufficiently on the company's management of the incident. Media coverage of these events was extensive and on an international scale. The possibility that other shipments to Switzerland and to Germany had contained suspect pellets was mooted. The Irish and Icelandic governments called for the closure of Sellafield. The Japanese, the Swiss and the Germans ban BNFL fuel imports. The NII inquiry report was highly critical of operations at Sellafield. The BNFL Chief Executive resigned four months after the initial report of the falsification. This was seen as too little, too late in most parts of the media. It was not seen as tackling the core structural organisational problems that created the mox incident. Almost two months later, three executive and six non-executive directors of the company were replaced and seventy new jobs were created to ensure safety. This management shake-up was not interpreted by the media as a sign of willingness to tackle the problems facing the company, but rather as further evidence of the depth of the original incompetence. The *Independent* concluded that the string of safety scares had led the government to shelve plans to privatise Sellafield for at least two years.

The mox incident was only one of several safety-related problems that BNFL had to face during this time. The apparent weakness of the safety culture within the company was reportedly linked with loss of income and with loss of UK government capacity to bring about the privatisation that was expected to deliver massive investment in the company.

This case is further analysed in Breakwell and Barnett (2001).

2.3   The safety culture of the regulator

Before leaving the regulator, it is necessary to stress that such agencies also can be characterised in terms of their own safety culture. In 2000, the British government published the report of the inquiry that has been established to review the history of the emergence and identification of BSE (bovine spongiform encephalitis – the so-called 'mad cow disease') and variant CJD (Creutzfeldt-Jakob Disease) in the UK and to determine what action was taken in response to it and the adequacy of that action (HMSO, 2000). By 2000, eighty people were dead or dying of variant CJD and the farming industry had seen the death or precautionary slaughter of hundreds of thousands of animals, together with calamitous loss of markets due to bans on exports of meat products. It is worth examining the inquiry conclusions, since they throw light on the safety culture of those parts of government charged with dealing with the farming industry and food safety at the time. The Executive Summary of the report states that:

At the heart of the BSE story lie questions of how to handle a hazard – a known hazard to cattle and an unknown hazard to humans. The Government took measures to address both hazards. They were sensible measures, but they were not always timely nor adequately implemented and enforced.

The rigour with which policy measures were implemented for the protection of human health was affected by the belief of many prior to early 1996 that BSE was not a potential threat to human life.

The Government was anxious to act in the best interests of human and animal health. To this end it sought and followed advice of independent scientific experts – sometimes when decisions could have been reached more swiftly and satisfactorily within government.

It goes on:

At times officials showed a lack of rigour in considering how policy should be turned into practice, to the detriment of the efficacy of the measures taken.

At times bureaucratic processes resulted in unacceptable delay in giving effect to policy.

The Government introduced measures to guard against the risk that BSE might be a matter of life and death not merely for cattle but also for humans, but the possibility of a risk to humans was not communicated to the public or to those whose job it was to implement and enforce precautionary measures.

The Government did not lie to the public about BSE. It believed that the risks posed by BSE to humans were remote. The Government was preoccupied with preventing an alarmist overreaction to BSE because it believed that the risk was remote. It is now clear that the campaign of reassurance was a mistake. When on 20 March 1996 the Government announced that BSE has probably been transmitted to humans, the public felt that they had been betrayed.

The report is identifying some of the more complex symptoms of a poor safety culture in a complex bureaucracy: unwillingness to acknowledge the significance of the risk of a novel hazard, failure to act swiftly or decisively on the identified risk, and failure to communicate appropriately about the risk. Several of these issues have emerged in discussions in Chapter 6, and will recur in Chapter 9.

2.4   Measuring safety culture

Although industry-specific guidelines for holistic assessments of safety culture have been developed (for instance, the ASCOT guidelines, IAEA-TECDOC-743 1994, for the nuclear industry), since safety culture is a complex construct (Berman et al., 1994, suggested it might have 130 attributes), reliable or valid measurement is not likely to be simple. Typically, researchers have chosen to index attitudes towards safety practices in a conventional fashion. Pre-dating the arrival of the safety culture concept, Zohar (1980) constructed and validated a measure of 'safety climate' which reflected employees' perceptions of the relative importance of safe conduct in their occupational behaviour. Scores on this measure correlated well with independent assessments of the safety of the companies studied. The items on the scale broke into two clusters: those dealing with management attitudes about safety, and those dealing with their own perceptions regarding the relevance of safety in general production processes. The separation of the beliefs about management attitudes to safety and their own attitudes to safety is a common finding in empirical research in this area (e.g. Dedobbeleer and Beland, 1991). This may suggest that it is overly simplistic to expect management attitudes to safety to drive employee attitudes to safety in any direct way. In turn, this might call into question the assumption that management will lead worker safety practices through example or through expression of concern. It suggests that there should be much more focused effort upon changing employee attitudes per se.

This is supported by the study from Cox and Cox (1991). They did an attitude-mapping exercise in a European company involved in the production and distribution of industrial gases. They found that employees' attitudes to safety could be explained in terms of five orthogonal factors: personal scepticism, individual responsibility, safeness of the work environment, effectiveness of the arrangements for safety and personal immunity. Interestingly, they noted that improving safety culture would depend upon extinguishing (or at least reducing) unconstructive and negative beliefs as much as enhancing the positive ones. The importance of perceived personal immunity as a reason for failing to follow safety precautions harks back to the findings concerning invulnerability that were considered in Chapters 3 and 4. It also ties in to Dejoy's (1994) suggestion that it would be useful to look at the role that attributions of causality play in predisposing workplace safety. Situational attributions of safety may militate against adopting safer work practices. Personal attributions of safety may facilitate safer practices.

There have been many other measures of safety culture that have been developed. Ostrom et al. (1993) developed one for the nuclear industry.

Donald and Canter (1994) developed another set of reliable scales to measure safety attitudes in the chemical industry and showed a significant relationship between safety attitudes and accident rates. Lee *et al.* (1993) developed a survey instrument to measure safety culture in the Sellafield reprocessing plant workforce. This comprised 172 attitude items that were found to cluster into 19 factors that could be grouped into 9 major areas: safety procedures, safety rules, permit to work system, risks, job satisfaction, ownership/participation, design, training and selection. They found that unwillingness to take risks at work was positively associated with a wide range of constructive attitudes towards safety measures and towards the work itself (Lee, 1995a).

Coyle *et al.* (1995) argue that measuring safety 'climate' can be a proactive management tool, allowing the identification of accidents that are waiting to happen and providing an opportunity to take pre-emptive action. Peterson (1993) claimed that ensuring attitude surveys were anonymous would improve the accuracy of self-disclosure among the workforce and would help management identify genuine problems. In recent years, measurement of safety culture or climate has become an integral part of the habitual processes of risk management in complex organisations. For instance, in offshore oil installations, whole system risk analysis (Bea, 2002) is conducted alongside safety climate assessment (Mearns *et al.*, 2001). In fact, Mearns *et al.* report a longitudinal study that allowed a careful examination of change in safety on North Sea oil and gas installations in consecutive years. They found that changes in perceived management commitment to safety were closely associated with changes in safety behaviour on the part of workers.

2.5   Improving safety culture

McDonald and Ryan (1992) argue that safety culture is a product of so many factors that are outside of the control of the organisation – for instance, societal, commercial and legal constraints – that the organisation itself can have only a limited impact upon it. This contrasts markedly with the numerous papers that offer recipes for improving safety culture (Geller, 1994, 1995; Arden, 1993). B. A. Turner (1991) effectively points out that the way to improve an organisation's safety culture is to institute those features of the working environment that characterise a good safety culture (for example, rewarding people if they behave in a safety-conscious manner, having management signal the importance of safety issues, explaining why safety matters, providing adequate resources so that safety can be achieved, and so on). The key to changing safety culture here is clearly seen to lie in the hands of management. Relatively simple changes in management style can be effective. For instance, Mattila *et al.* (1994) showed that foremen on building sites run by construction firms that gave their workers feedback about the consequences of their potentially unsafe practices were less likely to have accidents in their teams. Ekenes and Cameron (1993) report on an aluminium casting company that operated active safety culture management (i.e. improved safety training, evaluation of compliance with protective clothing guidelines, equipment checking, accident investigation and lesson-learning, etc.) and found very low levels of accident or injury. Shrader-Frechette and Cooke (2004) emphasise the role of providing adequate resources so that safety standards can be met.

Lee (1995b), having explained how important attitudes to risk are in predicting safety behaviour, examines whether such attitudes can be changed. Lee acknowledges that conformity pressures can induce inertia in systems. Bringing about an improvement in safety culture would therefore require a concerted and maintained intervention in the system. Rather like Turner, he argues that improved personnel policies, training and reward systems are needed. He also uses the voluminous literature on persuasive communication to suggest that the power of the intervention will be optimised if messages to the workforce are crafted to emanate from an appropriate influential source, in a structure and with a content that encourages motivated attention, and through a medium that has impact. It is a good reminder for risk managers that interventions should take account of what is known about persuasive communication (see also Chapter 6).

Going one step further, it seems that what the recommendations on changing safety culture have in common is a two-pronged attack: first, they say provide new information about the status quo (e.g. give feedback on attitudes, show the weakness of current safety practices, etc.) in the most persuasive format available; and, second, they say provide incentives for change (e.g. link safety to promotion prospects, offer immediate rewards through ongoing recognition schemes, remove disincentives such as blaming those who report problems, etc.). This is hardly surprising advice. What is surprising is that it is often ignored. Even major events sometimes fail to bring home the message that change is needed. For instance, on 23 March 2005, BP Product's refinery in Texas City suffered an explosion that killed 15 people and injured 170. As a result it was reported that $700 million was lost from BP's profits. Yet months later, when inspectors from the US Occupational Safety and Health Administration (OSHA) visited another BP refinery in Oregon, Ohio, they found unsafe working conditions similar to those associated with the explosion in Texas.

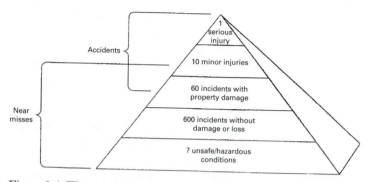

Figure 8.4 The safety pyramid

Phimister *et al.* (2003) provide a nice example of how information can be collected and used to change practice. They were interested in how 'near misses' (i.e. incidents that have the potential to, but do not, result in loss) could be analysed and then used to inform training in the chemical industry. Near misses provide insight into what *might* happen. Figure 8.4 shows a schematic Safety Pyramid which illustrates the ratio that might be expected of actual injury or loss to near misses.

The failure to take note of previous near misses has been catalogued in relation to a whole series of serious accidents. For instance, in 1986 the US Space Shuttle *Challenger* exploded. On previous missions dating back to 1982, it had been noted that O-ring seals degradation increased as ambient lift-off temperature decreased. Management was alerted the night before that ambient temperatures lower than 53 degrees Fahrenheit at take-off could result in catastrophic failure. Lift-off temperature was actually 36 degrees Fahrenheit. In 1997, sixty people died and more than 10,000 metric tons of petroleum-based products were released into the atmosphere or burned when the Hindustan refinery exploded. Management had been alerted earlier of corroded and leaking transfer lines where the explosion occurred. In the UK in 1999, thirty-one people died in the Paddington train crash when two trains collided because a signal that should have halted one of the trains was not acted on. From 1993 to 1999, eight near misses, or signals passed at danger (what the railway authorities called SPADS), had occurred at the location (signal 109) where the collision ultimately happened.

Getting organisations to learn the lessons of their near misses is clearly no simple business. Phimister *et al.* (2003) propose a seven-stage management system. These stages are: identification (recognise the incident has occurred); reporting, prioritisation and distribution (the incident is appraised and information about it transferred for assessment of follow-up); causal analysis (the underlying factors that might result in an accident are identified); solution identification (measures that might mitigate the likelihood or impact of an accident are pinpointed and corrective action taken); dissemination (information is broadcast to a wider audience to increase awareness); and resolution (corrective actions are implemented and evaluated, and where necessary other action taken).

The introduction of 'no-blame' reporting has been vital to enabling near misses to be identified. The concept is simple. Members of an organisation must believe that they will not be blamed or punished if they report an incident that could have, but did not, cause a loss. Where this belief pervades an organisation, it is said to have a 'no-blame' culture. Belief in no blame is thought to be tied to fuller and timelier disclosure of incidents. It is not easy to establish a no-blame culture. A single instance of punishment following disclosure can undermine belief in it. If no blame is to be taken seriously by all, it must be espoused explicitly, persistently and consistently by management. As Cox *et al.* (2006) state, management must have gained the trust of the workforce for no-blame assertions to have their effect on work practices. Clark and Payne (2006) suggest that such trust is intimately related to worker perceptions of their leaders as competent and consistent and, to a lesser extent, open. Of course, trust and distrust are not absolute or total, and it is possible to trust and distrust the same source. Cox *et al.* (2006) interestingly talk about the role of 'creative distrust' in the workplace. This occurs when workers doubt that their managers are right in the safety measures they introduce and as a consequence introduce their own improvements of the safety regime. This links to the Jeffcott *et al.* (2006) suggestion that trust that is based solely upon adherence to rules for safety may inhibit informed and self-conscious compliance. This newer research focuses attention on the active role of the workforce in ensuring safety and moves away from regarding them as merely reactive to management.

Of course, government departments in most industrialised countries are now engaged with the problem of ensuring that they, and the organisations that they regulate, are capable of learning from their mistakes in order to improve risk management. For instance, the Department of Health in the UK has analysed how the National Health Service should be learning from the adverse events that it experiences. In this analysis, the requirement for an organisational memory emerges strongly. This entails more than recording or investigating adverse events (for instance, causing patient harm by injecting the wrong drug or by failure to use the correct surgical procedure or through poor hygiene control). It entails ensuring that the knowledge about those events (and the reasons for them and the way to prevent them) is part of the active memory of the people working in the organisation. People need to be able to remember the events almost as if they had been personally involved. This is one way to make the hazard real and to motivate change in behaviour.

3   Trust and risk reputation

The public is increasingly willing to express its disapproval of companies that fail to put safety first. The sales losses from the American consumer boycott of Exxon petrol following the disastrous Exxon Valdez oil spill signalled that the public will not countenance supporting companies that behave carelessly. The case of the BNFL mox incident described above illustrated how complex the chain of consequences can be that flows from a single challenge to safety quality control. For BNFL the implications were damaging commercially, politically and technologically. Most large commercial organisations have learned the lesson well. They do everything within their power to minimise the loss to their reputation that any error over risk management might bring. Risk reputation management is now a vital element in total risk management.

Some good examples of the need for risk reputation management come from the food industry. It is a commonplace now to find that, when a manufacturer discovers some contaminant or pollutant has been introduced into their production line, they will withdraw all stocks of that product from supermarket shelves immediately and will publicise widely the fact that they have done so. The fact that their production line could be invaded by some pollutant or contaminant is itself not good for the reputation, but to be seen to react immediately and clearly with the public interests at heart, despite inevitable costs, can be good for the reputation. Interestingly, there is some evidence now that the company response to the discovery of a problem must be very rapid and totally comprehensive. When, in June 2006, Cadbury, the chocolate manufacturer, discovered that one of their production facilities was contaminated with salmonella, it issued a warning and withdrew stocks from stores. The estimated cost to the company by August 2006 was estimated at £20 million. Nevertheless, there were reports that it had acted to withdraw stock too slowly.

Even government departments have learned that their survival depends on their risk reputation. In Britain, the Ministry of Agriculture Fisheries and Food that presided over the BSE/CJD debacle was restructured soon after, though it did take the foot-and-mouth disease epidemic to precipitate its total replacement.

Trust and its relationship to the efficacy of risk communication have already been discussed in Chapter 6. But it returns in a different guise in relation to organisational risk reputation and total risk management. Poortinga and Pidgeon (2005) pose the fascinating question: Is trust in the risk regulator a determiner of acceptance of a risk or is prior perception of the risk a determiner of trust in the regulator? Effectively, they are asking: Is trust a cause or a consequence of risk acceptance? What they call the 'causal model of trust' would propose that trust affects perceptions of risk, which then affect acceptability of the risk.

An alternative is the 'associationist model of trust'. This postulates that acceptability pre-dates both trust and risk perception and affects both. Eiser *et al.* (2002) had found some support for the associationist model of trust. This second model ties into the arguments mentioned in Chapter 5 concerning the affect heuristic. Finucane *et al.* (2000) proposed that affect comes prior to, and directs judgements of, risks and benefits. People are held to have a general affective evaluation of an activity or technology and this operates as a filter for more specific evaluations. If specific risk judgements are indeed driven by general evaluative judgements, as the affect heuristic suggests, then it would seem reasonable to argue that a general willingness to accept a risk might shape willingness to trust a risk regulator or manager. Poortinga and Pidgeon (2005) tested this assertion empirically, studying trust in risk regulation, risk perception and acceptability of the risk associated with genetically modified food. They used data from a series of surveys and tested their hypothesis by comparing the impact of controlling for each variable on the bivariate zero order correlations between the others. While the statistical method is open to some debate, the trend in their data is interesting. They found evidence that acceptability of GM food seems to determine trust in regulation of GM food and levels of perceived risk. This clearly supports the associationist model.

This is a significant contribution to our modelling of the role of trust in risk management. However, it begs the question: How is the general acceptability of the hazard established in the first place? There is always a problem when tracing causal pathways in knowing when to stop. There is particular difficulty in deciding when to stop where those pathways may be circular over time. So, in this case, it is possible that current acceptability of GM food is actually a product of a history of distrust in regulation of the food industry in the past and not just in relation to GM food. The position of trust in any causal model would then shift according to the timescale that was being applied.

This is an important consideration for risk regulators and risk managers who are concerned with their risk reputation. Reputations are evolved over time, though they can change in any moment in time. Trust will only be retained if it is nurtured. Building up a bank of trustworthiness will be dependent upon accumulating credit, proving that you do what you say you will do and showing that what you say about things is true. However, trustworthiness is a complex product of accretions that have many sources, not just based on evidence of fairness and objectivity. Earle and Cvetkovich (1995) argue that, in arenas where trust is most important, for instance in relation to complex socio-technical systems that generate risk, most people will not have the resources to come to an informed decision about the level of trust to place in managers. Instead, trust is based on general agreement and perceived similarity of values. This has come to be known as the Salient Values Similarity theory. This holds that we trust those who are judged to share with us the values we deem appropriate in a particular risk management domain. In keeping with this theory, Earle (2004) found that risk managers were trusted more if their policies were congruent with the beliefs and values of the individuals who rated them. He also found that disagreement and distrust generated more conscious consideration of the arguments put by the risk manager. Distrust militated against uncritical acceptance of information. The makings of a vicious circle are evident.

Cvetkovitch *et al.* (2002) had already shown what they call the 'perseverance of trust' – that is, that established trust attributions persevere in the face of new information – so, for instance, individuals who distrust the nuclear industry are more likely to judge both good and bad news about the industry as less positive than those who are more trusting of it. Cvetkovitch *et al.* also showed partial evidence of the asymmetry principle (first mooted by Slovic): news about negative events has a much stronger effect on decreasing trust than does news about positive events on increasing it. Perseverance of trust seems to interact with the asymmetry principle. People who were less trusting of the nuclear industry treated bad news about it as more informative than those who were more trusting. The use of information provision to engender trust seems to be fraught, not least because information that risk managers might in the past have disclosed in order to prove that they had planned to deal with a hazard is now not disclosable for fear that it may be used by terrorists or others to prevent effective risk management (Beierle, 2004).

Recognising the complexity of the genesis and maintenance of trust, Poortinga and Pidgeon (2003) sought to explore the dimensionality of trust in risk regulation. Analysis of survey responses suggested two prime dimensions: general trust (or reliance) and scepticism. They suggested that these two dimensions interact to produce four types of trust in government:

high general trust + low scepticism = acceptance (trust)
high general trust + high scepticism = critical trust
low general trust + low scepticism = distrust
low general trust + high scepticism = rejection (cynicism)

This typology is good, because it focuses on the way reliance and scepticism can come together to produce critical trust. This is not frequently examined (e.g. Irwin *et al.*, 1996; Walls *et al.*, 2003), but intuitively it would seem likely to be useful in explaining how large numbers of people react to government attempts to manage risk. Critical trust may be what mature democracies should seek to foster in their citizenry. Critical trust may be the basis needed if participation of the public in risk decision-making is to progress.

Cvetkovich and Löfstedt (1999) presented a candid summary of the research on social trust and the management of risk. At that time they claimed that it was limited and inconclusive. They point out that some things seem well established. For instance, perceived openness and perceived competence can increase trust. However, as they say, achieving one may undermine the other: being open may reveal information that in the short term suggests lower competence. For those who need to manage their risk reputation, using the conclusions from research on trust is not in practice simple. It is hard to know what the leader of a complex organisation, public or private sector, might do to enhance trust.

Cvetkovich and Löfstedt propose three ways that a leader might develop trust. The first they call 'normal trust' and entails the leader talking and acting in ways that are judged to reflect that he or she shares the values of those whose trust must be won. This is sometimes called 'leadership by following', matching the leader's position to that of those who are to be led. There is some suggestion that, once the leader is established 'by following', it is possible in certain areas to go beyond or deviate from commonly held values or beliefs. The second type of approach involves trying to change the saliency of certain values, rather than the leader (and the organisation) changing – the wider stakeholder public is asked to change. This requires showing why the different set of values should be given primacy. The reasons will need to be powerful not only in objective or logical terms but also in affective terms. For instance, a national political leader might wish to gain trust in her government and its policies for tackling global poverty. This may require individuals to change their adherence to value systems that give priority to personal economic interest. The realignment of saliency in values will depend upon the leader being able to capture not just the minds but also the hearts of the public. The third type of approach that the leader can adopt is founded upon changing the very nature of the values that are brought to bear in assessing action priorities for risk management. This requires the leader to engage those whose trust is sought in the process of identifying and evolving the values that should be brought to bear in shaping the risk management strategy. In this approach trust emerges because the values are shared by being co-produced in the context of the controversy or the risk-management task. In this third approach, we are revisiting some of the suggestions that focus on achieving trust through participation that were discussed in Chapter 6.

Conclusion

In this discussion of trust we come full circle to the issues with which this chapter started. Complex organisations nowadays do not simply need to manage the hazards that they create. They must also manage the risks that surround their enterprise. Failing to be trusted represents a major risk. Ironically, much of the risk management that complex organisations do is aimed at ensuring that their trustworthiness remains as high as possible. Being trusted by shareholders in the commercial world, being trusted by voters in the political world and being trusted by stakeholders in the public sector is vital. Having a safety culture is important, but showing the world that you have a safety culture is even more important. Doing total quality risk management is important, but being known to do it is even more important.

9   Social amplification and social representations of risk

Chapter preview

This chapter introduces a systematic way to conceptualise how risk events, through social and psychological processes, can be amplified, or indeed dampened, and as a result can lead to a ripple of different consequences at various levels (for instance, economic, legal, cultural). This conceptual approach is known as the Social Amplification of Risk Framework (SARF). The basic tenets of SARF are described and the ways in which it has been used are summarised. Some of the recent elaborations of the approach are presented. The layering method is outlined as a tool for exploring amplification processes and ripple effects. The significance of hazard sequences, templates and negotiations with amplification and ripple processes are outlined. The chapter then proceeds to consider two theories that serve to explain some of the processes that underpin the amplification or attenuation of risk: Social Representations Theory and Identity Process Theory. Both theories are presented briefly and their usefulness in predicting risk perceptions and judgements and the ripple effects of risk events is assessed.

1   The Social Amplification of Risk Framework

The Social Amplification of Risk Framework (SARF) describes both the social and individual factors that act to amplify or attenuate perceptions of risk and then generate secondary effects such as regulatory changes, economic losses or stigmatisation of technologies. The SARF was first proposed in 1988 by Roger Kasperson, Ortwin Renn, Paul Slovic, Halina Brown, Jacques Emel, Robert Goble, Jeanne Kasperson and Samuel Ratick and has been subsequently elaborated (Kasperson *et al.*, 1988; Renn, 1991; Kasperson, 1992; Burns *et al.*, 1993; Kasperson and Kasperson, 1996; Kasperson *et al.*, 2003). The idea arose, according to Kasperson *et al.* (2003: 13), 'out of an attempt to overcome the fragmented nature of risk perception and risk communication research by developing an integrative theoretical framework capable of accounting for findings from a wide range of studies', including those from the psycho-metric and cultural schools of risk research and those from the media and organisational dynamics research traditions. Rosa (2003) argues that SARF is the most comprehensive tool available for the study of risk.

The framework particularly focuses upon the dynamic social processes that underlie risk perception and decisions. It highlights that certain events or hazards, which experts would state are relatively low in risk, can nevertheless become a focus of societal concern (risk amplification), whereas other hazards, which experts judge as more serious, attract less public attention (risk attenuation). In the UK, an example of amplification would be the response to the MMR vaccination (described in Chapter 6). An example of attenuation would be the reaction to naturally occurring sources of radiation, such as radon gas. It is worth emphasising that the SARF is about attenuation as well as amplification, because this is sometimes ignored.

The SARF proposes that risks (or risk events, which can be either real or hypothesised) will have an impact not only through their primary physical effects but also, and often more importantly, through the way people communicate them to others. The act of communication requires that the risk is translated into various 'risk signals' (images, symbols and signs) that will interact with a variety of psychological, social, institutional or cultural processes and this will result in the intensification or dampening of the perceptions of the risk and its manageability.

See Figure 9.1 for a summary of the factors SARF proposes are at play. The use of terms like 'social stations' in the figure occurs because the originators were using the metaphor of amplification from classical communications theory applied to physical systems. The notion of a 'station' implies that reshaping (e.g. filtering, re-emphasis, elaboration, glossing and so on) of information is involved as it moves through that node ('station') in the system. This can be seen to fit with all that we have said in earlier chapters about the cognitive and affective biases that operate at the individual level in the interpretation of risk. It also fits with what is known about the way groups and organisations behave when dealing with risk (see Chapter 8).

The figure makes it clear that the risk, or risk event, is given meaning through a complex and iterative process of interactions between different actors in the social structure. The meaning it is given will then determine the secondary, tertiary and subsequent effects that the risk can have upon different social entities (e.g. a local community or a company). It will also constrain the nature of the actions taken in response (e.g. legislative, organisational and economic).

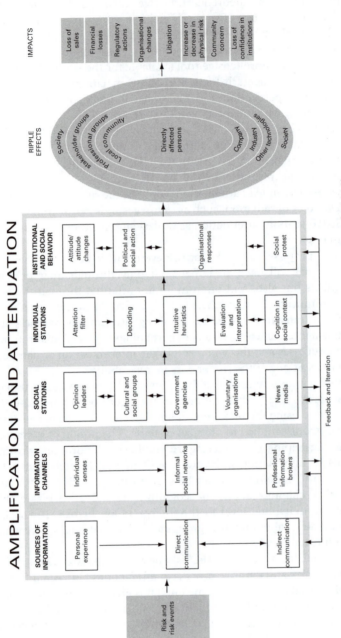

Figure 9.1 The social amplification of risk framework (from Kasperson *et al.*, 2003)

The 'ripple effects' can spread far beyond the originating risk event. This diffusion of impact indicates that there are many potential 'stations' that can contribute to the amplification or attenuation process. This suggests that the risk event will have no ultimate or consolidated interpretation. It will change over time as each element in the ripple system is brought into play. For some risks, the timescale for interpretation and reinterpretation may be very extended (i.e. over centuries). It is therefore possible that delayed or intermittent reinterpretation will stimulate different cycles of impact and will change the targets impacted.

It is worth noting that this figure, from the Kasperson *et al.* (2003) publication, is more explicit than earlier (e.g. 1988) models in detailing the iterative nature of the interactions between sources of information, the information channels, 'social stations', 'individual stations' and institutional and social behaviour. This is worth emphasising because it indicates that this is an evolving framework.

Box 9.1 uses the 10 August 2006 public announcement of a terrorist plot to blow up several passenger airliners over the Atlantic to illustrate in real time how a SARF analysis might work. It can be seen that SARF is a very useful way to organise the analysis of a complex event and its aftermath.

Box 9.1 Eleven days in August 2006: terrorist plot to bomb aircraft

A BRIEF SUMMARY OF THE EVENTS

At 11pm on **9 August,** the Home Secretary, responsible for home land security, was alerted to the possibility that the biggest terrorist attack of modern times was imminent, that the plot must be dismantled and that arrests would soon be under way. Britain was to be put on maximum alert.

On **10 August 2006,** the British police announced that twenty-four terrorist suspects were being questioned about an alleged plot to detonate suicide bombs on board five airliners bound for the United States. They claimed terrorists planned to conceal high-explosive bombs in false bottoms built into energy drink bottles, using explosives similar to that used in the 7 July 2005 attacks in the London Underground. A detonator would have been hidden in the flash mechanism of a disposable camera. The arrests followed an anti-terrorist operation that had been running for months. One of the suspects was released within twenty-four hours – said to be an innocent bystander in one of the

Box 9.1 (cont.)

raids. A martyrdom video apparently recorded by someone planning to become a suicide bomber was found at one of the addresses raided by the police. A further seventeen people were arrested in Pakistan.

The very act of foiling the attack brought chaos to airports in the UK, with a knock-on effect around the world. Hundreds of flights were cancelled or delayed and passengers bedded down on terminal floors with no idea as to when they might take off.

Media on **11 August** carried the story and its consequences:

Twenty-four terrorist suspects were detained. Counter-terrorist agencies had monitored the plotters for twelve months and had moved in after intelligence that the execution was imminent. Co-ordinated arrests were made in Pakistan. The government's emergency planning committee (Cobra) was told that the first wave of bombings would have targeted five aircraft leaving the UK in the next few days. A second wave of bombings was also planned, with greater numbers involved. The aim of the bombers, according to intercepted internet traffic, was to cause maximum death and destruction. The deputy commissioner for the London Metropolitan Police said that the aim of the terrorists was to commit 'mass murder on an unimaginable scale' and cause untold death and destruction. Reports from Pakistani intelligence suggested the direct involvement of senior Kashmiri militants linked to al-Qaeda (which had been held responsible for the 11 September 2001 attacks). The arrests had to be made when they were because an attack was deemed imminent.

The terrorists planned to hide micro-bombs in false bottoms of opaque energy drink bottles, enabling them to still drink from the bottle if needed. Experts were reported to suggest that the explosives were probably stable peroxide material, similar to that used in the 7 July attacks of 2005. While it would be difficult to blow up an airliner completely with a small liquid-based bomb, it could be done by concentrating on weak spots (such as windows) or by a combination of bombs on the same aircraft.

Raids were conducted in London, Birmingham and Buckinghamshire to detain suspects. The majority were young British Asian men of Pakistani descent, many holding dual nationality. At least one, however, was a white British convert to Islam. Some international media sources claimed that at least five terrorists were still at large.

The police teams were conducting a meticulous search of all properties associated with the suspects and also initiated a widespread search of their local neighbourhoods – including woods.

Box 9.1 (cont.)

The national threat level was raised to 'critical' – the highest possible – because Britain was still deemed to be at risk of an 'imminent' attack.

In SARF terminology, the risk event could be said to be the announcement of the terrorist plot and arrest of suspects. The declaration of the plot resulted in a series of secondary effects in quick succession. Strict security instructions were issued to airports and airlines on 10 August. They included a ban on all hand luggage, with the exception of essential items (e.g. medication). Gels and liquids were strictly banned, with the exception of baby milk (which parents were told they would have to taste before being allowed to take it on to the aircraft).

The immediate effect was chaos in airports. 185,000 people had been due to pass through Heathrow alone on 10 August. Hundreds of flights were cancelled and all delayed (some by many hours). All of this was happening at the height of the summer season. The CEO of the BAA, the airports operators, claimed that they had never before faced a security mandate of this scale and severity. Nevertheless, all seven of the BAA airports stayed open. Within the same day, most of the country's airports returned to normal, though delays persisted. The initial ban on short-haul flights into Heathrow was lifted by the end of 10 August, but by then many long-haul flights had also been cancelled. At Heathrow, crowds from the 314 cancelled flights were asked to leave, but it took hours for people to leave – many had packed car keys in checked-in baggage. The scene was replicated around Britain (at Manchester, Stansted, Gatwick, Birmingham, Glasgow, etc.).

Tightened security caused initial confusion among passengers with evidence that information and explanation was inadequate. Lengthy queues snaked around the terminal buildings. Passengers showed remarkable patience and restraint. Staff offered reassurance but had no information to supply. There was evidence of a resignation on the part of passengers that they must tolerate this chaos in the interests of dealing with the terrorists. The authorities were not blamed for the problems. But the media are quick to condemn airport authorities for not having security systems and technology that can detect the sort of threat posed by modern terrorists. In the absence of good systems, the heightened security requirements were said to be likely to result in chaos at airports for at least a month.

By 11 August, media reports included comments from those who knew some of the people arrested. They were reported variously to be

Box 9.1 (cont.)

well respected in the community, peaceful, religious, pleasant, and converts to a devout form of Islam.

Since the technology of detection in airports and the international standards of security it demands have changed very little in the past three decades, calls for a revamp appear immediately on 11 August. Reports anticipate that the new hand luggage curbs may become permanent. This possibly causes more anxiety among the travelling public than the original threat. Images of people carrying their small number of allowed hand baggage items in transparent plastic bags appear everywhere in the media. It is suggested that the scare could speed the introduction of full-body X-rays and the use of sniffer or puffer machines. Failures in the ability of the authorities to introduce these changes earlier are condemned. The case of the 1994 attempts by terrorists to blow up a Philippines airliner using liquid explosives is used to illustrate that security improvements have not occurred quickly enough.

Already on 11 August, the press were explaining that travellers who had suffered delays or cancellations would face a struggle to get compensation or to claim on their insurance policies from airlines.

Also on 11 August, *The Times* (and others) was reporting that Muslim community leaders in Britain were 'braced for a backlash' and were 'warning politicians and the press not to exacerbate resentment within their community through Islamophobic attacks'. They argued that, as a result of the discovery of the plot, Muslims would be further stigmatised. It should be noted here that a two-sided backlash was anticipated – both against the Muslim community and by the Muslim community against the authorities whom some believed to be victimising them.

The international dimension of the plot is explained. The Pakistan authorities confirmed the arrests were a result of active collaboration between themselves and the British intelligence forces. The importance for Pakistan to be seen to be dealing with this case is emphasised because it has been accused of failing the international community by harbouring and training terrorists. In many of the stories there is a reference to the 7 July 2005 bombing in London and the fact that the perpetrators were British Muslims and some had been trained at madrasas in Pakistan. The link between the new plot and the earlier attacks is made.

Also on 11 August, the press report that £220 million had been wiped off the share value of British Airways (the main airline carrier in

Box 9.1 (cont.)

the UK) on 10 August as it cancelled hundreds of flights. Its profits were predicted to fall by £10 million for every day of disruption. Other airlines reported massive losses (including EasyJet and Ryanair). Investors were worried by the long-term costs of this security threat. It is stated that airlines had only just recovered from the 9/11 attacks. Other share prices fell, but particularly those of travel-related companies. Accountants were reported to have estimated that the single day of the terror alert cost the UK economy about £3.2 million for every hour of disruption.

President Bush is reported to have said that the plot to set off multiple explosions in US aircraft should serve 'as a stark reminder that this nation is at war with Islamic fascists who will use any means to destroy those who love freedom'. The possible link of the plot to al-Qaeda is made repeatedly. The parallel is drawn with the Operation Bojinka plot in 1995 in the Philippines, in which improvised bombs using liquid in contact lens solutions containers would have been detonated on a dozen flights over the Pacific.

Despite the arrests of the accused plotters, there is repeated mention that the threat has not gone away – the security level is still critical. It is re-emphasised that the security services have foiled thirteen terrorist plots in the previous year.

Even on 11 August, the press is reflecting on the errors the police and security forces had made in handling the 7 July 2005 bombings and the more recent failures of intelligence that had led to a raid on the home and arrest of two Muslims who proved to be innocent. The damaging details of the shooting of an innocent man, Jean Charles de Menezes, in the London Underground, which had occurred following the July 2005 bombings, were retold. The possibility that the police intelligence might be in error about this new plot is raised. Members of the Muslim community are reported to be sceptical about the police claims that a plot existed, claiming that it was being used to distract attention from governmental policies on the Lebanon–Israel conflict (which had reached a critical point). Non-Muslims also voice the argument that, if Britain was not involved in Iraq, not allied to the US, not active in Afghanistan, and so on, it would not be a target for terrorists. They use the plot as a means of attacking government policies across a broad spectrum.

By **13 August**, one newspaper was reporting 'Britain is facing a horrifying Summer of War blitz from Muslim terrorists – the police fear last week's airline plot was just the beginning'. It then revealed the

Box 9.1 (cont.)

security services were 'secretly battling another 30 Islamist murder plots'. On the same day, this newspaper called for the use of passenger profiling at all airports, ID cards and tougher border controls and an increase to the time suspects can be held without charge. The language in other papers was more muted, but the message was the same: as many as 1,200 people in Britain were involved in terrorism, many dozens of plots were being hatched, and an apocalyptic wave of attacks was planned.

BAA, which runs the major UK airports, is attacked by both BA and Ryanair for allowing Heathrow to move to 'meltdown'. Three days into the event, BAA was ordering airlines to axe one in three flights from Heathrow. This was put down to the fact that BAA could not cope with the intensified security checks required. Each transatlantic flight cancelled could cost the carrier up to £300,000. BAA was also beleaguered by a massive slump in its retail sales from airport shops as a result of the security restrictions on take-on baggage. BAA claimed that if the security restrictions required by government were maintained, then the delays would continue. The potential importance of passenger-profiling techniques to fast-track low-risk travellers is strongly mooted. However, a further source of delay was identified as coming from the US, who required Advanced Passenger Information Screening to be done on all passengers outbound to the US before the plane was allowed to leave the airport. These checks were taking long periods.

Ministers are reported to actively reject the link between the terrorist plots and their foreign policy, particularly that in Iraq.

The broader significance of the arrests for the British Muslim community is reiterated. The need to address questions of integration, multiculturalism, religious separatism and so on is debated. The concept of the Muslim community having to deal with its own 'extremists' is promulgated.

14 August: Muslim leaders speak about their desire to modernise and to engage in the democratic process. The Home Secretary reports that the terror threat is still critical and further terrorist cells are being investigated. BAA explains that it cannot simply increase the numbers of security searches in order to reduce delays, because it takes a month to obtain security clearance for them. BAA indicates that the new security measures are not sustainable.

15 August: Government revises security rules to allow one small piece of hand luggage on the plane. A further terrorist suspect is arrested.

Box 9.1 (cont.)

16 August: Ryanair again attacks BAA for 'paralysing' Stansted airport. BAA criticise government security measures – pointing out that terrorists could just switch their focus to flights coming into Britain and would be subject to no stringent checks such as those imposed in the UK. Inconsistencies in security checks were reported to be the topic for a meeting of European security ministers that day. A common approach to airport security in Europe was to be developed. Duty-free industry and airport retail worldwide reported to have lost millions (mainly due to lost alcohol and perfume sales). Looting of lost luggage is reported – about 10,000–20,000 passenger bags had gone missing since the alert began. David Cameron, leader of the Conservative Party, is reported to have accused the government of doing too little to fight terrorism and extremism. He also urged the introduction of a new law to allow the use of intercept evidence in court, the creation of a single ministerial post in charge of counter-terrorism, and a dedicated border police force and a replacement of the Human Rights Act with a British Bill of Rights. The proposals for security profiling of passengers are accused of leading to problems if they are based on ethnicity or religion, since it would further alienate the Muslim community.

17 August: Authorities evacuate the terminal at the Tri-State Airport of Huntington in West Virginia after a test on two plastic containers carried by a female passenger showed a possible explosive. On another flight, a woman outbound from Heathrow was found to have managed to bring several banned items on board. She was behaving erratically and claimed connections with Pakistan. The captain declared an emergency and diverted to Boston airport, escorted by two US F16 fighter jets. BAA was accused of a lapse in security, having allowed her to board the flight with proscribed objects.

18 August: Virgin Atlantic airline calls for a Competition Commission inquiry into BAA. Analysts suggest that the airlines will use the disruptions associated with the terror event to support their case for the break-up of BAA. The airlines object to BAA because they argue that it is a multi-tier monopoly: it is the monopoly owner and operator of its airports; it controls seven airports across the country; and it controls the shops that go into the airports.

A suitcase full of bomb-making equipment is found by police searching a wood close to the homes of some of the suspects arrested.

20 August: Reports that holiday-makers refused to allow their UK-bound flight to leave Malaga airport until two men who were 'of Asian

Box 9.1 (cont.)

appearance' were removed. The men were found to represent no threat and were sent on a later plane. UK Muslim leaders use this to illustrate the prejudice to which innocent Muslims are subjected. Police reported to be trying to track down sixteen potential suicide bombers trained at an al-Qaeda camp on the Afghan–Pakistan border. The fact that BAA had been bought by a Spanish company in July 2006 is reported in the context of questions about its capacity to respond to what has been a national crisis. Warnings emerge that there will be further chaos at airports in a few days' time as Britain has a bank holiday and the numbers seeking to fly swell again. Another security lapse by BAA is reported – a man is allowed through several checkpoints with neither boarding card nor passport. The Home Secretary is reported to be seeking powers to detain terror suspects without trial and to be demanding much tougher anti-terrorism powers. Whitehall is reported to fear that the Metropolitan Police Force is using the case as a means of redressing the bad PR it had received for earlier botched operations. Details of the sorts of security screening that will be introduced (including behavioural analysis and technological scanning) in the future are described. The problems with passenger profiling that used race or religion as a criterion were again debated.

Failure to find evidence against a suspect detained in Pakistan and thought to be the 'mastermind' behind the plot stimulates further questions about the reality of the threat.

Share prices of BA and EasyJet show recovery; Ryanair has not recovered.

21 August: Eleven suspects arrested on 10 August are charged. Police disclose they have discovered bomb-making and martyrdom videos (i.e. recordings made for broadcast after the suicide bombings have occurred). Eight of the eleven were charged with conspiracy to murder and a new offence of preparing acts of terrorism. The other three were charged with offences under the Terrorism Act 2000. Eleven other suspects remain in custody. One woman is released without charge. Very full details of the investigations conducted by the police are reported, including indications of the huge volume of evidence collected.

National state of alert reported to have been lowered to 'severe'.

This is the point where we choose to arbitrarily cut off the description of this illustration. In reality, it would not be too far-fetched to say that the effects and the reinterpretations of the risk event will continue

Box 9.1 (cont.)

for many years. The line has to be drawn somewhere for the sake of practicality – even though it would be fascinating to follow it further.

A BRIEF SARF ANALYSIS

Using the SARF approach to the analysis of even this small amount of data on the events that took place in the eleven-day period focuses attention upon the way the original risk event (the announcement of the plot) was followed by a complex set of amplification and attenuation processes, and by rippled secondary effects. The first interesting feature to notice is how quickly the amplification/attenuation processes start to have an effect, but also how very quickly the secondary effects occur. Within twenty-four hours we see the plot is not an isolated incident – there are many other terrorist activities under investigation – and the plot is just the tip of an iceberg of threat from the Islamic extremists. The plot is contextualised within a constellation of other thwarted and successful attacks and is talked about as being much worse than any other. It is even located within 'the war on terror'.

We also see immediate secondary political (nationally and internationally – particularly relating to foreign policy on Iraq, Lebanon and Afghanistan) impacts, economic impacts (e.g. airline share values), regulatory changes (e.g. security protocols), calls for legislative change (e.g. with regard to anti-terrorism laws), pressure for commercial restructuring (e.g. claims that BAA 'monopoly' should be dismantled), and intergroup tension increases (e.g. the response towards and by the Muslim community). Reputational issues come to the fore: the motives of the police; the competence of the airport authority; and trustworthiness or foreign policy probity of political leaders. It is quite startling to realise how quickly these secondary effects can occur.

The second interesting feature to note is that the secondary effects themselves serve to amplify and change the meaning of the original risk event. For instance, the fact that, under the increased pressure of changed regulations, there are failures of airport security, suggests that air travellers really are at greater risk of a successful terrorist attack. Also, the looting of lost baggage makes the risk event seem more grievous in its personal consequences; so does the problem identified with compensation and insurance claims.

The sequence of events also serves to highlight that it is necessary to consider the ripple effects for different groups of people and

Box 9.1 (cont.)

institutions. Every single target identified in Figure 9.1 as possibly affected through rippling was affected here. This risk event had global implications but also massive individual effects.

The third interesting feature to consider is the stigmatisation process that occurs for the Muslim community. It is particularly worth noting that not only does this occur (illustrated dramatically by the ejection of the two men from the Malaga flight and also by the calls for passenger profiling), but it is also anticipated by the Muslim community itself. This risk event is not the start of stigmatisation; it is just another basis for sustaining and extending it.

The fourth feature concerns the countervailing attenuation processes that were evident in some parts of the Muslim community. Some people were claiming that the accusations were false, that those arrested were not the sort of people who would be involved in an attack, that the security forces were engaged in a face-saving exercise and there really was no evidence of any plot. The Muslim community was not alone in voicing scepticism. Others were audibly questioning whether the security forces had evidence and whether the supposed bomb-making method could possibly work in a modern aircraft. This representation might be seen to have a longer-term advantage: it attenuates the risk and would justify a return to the use of air travel.

This pattern supports the SARF assertion that amplification and attenuation can be going on simultaneously, driven by different interest groups. It may be important to recognise that this attenuation effort was concerned solely with the alleged plot itself (the original risk event); it did not extend to an attempt to reinterpret the secondary effects of the risk event (except in so far as passenger profiling using ethnicity was claimed to be victimisation). The amplification process was much more widespread: secondary effects were themselves treated as risk events in their own right and were then subject to amplification. For example, the effect of disruption on the airlines was identified as the genesis of a long-term and escalating risk for them in terms of profitability, but also for their customers because increased costs would be passed on in airfares.

This example of the unfurling of a risk event also suggests that if the processes at work in amplification and rippling are to be understood fully, a complex array of data would need to be collected in the wake of any risk event. The layering method described in this chapter offers one way to do this.

Box 9.1 (cont.)

The final point worth emphasising here is that the example points to the significance of hazard sequences in determining the way amplification or attenuation works. This risk event was systematically described, and its importance calibrated, against other relevant events. Amplification of the risk looked at it in comparison with other attempts (like the planned Philippines aircraft bombing) or attacks (like the 7 July 2005 bombs in London or those of 11 September 2001 in the USA) – the similarities and differences were highlighted and the lessons and predictions that could be taken from the previous incidents were elaborated. The 10 August risk event was interpreted in the frame of these sequences. Similarly, the attenuation process used the same approach. The risk event was set against in this case a whole array of security and police force errors in accusations and actions against Muslims in the UK and internationally. The hazard sequence used was different, because this frame interpreted the risk event in terms of victimisation. Understanding further the use of hazard sequences in establishing the bases for amplification/attenuation would seem to be valuable.

2   Research based on SARF

Kasperson *et al.* (2003) provide an excellent review of some of the empirical studies to which SARF has given rise, and the presentation here owes a lot to their summary. It would be inappropriate to suggest that the studies 'test' SARF. Since SARF itself is not a theory and specifies no unambiguous testable hypotheses, it would be inappropriate to conceive of these studies as attempts to prove (or disprove) SARF. Instead, they are illustrations of some of the relationships that SARF considers important. Essentially, the studies suggest:

- **Risk signals**

  Hazards generate different signals (i.e. messages embedded in symbols, metaphors and images) over time – for instance, Kasperson *et al.* (1992) examined the 'signal stream' associated with the proposed siting of a nuclear waste repository at Yucca Mountain in the USA between 1985 and 1989 that appeared in a local newspaper, and showed that a shift occurred during this period from a focus on the specific risk itself to issues of victimisation, distrust, villainy and unfairness. One can see something akin to this shift occurring in the case study presented in Box 9.2.

Box 9.2 The layering method

Indices of each theoretically important element in the amplification/ attenuation or ripple processes should be mapped on the timeline. For instance, a not exhaustive list:

- assessment of estimated risk of the hazard and levels of concern (perhaps by each or at least several significant 'stations')
- physical assessments of the risk event impact (e.g. number of deaths, number ill, area evacuated, etc.)
- volume of messages about the risk event and its implications (identified by source)
- valence of messages about the risk event and its implications (identified by source
- economic consequences of the risk event
- political consequences of the risk event
- legal consequences of the risk event.

. . . .

Time Zero   End Point
Timeline (measured in whatever unit seems appropriate
– hours, days, weeks, months, years, etc.)

Time Zero may be the point immediately after the risk event occurs, but it could be earlier if data are available. This may be enormously valuable, because then the nature of the impact of the risk event upon ongoing processes can be better estimated.

Preferably these indices should be mapped on to the timeline graphically. Juxtaposing each of the indices chosen on the timeline graphically may be artificial, since the scales on which each index will be measured will probably differ. However, that sort of superimposition of the profiles of each of the indices in terms of the same timeline is very informative. It highlights the simultaneity or disjuncture of the amplification/attenuation and ripple effects. It can throw into stark relief the way sometimes different 'stations' are moving in opposite directions. For instance, had the layering method been used to examine the case of the 10 August 2006 terrorist plot, it could have exposed the way elements of the Muslim community tended to attenuate and elements of other communities tended to amplify the hazard.

The layering method is also most likely to reveal feedback loops and interactions in the amplification/attenuation process, because it requires the researcher to look over time and beyond bivariate relationships. This is an advantage to those working with SARF, because there have been claims in the past that they treat the amplification process as unidirectional.

There is also a suggestion that some hazards have greater 'signal strength'. Slovic *et al.* (1985) report that those hazards located in the top right quadrant of the dread/known factor space (see Figure 2.5) have a greater capacity to generate symbols and images with high impact, perhaps linked to their perceived capacity to produce more serious secondary and tertiary effects. This suggestion seems plausible; however, direct evidence on 'signal strength' is not available.

- **Hidden hazards**

A corollary to the argument that hazards generate different signal strengths is the proposition that some can be hidden by the process of attenuation. This is a very interesting and useful notion. Kasperson and Kasperson (1991) offer an explanation for the existence of 'hidden hazards'. They describe five aspects of such hazards that motivate attenuation:

  ○ *Global elusive hazards* – involve a series of complex problems (international interactions, long time lags, diffuse effects, etc.) and their signal power is muted in many societies by the inequalities and fragmentation between nations and cultures.
  ○ *Ideological hazards* – lie embedded in a system of beliefs and values that attenuates the consequences of the hazard.
  ○ *Marginal hazards* – affect people who are at the margins of society, who have little power, and whose problems are not a focus of attention for mainstream society.
  ○ *Amplification-driven hazards* – occur as a secondary consequence of other hazards and exist below the threshold of recognition (this can of course be a temporary phase in the life of a hazard).
  ○ *Value-threatening hazards* – alter lifestyles and basic values but are not recognised because societal attention is elsewhere (e.g. concerned with what are considered to be more important issues, such as conflicts, profit and physical survival).

In analyses of environmental degradation and delayed societal responses, Kasperson *et al.* (1995) have illustrated the existence of such distinct hazard types.

- **Factors affecting amplification/attenuation**

Kasperson (1992) reports six case studies of nuclear accidents. The conclusions were:

  ○ The risk events were not predictably linked to amplification or genesis of secondary effects, and such effects seem to be mediated by pre-accident trust in the relevant authorities and by the way the actual event was handled. Several factors may need to be present before an event will trigger an amplification process intense enough to initiate secondary effects.

○ Amplification/attenuation may occur simultaneously but at different levels in the social structure (e.g. attenuation may occur locally but amplification happen nationally).

○ If the risk is associated with economic benefits, attenuation may result.

There have been other studies that examine the factors that may affect amplification. For instance, McComas (2003) conducted a longitudinal study of members of a community facing the expansion of an existing solid waste landfill. She found that community members who attended initial public meetings about the proposal manifested intensification of the risk perceived and erosion of trust in those managing the site. There are many studies that show in relation to specific hazards that particular factors affect the representation of the risk. There is, however, no coherent pattern to these findings.

• **Role in deliberate risk-taking**

Machlis and Rosa (1990) and Rosa (1998, 2003) suggested that the SARF could be used to explain how desired risks or deliberate risk-taking are interpreted. While some of the terminology in the framework (e.g. the use of the label 'victims') can be seen to be inappropriate for desired risk, the overall approach is applicable.

• **Role of the mass media**

In the SARF, which focuses upon the significance of interpretation of risk through communication, it is inevitable that the mass media might be expected to play a fundamental role. There have been many analyses of the way the media report risks and risk events (see Chapter 6). Specifically in relation to the propositions of SARF, the work of Mazur (1990) is interesting. He analysed mass media coverage of nuclear power and chemical hazards and proposed a model with four interrelated propositions: (1) it is important to distinguish between the substantive content of a news story about a risk and the simpler image (signal) that the story conveys; (2) public concern about a risk rises as media coverage increases; (3) public action to deal with the risk increases or decreases in line with the volume of media coverage; (4) a small number of national media organisations are very influential in choosing which hazards receive attention at any one time. It is important to recognise that Mazur is not suggesting that any one of these propositions can be seen to capture the role of the media in the processes of amplification/attenuation. For instance, volume of coverage alone will not trigger heightened public concern. As Renn (1991) asserts, volume is only one route through which the media can affect public (or indeed institutional) concern. There are many elements in the presentation of the story, especially one which runs over an extended period of time, which will influence the way the risk is perceived. They include:

o the precise content of the information – particularly its capacity to arouse emotional responses or trigger associations with other concerns

o the format of the information – for instance, the order in which it occurs in a news bulletin or in the newspaper will signal importance

o contextualisation matters – for instance by juxtaposing a risk story with another that is also high risk, both stories could achieve heightened impact.

Frewer *et al.* (2002a, 2002b) illustrated the operation of the media in relation to amplification concerning genetically modified foods, arguing that people's risk perceptions do increase or decrease in accordance with the complex interaction of the volume of risk information provided by the media, the independent accuracy and actual content of the information, the evident disagreement between various actors in the risk debate, the extent of dramatisation of the risk information, and the symbolic connotations incorporated into the coverage.

However, as a general rule, as was indicated in Chapter 6, it is not sensible to talk about 'the' effects of 'the' mass media. The mass media are highly differentiated (not just between types of media – the press, the radio and TV, and increasingly the web-based providers – but between forms within these types). If there is one rule to be applied to them, it is that no single rule can be applied to them. Since the structure of media provision has changed so much in the last few years as information technologies and the public uptake of those technologies has changed, it is truly uncertain how the media work to amplify risk or to generate ripple effects. That they do have these effects is undoubted (Vaughan and Seifert, 1992). The real question is how they have these effects in an era of twenty-four-hour news and immediate access through personal electronic communication.

• *The role of complex organisations*

SARF specifies that organisations and institutions will play a role in amplification and attenuation of risk events but will also be the recipients of the impacts, through the ripple effects, of those events. We have already seen in Chapter 8 many of the ways in which complex organisations moderate and mediate the risk event: through the way they plan for it, the way they manage it, the way they recover from it, even through the way they may deny or hide it. Freudenburg (1992) examined the characteristics of organisations that serve to attenuate risk signals. They include lack of commitment to the risk-management function, bureaucratic slowness in the flow of news (particularly bad news), the existence of gaps in corporate responsibility for hazard vigilance, mismatches in resource allocation and goal-setting, and a culture of risk-taking by the workforce.

• *Stigmatisation*
Kasperson *et al.* (1988) hypothesised that stigmatisation was one of the four major mechanisms (the others being: the use of heuristics and value filters, changes in intergroup relationships and modification in risk signal values) whereby the amplification process can generate ripple and secondary effects. In the past, stigma has been used to refer to the negative imagery associated with undesirable individuals or social groups. Kasperson *et al.* proposed that hazards could also be stigmatised. Hazards that are stigmatised would be shunned and attacked in the same way that other stigmatised objects are treated. The role of stigmatisation is further considered in Chapter 6. It is important not to become mesmerised by the word 'stigmatisation'. Essentially, all we are talking about is the fact that negative images are attached to hazards. Once attached, these images have the power to attract other negative images to the hazard. The package of negative images stimulates not only negative emotions but also biases in cognitive processing of information. However, the stigma is not necessarily just attached to the hazard itself; it can transfer to places, people, products or technologies associated with the hazard. Thus the geographical location of a GM crop, the tomato sauce produced by those GM crops and the firm that makes the tomato sauce can all find themselves stigmatised by the process that assigns stigma to GM technologies. This form of 'stigma contamination' is a secondary effect of risk amplification.

Kasperson *et al.* (2001) extended the social amplification framework to focus upon stigmatisation. In this version, the risk event generates a flow of communication that influences risk perceptions and images, but this simultaneously 'marks' associated places, products and technologies. 'Marking' is said to involve the selection of some attribute of the object. This can be tied to labelling the attribute (for example, 'Frankenstein food' was a label attached to GM food). Marking pinpoints the negative aspects of the identity of the product, place or technology that has been derived from the hazard. It is this, usually easy-to-remember, label that is reused in the communication process and which shifts the balance of the evaluation of the object towards the negative. The stigma is thus attached to the object and can stimulate further secondary effects – for instance, in the public acceptability of the object or in regulatory impositions upon it. Since stigmatisation is a potent process, and one which is relatively uncontrollable once initiated, it needs to be researched further.

- *The role of trust and confidence*

Kasperson *et al.* (2003) point out that trust was not a factor included in the original framework as a determiner of the amplification process. They argue that it should have been. The significance of trust in the source of a message in determining the impact of risk communications has been examined in Chapter 6.

It is worth reiterating here that the efficacy of any communication will be driven by the extent to which the communicator is trusted, but the relationship between trust and amplification/attenuation is not mapped out. While it is possible to study the relationship between trust in a communicator and belief in their message or compliance with their instructions at an individual or societal level, it is not so simple to study systematically the relationship between trust and amplification/attenuation. This is because the process of amplification/attenuation is one that occurs through the interaction of many communicators (many stations). To isolate one message source and to examine the extent to which it is trusted might be possible. To examine every relevant message source and determine how their relative trustworthiness affects the way their messages are received might be possible. However, to assess the overall, dynamic, interactive level of trust in the multitudinous sources of communication in the aftermath of the risk event might be rather difficult, not just empirically, but also because we have no model of how trust in a complex network of often conflicting sources is generated or changed. There is the added complexity that, when dealing with risk amplification and ripple effects, we are not just dealing with individual reactions to this complex panoply of sources. We are dealing with institutional and organisational responses, sometimes internationally. Estimating levels of trust in any coherent way would be challenging, to put it mildly. Add to this the fact that the dependent measure is not an individual's changed perceptions or behaviour (or even an institution's changed perceptions or behaviour) but rather the entire system's amplification of risk and the broader ripple effects. This does make an empirically tested model of the relationship between trust and amplification seem a remote prospect.

Nevertheless, there is no need to abandon the examination of trust and amplification. The task has to be broken into its component parts. Particularly promising is the work that explores what happens when an observable and quantifiable decrement in trust occurs with regard to one element in the complex communications network. As stated in Chapter 6, Slovic (1993) suggested that trust is slow to develop and easy to destroy. He posits the asymmetry principle to explain why it is easier to destroy than to earn trust: negative events are more visible than positive events because they are often more specific and less indistinct. Negative events are the basis for the erosion of trust and, since they are more likely to grab attention than positive events, trust is more likely to be destroyed than built. Since risk events are typically negative, it does suggest that trust will be eroded at the very moment that risk amplification processes will come into play.

- *Ripple effects*
Kasperson *et al.* (2003) recognise that there has been little empirical research that has specifically explored the relationship between the amplification/attenuation processes and ripple effects. There is obviously research that explores the secondary effects of a risk event. There are many examples elsewhere in this book that illustrate how organisations, economies and regulatory systems have been changed following a risk event (e.g. the Chernobyl accident, the BSE inquiry, the mox incident, etc.). However, these examples do not have a detailed analysis of how amplification occurred and how this directly induced secondary effects. It can be assumed that it did and that information flows in these events were shaped in the way SARF suggests. Yet what elements of the amplification process are causally linked to which secondary effects?

There is a further empirical lacuna: little is known about the relationship between different secondary effects – either in terms of the groups/ institutions affected or the types of effect.

3   Critiques of SARF

There have been various critiques of SARF. Many have been based upon a misunderstanding of the purpose of the framework. Some of these have criticised it for not being a theory (i.e. complete with predictive relationships between component concepts). Since SARF did not set out to be a theory in the first place, this is rather unfair. It is reminiscent of criticising a leopard for not being a horse.

However, beyond that form of criticism there are some other types of attack on SARF. For instance, Rayner (1988) did not like the metaphor on which SARF is based. He thought that it could be taken to imply that there is an underlying 'real' risk that is then 'distorted' by social communication processes. He also considered the framework implies passivity on the part of those receiving communications. Neither of these two implications was actually intended by SARF researchers. In fact, a moment's consideration of the framework should reveal that there is a fundamental social constructivist assumption in it. There is no suggestion that amplification produces a distortion in the sense of something that is incorrect or in error. Amplification/attenuation produces representation of the risk event. The framework is not concerned with evaluating whether these representations are right or distorted. The representations once generated are the functional reality.

This in turn is not meant to imply that a risk event is 'merely' a social construct. According to SARF, risk events have real consequences and these may be direct (the physical changes induced) and indirect (derived from the social processing of the risk – stigmatisation, group conflict, loss of trust, etc.). Rosa (2003) presents a detailed unpacking of the logical and philosophical status of the risk concept as it is used in SARF. He points out that there is a tendency in SARF expositions to avoid dealing with the question of whether the risk is 'real' by dealing with whether its consequences are 'real'. According to Rosa, this leaves the question: What is the object of amplification? Rosa proposes that SARF should clearly embrace a realist definition of risk as its starting point (based on ontological realism – i.e. the assumption that the world exists independent of percipient actors) and then be explicit about the social and cognitive processes that transform it into a social construct. While his argument is well made, it may be a retrograde step to seek to revisit these definitional and philosophical questions. Rosa, in turn, would need to be able to answer the question he originally posed: 'What is the real risk?' Empirically, how can he identify the real risk prior to any social representation of that risk? Surely, the moment that an individual is conscious that a physical event has occurred, representation processes are already implicated. This is not to assume that there is no world other than the one we create through representations. But it is to assume that in order to analyse that world we must have engaged in representation of it. The epistemological and ontological debate would seem to be never-ending. Perhaps a more useful way to proceed is to agree that the task is to properly understand the cognitive and social processes that are at work from that first moment of awareness. This is not unlike the position taken by the Astronomer Royal, Sir Martin Rees, about the genesis of the universe. He accepts that we do not know what preceded the big bang – and cannot therefore dismiss the possibility that God was at work – but the task is to map everything that happened subsequently without being too concerned about what the deity may have been doing.

Another form of attack, derived from the accusation that it is not a theory, is that the framework is incapable of offering any new insights beyond what other models already offer (Wåhlberg, 2001). The counter to this is provided by Kasperson (1992) when he says that SARF is designed to bring competing theories and small-scale models into direct conjunction or confrontation and allow their relative contributions to be explored, to provide a structure in which an array of fragmented empirical findings can be subjected to comparative interpretation, and to motivate new questions about the relationships between its conceptual elements. In fact, Kasperson et al. (2003) claim that a particular strength of the framework for developing policy interventions is its capacity to mesh together emerging findings from different avenues of risk research.

Other commentators have highlighted the relative simplicity of the model of risk communication that it encompasses. Handmer and Penning-Rowsell (1990) criticise the apparent one-way transfer of information that is assumed in SARF. This misconception may be forgiven because the original 1988 article was not explicit about the complexity of interaction feedback loops in the amplification process. The Kasperson et al. (2003) figure (Figure 9.1) representing the SARF eliminates the scope for this misreading of the original intention by showing the feedback channels.

Some (Rip, 1988; Svenson, 1988) have argued that the SARF is too focused upon individual level dynamics and not enough on the societal level. This criticism may apply less in the first decade of the twenty-first century after the further specification in the framework of the role of stigmatisation and social trust besides the work on organisational inputs to the amplification and ripple processes.

A final criticism probably has more substance. The SARF is said to underanalyse the way the mass media work in the amplification and ripple processes. Of course, the development of this analysis can be seen as ongoing. Kasperson et al. (2003) admit that the framework should be able to describe the amplification and attenuation rules used by the media institutions in their role between government and sections of society. Indeed, it should also be able to identify the amplification and attenuation rules that apply to other institutions.

Breakwell and Barnett (2001) have argued that some refinement of the description of amplification processes might help to eradicate some of the difficulties that people have, both with the metaphor underlying SARF and with the movement towards using it to make predictions of what will happen following a risk event. Kasperson et al. (1988) in their original paper stated that amplification denotes the process of intensifying or attenuating signals during the transmission of information from an information source. In saying this, they were following the classic communications system terminology. However, in their own work they were actually using amplification to mean something more than quantitative intensification or attenuation. In fact, they use the concept to refer to

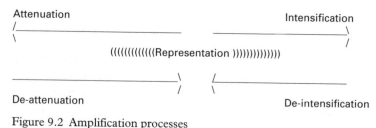

Figure 9.2 Amplification processes

qualitative restructuring of the signal (message) – a change in its meaning or significance, not just a change of degree.

Breakwell and Barnett suggested that the variety of different modifications that amplification can bring about should be better explained. They started by suggesting that, as a bare minimum, amplification should be treated as the generic term for these processes and intensification should be recognised as a discrete process. They also argued that intensification and attenuation inevitably (because of their common language meanings) are interpreted to be concerned with quantity. They proposed that some communication following a risk event will be concerned with establishing the 'representation' of the hazard and this may be predominantly about the characteristics or qualities of the hazard not its severity. They also point out that there are separate processes of de-intensification and de-attenuation that can occur. De-attenuation is not quite equivalent to amplification because it can be a process of pulling the image of the risk back from a low level but not reaching the point at which it started. Similarly, but obversely, de-intensification is not the simple equivalent to attenuation. Figure 9.2 presents the relations of these processes. Following Breakwell and Barnett, it would be useful to ensure that separate measures of intensification, attenuation, representation, de-intensification and de-attenuation are considered in empirical studies of amplification processes. In fact, Poumadère et al. (2005) provide an interesting example of how de-attenuation can occur. They describe how the dangers of heatwaves have been attenuated in France in the past but, as a result of the 2003 heatwave in that country, have been de-attenuated.

4   The layering method

It is easy to see from the Box 9.1 illustration that any researcher who wishes to fully understand amplification and ripple processes involved in a significant risk event will need to collect data at many levels: the psychological, sociological, political, economic, legal, technological and scientific – to identify only the main requirements. Arguments made here would also suggest that historical data would be vital. Such multi-level data collections are rare. They are time-consuming, they require enormous resources if they are to be done properly, and they require multi-disciplinary expertise. Even when researchers see the value of such an analysis, they can be dissuaded by the practical difficulties it entails.

Nevertheless, when it can be done, it may be the route to a thorough exploration of amplification and ripple phenomena. Breakwell and Barnett (2003b) have suggested one approach that might be more regularly used. This method, which they have called 'the layering method', entails:

- Collection of data that are situated at various levels of analysis. At the individual level this may include evidence of cognitions, affect and behaviour. At the societal level it might use data at both structural and processual levels. For instance, it could include evidence of shifts in political policy, the structure of groups, the relationships between groups, communication patterns, economic indicators, scientific and technological innovation or practices, and so on. Effectively, the task is to collect data which reflect what is happening to the individuals and institutions (defined broadly) that might be affected by the risk event.
- Data from these different levels are 'layered' such that it is possible to see for one moment in time the data at each of the levels that are relevant to the amplification and ripple effects of the risk event.
- Data from each of the levels are also collected over time, allowing multiple time-points to be compared. These comparisons can be between different times on the same level of analysis. For instance, attitudes might be tracked over time. In addition, these comparisons can be between levels of analysis over time. This entails identifying the temporal profiles in data across levels of analysis. For instance, while attitudes (e.g. health attitudes) are tracked over time, the incidence of a particular illness is also tracked with the same data sampling time-points.

The method generates layers of data arranged at different levels of analysis tied together by a clearly defined time frame. The method does not stipulate which levels of analysis should be used. It does not determine how data should be collected. It does not require a particular type of statistical analysis. The method is rather a way of getting researchers to think about relationships between data at different levels of analysis and ensuring that they take temporal sequences in data seriously. It is, in some ways, ideally suited to the SARF approach. SARF requires multi-dimensional approaches to data collection if it is to evolve towards predicting amplification/attenuation and ripple effects. The layering method can be used to identify the relationships between the various components in the SARF. For instance, it can be used to look at how, following a risk event, the various 'stations' react and interact, the information sources and channels are used, the behaviour patterns of individuals and institutions change, and the legislative, economic, political, etc., effects appear. Box 9.2 illustrates the sort of structure for data collection that the layering method generates.

Breakwell and Barnett (2003b) present two examples of the use of the layering method, analysing data concerning developments following the official notifications of, first, the BSE/CJD hazard (1988–2000) and, second, the HIV/AIDS hazard (1984–2000). They show how the formal history of the diseases unfolds in terms of government pronouncements and actions. They show how the media represent the diseases throughout this time. They provide evidence of public attitudes towards the diseases during the period. Economic and medical data relevant to the diseases through the period are presented. Since their analyses are reliant upon a variety of sources (e.g. individual research projects, government statistics, information from commercial sources, etc.), there are problems in matching perfectly the time frames over which data were collected. Nevertheless, the examples given illustrate that the layering method could be a powerful tool in examining amplification and ripple effects. For instance, they show from their BSE/CJD analyses that levels of public anxiety about food hazards are not related directly to the volume of media reportage of those hazards. They show that apparent levels of public concern are highly dependent upon the method used to elicit information and provide evidence that different subsections of the public move in opposite directions over time in the level of their concern. They also indicate that the amount of government spending on research concerning CJD/BSE is not related in any simple way to public concern levels and suggest that this pattern of government spend on research into these diseases is not simply related to the number of cases of the diseases – at certain points in the cycle, the rate of disease declines and the amount of research expenditure increases. Their analysis is correlational and inevitably partial, given its reliance upon secondary sources, but the study provides some sense of the scope that could be achieved by research that adopted the layering method.

5   Hazard sequences, hazard templates and hazard negotiations

Following detailed studies of a series of risk events using the SARF approach and implementing the layering method, Breakwell and Barnett (2001) suggested that there were certain discernible regularities in the way in which amplification processes worked that could provide the basis for the development of a more predictive model. They highlighted the roles of what they labelled 'hazard sequences', 'hazard templates' and 'hazard negotiations'.

- *Hazard sequences*

  This is a simple notion: any one risk event is often represented or conceptualised as part of a sequence of risk events that share common features. So, for instance, a train crash will be viewed within the frame of a series of other train crashes, just as the terrorist plot against aircraft used in the Box 9.1 illustration was referenced in terms of other terrorist attempts and attacks. Barnett and Breakwell (2003) report how the 1995 oral contraception pill scare was reported and was interpreted in terms of other health scares that concerned either oral contraceptives or hormone replacement therapies. The existence of the hazard sequence allows the new risk event to be located in terms of its severity and meaning because it offers the backcloth of knowledge about similar events in the past. Reference to other past risk events can also provide the emotional connotations necessary to achieve either intensification or attenuation.

  Following any risk event, there is the scope for interested 'stations' to seek to construct the hazard sequence that works best for their own purposes. The hazard sequences that are chosen and the way they are used should be the object of research. There may be certain obvious similarities between the substance of a series of hazards (e.g. they are all bomb plots) that encourage their use in a hazard sequence. They have to be readily identifiable as falling within the same category in some respects, because otherwise the sequence could not be used to add value and ease to communications about the risk event. However, sometimes the link between the hazards used in a sequence is more tenuous. For instance, in the case of the mox incident at Sellafield (described in Chapter 8), the hazard sequence concerned not just safety lapses (which are similar in substance to the risk event) but also risks associated with the financial viability of the company. Together the safety and financial risks were used to intensify concern about the new risk event. The point to remember is that hazards in a sequence can be of totally different types: technical, managerial, financial, etc.

- *Hazard templates*

  This idea to some extent flows from the notion of hazard sequences. Breakwell and Barnett (2001) suggest that, when a new risk event occurs, the way it will be represented will be determined by the 'templates' that already exist for the representation of that type of risk. The template will provide a ready-made phrase to be used about it. It will provide common explanations for the origin of the risk event, the individuals, groups or institutions who should be held responsible, the forms of remedial or punishment action that should be taken, etc. The form of the template is roughly common across hazards, but the substantive content will differ widely. So, for instance, the template for a multi-car smash on the motorway in fog (e.g. reckless drivers, driving too close and too fast; poor signage; overcrowded motorways causing increasing occurrence; need for improved driver training and motorway control; efficient response of the emergency services who worked tirelessly; etc.) is different from the template for an outbreak of food poisoning in a hotel (e.g. poor hygiene, poor management, inadequate regulatory controls, increasing incidence of such cases, etc.). Nevertheless, some underlying similarities emerge: the cause, the significance, the responsibility and the redress.

These templates are commonly used by the mass media to structure their stories but they are also the frameworks that lay people use when they come to talk about a new risk event. They appear to have a risk vocabulary and rhetoric that is built upon understandings and expectations of the way different hazards work. These understandings and expectations are shared to varying degrees. The issues of how, and why, and when they are shared are considered further in this chapter.

Breakwell and Barnett (2001) note that the same template will often be used for different hazards identified to be part of a sequence. Also, the template will affect the type and amount of information which is sought and used.

- *Hazard negotiations*

Following a risk event, all those affected, directly or indirectly, are likely to have something to say about it. While the channels available to them to 'have their say' will vary in salience, there will be multitudinous voices. Amplification processes (*note*: they are taken by Breakwell and Barnett to encompass intensification, attenuation, representation, de-intensification and de-attenuation) will consequently involve the probably simultaneous presentation of varying messages about the risk event. The extent to which they are at variance will inevitably differ across risk events. However, to the extent that the sources of messages are aware that other messages are promulgated, they have the task of responding to these alternatives. This is where the concept of hazard negotiation has a role.

When 'stations' find that they are broadcasting messages about a risk event that are at variance with each other, there is scope for them to attempt to negotiate a common interpretation or, if this proves impossible, at least to seek a compatible set of interpretations. There are endless examples of the ways experts and lay publics differ in the representations that they generate about risk events. Many have been illustrated in this book (e.g. MMR, GM foods, naturally occurring radon gas, etc.). Often the differences in representation of the hazard are not reconciled. The public consultation mechanisms described in Chapter 6 can be seen as one route through which attempts to reconcile them are made. Such 'hazard negotiations' are formally structured exchanges with clear rules of engagement.

Yet often the exchanges are less peaceable; the negotiation takes place within conflict. For instance, this may be the case where protesters resist some change in their environment. The siting of mobile telecommunications masts has incited enormous resistance in recent years. Local residents claim health hazards associated with the masts, while the telecoms companies insist there is no significant hazard. Under these circumstances, the representations of the hazard may simply co-exist in opposition, but they may also evolve to take account of each other's existence. The protesters' representation of the hazard is refined to protect itself against the company's representation – and vice versa. This is a form of hazard negotiation. It is not a negotiation that leads to reconciliation and agreement. In fact, it is one which may even solidify and strengthen the opposing representations. Hazard negotiation is the dynamic process whereby different agents reform their own representation of the hazard while simultaneously influencing the representations that others hold of the hazard.

Breakwell and Barnett illustrate one way in which this occurs in a study of the reactions to the decision by Shell to expand their natural gas liquids facility in Fife, Scotland. An action group had originally opposed the establishment of the facility during the period 1977–9. Their representation of the risk levels was rejected at public inquiry and the facility was approved in 1979. The local risk was said to be outweighed by the national benefits, the positive local socio-economic impacts, and the argument that the plant could be designed to operate within an acceptable level of hazard. The action group focused their representation of the hazard upon the health and safety risks it entailed, but also the negative impact the plant would have upon the environment (i.e. noise, visual and marine pollution, interference with tourism and agricultural and heritage loss). In response to the action group's protests, planning permission for the facility imposed conditions to minimise environmental impact. The two representations of the hazard remained at variance: the action group viewed it as a real and present health and safety risk and threat to the environment; the company (and planners) regarded it as a manageable, controlled hazard with enormous social and economic benefits. The action group succeeded in making the company respond to its concerns in terms of design and operational constraints. This of course served to re-emphasise the representation of the site promulgated by the company that it was indeed safe. In 1994–6, Shell made an attempt to extend the facility. The same action group was revived. On this occasion the representation of the hazard that it presented differed. The action group emphasised the danger to air quality, arising specifically from benzene, which has been alleged to have carcinogens and to be linked to leukaemia. The action group also used a risk event that had occurred recently to reinforce their safety fears (a liquid petroleum gas tanker had broken loose from its moorings at the Shell jetty and, although no serious injuries resulted, it could be used as an exemplar of what was possible). Interestingly, on this occasion, Shell was asked to carry out a Societal Risk Assessment (SRA) of their operations in the area and to analyse the probability of large numbers of fatalities resulting from any accident. Before the SRA was complete, Shell decided to withdraw its application to develop the site. In order to limit damaging speculation, Shell finished and publicised the SRA, which concluded that the risk levels from the shipping operations to the local community were very low and well within limits used by the Health and Safety Executive (the relevant regulator). Shell furthermore decided to develop a strategy for active dialogue with the local community in the interests of improving understanding and acceptance of their operations. In terms of hazard negotiation, the Shell example offers two clear insights: the action group chose to shift its representation of the hazard over time in order to pursue its resistance; and the company sought to improve the flow of communication and allow 'negotiation' of the representation of the hazard in order to pursue its business. The example also serves to show how the hazard negotiation can be extended in time (close to twenty years, in this case). Finally, the example illustrates how vital pressure groups can be in imposing the need for hazard negotiation. The role of minority influence or pressure groups is considered further elsewhere in this book.

Although it is probably obvious, it may be worth being explicit that all aspects of the processes of amplification (including representation) will in large part determine the mental models (Bostrom *et al.*, 1992, 1994a, 1994b) that individuals hold about a hazard.

6   Social representation and identity processes

Given that SARF is not itself a theory, it may be worth considering whether theories originating elsewhere could be used to explain and predict some of the findings that it has generated. A variety of theories from social psychology could be used in this way. For instance, theories of intergroup relations (e.g. Turner and Giles, 1981) or social influence (e.g. J. C. Turner, 1991) would seem potentially valuable in providing the explanations for the way hazards are negotiated or the form that ripple effects take. However, two theories seem particularly useful in offering interpretations of the way risk events are amplified and the ripple effects that they have: Social Representations Theory and Identity Process Theory.

6.1   Social Representations Theory

Social Representations Theory (SRT) (Moscovici, 1988; Moscovici and Farr, 1984), one of the major social psychological theories of social influence processes, can provide the basis for explaining how an individual may acquire a representation (or mental model) of a hazard. In this theory, social representations can be both products and processes. As a product, a social representation is defined as a widely shared set of beliefs, a systematic framework for explaining events and evaluating them. As a process, social representation is the whole package of activity (communication, exchange and argumentation) in which individuals and groups engage to make meaningful changes in their physical and social environment. According to Moscovici, social representation operates with two prime processes:

- objectification
- anchoring.

Objectification entails translating something that is abstract into something which is almost concrete, gaining a density of meaning which ultimately makes it a common and 'natural' part of thinking about the object. Anchoring entails categorising a new object into pre-existing cognitive frameworks in order to render them familiar – reducing the strange and unfamiliar object to the level of an ordinary object set in a familiar context.

The theory of social representations may be particularly relevant to explaining why particular images or mental models of hazards evolve, because it was initially developed to explain what happens when people are faced with having to make sense of, or give meaning to, ideas or data which are novel to them, under conditions of uncertainty and where claims are contested. Plainly these are qualities that characterise the initial interface between people and information about hazards. Indeed, it might be argued that encountering a newly identified hazard inevitably triggers social representation processes. Breakwell (2001a) suggests that the novel, normally abstract, scientific specification of the hazard typically requires such objectification and anchoring. Castro and Gomes

(2005) illustrated this through an analysis of the way the media discussion of GMOs (genetically modified organisms) developed in the Portuguese newspapers between 1999 and 2001. They showed anchoring in prior ideological systems concerning agriculture and scientific innovation.

The processes of objectification and anchoring could account for the structure, often evident, in representations or mental models of hazards held by lay members of the public. Frequently, systematic empirical investigations expose lay representations of a novel hazard that are characterised by objectification (the abstract properties of the hazard being translated into commonly understood metaphors or represented through tangible, if tangential, exemplars) and by anchoring (being given meaning through association or through claiming similarity with other types of explanation that are more familiar). SRT would suggest that the representation that is constructed of any hazard will be determined by the proclivities of the individual for particular forms of objectification and anchoring.

However, SRT would emphasise that the representation (or mental model) produced of any hazard is not idiosyncratic or purely individualised. SRT states that objectification and anchoring are not individual processes. They are processes that normally involve social interaction and the establishment of shared meaning and consensus through communication among people. If mental models of hazards are generated through processes of social representation, they will be substantially shared by members of discrete subcultures. This idea that the mental model of a hazard is in many respects the product and property of a group or subculture should not be regarded as particularly novel. In fact, much of the research on mental models in the cognitive psychology literature on decision-making has focused upon shared mental models of complex systems and their implications for maintaining team effectiveness in the workplace (Cannon-Bowers et al., 1990; Castellan, 1993). Joffe and Lee (2004) adopted the social representations approach to the study of images that local women produced of the 2001 Hong Kong avian flu epidemic. They showed that the images of the epidemic were structured around explanations of its origins, anchors for it, emotions about it and graphic images of its effects. Aspersions concerning the lack of hygiene of mainland Chinese chicken farmers and chicken sellers in Hong Kong dominated the images. Other environmental factors were also stressed, as was regulation leniency and drive to profit. Comparisons between old traditions and newer practices formed a central feature of the representation. The study shows the significance of intergroup stereotypes and cultural expectations in the rapid and consensual development of a representation of new hazard. In a cross-national study of the social representations of HIV/AIDS, Goodwin et al. (2003; 2004b) described significant cultural and gender differences in the structure of the representations and their relationship to sexual risk-taking.

This does not mean that all members of the subculture would hold absolutely identical mental models of a hazard but rather that their mental model would share certain common core elements. Individuals within the subculture might then have mental models that incorporate some minor peripheral elements that are not shared. Abric (1994) has argued that social representations comprise a central core (an indispensable combination of basic underlying components linked in a specific constellation and tied systematically to a set of values and norms associated with the group espousing the social representation) and the peripheric elements (the way the representation is articulated in concrete terms depending upon context). Abric argues that the core is resistant to change but that the peripheric elements are responsive to changing context. By adapting, the peripheric elements can protect the core from having to change. Following Abric might lead one to conclude that individuals will be different from each other in the personal representations they construct, not in the core, but in the peripheric elements. Empirically, problems in differentiating core from periphery make testing this hypothesis difficult. It is, however, worth pursuing. To do so would, of course, demand an operational definition of peripheric elements which did not depend upon the extent to which they are consensually included in the representation. Moliner and Tafani (1997) have made an interesting start in this direction by examining how far components of a social representation can be ordered in terms of an evaluative dimension.

SRT suggests that subcultures (and social categories and groups) shape the social representations that they develop to serve their self-interests. Thus the construction of a mental model of a hazard by a subculture will be purposeful, motivated to achieve particular objectives. There is overwhelming evidence that risk in general is fertile ground for contested social representation, and competing mental models of hazards are common. Moscovici (1988) notes the scope for groups to use social representations strategically and identifies three types of representation:

- *Hegemonic representations* – these are shared by all members of a highly structured group without them having been produced by the group; they are uniform and coercive.
- *Emancipated representations* – these are the outgrowth of the circulation of knowledge and ideas belonging to subgroups that are in more or less close contact – each subgroup creates and shares its own version.
- *Polemical representations* – these are generated in the course of social conflict or controversy, and society as a whole does not share them;

they are determined by antagonistic relations between its members and are intended to be mutually exclusive.

The representation of a specific hazard could fall into any of these categories of social representation.

This SRT interpretation of the genesis of the representation of hazards has significant implications for explanations of how intensification or attenuation might work. It suggests that the subcultural base for any individual's representation of a hazard will influence their susceptibility to any reframing attempts, including official interventions aimed at changing risk perceptions. It is necessary as a precursor to any intervention to understand why the representation takes the form that it does. More specifically, it highlights that, where the representation is *hegemonic*, the intervention must take account of the fact that the representation is not a product of the subculture but is substantially shared by everyone in it. This suggests that changing the representation (or mental model) of the hazard may require the use of one of three prime alternative strategies:

- showing that the source of the original representation has recanted and changed its beliefs about the hazard
- showing that an equally powerful alternative source would support the target subculture changing its representation
- giving the target subculture (or some subset of individuals in it) the informational and motivational basis for rejecting the original representation.

Where the representation is *emancipated*, the intervention must provide a basis for changing it that emphasises the self-interest of the target subculture that has developed it and should encourage the regular communication within that subculture to rehearse and re-emphasise the changes required. Where the representation is *polemical*, the intervention must show how changing it would serve the target subculture's interests in the context of subcultural conflict. In all cases, these interventions would require more than a simple information-deficit correction approach targeted at the individual. They involve acknowledgement of the motivational and subcultural dynamics that underpin the development of the original representation.

Studies of the social representations of hazards are now growing in number (Goodwin *et al.*, 2004a; Joffe, 2003; Canelon and Rovira, 2002; Simarra *et al.*, 2002; de Souza, 2001).

6.2   Identity processes

Although social representations have been defined at one level as being a widely shared set of beliefs, it is not the case that beliefs are accepted and used by individuals in their entirety. Among alternative competing social representations, the hazard representations of which an individual is aware, will accept and may use will firstly depend upon the significance they have for identity. That is, the content and usage of a social representation (or mental model) can be predicted in relation to its likely impact upon the demands of individual identity requirements. Identity Process Theory (Breakwell, 1986, 1993, 2001a), which links social representation and identity models to predict risk perceptions, proposes that the extent to which any message about the risk will be received and incorporated into belief systems is affected by the ways in which this may threaten their identity.

The individual's relationship to any social representation can be described along a number of dimensions:

- *Awareness* – individuals will differ in their awareness of the social representation; some individuals will simply not know that there is a social representation in existence, others will know only part of its scope, and yet others will be fully aware of its structure and content. For instance, at any one time awareness of the available social representations of pandemic influenza will differ across people. Awareness is likely to be determined, in part, by previous personal experience, which, in turn, will be controlled to some extent by membership of different groups or communities. But awareness will also be determined by the significance of the object of the representation. If the target changes in significance due to some change of social or physical circumstances, awareness of existing social representations will alter. For example, with reports of scientific estimates of the growth of the hole in the earth's ozone layer and the consequent global warming, the significance of social representations previously generated by environmentalist activists was heightened.

- *Understanding* – individuals will differ in the extent to which they actually understand the social representations of which they are aware. There is ample evidence that individuals are capable of reproducing a dominant social representation even though they cannot explain how or why its elements fit together and, if challenged, they cannot justify it. For instance, in the late 1990s many people were aware of the social representation of the Millennium Bug (or Year Two Thousand Problem). This entailed the predicted collapse of systems dependent upon computers as midnight on 31 December 1999 chimed in the new century, because these computers were not programmed to recognise dates after that day. The social representation was interesting because it was elaborated to include what one must do to protect oneself from the effects of the collapse (e.g. avoid air journeys at that time, take out plenty of cash in advance because the banking systems would cease to function, etc.). While many people could detail these elements of the social representation, equally many could not explain why the computers would fail just because the date was wrong.

- *Acceptance* – individuals will differ in the extent to which they believe or accept a social representation even if they are fully aware of it. Typically, people can say: this is what is generally believed but, nevertheless, this is what I believe. For instance, I might know that other people believe the world is round, but I believe it is pear-shaped and the rivers run out of the stalk. Similarly, I might say that I know that the majority of people believe that microwave ovens are safe and useful, but personally I have a theory that they are dangerous and liable to fry your eyeballs because they leak waves that no one can detect. People can not only know (in the sense of being able to reproduce at will) contradictory social representations of the same target but also be able to identify at the same time a separate representation of it which is their own. This personal representation may be unique only in the specifics and may share many of the common features of the social representation, but it has been intentionally personalised. The extent to which the personal representation echoes the social representation reflects in part the degree to which the latter is accepted. The importance of being able to personalise the social representation so that it appears individualised should not be ignored. While seeking identification and community membership at one level, people also simultaneously seek distinctiveness and differentiation. The personalising of social representations is part of that process of establishing and protecting an accepted but also a unique identity.

- *Assimilation* – the individual does not accept (to whatever extent it is accepted) the social representation in some clinically detached way. It will be assimilated to pre-existent systems of personal representation (developed originally within the operation of idiosyncratic cognitive biases and capacities). This substratum of already extant personal representations will differ across individuals and the ultimate shape of the new personal representation will be influenced by it differentially for each individual. Just as social processes ensure that the new social representation is anchored in prior social representations, at the individual level cognitive and emotional processes ensure that it is anchored in prior personal representations. In fact, there must be an intimate connection between the social processes of anchoring and objectification and their parallel individual processes. The social communication which ensures that novel events and ideas are interpreted in terms of existing systems of meaning is generated by individuals using prior knowledge mediated through cognitive and conative networks. The social exchange can produce understandings which no single participant to the interaction might be able to create, but at some level even these emergent representations are limited in some ways by the capacities of the individuals involved to anchor and objectify.

- *Salience* – the salience of a social representation will differ across people and for the same person across time and contexts. The salience of the social representation, for instance, may increase if the group or community which generates it is important to the individual. Similarly, it may increase if the social representation becomes relevant to the individual's ongoing activity. At the level of the community, if the target for social representation is non-salient, it is likely that the social representation will be difficult to elicit, simple, undifferentiated and relatively unconnected with other components of the community's belief system. For instance, Hassan (1986) did a study of the social representations held of female circumcision by British, rural Sudanese and urban Sudanese. She found that the British had a rudimentary social representation of female circumcision, but one which was consensually held; in the Sudan (where the practice was widespread) there were very complex social representations which attributed religious and social significance to the procedure and, importantly, there were a number of variations in the social representation, each associated with different parts of the community (urban vs rural; male vs female). At the level of the individual, the salience of the social representation will be likely to influence how accurately and completely personal representation mirrors it.

It is notable that some of the dimensions which shape the personal representation are potentially non-volitional (for example, awareness and understanding); others are volitional (for example, acceptance). However, this distinction may be rightly regarded as arbitrary. Even those that appear volitional are largely predisposed by prior social experiences and constrained by identity requirements.

The nature of, and scope for, individual impact upon the social representational process depends in some ways upon the type of social representation concerned and upon the structure of the social representation itself. It will vary across hegemonic, emancipated and polemical types of representation because they reflect different power relationships within and between groups or subcultures. The hegemonic representation supposes little individual variation. The emancipated representation supposes individual variation based upon differential exposure within group contexts. The polemical representation supposes individual variation based upon the prevailing conditions of intergroup conflict. Of course, it is the scope for personalising representations which emerges when emancipated or polemical representations prevail about a target that is one of the necessary conditions for innovation and change. This assertion is not meant to trivialise or ignore the real differentials between individuals in their power to maintain or to proselytise their personal representations. One of the things which this perspective emphasises is that personal representations will be perpetually under pressure to change from the social representations which surround them. Individuals who are powerful (through position, expertise or some other route) are more likely to be able to retain their own personal representations and to be able to influence the development of social representations shared by others.

IPT (Breakwell, 1993) argues that identity requirements are important determinants of awareness, understanding, acceptance, assimilation and salience of social representations (and, by extension, of mental models of hazards). IPT postulates that individuals are motivated to achieve certain characteristics in their identity structure: continuity, distinctiveness, self-efficacy and self-esteem. These four motives vary in their relative and absolute salience over time and across situations. A threat to identity occurs when these motives cannot be satisfied. If they find that esteem, continuity, distinctiveness or efficacy are threatened, individuals will use a variety of strategies to protect or regain them. IPT has now generated an extensive series of studies which illustrate that individuals in the same social category will accept and use (i.e. reproduce or act in accordance with) a particular social representation to differing degrees depending upon its potential impact upon their identity esteem, continuity, distinctiveness and efficacy.

Many of these studies have concerned social representations of hazards. For example, Joffe and Bettega (2003) explored the social representations of AIDS among Zambian adolescents. They found that the structure of the social representation of the danger of AIDS served to protect the identity of the participants but also to justify current social practices. Similarly, individuals will reject social representations of their local environment as being polluted (despite objective evidence that it is) if attachment to that place features as an important aspect of their personal sense of distinctiveness (Bonauito et al., 1996). This study involved estimates of risk in relation to the levels of beach pollution (locally and nationally) in six English coastal resorts. The entire sample lived in towns where beaches had been officially declared either clean or polluted by the European Union. If beaches are declared clean by the European Union, they are given what is called a blue flag. Having this accolade has a significant impact on the marketability of the town for tourism. The sample was asked to indicate how far they were attached to their locality (place identification), and their nationalist sentiments were also assessed. They were further asked to index the extent of the pollution of which they were aware on their local beaches. Finally, they were asked to rate the level of beach pollution locally and the level of beach pollution nationally. Essentially, the data showed that, over and above the impact of the rating of pollution that was given by the European Union, local attachment to the place and nationalism predicted representations of the extent of pollution locally and nationally. The requirements of place identity are associated with a rejection of the representation of the risk of pollution in the area that is generated formally by European Union legislation. Given the generally negative feelings of the British people towards the European Union, it should hardly be surprising that nationalism was associated with a rejection of the European Union's evaluation of the British environment. More surprisingly, both attachment to the locale and nationalism were associated with a reduction in the perceived 'objective evidence' of beach pollutants, and both had a direct impact upon the perceived level of local beach pollution. This study illustrated that processes of identification limit willingness to accept social representations of hazards (in fact, it seems they affect the mental model of the hazard). It suggests that they tend to construct personal representations that are consonant with the identity requirements – in this case, those aspects of identity dependent upon affiliation to place.

Such studies would suggest that polemical social representations of hazards are most significantly mediated by identity processes. Many environmental hazards generate polemical social representations of hazards, created by agencies or groups in conflict. Under these circumstances the social representations of hazards that the individual chooses will be highly influenced by identity requirements. An example comes from a study of how a community responded to a potentially hazardous waste incinerator being sited locally (Twigger-Ross and Breakwell, 1999). The company wishing to introduce the development wanted to do so in an area that was already highly industrialised and where they had a well-established chemical processing complex. The introduction of this new waste incinerator was opposed by various environmental groups, including Greenpeace and Friends of the Earth. This community was studied throughout the lengthy process of gaining legal planning consent for the new incinerator. In a survey of local residents, indices were taken of the extent to which individuals perceived that there would be a risk arising from the development of the new waste incinerator, their trust in the governmental regulation of such risks, the image they held of the company, and their concern for the environment and their acceptance of

'Green' beliefs. Residents varied in their representation of the hazard and its risk. The representation that they reproduced depended upon the extent to which they identified with environmentalist groups, but also upon the extent to which they identified with the company as a trusted and traditional employer in the area. In a more recent study, Masuda and Garvin (2006) similarly analysed the significance of pre-existing patterns of social representation (what they called cultural world-views) in determining how the risks surrounding industrial development were viewed in a region of Canada located at the rural–urban interface. They concluded that patterns of risk intensification and attenuation were based on conflicting cultural world-views.

Essentially, in both of these studies, individuals were found to reject social representations that might threaten important aspects of their identity. However, it is probably too simplistic to use the term 'rejection' when examining how identity constraints motivate the way a social representation is treated. What often happens is that the social representation is subtly modified in personal use. For instance, it can be slightly re-anchored or there is a minor tweak to the objectification (often through use of different exemplars). Yet, in effect, individuals who are actively engaged in identity maintenance and development are also perforce engaged in social representation creation and change. Of course, whether or not their renovation of the social representation gains common acceptance or use is a function of the processes outlined in the theory of social representations itself. The significant point that all these studies have shown is that there is never total consensus upon a social representation. All the research illustrates variety among individuals despite elements of agreement and consensus. Empirical studies emphasise divergence amidst universalism. Moreover, the divergence is not random. It is lawful and, in part, predictable in terms of IPT expectations concerning the desire to achieve and maintain esteem, efficacy, distinctiveness and continuity for identity.

The recognition that identity processes moderate, at the level of the individual, the structure of the personal representation (or mental model) of the hazard has implications for risk communication interventions. It suggests that the role of the specific representation of the hazard in maintaining the individual's self-esteem, efficacy, continuity and distinctiveness should be identified. Methods for presenting an alternative representation of the hazard should avoid threatening self-esteem, efficacy, continuity and distinctiveness as far as possible. In designing a risk communication intervention, there should always be a phase which considers likely identity implications for the targets, and estimates the possible barriers to achieving change that may be involved. This sort of assessment may provide a basis for focusing effort upon targets who are most likely to change or upon those who require greater attention. It will almost certainly suggest how information could be best presented and allow avoidance of the most obvious pitfalls (see Breakwell, 2001a).

This approach to risk communication is particularly relevant in the context of current societal concerns to access those members of the community who are typically unresponsive to general media campaigns (e.g. the elderly, those with disabilities, ethnic minorities, those with learning difficulties). This approach argues for a more differentiated approach to risk communication that takes systematic account of the personal and subcultural concerns of the target audience.

The implications of this approach for risk communication in the work-place are also important. Recognising that mental models of hazards will be substantially a product of subcultural dynamics that are modified by individual identity motivations suggests that interventions in the work-place must be founded upon a clear appreciation of the group or team's shared representations of the hazard. However, the significance of the informal influence networks and the implicit reinforcers for the original representation of the hazard cannot be minimised. In fact, the social representation and identity process approach provides a framework within which such resistances to change in the mental model of the hazard can be analysed. It particularly points to the need to pay attention to the subcultural advantages of the existing mental model of the hazard when devising any intervention.

Conclusion

The SARF provides a useful platform for the systematic analysis of the consequences of a risk event. The research it has stimulated has been particularly influential in allowing us to understand stigmatisation and, increasingly, the role of the mass media in promulgating hazard repre-sentations. The SARF is a comprehensive approach to the analysis of the risk event. It pushes researchers towards a whole life-cycle examination of the hazard, recognising that it exists as part of hazard sequences. It makes it clear that the impacts of a risk event cannot be meaningfully said to lie at any one level of analysis. As a consequence, it is requiring the use of multi-disciplinary methodological tools. The layering method, described here, represents one systematic approach to direct data collection that is appro-priate to the SARF.

As more empirical work is done, the absence within the SARF of a predictive model has become more concerning. Patterns in the processes of amplification and rippling that the research reveals are calling for explanation and interpretation. This inevitably encourages ad hoc and post hoc theorising. The two theories presented in this chapter (SRT and IPT) would seem together to offer a meta-theoretical structure that could be used by SARF researchers. These theories are targeted precisely at the factors that should determine the nature of amplification (including intensification, attenuation, representation, de-attenuation and de-intensification) and rippling processes. Used in conjunction, IPT and SRT range across the spectrum of intra-personal, group and intergroup processes that affect the development of the representation of the hazard and its subsequent secondary impacts. These theories will generate hypotheses that are testable within the SARF. It is, however, vital to recognise that these are essentially theories at the social psychological level of analysis. In order to generate robust hypotheses, the SARF demands that the relevance of theories from other levels of analysis (e.g. the economic) should be incorporated. It would be fascinating to see a worked example, using the aftermath of a single risk event, which attempted to show how these social psychological models could be used in conjunction with economic models (or, indeed, models at other levels of analysis) to predict the course of events. The layering method would provide the relevant data. The challenge lies in achieving the conceptual integration of theories. Such an approach might mean that it is possible to explain not only how representations of a hazard evolve over time, but also how representation is related to behaviour not just at the individual but also at the organisational and community levels. An explicit model of the relationships between representations, decision-making and action is long overdue.

10   Changing risk responses

Chapter preview

This chapter summarises some of the most salient empirically founded conclusions that can be drawn from the research presented in this volume. It relates these conclusions to the framework for the social psychological analysis of risk suggested in Chapter 1. It considers how these conclusions might be used for bringing about change in risk reactions. Some generic principles for the effective introduction of change are outlined. The ethical issues associated with deliberate interventions to change risk responses are raised.

1   Firm suspicions and robust conclusions

It is tempting when faced with the volume of empirical data that risk researchers have generated to become lost in the detail. Emersion in each fragment of the findings is rewarding and fascination with the specific can result in missing the bigger picture. Chapter 1 proposed that a systematic framework for structuring the social psychological analysis of risk should be adopted that could guide the integration of diverse data streams. The framework calls for data at several levels of analysis – the intra-psychic (including the cognitive, conative and oretic); the interpersonal and intra-group; the intergroup and societal (including the institutional, ideological and social representational, and the socio-historical); and the physical/environmental (the material). The framework expects eclecticism in methods of data collection and analysis – moving from qualitative to quantitative, as appropriate for the subject matter. It also requires explanations of the relationships between data at the different levels of analysis; that is, it does not merely expect description, but interpretation and ultimately prediction.

With regard to risk, the framework was said to lead to a series of basic questions:
- What do individuals believe about hazards and risks?
- How do individuals differ in their beliefs about hazards and risks – what personal and social factors predict these differences?

- What factors, social and psychological, influence decision-making about hazards and risks at either the individual or institutional levels?
- What role does affect or emotion play in individual reactions to hazards and risks?
- How do actions with respect to hazards and risks reflect the beliefs, emotions or intentions of individuals?
- How is risk communicated within the matrix of sources of social influence and prevailing interpersonal and institutional affordances – what normative pressures operate?
- How does human action, at the levels of individuals or institutions, create hazards unintentionally, and what socio-historical or physical-environmental factors influence the effects of such action?
- How do institutions or complex organisations deal with hazards and risks?
- What are the sequences of processes that transform a material object that has potentially harmful consequences into a socially recognised, if contested, hazard with its associated risk?

In the intervening chapters, the research evidence relevant to these questions has been summarised. There are some relatively robust conclusions that can be drawn from the research base. Also some firm suspicions emerge that await further confirmation. What follows is a limited selection of these robust conclusions and firm suspicions that seem to be of prime importance for the social psychological analysis of risk.

- Beliefs about hazards are structured and revolve around two underlying dimensions – whether the hazard is dreaded (i.e. severe, uncontrollable, catastrophic, hard to prevent, fatal, affecting future generations, not easily remediated, increasing, involuntary and personally threatening) and whether it is known (i.e. novel, observable, with immediate consequences, understood by experts). However, this is in effect a generic statement about structure. With regard to specific hazards, it has been shown that people hold sometimes very complex mental models that encompass detailed beliefs about the composition of the hazard, its origins and potential effects.
- While the underlying generic structure of beliefs about hazards has been characterised and appears regularly over time and across populations, there are significant differences between individuals and between different groups or social categories in the specific beliefs held about particular hazards. Such differences have not been fully categorised. There is a suspicion that, when there is more systematic evidence, the significance of differential vulnerability in predisposing differences in beliefs about hazards and risk perception will emerge. Two types of vulnerability appear relevant. Psychological vulnerability

would include enduring anxiety levels, cognitive style biases, and pro-clivity to seek novelty. Material vulnerability would include limitations in control over exposure to the hazard as a consequence of social position. Vulnerability does not in itself explain risk perception differentials. But it could be a vital ingredient in determining the mental model of a hazard that an individual or group would accept as appropriate or, indeed, help to create. The less vulnerable might be more likely to accept a model of the hazard that posits that it can and will be controllable. This type of explanation for differences in risk perception relies upon the assumption that people are actively engaged in the interpretation of hazards but they are constrained in how they do this by the psychological, interpersonal, societal and material resources (i.e. affordances) that they have available. The interpersonal and societal resources that are differentially available will include access to particular mental models of risk or specific social representational or ideological systems relevant to the hazard.

- Human inference processes in conditions of uncertainty are riddled with biases – that is, systematic deviations from what would be expected if the inferences were based on mathematical or formal propositional rules for probability estimation. Moreover, the catalogue of biases now established (availability, representativeness, anchoring, optimism, hindsight and prospect) is unlikely to capture all that exist. These biases affect hazard interpretation and risk estimation. Why do these biases occur? There are two probably interconnected routes: cognitive and motivational. Limitations in computational capacity, mostly derived from the weaknesses of memory or the inadequacies of information available, generate biases that also serve motivational ends – primarily enhancing self-esteem. The problem with coming to any firm conclusion about the reasons that these biases appear lies in the relative unpredictability of their occurrence. Optimistic and hind-sight biases seem particularly susceptible to variation according to circumstance. Nevertheless, the robust conclusion is that explanations solely in terms of cognitive factors are inadequate.

- Small, face-to-face groups do behave differently to individuals when it comes to risk estimations and choices. The 'shift to risk' or group polarisation phenomena are robust effects. However, the significance of group membership (as opposed to social category membership like nationality or gender) and, indeed, intergroup relationships in risk perception and reactions, is not sufficiently extensively researched. There is, nonetheless, a reasonable suspicion that explanations of the impact of group and intergroup dynamics upon individual risk reactions will need to encompass cognitive, emotional and motivational components.

- Since most of the studies that examine decision-making in uncertainty are concerned with the ways in which heuristics, biases and mental models, and so on, affect risk estimations rather than choices, it would be reasonable to ask whether they address decision-making per se at all. Not all studies ignore actual choices (e.g. the work on prospect theory), but most do. This is non-trivial because there is a substantial body of literature that shows that risk estimation is not directly related to the intention (i.e. stated decision) to take a risk. Moreover, intentions concerning risk-taking are not related to actual risk-taking in any simple fashion. This suggests that there is a very real need for studies that follow the decision-making process from risk estimation (linked to biases, etc.) to risk-taking. Risk-taking in such research would need to be broadly conceptualised – being concerned not just with individual choices regarding risk but also with societal decisions about the tolerability of particular risks. The psychological risk literature is surprisingly lacking in studies of purposive (i.e. goal-directed) behaviour towards hazards or risks. Thus, while the bilateral links between cognitive and conative processes are being plotted, their links with oretic processes are not.

- Emotion is a significant determinant of risk perception and risk decision-making – either through the affect attached to the hazard itself or through the emotional state of the individual reacting to the hazard. It is not appropriate to talk about the global primacy of either cognitive or affective components in the determination of risk reactions, yet it is still rare for research to provide an integrative analysis of both the cognitive and the affective factors. Of course, the framework for the social psychological analysis of risk that is used here requires both to be considered.

- Risk communication and social influence (e.g. persuasion) processes have been explored. Factors likely to influence the persuasiveness of a message have been catalogued (the source characteristics, the message's content and structure, the medium of communication and audience characteristics). The value of targeting risk communication in full awareness of the prior risk mental models held by the audience has been established, and methods for doing this have been specified. Factors that have been extensively examined that may affect the efficacy of risk communications include fear induction and levels of trust in the origin of the message. The firm suspicions are that fear appeals can be effective (but are difficult to design and control) and trust is vital (but not open to simple manipulation). A robust conclusion from the risk communication research is that uncertainty (in its various forms) is difficult to explain accurately and, once evident, will affect both risk perceptions and trust in the message source. The nature of its effects vary massively according to context. Research on the communication of uncertainty is badly needed. Ignoring uncertainty in risk communication is not a realistic proposition.

- Research on the role of the mass media in risk communication is extensive. The scope of its involvement in risk messaging has been examined qualitatively and quantitatively. Hazards and risk stories are omnipresent in all media. The editorial bases for decisions on risk coverage have been described in terms of the ideological stance of the particular organ of the media and general 'news' preoccupations (e.g. with infotainment, with dramatic memorable imagery, with running with the pack but also leading it, with hazard templates, and with maintained circulation, and so on). There is a firm suspicion that volume of media coverage of a hazard correlates positively with public concern about the hazard (though the direction of causality may be open to debate). There is an equally firm suspicion that the media provide the rhetorical fodder for the construction of vivid representations of the hazard. The images and vocabulary chosen by the media are designed to have impact, to engage their chosen audience; by doing so they ready-make shared representations and mental models of the hazard. The robust conclusion of the research in this area is that the public is by no means a passive recipient of media hazard representations. The way that the media message is treated (accepted, rejected, and modified) will depend on all of those other elements that are built into the social psychological framework for analysis (i.e. including the intra-psychic factors, interpersonal, group, societal and material).

- The control of risk communications does not lie solely in the hands of institutions or experts. The role of minorities and pressure groups in social influence processes concerning risk is now recognised as important. It is not yet adequately understood.

- The robust conclusion from all the research on risk communications is that they will be more effective if they are part of a genuine exchange between the originators of the message and the users of the message. There are many ways of achieving this. An essential ingredient to all of them is engendering the belief on the part of those who are called to participate that their thoughts, feelings and desires (that is, motives) matter. These consultation and participation processes are actually linking the cognitive, conative and oretic processes at the level of the individual and small group, together with social influence and normative processes at the level of the institution and society.

- People are often the originators of hazards. Human error is a prime source of hazards but researchers have shown that violations (deliberate breaches of rules or safety codes) are also important. There is no good model that explains the relationship between risk estimation, risk-taking and willingness to make violations. Errors not only produce risks – they can be the product of risks – however, the relationship of error rate and intensity of perceived risk is not specified in the literature. Major accidents affect the social representation of a hazard type – for an indeterminate period, but not for ever. Risk homeostasis, motivated error and error proneness are all concepts that have limited empirical support. The analysis of errors, accidents and emergencies is no simple task. The work on the origins and nature of errors is very sophisticated and has resulted in some strong predictive models. The work on accidents has led to less theory and more detailed descriptions of the circumstances surrounding specific events. There is less work on emergencies and this is also often atheoretical. There is a real challenge here for psychologists to provide useful, valid models.
- For complex organisations and institutions, managing risk and being trusted to manage it are now of fundamental importance. There are robust conclusions that can be drawn about how risk should be managed: for instance, through risk mapping and registers, the introduction of a safety culture, business continuity planning and risk reputation maintenance. The suspicion is that much risk management in complex organisations is aimed at ensuring their trustworthiness remains as high as possible. Being trusted by shareholders in the commercial world, by voters in the political world, and by stakeholders in the public sector, is vital. Having a safety culture is important but showing the world that you have a safety culture is even more important, just as doing total quality risk management is important but being known to do it is even more important.
- Research on the social amplification of risk and the social representation of risk has proven a fruitful arena for robust conclusions and firm suspicions. This research has highlighted the role of stigmatisation in hazard contexts and has required careful examination of the role of the mass media. Social amplification processes are basically underpinned by communication. In this area the findings on risk communication (e.g. the role of trust) are used to explain the basis for the social influences that result in amplification. Researchers have begun to explore the whole life cycle of the hazard, locating it often as part of a hazard sequence and hazard negotiations that will affect the way it is understood and the reactions it generates. Social amplification of risk has to be examined at a variety of levels of analysis (intra-psychic to

societal). This is evident when there is any attempt to examine the ripple effects (i.e. secondary and tertiary impacts) of a risk event. These can occur at any level (for example, economic, fiscal, legal, etc.) and the analytic methods to track them must be chosen appropriately. The layering method has been developed to achieve this end.

- Social Representations Theory offers a coherent and comprehensive account of how beliefs about hazards and their associated risks may come into being. It is a theory of social influence processes – one which is particularly interested in the role of conflict between individuals, groups (including minorities) or institutions in generating widely shared sets of beliefs that represent a framework for explaining and evaluating events. The social processes of objectification and anchoring (operating through communication and argumentation) are said to account for the structure of mental models held of hazards by lay members of the public.

- Acknowledging the role of social representational processes in creating the shared risk representation, Identity Process Theory offers a way of explaining why individuals quite often do not accept the social representation of a risk in its entirety. Identity Process Theory shows how the content and usage of a social representation (or mental model) can be predicted in relation to its likely impact upon the demands of individual identity requirements. It proposes that the extent to which any message about the risk will be received and incorporated into belief systems is affected by the ways in which this may threaten identity (specifically, its esteem, efficacy, distinctiveness or continuity). Identity Process Theory is a model that analyses individual cognitive, conative and oretic processes in relation to social influences and societal affordances, and as such complies with the expectations of model-building laid down in Chapter 1.

- Used in conjunction, Identity Process Theory and Social Representations Theory range across the spectrum of intra-personal, group and intergroup processes that affect the development of the representation of the hazard and its subsequent secondary impacts.

In relation to the demands of the framework for the social psychological analysis of risk suggested in Chapter 1, the data accumulated and the conclusions that can be drawn from them are not inconsiderable. We have evidence on cognitive and conative processes, with less on oretic processes. There is some information on individual and institutional action and prior action patterns. We have evidence on social influence sources and normative pressures. There are data on social representations. Institutional affordances are examined, as are interpersonal affordance, if to a lesser extent. The socio-historical and the physical/

environmental contexts are considered, patchily. The problem, quite obviously, is that no single study offers evidence for all elements in the framework. No holistic empirical test of any model based on the framework has been conducted – though those based on Social Representations Theory and Identity Process Theory may get closest. It is thus impossible to trace the patterns of influence that run from the socio-historical context through to individual action in relation to a particular hazard. A full social psychological analysis of risk is not available. This is probably too much ever to expect, but recognising its absence makes it feasible to see the limitations and range of applicability of those models that are current. The explanatory models that have been described have limited predictive powers, because they deal with relationships between relatively limited ranges of variables that are influenced by others residing outside of the model. No model can encompass all variables. However, knowing which types of variable may be relevant but are excluded does aid the interpretation of any findings that a model generates. The framework for the social psychological analysis of risk usefully points attention at the missing constructs in any model.

2   Changing risk responses

The idea that the psychological analysis of risk is capable of being translated into a new technology for the deliberate, systematic and predictable restructuring of risk perception or acceptance is fanciful. Despite the robust conclusions summarised above, the theoretical models are too underspecified and lack predictive power. However, while a new technology is not waiting in the wings for delivery, there are innumerable lower-level generalisations that could feed into attempts to change risk responses. For instance, using the appropriate framing in a risk message could improve its chances of success; working with the cognitive and affective biases when providing information or advice rather than against them would not be a bad idea; recognising the imperatives that direct media risk story coverage when shaping a public announcement is sensible; anticipating that the ripple effects of a risk event cannot go amiss; using indicators of safety culture when predicting organisational accidents or errors is effective; customising the message to take account of mental models of risk aids efficacy; and so on. Virtually all of the data reported in this book can be translated into a hint or a clue as to how risk responses can be changed. These would not be universal recipes for enhanced control over changing risk responses – they are the sensible, practical implications for efforts to bring about change of the findings so far. The value of the hints and clues is limited by a number of things, including:

- *How good the original research was* – was it designed properly, were the data defined effectively, was the collection of information unbiased, were the analyses correct and was the conclusion drawn appropriate?
- *How far the translation of the original finding into a recommendation for subsequent interventions to change risk responses is appropriate* – does the recommendation go too far beyond the original finding because it is over-extended in terms of populations to which it might be applied, type of hazard, timescale, and so on?
- *How far the recommendation is understood by the potential user* – does it assume implicit knowledge or expertise not possessed by the user?

It could be asked: Are there no superordinate principles that should be adopted when trying to bring about change in risk responses? Some key candidates that come to mind might be:

- simplicity, consistency and persistency in message (information, emotional tone, imagery, advice and instructions) provided
- measures to ensure establishment and maintenance of both trust and credibility
- customise the message to the condition of its audience (knowledge, beliefs, emotional state, action intentions, goals, identity, sense of control, and so on)
- engagement with the audience (through consultative or participation processes) to ensure own responsiveness to their concerns, but also to make responsiveness evident.

Such generic guidance is hardly difficult to produce. The problem lies in the translation process again. How does the practitioner or policy-maker who is faced with changing a risk response to a specific hazard know how to use this advice? How do you customise the message to the condition of the audience? For instance, how do you know the condition of the audience? What is more, how do you know the condition of the audience quickly enough to bring about a change in risk responses in a crisis situation?

Perhaps it is unrealistic to expect practitioners and policy-makers to do the translation alone. Possibly the only way to make the social psychological analysis of risk predictably and genuinely useful is to have the researchers working alongside the practitioners and policy-makers to develop intervention strategies. This is not so novel an idea. It works in other domains all the time. Examples abound: the research physicist who works with the manufacturer to produce a laser that can revolutionise the treatment of cancer; the electronic engineer who works with industry to produce the next-generation satellite; the biochemist who helps government departments to introduce a radical approach to hospital-based infections; and so on. Clinical and health psychologists already work on a daily basis using these risk research findings to improve the way patients are told about health hazards and the things they can do to protect themselves. These are frequently practitioner-researchers, developing the knowledge base as they apply it. The model is extendable and could massively benefit our understanding of how risk reactions are changed. By working with the agencies and institutions that seek to change risk responses, the researcher would be able to acquire additional invaluable insight and data.

Practitioners and policy-makers reading this book will undoubtedly have taken what they need for the problems that they are currently addressing in dealing with risk reactions. The recommendations derived from the research evidence are not, and should not be, the preserve of the researchers to create. The evidence presented in this volume is open to interpretation or use by everyone. Others should, of course, be under the same constraints as the original researchers to use the data properly. It is not easy to do this at second-hand. Often, insufficient detail is offered. It is consequently an obligation upon researchers to be as clear as they can in describing their work where the boundaries of applicability lie. This is perhaps particularly true in relation to risk research where the misapplication of some finding could be so hazardous.

The ethical implications of application of the risk research findings should not be overlooked. In talking about changing a risk reaction, we are talking about some form of manipulation. It is an explicit attempt at social influence. Normally, it may be argued that it is in the interests of the person or people manipulated – protecting their health, protecting their environment, protecting their livelihood, and so on – but this does not make the decision to support it any less than one that requires an ethical evaluation. Actively using one's knowledge of risk responses to aid someone else to influence others should only be done after a thorough evaluation of the ethical issues. Indirectly, through publication of findings, allowing others to use one's knowledge to achieve the same end, has an equivalent imperative for ethical appraisal. Using or making available for use expertise in changing risk responses always has a moral dimension. Pretending that we can evade or avoid the ethical considerations just because our powers of prediction are limited or our models are incomplete is unacceptable. Working through the ethical problems is a first indicator of the recognition that the analysis of the psychology of risk might have something very serious to say to practitioners and policy-makers.

Conclusion

The analysis of the psychology of risk does have something seriously to contribute not just to practitioners and policy-makers but to everybody.

We have achieved a sophisticated, multi-layered understanding of how individuals and institutions think, feel and act about hazards and their associated risks. In large part, we understand the influence processes that are at work in the social construction of hazards and risks. If society does now define itself in terms of risks on a global scale, then this psychological analysis of risk – not just at the individual, but at institutional and societal levels – is pertinent to everyone. The analysis can be used: by individuals who want to better understand their own risk reactions; by organisations and institutions that want to improve their risk management; by pressure groups that want to sensitise others to their concerns; and by governments facing the need to communicate with their publics in the context of a chronic disaster. The only obligation on any who would use this analysis is to do so appropriately, with respect for its own limitations and with awareness of the ethical issues its application entails.

References

HMSO (2000). *The BSE Inquiry*. London: The Stationery Office.

HSE (1993). *ACSNI Study Group on Human Factors. Third Report: Organising for safety*. London: HMSO.

HSE (2001). *Reducing Risks, Protecting People: HSE's decision-making process*. London: HMSO.

Abbey, A., Saenz, C. and Buck, P. O. (2005). The cumulative effects of acute alcohol consumption, individual differences and situational perceptions on sexual decision making. *Journal of Studies on Alcohol*, 66, 82–90.

Abele, A. and Hermer, P. (1993). Mood influences on health-related judgments: appraisal of own health versus appraisal of unhealthy behaviors. *European Review of Social Psychology*, 23, 613–25.

Abelson, R. P. and Levi, A. (1985). Decision-making and decision theory. In G. Lindzey and E. Jason Aronson (eds), *Handbook of Social Psychology* (pp. 231–309). New York: Random House, 19th edition.

Abrams, D., Wetherell, M. S., Cochrane, S., Hogg, M. A. and Turner, J. C. (1990). Knowing what to think by knowing who you are: self-categorisation and the nature of norm formation, conformity and group polarization. *British Journal of Social Psychology*, 29, 97–119.

Abric, J. C. (1994). Les Représentations sociales: aspectes théoretiques. In J. C. Abric (ed.), *Pratiques Sociales et Représentations*. Paris: Presses Universitaires de France.

Agha, S. (2003). The impact of mass media campaign on personal risk perception, perceived self-efficacy and on other behavioural predictors. *AIDS Care*, 15, 749–62.

Ahern, J., Galea, S., Resnick, H. and Vlahov, D. (2004). Television images and probable post-traumatic stress disorder after Sept 11: the role of background characteristics, event exposure and perievent panic. *Journal of Nervous and Mental Diseases*, 192, 3, 217–26.

Alhakami, A. S. and Slovic, P. (1994). A psychological study of the inverse relationship between perceived risk and perceived benefit. *Risk Analysis*, 14, 1085–96.

Alicke, M. D., Klotz, M. L., Breithenbecher, D. L., Yurack, T. J. and Vredenburg, D. S. (1995). Personal contact, individualisation and the better than average effect. *Journal of Personality and Social Psychology*, 68, 804–25.

Allen, P. T. (1998). Public participation in resolving environmental disputes and the problem of representiveness. *Risk: Health, Safety & Environment*, 9, 297–308.

Anderson, C. and Galinsky, A. D. (2006). Power, optimism, and risk-taking. *European Journal of Social Psychology*, 36, 511–36.

Ansell, J. (1992). Reliability, industrial risk assessment. In J. Ansell and F. Wharton (eds), *Risk: Analysis, Assessment and Management*. Chichester: John Wiley and Sons.

Appleton-Knapp, S. L. (2003). Memory dynamics in hindsight biases. *Dissertation Abstracts International*, Section B, *The Sciences and Engineering*, 63 (7-B), 3488.

Ardelt, M. (2000). Still suitable after all these years? Personality stability theory revisited. *Social Psychology Quarterly*, 63, 392–405.

Arden, P. (1993). Create a corporate safety culture. *Safety & Health*, 60–63.

Arkes, H. R. (1991). Costs and benefits of judgment errors: implications for debiasing. *Psychological Bulletin*, 110, 486–98.

Arnstein, S. R. (1969). A ladder of citizen participation. *AIP Journal*, 216–24.

Aronson, E. (1997). Bring the family. *APS Observer*, July/August, 17.

Atman, C. J., Bostrom, A., Fischhoff, B. and Morgan, M. G. (1994). Designing risk communications: completing and correcting mental models of hazards processes, part I. *Risk Analysis*, 14, 779–88.

Bakker, A. B., Buunk, B. P. and Manstead, A. S. (1997). The moderating role of self-efficacy beliefs in the relationship between anticipated feelings of regret and condom use. *Journal of Applied Social Psychology*, 27, 2001–14.

Balzano, Q. and Sheppard, A. R. (2002). The influence of the precautionary principle on science-based decision-making: questionable applications to risks of radiofrequency fields. *Journal of Risk Research*, 5, 351–69.

Bandura, A. (1997). *Self-Efficacy: The Exercise of Control*. New York: Freeman.

Barke, R. and Jenkins-Smith, H. (1993). Politics and scientific expertise: scientists, risk perception, and nuclear waste policy. *Risk Analysis*, 13, 425–39.

Barlow, D. H., Rapee, R. M. and Brown, T. A. (1992). Behavioural treatment of generalized anxiety disorder. *Behaviour Therapy*, 20, 261–82.

Barnett, J. and Breakwell, G. M. (2001). Risk perception and experience: hazard personality profiles and individual differences. *Risk Analysis*, 21, 171–7.

(2003). The social amplification of risk and the hazard sequence: the October 1995 oral contraceptive pill scare. *Health, Risk & Society*, 5, 301–13.

Baron, J., Hershey, J. C. and Kunreuther, H. (2000). Determinants of priority for risk reduction: the role of worry. *Risk Analysis*, 20, 413–27.

Barratt, E. O., Cabal, L. F. and Moeller, F. G. (2004). Impulsivity and sensation seeking: a historical perspective on current challenges. In R. M. Stelmack (ed.), *On the Psychobiology of Personality: Essays in Honor of Marvin Zuckerman* (pp. 3–15). New York: Elsevier.

Bartholomew, R. E. and Wessely, S. (2002). Protean nature of mass sociogenic illness: from possessed nuns to chemical and biological terrorism fears. *British Journal of Psychiatry*, 180, 300–6.

Bartlett, F. C. (1932). *Remembering*. Cambridge University Press.

Basili, M. and Franzini, M. (2006). Understanding the risk of an avian flu pandemic: rational waiting or precautionary failure? *Risk Analysis*, 26, 617–30.

Bateman, I. J., Langford, I. H., Turner, R. K., Willis, K. G. and Garrod, G. D. (1995). Elicitation and truncation effects in contingent valuation studies. *Ecological Economics*, 12, 161–79.

Bea, R. G. (2002). Human and organizational factors in reliability assessment and management of offshore structures. *Risk Analysis*, 22, 29–45.

Beck, U. (1992). *Risk Society: Towards a New Modernity*. London: Sage Publications. (2006). Living in the world risk society. *Economy and Society*, 35, 329–45.

Begum, H. A. and Ahmed, E. (1986). Individual risk-taking and risky shift as a function of cooperation – competition proneness of subjects. *Psychological Studies*, 31, 1, 21–5.

Beierle, T. C. (2004). The benefits and costs of disclosing information about risks: what do we know about right-to-know? *Risk Analysis*, 24, 335–46.

Benthin, A., Slovic, P. and Severson, H. (1993). A psychometric study of adolescent risk perception. *Journal of Adolescence*, 16, 153–68.

Bergstrom, R. L. and McCaul, K. D. (2004). Perceived risk and worry: the effects of 9/11 on willingness to fly. *Journal of Applied Social Psychology*, 34, 1846–56.

Berman, J., Brabazon, P., Bellamy, L. and Huddleston, J. (1994). *The Regulator as a Determinant of the Safety Culture*. London: HSE Report.

Bernoulli, D. (1954). A new theory on the measurement of risk, trans. L. Sommer. *Econometrica*, 22, 36. Original work published 1738.

Bernstein, N. R. (1990). Fire. In R. Coddington and J. D. Noshpitz (eds), *Stressors and the Adjustment Disorders* (pp. 260–77). Oxford: John Wiley and Sons.

Blume, S. (2006). Anti-vaccination movements and their interpretations. *Social Science & Medicine*, 62, 628–42.

Boholm, A. (1996). Risk perception and social anthropology: critique of cultural theory. *Ethnos*, 61, 64–84.

Bonaiuto, M., Breakwell, G. M. and Cano, I. (1996). Identity processes and environmental threat: the effects of nationalism and local identity upon perception of beach pollution. *Journal of Community & Applied Social Psychology*, 6, 157–75.

Boney-McCoy, S., Gibbons, F. X., Reis, T. J., Gerrard, M., Luus, C. A. E. and Sufka, A. V. W. (1992). Perceptions of smoking risk as a function of smoking status. *Journal of Behavioral Medicine*, 15, 469–88.

Bord, R. J. and O'Connor, R. E. (1990). Risk communication, knowledge, and attitudes: explaining reactions to a technology perceived as risky. *Risk Analysis*, 10, 499–506.

(1992). Determinants of risk perceptions of a hazardous waste site. *Risk Analysis*, 12, 411–16.

(1997). The gender gap in environmental attitudes. *Social Science Quarterly*, 78, 4, 830–40.

Boscarino, J. A., Adams, R. E. and Figley, C. R. (2004). Mental health service use 1 year after the World Trade Center disaster: implications for mental health care. *General Hospital Psychiatry*, 26, 346–58.

Bostrom, A., Fischhoff, B. and Morgan, M. G. (1992). Characterizing mental models of hazardous processes: a methodology and an application to radon. *Journal of Social Issues*, 48, 85–100.

Bostrom, A., Atman, C., Fischhoff, B. and Morgan, M. (1994a). Evaluating risk communications: completing and correcting mental models of hazardous processes, Part 2. *Risk Analysis*, 14, 789–98.

Bostrom, A., Morgan, M. G., Fischhoff, B. and Read, D. (1994b). What do people know about global climate-change. 1. Mental models. *Risk Analysis*, 14, 959–70.

Bouyer, M., Bagdassarian, S., Chaabanne, S. and Mullet, E. (2001). Personality correlates of risk perception. *Risk Analysis*, 21, 457–65.

Bradfield, A. and Wells, G. L. (2005). Not the same old hindsight bias: outcome information distorts a broad range of retrospective judgments. *Memory and Cognition*, 33, 120–30.

Brauer, M., Judd, C. M., and Gliner, M. D. (1995). The effects of repeated expressions on attitude polarization during group discussion. *Journal of Personality and Social Psychology*, 68, 1014–29.

Breakwell, G. M. (1986). *Coping with Threatened Identities*. London: Methuen.

(1993). Integrating paradigms, methodological implications. In G. M. Breakwell and D. V. Canter (eds), *Empirical Approaches to Social Representations* (pp. 180–201). Oxford University Press.

(1994). The echo of power: a framework for social psychological research. *The Psychologist*, 17, 65–72.

(1996). Risk estimation and sexual behaviour: a longitudinal study of 16–21 year olds. *Journal of Health Psychology*, 1, 79–91.

(2000). Risk communication: factors affecting impact. *British Medical Bulletin*, 56, 1, 110–20.

(2001a). Mental models and social representations of hazards: the significance of identity processes. *Journal of Risk Research*, 4, 341–51.

(2001b). What makes innovation acceptable? In J. P. Toutant and I. Balazc (eds), *Molecular Farming*. Springer-Verlag.

Breakwell, G. M. and Barnett, J. (2000). Social influence processes and their effect on risk amplification. In M. P.Cottam, D. W. Harvey, R. P. Pape and J. Tait (eds), *Foresight and Precaution* (pp. 1181–7). Rotterdam: A. A. Balkema.

(2001). *The Impact of Social Amplification on Risk Communication*. Contract Research Report 322/2001. Sudbury: HSE Books.

(2003a). The significance of uncertainty and conflict: developing a social psychological theory of risk communication. *New Review of Social Psychology*, 2, 107–14.

(2003b). Social amplification of risk and the layering method. In N. Pidgeon, R. Kasperson and P. Slovic (eds), *The Social Amplification of Risk* (pp. 80–101). Cambridge University Press.

Breakwell, G. M. and Petts, J. (2000). *Stakeholder Participation Methods – Scoping Study*. Report to the HSE. RSU Ref 4072/R64.063.

Breakwell, G. M. and Rowett, C. (1982). *Social Work: The Social Psychological Approach*. Wokingham: Van Nostrand Reinhold.

Breakwell, G. M., Millward, L. and Fife-Schaw, C. R. (1994). Commitment to 'safer' sex as a predictor of condom use amongst 16–20 year olds. *Journal of Applied Social Psychology*, 24, 189–217.

Brenot, J. and Bonnefous, S. (1995). *Approche socio-culturelle de la perception des risques.* Fontenay-aux-Roses, France: Institut de Protection et de Sûreté Nucléaire.

Brockner, J., Wiesenfeld, B. M. and Martin, C. L. (1995). Decision frame, procedural justice, and survivors' reactions to job layoffs. *Organizational Behaviour and Human Decision Process*, 63, 59–68.

Brody, C. J. (1984). Differences by sex in support for nuclear power. *Social Issues*, 63, 209–28.

Broers, A. N. (2005). The nuclear energy option – will we still need it – and if so – when? *Science in Parliament*, 62, 16–17.

Bromiley, P. and Curley, S. P. (1992). Individual differences in risk taking. In J. F. Yates (ed.), *Risk-Taking Behaviour* (pp. 87–132). Chichester: John Wiley and Sons.

Bronfman, N. C. and Cifuentes, L. A. (2003). Risk perception in a developing country: the case of Chile. *Risk Analysis*, 23, 1271–85.

Brosius, H. B. and Weimann, G. (1996). Who sets the agenda?: agenda-setting as a two-step flow. *Communication Research*, 23, 561–80.

Brown, J. M., Henderson, J. and Armstrong, M. P. (1987). Children's perceptions of nuclear power stations as revealed through their drawings. *Journal of Environmental Psychology*, 7, 189–99.

Brun, W. (1992). Cognitive components in risk perception: natural versus manmade risks. *Journal of Behavioural Decision Making*, 5, 117–32.

Bryant, F. B. and Guilbault, R. L. (2002). 'I knew it all along' eventually: the development of hindsight bias in reaction to the Clinton impeachment verdict. *Basic and Applied Social Psychology*, 24, 27–41.

Bull, R. and Carson, D. (eds) (2001). *Handback of Psychology in Legal Contexts.* Chichester: Wiley.

Burger, J. M. and Burns, L. (1988). The illusion of unique invulnerability and the use of effective contraception. *Personality and Social Psychology Bulletin*, 14, 270.

Burns, W. J., Slovic, P. and Kasperson, R. E. (1993). Incorporating structural models into research on the social amplification of risk: implication for theory construction and decision making. *Risk Analysis*, 13, 611–24.

Burnstein, E. and Vinokur, A. (1977). Persuasive argumentation and social comparison as determinants of attitude polarization. *Journal of Experimental Social Psychology*, 13, 315–32.

Burt, R. S. (1999). The social capital of opinion leaders. *Annals of the American Academy of Political and Social Science*, 566, 37–54.

Buunk, B. P., Bakker, A. B., Siero, F. W., Eijinden, R. J. and Yzer, M. C. (1998). Predictors of AIDS-preventive behavioural intentions among adult heterosexuals at risk for HIV-infection: extending current models and measures. *AIDS Education and Prevention*, 10, 149–72.

Caffray, C. M. and Schneider, S. L. (2000). Why do they do it? Affective motivators in adolescents' decisions to participate in risk behaviours. 14(4), 576.

Calman, K. C. (2002). Communication of risk: choice, consent and trust. *Lancet*, 360, 166–8.

Campbell, J. D. and Tesser, A. (1983). Motivational interpretations of hindsight bias: an individual difference analysis. *Journal of Personality*, 51, 605–20.

Campbell, L. F. and Stewart, A. E. (1992). Effects of group membership on perception of risk for AIDS. *Psychological Reports*, 70, 1075–92.

Canelon, M. L. and Rovira, D. P. (2002). Representaciones sociales de la enfermedad de Chagas en comunidades en riesgo: creencias, actitudes y prevención. *Revista Interamericana de Psicologia*, 36, 215–36 (Social representation of Chagas Disease in at-risk communities: beliefs, attitudes and prevention).

Cannon-Bowers, J. A., Salas, E. and Converse, S. A. (1990). Cognitive psychology and team training: training shared mental models of complex systems. *Human Factors Bulletin*, 33, 1–4.

(1993). Shared mental models in expert team decision-making. In N. J. Castellan (ed.), *Individual and Group Decision Making: Current Issues*. New Jersey: LEA.

Cantor, N. and Mischel, W. (1977). Traits as prototypes: effects on recognition memory. *Journal of Personality and Social Psychology*, 35, 38–48.

Carnes, S. A., Schweitzer, M., Peelle, E. B., Wolfe, A. K. and Munro, J. F. (1998). Measuring the success of public participation on environmental restoration and waste management activities in the US Department of Energy. *Technology in Society*, 20, 385–406.

Carney, R. E. (1971). Attitudes towards risk. In R. E. Carney (ed.), *Risk Taking Behaviour: Concepts, Methods, and Applications to Smoking and Drug Abuse* (pp. 1–27). Springfield, IL: Charles C. Thomas.

Carson, L. (1999). In a sneak preview of the referendum, your average Australian voted yes. *University of Sydney News*, 6.

Carter, D. A. (1991). Aspects of risk assessment for hazardous pipeline containing flammable substances. *Journal of Loss Prevention in the Process Industries*, 4, 68.

Carvalho, A. and Burgess, J. (2005). Cultural circuits of climate change in UK broadsheet newspapers. *Risk Analysis*, 25, 252.

Castellan, N. J. (1993). *Individual and Group Decision Making: Current Issues*. New Jersey: LEA.

Castro, P. and Gomes, I. (2005). Genetically modified organisms in the Portuguese press: thematization and anchoring. *Journal for the Theory of Social Behaviour*, 35, 1–17.

Chapman, G. B. and Coups, E. J. (2006). Emotion and preventative health behaviour: worry, regret, and influenza vaccination. *Health Psychology*, 25, 444.

Cherpitel, C. J. (1993). Alcohol, injury and risk-taking behaviour: data from a national sample. *Alcoholism Clinical and Experimental Research*, 17, 762–6.

Chess, C. and Purcell, K. (1999). Public participation and the environment: do we know what works? *Environmental Science & Technology*, 33, 2685–92.

Clark, M. C. and Payne, R. L. (2006). Character-based determinants of trust in leaders. *Risk Analysis*, 26, 1161–73.

Cliff, S. M., Wilkins, J. C. and Davidson, E. A. F. (1993). Impulsiveness, venturesomeness and sexual risk-taking among heterosexual GUM clinic attenders. *Personality and Individual Differences*, 15, 403–10.

Costa, P. T., Jr. and McCrae, R. R. (1992). Revised NEO Personality Inventory (NEO-PI-R) and NEO Five Factor Inventory (NEO-FFI) professional manual. Odessa, FL: Psychological Assessment Resources.

Cotgrove, S. (1982). *Catastrophe or Cornucopia: The Environment, Politics and the Future*. Chichester: Wiley.

Cowley, S. and Billings, J. R. (1999). Identifying approaches to meet assessed needs in health visiting. *Journal of Clinical Nursing*, 8, 527–34.

Cox, P., Fischhoff, B., Gerrard, S., Niewöhner, J., Pidgeon, N. and Riley, D. (2001). *Developing a Methodology for Designing Messages about Chemical Risks in the Workplace Using the Mental Models Approach*. Report to the Health and Safety Executive.

Cox, S. and Cox, T. (1991). The structure of employee attitudes to safety: a European example. *Work & Stress*, 5, 93–106.

Cox, S., Jones, B. and Collinson, D. (2006). Trust relations in high-reliability organizations. *Risk Analysis*, 26, 1123–38.

Coyle, I., Sleeman, S. and Adams, D. (1995). Safety climate. *Journal of Safety Research*, 22, 247–54.

Crane, S. F. and Carswell, J. W. (1992). A review and assessment of nongovernmental organization-based STD/AIDS education and prevention projects for marginalized groups. *Health Education Research*, 7, 175–94.

Crisp, B. R. and Barber, J. G. (1995). The effect of locus of control on the association between risk perception and sexual risk-taking. *Personality and Individual Differences*, 19, 841–5.

Crossland, B., Bennett, P. A., Ellis, A. F., Farmer, F. R., Gittus, J., Godfrey, P. S. et al. (1992). *Estimating Engineering Risk*. London: Royal Society.

Cvetkovich, G. (1999). The attribution of social trust. In G. Cvetkovich and R. E. Lofstedt (eds), *Social Trust and the Management of Risk* (pp. 53–61). London: Earthscan.

Cvetkovich, G. and Earle, T. C. (eds) (1991). *Journal of Cross-Cultural Psychology*, special issue: Risk and Culture, 22, 11–149.

Cvetkovich, G. T. and Löfstedt, R. E. (1999). *Social Trust and the Management of Risk*. London: Earthscan.

Cvetkovich, G., Siegrist, M., Murray, R. and Tragesser, S. (2002). New information and social trust: asymmetry and perseverance of attributions about hazard managers. *Risk Analysis*, 22, 359–67.

Dake, K. (1991). Orienting dispositions in the perception of risk: an analysis of contemporary worldviews and cultural biases. *Journal of Cross-Cultural Psychology*, 22, 61–82.

Dake, K. and Wildavsky, A. (1991). Individual differences in risk perception and risk-taking preferences. In B. J. Garrick and W. C. Gekler (eds), *The Analysis, Communication and Perception of Risk* (pp. 98–117). New York: Plenum.

Das, E., de-Wit, J. and Stroebe, W. (2003). Fear appeals motivate acceptance of action recommendations: evidence for a positive bias in the processing of persuasive messages. *Personality and Social Psychology Bulletin*, 29, 650–64.

Davidson, D. J. and Frendenburg, W. R. (1996). Gender and environment risk concerns: a review and analysis of available research. *Environment and Behaviour*, 28, 3, 302–39.

Davies, M. F. (1993). Field dependence and hindsight bias: output interference in the generation of reasons. *Journal of Research in Personality*, 27, 222–37.

Davis, M. A. and Bobko, P. (1986). Contextual effects on escalation processes in public sector decision-making. *Organizational Behaviour and Human Decision Processes*, 37, 121–38.

de Hoog, N., Stroebe, W. and de-Wit, J. B. F. (2005). The impact of fear appeals on processing and acceptance of action recommendations. *Personality and Social Psychology Bulletin*, 31, 24–33.

de Man, A. F., Simpson-Housley, P. and Curtis, F. (1984). Trait anxiety, perception of potential nuclear hazard, and state anxiety. *Psychological Reports* 54, 3, 791–4.

de Man, A., Simpson-Housley, P., Curtis, F., and Smith, D. (1984). Trait anxiety and response to potential disaster. *Psychological Reports*, 54, 507–12.

de Souza, L. C. G. (2001). The social representations of the car and the traffic behaviour of youths/as representacoes sociais do carro e o comportamento dos jovens no transito. *Arquivos Brasileiros de Psicologia*, 53, 125–37.

de-Wit, J., Teunis, N., Van Griensven, G. and Sandfort, T. H. (1994). Behavioral risk reduction strategies to prevent HIV infection among homosexual men: a grounded theory approach. *AIDS Education and Prevention*, 6, 493–505.

Dedobbeleer, N. and Beland, F. (1991). A safety climate measure for construction sites. *Journal of Safety Research*, 22, 97–103.

Deery, H. A. and Love, A. W. (1996). The effect of a moderate dose of alcohol on the traffic hazard perception profile of young drink-drivers. *Addiction*, 91, 815–27.

Deitz, S. R. E. and Thoms, W. E. E. (1991). *Pilots, Personality, and Performance: Human Behaviour and Stress in the Skies*. New York: Quorum Books.

Dejoy, D. M. (1989). An attribution theory perspective on alcohol-impaired driving. *Health Education Quarterly*, 16, 359–72.

(1992). An examination of gender differences in traffic accident risk perception. *Accident Analysis and Prevention*, 24, 237–46.

(1994). Managing safety in the workplace: an attribution theory analysis and model. *Journal of Safety Research*, 25, 3–17.

Dekker, S. W. A. (2004). The hindsight bias is not a bias and not about history. *Human Factors and Aerospace Safety*, 4, 87–99.

Department of Health (1997). *Communicating about Risks to Public Health: Pointers to Good Practice*. Department of Health.

Dockins, C., Jenkins, R. R., Owens, N., Simon, N. B. and Bembenek Wiggins, L. (2002). Valuation of childhood risk reduction: the importance of age, risk preferences, and perspective. *Risk Analysis*, 22, 335–46.

Doise, W. (1982). *Levels of Explanation in Social Psychology*. Cambridge University Press.

Dolinski, D., Wojciech, G. and Zawisza, E. (1987). Unrealistic pessimism. *Journal of Social Psychology*, 127, 511–16.

Donald, I. and Canter, D. (1994). Employee attitudes and safety in the chemical industry. *Journal of Loss Prevention in the Process Industries*, 7, 208.

Donohew, L., Bardo, M. T. and Zimmerman, R. S. (2004). Personality and risky behaviour: communication and prevention. In R. M. Stelmack (ed.), *On the Psychobiology of Personality: Essays in Honor of Marvin Zuckerman* pp. 223–45. New York: Elsevier.

Dorn, L. and Matthews, G. (1995). Prediction of mood and risk appraisals from trait measures: two studies of simulated driving. *European Journal of Personality*, 9, 25–42.

Dorner, D. (1987). On the difficulties people have in dealing with complexity. In J. Rasmussen, K. Duncan and J. Leplat (eds), *New Technologies and Human Error* (pp. 97–109). New York: Wiley.

Dosman, D. M., Adamowicz, W. L. and Hrudey, S. E. (2001). Socioeconomic determinants of health – and food safety – related risk perceptions. *Risk Analysis*, 21, 307–17.

Douglas, M. (1982). *Essays in the Sociology of Perception*. London: Routledge and Kegan Paul.

(1986). *Risk Acceptability according to the Social Sciences*. London: Routledge and Kegan Paul.

Douglas, M. and Calvez, M. (1990). The self as risk taker: a cultural theory of contagion in relation to AIDS. *Sociological Review*, 38, 445–64.

Douglas, M. and Wildavsky, A. (1982). *Risk and Culture: An Essay on the Selection of Technological and Environmental Dangers*. Berkeley: University of California Press.

Drottz-Sjöberg, B. M. and Sjöberg, L. (1990). Risk perception and worries after the Chernobyl accident. *Journal of Environmental Psychology*, 10, 135–49.

Dunegan, K. J. (1993). Framing cognitive modes, and image theory: toward an understanding of a glass half full. *Journal of Applied Psychology*, 78, 503.

Durodie, B. and Wessely, S. (2002). Resilience or panic? The public and terrorist attack. *Lancet*, 360, 1901–2.

Earle, T. C. (2004). Thinking aloud about trust: a protocol analysis of trust in risk management. *Risk Analysis*, 24, 169–83.

Earle, T. C. and Cvetkovich, G. T. (1995). *Social Trust: Toward a Cosmopolitan Society*. Westport, CT: Praeger.

Eiser, J. R. and Arnold, B. W. A. (1999). Out in the midday sun: risk behaviour and optimistic beliefs among residents and visitors on Tenerife. *Psychology and Health*, 14, 529–44.

Eiser, J. R., Miles, S. and Frewer, L. J. (2002). Trust, perceived risk, and attitudes toward food technologies. *Journal of Applied Psychology*, 32, 2423–33.

Ekenes, J. M. and Cameron, S. (1993). Fostering a safety culture. *Light Metals* 21–5, 883–7.

El-Hajje, E. and Ahmed, R. (1997). The effect of mood on group decision-making. *Dissertation Abstracts International*, Section B, *The Sciences and Engineering*, 57, 5976.

Engen, T. (1972). Psychophysics. In J. W. Kling and L. A. Riggs (eds), *Experimental Psychology* (pp. 1–46). New York: Holt, Rinehart and Winston, 3rd edition.

Englander, T., Farago, K., Slovic, P. and Fischhoff, B. (1986). Comparative analysis of risk perception in Hungary and the United States. *Social Behaviour*, 1, 55–66.

Eysenck, H. (1967). *The Biological Basis of Personality*. Springfield: C. C. Thomas.

Eysenck, S. B. G. and Abdel-Khalex, A. M. (1992). Cross-cultural comparisons of the I-sub-7 impulsiveness scales for Egyptian and English adults. *European Journal of Psychological Assessment*, 8, 149–53.

Eysenck, S. B. G. and Eysenck, H. J. (1963). On the dual nature of extraversion. *British Journal of Social and Clinical Psychology*, 2, 46–55.

(1978). Impulsiveness and venturesomeness: their position in a dimensional scale of personality description. *Psychological Reports*, 43, 1247–55.

(1980). Impulsiveness and venturesomeness in children. *Personality and Individual Differences*, 1, 73–8.

Eysenck, S. B. G., Daum, I., Schugens, M. M. and Diehl, J. M. (1990). A cross-cultural study of impulsiveness, venturesomeness and empathy: Germany and England. *Zeitschrift für Differentielle und Diagnostische Psychologie*, 11, 209–13.

Eysenck, S. B. G., Pearson, P. R., Easting, G. and Allsopp, J. F. (1985). Age norms for impulsiveness, venturesomeness and empathy in adults. *Personality and Individual Differences*, 6, 613–19.

Facione, N. C. (2002). Perceived risk of breast cancer. Influence of heuristic thinking. *Cancer Practice*, 10, 256–62.

Feigenson, N. R. and Bailis, D. S. (2001). Air bag safety: media coverage, popular conceptions, and public policy. *Psychology, Public Policy, and Law*, 7, 444–81.

Ferguson, N. M., Cummings, D. A. T., Cauchemez, S. and Fraser, C. (2005). Strategies for containing an emerging influenza pandemic in Southeast Asia. *Nature*, 7056, 209–14.

Ferguson, N. M., Cummings, D. A. T., Fraser, C., Cajka, J. C., Cooley, P. C. and Burke, D. S. (2006). Strategies for mitigating an influenza pandemic. *Nature*, 7101, 448–52.

Fife-Schaw, C. and Barnett, J. (2003). Measuring optimistic bias. In G. M. Breakwell (ed.), *Doing Social Psychology Research*. Oxford: Blackwell.

Fife-Schaw, C. and Rowe, G. (1996). Public perceptions of everyday food hazards: a psychometric study. *Risk Analysis*, 16, 487–500.

Finucane, M. L., Alhakami, A. S., Slovic, P. and Johnson, S. M. (2000). The affect heuristic in judgments of risk and benefits. *Journal of Behavioural Decision Making*, 13, 1–17.

Fischhoff, B. (1975). Hindsight? Foresight: the effect of outcome knowledge on judgment under uncertainty. *Journal of Experimental Psychology: Human Perception and Performance*, 1, 288–99.

(1994). The psychology of risk characterization. In N. E. Sahlin and B. Brehmer (eds), *Future Risks and Risk Management* (pp. 125–39). New York: Kluwer Academic/Plenum Publishers.

(1998). Risk Communication. In R. Löfstedt and L. Frewer (eds), *Risk and Modern Society*. London: Earthscan.

(1999). Why (cancer) risk communication can be hard. *Journal of the National Cancer Institute Monographs*, 25, 7–13.

(2001). Defining stigma. In J. Flynn, P. Slovic and H. Kunreuther (eds), *Risk, Media and Stigma: Understanding Public Challenges to Modern Science and Technology* (pp. 361–8). London: Earthscan.

Fischhoff, B., Bostrom, A. and Quadrel, M. J. (2000). *Risk Perception and Communication*. New York: Cambridge University Press, 2nd edition.

(1997). *Risk Perception and Communication*. Oxford University Press.

Fischhoff, B., Gonzalez, R. M. and Lerner, J. S. S. D. A. (2005). Evolving judgments of terror risks: foresight, hindsight, and emotion. *Journal of Experimental Psychology: Applied*, 11, 124–39.

Fischhoff, B., Slovic, P. and Lichtenstein, S. (1978a). Fault trees: sensitivity of estimated failure probabilities to problem representation. *Journal of Experimental Psychology: Human Perception and Performance*, 4, 330–44.

Fischhoff, B., Hohenemser, C., Kasperson, R. E. and Kates, R. W. (1978b). Can hazard management be improved? *Environment*, 20, 16–20, 32–37.

Fischhoff, B., Slovic, P., Lichtenstein, S., Read, S. and Combs, B. (1978c). How safe is safe enough? A psychometric study of attitudes towards technological risks and benefits. *Policy Sciences*, 9, 127–52.

Florig, H. K., Granger Morgan, M., Morgan, K. M., Jenni, K. E., Fischhoff, B., Fischbeck, P. S. *et al.* (2001). A deliberative method for ranking risks (1): overview and test bed development. *Risk Analysis*, 21, 913–22.

Floyd, D. L., Prentice-Dunn, S. and Rogers, R. W. (2000). A meta-analysis of research on protection motivation theory. *Journal of Applied Social Psychology*, 30, 407–29.

Flynn, J., Slovic, P. and Mertz, C. K. (1993). The Nevada Initiative: a risk communication fiasco. *Risk in File*, 138, 497–502.

(1994). Gender, race, and perception of environmental health risks. *Risk Analysis*, 14, 1101–8.

Flynn, J., Peters, E., Mertz, C. K. and Slovic, P. (1998). Risk, media, and stigma at Rocky Flats. *Risk Analysis*, 18, 715–27.

Flynn, J., Slovic, P. and Kunreuther, H. (eds) (2001). *Risk, Media and Stigma: Understanding Public Challenges to Modern Science and Technology*. London: Earthscan.

Fontaine, K. and Snyder, L. B. (1995). Optimistic bias in cancer risk perception: a cross national study. *Psychological Reports*, 77, 143–6.

Forgas, J. P. E. (2000). *Feeling and Thinking: The Role of Affect in Social Cognition*. Cambridge University Press.

Franco, K., Belinson, J., Casey, G., Plummer, S., Tamburrino, M. and Tung, E. (2000). Adjustment to perceived ovarian cancer risk. *Psychooncology*, 9, 411–17.

French, D. P., Gayton, E. L., Burton, J., Thorogood, M. and Marteau, T. M. (2002). Measuring perceptions of synergistic circulatory disease risk due to smoking and the oral contraceptive pill. *Risk Analysis*, 22, 1139.

Freudenburg, W. R. (1992). Nothing succeeds like success? Risk analysis and the organizational amplication of risks. *Risk: Issues in Health and Safety*, 3, 1–53.

Frewer, L. (1999a). *Demographic Differences in Risk Perception and Public Priorities for Risk Mitigation*, Ministry of Agriculture Fisheries and Food, UK Government.

(1999b). Risk perception, social trust, and public participation in strategic decision making: implications for emerging technologies. *Ambio*, 28, 569–74.

Frewer, L. J. and Miles, S. (2003). Temporal stability of the psychological determinants of trust: implications for communication about food risks. *Health, Risk & Society*, 5, 259–71.

Frewer, L., Miles, S. and Marsh, R. (2002a). The GM foods controversy: a test of the social amplification of risk model. *Risk Analysis*, 22, 713–23.

(2002b). The media and genetically modified foods: evidence in support of social amplification of risk. *Risk Analysis*, 22, 701–11.

Frewer, L., Raats, M. and Shepherd, R. (1994). Modelling the media: the transmission of risk information in the British quality press. *Journal of the Institute of Mathematics and its Applications to Industry*, 5, 235–47.

Frewer, L. J., Scholderer, J. and Bredahl, L. (2003). Communicating about the risks and benefits of genetically modified foods: the mediating role of trust. *Risk Analysis*, 23, 1117–33.

Frewer, L., Howard, C., Hedderley, D. and Shepherd, R. (1996). What determines trust in information about food-related risks? Underlying psychological constructs. *Risk Analysis*, 16, 473–86.

Frost, S., Myers, L. B. and Newman, S. P. (2001). Genetic screening for Alzheimer's disease: what factors predict intentions to take a test? *Behavioural Medicine*, 27, 101–9.

Gadomska, M. (1994). Risk communication. In *Radiation and Society: Comprehending Radiation Risk. International Atomic Energy Agency Proceedings, Vienna*, vol. I, pp. 147–66.

Galanter, E. (1990). Utility functions for nonmonetary events. *American Journal of Psychology*, 105, 449–70.

Galanter, E. and Pliner, P. (1974). Cross-modality matching of money against other continua. In H. Moskowitz, B. Sharf and J. C. Stevens (eds), *Sensation and Measurement: Papers in Honour of S. S. Stevens* (pp. 65–76). Dordrecht: Reidel.

Ganzach, Y. (2001). Judging risk and return of financial assets. *Organizational Behaviour and Human Decision Processes*, 83, 353–70.

Gardner, G. T. and Gould, L. C. (1989). Public perceptions of the risks and benefits of technology. *Risk Analysis*, 9, 225–42.

Garvin, T. (2001). The epistemological distances between scientists, policy makers and the public. *Risk Analysis*, 21, 443–55.

Gasper, K. and Clore, G. L. (1998). The persistent use of negative affect by anxious individuals to estimate risk. *Journal of Personality and Social Psychology*, 74, 1350–63.

(2000). Do you have to pay attention to your feelings to be influenced by them? *Personality and Social Psychology Bulletin*, 266, 711.

Geller, E. S. (1994). Ten principles for achieving a total safety culture. *Professional Safety*, 39, 18–24.

(1995). Key to achieving a total safety culture. *Professional Safety*, 40, 16–22.

Geller, S., Burns, S. E. and Brailer, D. J. (1996). The impact of nonclinical factors on practice variations: the case of hysterectomies. *Health Services Research*, 30, 723–50.

Gescheider, G. A. (1976). *Psychophysics: Method and Theory*. Hillsdale, NJ: Erlbaum.

Giddens, A. (1990). *The Consequences of Modernity*. Cambridge: Polity Press. (1991). *Modernity and Self-Identity*. Cambridge: Polity.

Gigerenzer, G. (2006). Out of the frying pan into the fire: behavioural reactions to terrorist attacks. *Risk Analysis*, 26, 2, 347–57.

Gigone, D. and Hastie, R. (1993). The common knowledge effect: information sharing and group judgment. *Journal of Personality and Social Psychology*, 65, 974.

Girandola, F. (2000). Peur et persuasion: présentations des recherches (1953–1998) et d'une nouvelle lecture. *Année-Psychologique*, 100, 333–76 (Fear and persuasion: review and re-analysis of the literature (1953–1998)).

Glass, T. A. (2001). Understanding public response to disasters. *Public Health Reports*, 116, 69–73.

Glass, T. A. and Schoch-Spana, M. (2002). Bioterrorism and the people: how to vaccinate a city against panic. *Clinical Infectious Diseases*, 34, 217–23.

Goldberg, L. R. (1993). The structure of phenotypic personality traits. *American Psychologist*, 48, 1, 26–34.

Goma-i-Freixanet, M. (2004). Sensation seeking and participation in physical sports. In R. M. Stelmack (ed.), *On the Psychobiology of Personality: Essays in Honor of Marvin Zuckerman* (pp. 185–201). New York: Elsevier.

Goodwin, R., Kozlova, A., Kwiatkowska, A., Luu, L. A. N., Nizharadze, G., Realo, A. *et al.* (2003). Social representations of HIV/AIDS in Central and Eastern Europe. *Social Science and Medicine*, 56, 1373–84.

Goodwin, R., Kozlova, A., Nizharadze, G. and Polyakova, G. (2004a). HIV/AIDS among adolescents in Eastern Europe: knowledge of HIV/AIDS, social representations of risk and sexual activity amongst school children and homeless adolescents in Russia, Georgia and the Ukraine. *Journal of Health Psychology*, 9, 381–96.

Goodwin, R., Kwiatkowska, A., Realo, A., Kozlova, A., Luu, L. A. N. and Nizharadze, G. (2004b). Social representations of HIV/AIDS in five central European and eastern European countries: a multidimensional analysis. *AIDS Care*, 16, 669–80.

Gordon, K. E., Dooley, J. M., Camfield, P. R., Camfield, C. S. and MacSween, J. (2002). Parents of children with epilepsy are optimistic for their children's health, but relatively pessimistic when compared with other parents. *Epilepsy and Behaviour*, 3, 262–5.

Gorman, J. M. (2005). In the wake of trauma. *CNS Spectrums*, 10, 81–5.

Goszczynska, M., Tyszka, T. and Slovic, P. (1991). Risk perception in Poland: a comparison with three other countries. *Journal of Behavioural Decision Making*, 4, 179–93.

Gould, L. C., Gardner, G. T., Deluca, D. R., Tiemann, A. R., Doob, L. W. and Strolwijk, J. A. J. (1988). *Perceptions of Technological Risks and Benefits*. New York: Russell Sage Foundation.

Graham, J. D. (2001). Decision-analytic refinements of the precautionary principle. *Journal of Risk Research*, 4, 2, 127–42.

Graham, J. D. and Hsia, S. (2002). Europe's precautionary principle: promise and pitfalls. *Journal of Risk Research*, 5, 371–90.

Grasso, B. C., Rothschild, J. M., Jordan, C. W. and Jayaram, G. (2005). What is the measure of a safe hospital? Medication errors missed by risk management, clinical staff, and surveyors. *Journal of Psychiatric Practice*, 11, 268–73.

Grendstad, G. and Grendstad, P. S. (1994). Kultur som Levemate. *Politica*, 26, 420–38.

Grendstad, G. and Selle, P. (1995). Cultural theory and the new institutionalism. *Journal of Theoretical Politics*, 7, 1, 5–27.

Grobe, D., Douthitt, R. and Zepeda, L. (1999). A model of consumers' risk perceptions toward recombinant bovine growth hormone (rbgh): the impact of risk characteristics. *Risk Analysis*, 19, 661–73.

Grunert, K. G., Brunso, K., Bredahl, L. and Beck, A. C. (2001). Food-related lifestyle: a segmentation approach to European food consumers. In L. J. Frewer, E. Risvik and R. Schifferstein (eds), *Food, People and Society* (pp. 211–30). Berlin: Springer Verlag.

Gurmankin, A. D., Baron, J. and Armstrong, K. (2004). Intended message versus message received in hypothetical physician risk communication: exploring the gap. *Risk Analysis*, 24, 1337–47.

Gustafson, P. E. (1998). Gender differences in risk perception. *Risk Analysis*, 18, 6, 805–12.

Gutteling, J. M. and Kuttschreuter, M. (1999). The millennium bug controversy in the Netherlands. Expert views versus public perception. In L. H. J. Goossens (ed.), *Proceedings of the Ninth Annual Conference on Risk Analysis: Facing the New Millennium*. Delft University Press.

(2002). The role of expertise in risk communication: lay people's and experts' perception of the millennium bug risk in the Netherlands. *Journal of Risk Research*, 5, 35–47.

Gutteling, J. M. and Wiegman, O. (1993). Gender specific reactions to environmental hazards in the Netherlands. *Sex Roles*, 28, 433–77.

Gwartney-Gibbs, P. A. and Lach, D. H. (1991). Sex differences in attitudes toward nuclear war. *Journal of Peace Research*, 28, 161–74.

Hakes, J. K. and Viscusi, W. K. (2004). Dead reckoning: demographic determinants of the accuracy of mortality risk perceptions. *Risk Analysis*, 24, 651–64.

Halpern-Felsher, B. L., Millstein, S. G., Ellen, J. M., Adler, N. E., Tschann, J. M. and Biehl, M. (2001). The role of behavioural experience in judging risks. *Health Psychology*, 20, 120–6.

Hammitt, J. K., Wiener, J. B., Swedlow, B., Kall, D. and Zhou, Z. (2005). Precautionary regulation in Europe and the United States: a quantitative comparison. *Risk Analysis*, 25.

Hammond, S. (2000). Using psychometric tests. In G. M. Breakwell, S. Hammond and C. Fife-Schaw (eds), *Research Methods in Psychology* (pp. 182–209). London: Sage, 2nd edition.

Hampson, S. E., Andrews, J. A., Barckley, M., Lee, M. E. and Lichtenstein, E. (2003). Assessing perceptions of synergistic health risk: a comparison of two scales. *Risk Analysis*, 23, 1021–9.

Hampson, S. E., Andrews, J. A., Lee, M. E., Foster, L. S., Glasgow, R. E. and Lichtenstein, E. (1998). Lay understanding of synergistic risk: the case of radon and cigarette smoking. *Risk Analysis*, 18, 343–50.

Handmer, J. and Penning-Rowsell, E. (1990). *Hazards and the Communication of Risk*. Aldershot: Gower.

Hanekamp, J. C. (2006). Precaution and cholera: a response to Tickner and Gouveia-Vigeant. *Risk Analysis*, 26, 1013–19.

Hanekamp, J. C., Vera-Navas, G. and Verstegen, S. W. (2005). The historical roots of precautionary thinking: the cultural ecological critique and 'The Limits to Growth'. *Journal of Risk Research*, 8, 295–310.

Hare, R. D. (1991). *The Hare Psychopathology Checklist Revised*. Toronto: Multi-Health Systems.

Harris, G., Rice, M. and Quincy, V. (1993). Violent recidivism of mentally disordered offenders: the development of a statistical prediction instrument. *Criminal Justice Behaviour*, 20, 315–35.

Harris, P., Middleton, W. and Joiner, R. (2000). The typical student as an ingroup member: eliminating optimistic bias by reducing social distance. *European Journal of Social Psychology*, 30, 235–54.

Haselton, M. G. and Buss, D. M. (2001). Emotional reactions following first-time sexual intercourse: the affective shift hypothesis. *Personal Relationships*, 8, 357–69.

Hashiguchi, K. (1974). The number of decision makers and the level of risk taking within a group. *Japanese Journal of Experimental Social Psychology*, 14, 123–31.

Hassan, A. (1986). Circumcision in the Sudan. Unpublished MSc dissertation, University of Surrey, Guildford.

Hastings, G., Stead, M. and Webb, J. (2004). Fear appeals in social marketing: strategic and ethical reasons for concern. *Psychology & Marketing*, 21, 961–86.

Health and Safety Commission (1991). *Major Hazard Aspects of the Transport of Dangerous Substances*. London: HMSO.

Heath, R. L. & Palenchar, M. (2000). Community relations and risk communication: a longitudinal study of the impact of emergency response messages. *Journal of Public Relations Research*, 12, 131–61.

Heaven, P. C. (1991). Venturesomeness, impulsiveness, and Eysenck's personality dimensions: a study among Australian adolescents. *Journal of Genetic Psychology*, 152, 91–9.

Hedge, B. (1989). Worried well and psychological issues. *AIDS Care*, 1, 193–4.

Heilbrun, K. (1999). Basic and advanced issues in risk assessment. Paper at Workshop of the Department of Public Welfare, Commonwealth of Pennsylvannia.

Heine, S. J. and Lehman, D. R. (1995). Cultural variation in unrealistic optimism: does the west feel more invulnerable than the east? *Journal of Personality and Social Psychology*, 68, 595–607.

Helsloot, I. and Ruitenberg, A. (2004). Citizen response to disasters. *Journal of Contingencies and Crisis Management*, 12, 98–111.

Helweg-Larsen, M. (1999). (The lack of) optimistic biases in response to the 1994 Northridge earthquake: the role of personal experience. *Journal of Basic and Applied Social Psychology*, 21, 110–29.

Henderson, V. R., Hennessy, M., Barrett, D. W., Curtis, B., McCoy-Roth, M., Trentacoste, N. *et al.* (2005). When risky is attractive: sensation seeking and romantic partner selection. *Personality and Individual Differences*, 38, 311–25.

Hendrick, S. and Hendrick, C. (1987). Love and sex attitudes, self-disclosure and sensation-seeking. *Journal of Social and Personal Relationships*, 4, 281–97.

Hertwig, R., Fanselow, C. and Hoffrage, U. (2003). Hindsight bias: how knowledge and heuristics affect our reconstruction of the past. *Memory*, 11, 357–77.

Hess, A. K. and Weiner, I. B. (eds) (1999). *Handbook of Forensic Psychology*. New York: Wiley, 2nd edition.

Higbee, K. L. (1972). Group risk taking in military decisions. *Journal of Social Psychology*, 88, 55–64.

Highhouse, S. and Paese, P. W. (1996). Problem domain and prospect frame: choice under opportunity versus threat. *Personality and Social Psychology Bulletin*, 22, 124–32.

Hillier, L. M. and Morrongiello, B. A. (1998) Age and gender differences in school-age children's appraisals of injury risk. *Journal of Pediatric Psychology*, 23, 4, 229–38.

Himiob-de-Marcano, M. (2000). When panic seizes everybody: how to remain calm to help our fellow-men directly traumatized. *Tropicos: Revista de Psicoanalisis*, 8, 149–52 (Cuando el panico es de todos: como conservar la calma para ayudar a nuestros hermanos directamente traumatizados).

Hinman, G. W., Rosa, E. A., Kleinhesselink, R. R. and Lowinger, T. C. (1993). Perceptions of nuclear and other risks in Japan and the United States. *Risk Analysis*, 13, 449–55.

Hiraba, J., Bao, W. N., Lorenz, F. O. and Pechacova, Z. (1998). Perceived risk of crime in the Czech Republic. *Journal of Research in Crime and Delinquency*, 35, 225–42.

Hoffrage, U., Hertwig, R. and Gigerenzer, G. (2000). Hindsight bias: a by-product of knowledge updating? *Journal of Experimental Psychology: Learning, Memory and Cognition*, 26, 566–81.

Hogg, M. A. and Vaughan, G. M. (1998). Leadership and group decision-making. In M. A. Hogg and G. M. Vaughan (eds), *Social Psychology: An Introduction* (pp. 300–6) London: Prentice-Hall, 2nd edition.

Hogg, M. A., Turner, J. C. and Davidson, B. (1990). Polarized norms and social frames of reference: a test of the self-categorization theory of group polarization. *Basic and Applied Social Psychology*, 11, 77–100.

Hohenemser, C. and Renn, O. (1988). Chernobyl's other legacy: shifting public perceptions of nuclear risk. *Environment*, 30, 3, 4–11.

Holzl, E. and Kirchler, E. (2005). Causal attribution and hindsight bias for economic developments. *Journal of Applied Psychology*, 90, 167–74.

Horlick-Jones, T., Rosenhead, J., Georgiou, I., Ravetz, J. and Löfstedt, R. (2001). Decision support for organisational risk management by problem structuring. *Health, Risk & Society*, 3, 141–65.

Hornig, S. (1992). Framing risks: audience and reader factors. *Journalism Quarterly*, 69, 679–90.

Hornig Priest, S. (1999). The never-ending story of dioxin. In S. M. Friedman, S. Dunwoody and C. L. Rogers (eds), *Communicating Uncertainty, Media Coverage of New and Controversial Science* (pp. 190–201). New York: LEA.

Horswill, M. S. and McKenna, F. P. (1999a). The effect of interference on dynamic risk taking judgments. *British Journal of Psychology*, 90, 189–99.

(1999b). The effect of perceived control on risk taking. *Journal of Applied Psychology*, 29, 377–91.

Horvath, P. and Zuckerman, M. (1993). Sensation seeking, risk appraisal, and risky behaviour. *Personality and Individual Differences*, 14, 41–52.

Hossain, F. and Onyango, B. (2004). Product attributes and consumer acceptance of nutritionally enhanced genetically modified foods. *International Journal of Consumer Studies*, 28, 255–67.

Houlding, C. and Davidson, R. (2003). Beliefs as predictors of condom use by injecting drug users in treatment. *Health Education Research*, 18, 145–55.

Howel, D., Moffatt, S., Prince, H., Bush, J. and Dunn, C. E. (2002). Urban air quality in North-East England: exploring the influences on local views and perceptions. *Risk Analysis*, 22, 121–30.

HSE, ACSNI and Human Factors Study Group (1993). *Organising for Safety*. Report 3. Suffolk: HSE Books.

Hsee, C. K. and Weber, E. U. (1999). Cross-national differences in risk preference and lay predictions. *Journal of Behavioural Decision Making*, 12, 2, 165–79.

Humphrey, J. C. (1998). Self organise and survive: disabled people in the British trade union movement. *Disability and Society*, 13, 587–602.

Hunton, J. and Rose, J. M. (2005). Cellular telephones and driving performance: the effects of attentional demands on motor vehicle crash risk. *Risk Analysis*, 25, 4, 855–66.

Hutter, B. M. (2001). *Regulation and Risk: Occupational Health and Safety on the Railways*. New York: Oxford University Press.

Imrie, R. (1999). The role of access groups in facilitating accessible environments for disabled people. *Disability and Society*, 14, 463–82.

International Nuclear Safety Advisory Group (1991). *Safety Series No 75-INSAG-4*. Vienna: IAEA.

Irwin, W., Davidson, R. J., Lowe, M. J., Mock, B. J., Sorenson, J. A. and Turski, P. A. (1996). Human amygdala activation detected with echo-planar functional magnetic resonance imaging. *NeuroReport*, 7, 1765–9.

Isenberg, D. J. (1986). Group polarization: a critical review. *Journal of Personality and Social Psychology*, 50, 1141–51.

Janis, I. L. (1971). Groupthink. *Psychology Today* 43–6, 344.

(1972). *Victims of Groupthink*. Boston: Houghton Mifflin.

Janoff-Bulman, R. and Frieze, I. H. (1983). A theoretical perspective for understanding reactions to victimization. *Journal of Social Issues*, 39, 1–17.

Jeffcott, S., Pidgeon, N., Weyman, A. and Walls, J. (2006). Risk, trust, and safety culture in the U.K. train operating companies. *Risk Analysis*, 26, 1105–21.

Jianguang, Z. (1993). Environmental hazards in the Chinese public's eyes. *Risk Analysis*, 13, 509–14.

Joffe, H. (2003). Risk: from perception to social representation. *British Journal of Psychology*, 42, 55–73.

Joffe, H. and Bettega, N. (2003). Social representations of AIDS among Zambian adolescents. *Journal of Health Psychology*, 8, 616–31.

Joffe, H. and Haarhoff, G. (2002). Representations of far-flung illnesses: the case of Ebola in Britain. *Social Science and Medicine*, 54, 955–69.

Joffe, H. and Lee, L. (2004). Social representation of a food risk: the Hong Kong avian bird flu epidemic. *Health Psychology*, 9, 517–33.

Johnson, B. B. (2002a). Gender and race in beliefs about outdoor air pollution. *Risk Analysis*, 22, 725–38.

(2002b). Stability and inoculation of risk comparisons' effects under conflict: replicating and extending the 'Asbestos Jury' study by Slovic *et al*. *Risk Analysis*, 22, 777–88.

(2004a). Risk comparisons, conflict, and risk acceptability claims. *Risk Analysis*, 24, 131–45.

(2004b). Varying risk comparison elements: effects on public reactions. *Risk Analysis*, 24, 103–14.

Johnson, B. B. and Slovic, P. (1994). 'Improving' risk communication and risk management: legislated solutions or legislated disasters? *Risk Analysis*, 14, 905–6.

Jungermann, H., Schutz, H. and Thuring, M. (1988). Mental models in risk assessment: informing people about drugs. *Risk Analysis*, 8, 147–55.

Kahneman, D. and Tversky, A. (1979). Prospect theory: an analysis of decision under risk. *Econometrica*, 47, 291.

Kahneman, D. and Tversky, A. (eds) (2000). *Choices, Values and Frames*. New York: Cambridge University Press.

Kahneman, D., Slovic, P. and Tversky, A. (1982). *Judgment under Uncertainty: Heuristics and Biases*. New York: Cambridge University Press.

Kalichman, S. C. (1994). Magic Johnson and public attitudes toward AIDS: a review of empirical findings. *AIDS Education and Prevention*, 6, 542–57.

Kallmen, H. (2000). Manifest anxiety, general self-efficacy and locus of control as determinants of personal and general risk perception. *Journal of Risk Research*, 3, 111–20.

Kasperson, J. and Kasperson, R. E. (2001). Transboundary risks and social amplification. In J. Linnerooth-Bayer and R. Löfstedt (eds), *Cross-National Studies of Transboundary Risk Problems* (pp. 207–43). London: Earthscan.

Kasperson, J., Kasperson, R. E. and Turner, B. L. (1995). *Regions at Risk: Comparisons of Threatened Environments*. Tokyo: United Nations University.

Kasperson, J., Kasperson, R. E., Pidgeon, N. and Slovic, P. (2003). *The Social Amplification of Risk: Assessing 15 Years of Research and Theory*. Cambridge University Press.

Kasperson, R. E. (1992). The social amplification of risk: progress in developing an integrative framework of risk. In S. Krimsky and D. Golding (eds), *Social Theories of Risk* (pp. 119–32). CT: Praeger.

Kasperson, R. E. and Kasperson, J. (1991). Hidden hazards. In D. G. Mayo and R. D. Hollander (eds), *Acceptable Evidence: Science and Values in Risk Management* (pp. 9–28). New York: Oxford University Press.

(1996). The social amplification and attenuation of risk. *The Annals of the American Academy of Political and Social Science*, 545, 95–105.

Kasperson, R. E., Golding, D. and Tuler, S. (1992). Social distrust as a factor in siting hazardous facilities and communicating risks. *Journal of Social Issues*, 48, 161–87.

Kasperson, R. E., Jhaveri, N. and Kasperson, J. (2001). *Stigma, Places, and the Social Amplification of Risk: Toward a Framework of Analysis*. London: Earthscan.

Kasperson, R. E., Renn, O., Slovic, P., Brown, H., Emel, J., Goble, R. *et al.* (1988). The social amplification of risk: a conceptual framework. *Risk Analysis*, 8, 177–87.

Kathlene, L. and Martin, J. A. (1991). Enhancing citizen participation: panel designs, perspectives, and policy formation. *Journal of Policy Analysis and Management*, 10, 46–63.

Katsuya, T. (2001). Public response to the Tokai nuclear accident. *Risk Analysis*, 21, 1039–46.

Katz, E. and Lazarsfeld, P. F. (1955). *Personal influence: the part played by people in the flow of mass communications. Foundations of Communications Research, 2.* A report of the Bureau of Applied Social Research, Columbia University. Glencoe, IL: Free Press.

Keller, C., Siegrist, M. and Gutscher, H. (2006). The role of the affect and availability heuristics in risk communication. *Risk Analysis*, 26, 4, 971–9.

Keller, P. A. (1999). Converting the unconverted: the effect of inclination and opportunity to discount health-related fear appeals. *Journal of Applied Psychology*, 84, 403–15.

Kelley, H. H. (1972). Causal schemata and the attribution process. In E. E. Jones, D. E. Kanouse, H. H. Kelley, R. E. Nisbett, S. Valmis and B. Weiner (eds), *Attribution: Perceiving the Causes of Behaviour* (pp. 41–58). Morristown, NJ: General Learning Press.

Keown, C. F. (1989). Risk perceptions of Hong Kongese vs. Amercians. *Risk Analysis*, 9, 401–5.

Kitchin, R. (2000). The researched opinions on research: disabled people and disability research. *Disability and Society*, 15, 25–47.

Klar, Y. and Ayal, S. (2004). Event frequency and comparative optimism: another look at the indirect elicitation method of self–others risks. *Journal of Experimental Social Psychology*, 40, 805–14.

Klein, C. T. F. and Helweg-Larsen, M. (2002). Perceived control and the optimistic bias: a meta-analytic review. *Psychology and Health*, 17, 437–46.

Kleinhesselink, R. R. (1992). Risk perceptions, risk regulatory motivations, and personality: US/Japan comparisons. *International Journal of Psychology*, 27, 308–11.

Kleinhesselink, R. R. and Rosa, E. A. (1991). Cognitive representation of risk perceptions – a comparison of Japan and the United States. *Journal of Cross-Cultural Psychology*, 222, 11–28.

Kogan, N. and Wallach, M. A. (1967). Risky-shift phenomenon in small decision-making groups: a test of the information-exchange hypothesis. *Journal of Experimental Social Psychology*, 3, 75–82.

Kovacs, D. C., Fischhoff, B. and Small, M. J. (2001). Perceptions of PCE use by dry cleaners and dry cleaning customers. *Journal of Risk Research*, 4, 353–75.

Krause, N. and Slovic, P. (1988). Taxonomic analysis of perceived risk: modeling individual and group perceptions within homogeneous hazard domains. *Risk Analysis*, 8, 435–55.

Krause, N., Malmfors, T. and Slovic, P. (1992). Intuitive toxicology: expert and lay judgments of chemical risks. *Risk Analysis*, 12, 215–32.

Krewski, D., Slovic, P., Bartlett, S., Flynn, J. and Mertz, C. K. (1995a). Health risk perception in Canada I: rating hazards, sources of information and responsibility for health protection. *Human and Ecological. Risk Assessment*, vol. II, pp. 117–28.

(1995b). Health risk perception in Canada II: worldviews, attitudes and opinions. *Human and Ecological. Risk Assessment*, vol. III, pp. 231–48.

Kunreuther, H., Easterling, D., Desvousges, W. and Slovic, P. (1990). Public attitudes toward siting a high-level nuclear waste repository in Nevada. *Risk Analysis*, 10, 469–84.

Kuttschreuter, M. and Gutteling, J. M. (2004). Experience based processing of risk information: the case of the millennium bug. *Journal of Risk Research*, 7, 3–16.

Laforet, S. and Saunders, J. (2005). Managing brand portfolios: how strategies have changed. *Journal of Advertising Research*, 45, 314–27.

Laird, F. N. (1989). The decline of deference: the political context of risk communication. *Risk Analysis*, 9, 543–50.

Lane, J. and Meeker, J. W. (2003). Ethnicity, information sources, and fear of crime. *Deviant Behaviour*, 24, 1–26.

Lang, J. T. and Hallman, W. K. (2005). Who does the public trust? The case of genetically modified food in the United States. *Risk Analysis*, 25, 4, 1241–52.

Langford, I. H., Georgiou, S., Day, R. J. and Bateman, I. J. (1999). Comparing perceptions of risk with willingness to pay. *Risk Decision and Policy*, 4, 201–20.

Larrain, P. and Simpson-Housley, P. (1990). Geophysical variables and behaviour, Lonquimay and Alhme, Chile: tension from volcanic and earthquake hazard. *Perceptual and Motor Skills*, 70, 296–8.

Larson, J. R., Jr, Foster-Fishman, P. G. and Keys, C. B. (1994). Discussion of shared and unshared information in decision-making group. *Journal of Personality and Social Psychology*, 67, 446–61.

Lavery, B., Siegel, A. W., Cousins, J. H. and Rubovits, D. S. (1993). Adolescent risk-taking: an analysis of problem behaviours in problem children. *Journal of Experimental Child Psychology*, 55, 277–94.

Lazo, J. K., Kinnell, J. C. and Fisher, A. (2000). Expert and layperson perceptions of ecosystem risk. *Risk Analysis*, 20, 179–93.

Lee, T. (1993). Seeking a safety culture: psychological aspects of safety in the nuclear industry. *Atom*, 429, 20–3.

Lee, T. R. (1995a). The role of attitudes in the safety culture. Paper Presented at the Conference of the American Nuclear Society. International Topical Meeting, Washington.

Lee, T. (1995b). The roles of attitudes in the safety culture and how to change them. Paper presented to the Conference on Understanding of Risk Perception, Aberdeen.

Lee, T. R. (1995c). Social and psychological consequences of the Chernobyl accident: an overview of the first decade. Paper presented at the International Conference on Health Consequences of the Chernobyl and other Radiological Accidents, Geneva.

Lee, T. R., Macdonald, S. M. and Coote, J. A. (1993). Perceptions of risk and attitudes to safety at a nuclear reprocessing plant. Paper presented to the Society for Risk Assessment (Europe) Fourth Conference, Rome.

Lefcourt, H. M. (1982). *Locus of Control: Current Trends in Theory and Research.* Hillsdale, NY: Erlbaum, 2nd edition.

Leiserowitz, A. A. (2005). American risk perceptions: is climate change dangerous? *Risk Analysis*, 25, 6, 1433–42.

Lek, Y. and Bishop, G. D. (1995). Perceived vulnerability to illness threats. *Psychology and Health*, 10, 205–19.

Lerner, J. S. and Keltner, D. (2000). Beyond valence: toward a model of emotion-specific influences on judgment and choice. *Cognition and Emotion*, 14, 473–93.

Leventhal, H. (1970). Findings and theory in the study of fear communications. In L. Berkowitz (ed.), *Advances in Experimental Social Psychology*, vol. V. London and New York: Academic Press.

(1984). A perceptual-motor theory of emotion. *Advances in Experimental Social Psychology*, 17, 117–82.

Levin, I. P. and Gaeth, G. J. (1988). Framing of attributes information before and after consuming the product. *Journal of Consumer Research*, 15, 374–8.

Levin, I. P., Schneider, S. L. and Gaeth, G. J. (1998a). All frames are not created equal: a typology and critical analysis of framing effects. *Organizational Behaviour and Human Decision Processes*, 76, 149–88.

Levin, I. P., Schnittjer, S. K. and Thee, S. L. (1988b). Information framing effects in social and personal decisions. *Journal of Experimental Social Psychology*, 122, 173–81.

Levine, J. M. and Moreland, R. L. (1999). Knowledge transmission in work groups: helping newcomers to succeed. In L. L. Thompson, J. M. Levine and D. M. Merrick (eds), *Shared Cognition in Organisations: The Management of Knowledge* (pp. 267–96). Mahwah, NJ: LEA.

Levy-Leboyer, C. (1988). Success and failure in applying psychology. *American Psychologist*, 43, 779–85.

Lichtenstein, S., Slovic, P., Fischhoff, B., Layman, M. and Combs, B. (1978). Judged frequency and lethal events. *Journal of Experimental Psychology: Human Learning and Memory*, 4, 551–78.

Lima, M. L. (2004). On the influence of risk perception on mental health: living near an incinerator. *Journal of Environmental Psychology*, 24, 71–84.

Lima, M. L., Barnett, J. and Vala, J. (2005). Risk perception and technological development at a societal level. *Risk Analysis*, 25, 5, 1229–39.

Lindell, M. K. and Earle, T. C. (1983). How close is close enough: public perception of the risks of industrial facilities. *Risk Analysis*, 3, 4, 245–53.

Lindell, M. K. and Perry, R. W. (1990). Effects of the Chernobyl accident on public perceptions of nuclear plant accident risks. *Risk Analysis*, 10, 3, 393–9.

Linville, P. W., Fisher, G. W. and Fischhoff, B. (1993). AIDS risk perceptions and decision biases. In J. B. Pryor and G. D. Reeder (eds), *The Social Psychology of HIV Infection* (pp. 5–38). Hillsdale, NJ: Erlbaum.

Loewenstein, G. F., Weber, E. U., Hsee, C. K. and Wells, G. L. (2001). Risk as feelings. *Psychological Bulletin*, 127, 267–86.

Lowrance, W. W. (1976). *Of Acceptable Risk: Science and the Determination of Safety*. Los Altos, CA: William Kaufman.

Lyons, E. (1996). Changing European identities: social psychological analyses of social change. In G. M. Breakwell and E. Lyons (eds), *Coping with Social Change: Processes of Social Memory in the Reconstruction of Identities* (pp. 31–9). Chichester: Butterworth-Heinemann.

Maass, A. and Clark, R. D. (1984). Hidden impact of minorities: fifteen years of minority influence research. *Psychological Bulletin*, 95, 428–50.

McComas, K. A. (2003). Public meetings and risk amplification: a longitudinal study. *Risk Analysis*, 23, 1257–70.

McCrae, R. R. and Terracino, A. (2005). Members of the personality profiles of cultures project (2005) universal features of personality traits from the observer's perspective: data from 50 cultures. *Journal of Personality and Social Psychology*, 88, 547–61.

McDaniels, T. L., Axelrod, L. J., Cavanagh, N. S. and Slovic, P. (1997). Perception of ecological risk to water environments. *Risk Analysis*, 17, 341–52.

McDaniels, T. L., Gregory, R. S. and Fields, D. (1999). Democratizing risk management: successful public involvement in local water management decisions. *Risk Analysis*, 19, 497–510.

McDonald, N. and Ryan, F. (1992). Constraints on the development of safety culture: a preliminary analysis. *Irish Journal of Psychology*, 273–81.

McDougall, W. (1918). *An Introduction to Social Psychology*. Boston: J. W. Luce and Co.

MacGregor, D., Slovic, P., Mason, R. G. and Detweiler, J. (1994). Perceived risks of radioactive waste transport through Oregon: results of a statewide survey. *Risk Analysis*, 14, 1, 5–14.

Machlis, G. E. and Rosa, E. A. (1990). Desired risk: broadening the social amplification of risk framework. *Risk Analysis*, 10, 161–7.

Macintyre, K., Rutenberg, N., Brown, L. and Karim, A. (2004). Understanding perceptions of HIV risk among adolescents in KwaZulu Natal. *AIDS and Behaviour*, 8, 237–50.

McKenna, F. P. (1985). Do safety measures really work? An examination of risk homoeostasis theory. *Ergonomics*, 28, 489–98.

  (1988). What role should the concept of risk play in theories of accident involvement? *Ergonomics*, 31, 469–84.

McKenna, F. P. and Albery, I. P. (2001). Does unrealistic optimism change following a negative experience? *Journal of Applied Social Psychology*, 31, 1146–57.

McKenna, F. P. and Horswill, M. S. (2006). Risk taking from the participant's perspective: the case of driving and accident risk. *Health Psychology*, 25, 163–70.

McKenna, F. P. and Myers, L. B. (1997). Illusory self-assessments – can they be reduced? *British Journal of Psychology*, 88, 39–51.

McKenna, F. P., Warburton, D. M. and Winwood, M. (1993). Exploring the limits of optimism: the case of smokers' decision making. *British Journal of Psychology*, 84, 389–94.

McMath, B. F. and Prentice-Dunn, S. (2005). Protection motivation theory and skin cancer risk: the role of individual differences in responses to persuasive appeals. *Journal of Applied Social Psychology*, 35, 631–43.

Maddux, J. E. and Rogers, R. W. (1983). Protection motivation and self-efficacy: a revised theory of four appeals and attitude change. *Journal of Experimental Social Psychology*, 19, 469–79.

Marquis, D. G. (1962). Individual responsibility and group decisions involving risk. *Industrial Management Review*, 3, 8–23.

Marris, C., Langford, I. H. and O'Riordan, T. (1998). A quantitative test of the cultural theory of risk perceptions: comparisons with the psychometric paradigm. *Risk Analysis*, 18, 635–48.

Masuda, J. R. and Garvin, T. (2006). Place, culture and the social amplification of risk. *Risk Analysis*, 26, 437.

Matsumoto, T., Shiomi, T. and Nakayachi, K. (2005). Evaluation of risk communication from the perspective of the information source: focusing on public relations officers for nuclear power generation. *Japanese Journal of Social Psychology*, 20, 201–7.

Mattila, M., Rantanen, E. and Hyttinen, M. (1994). The quality of work environment, supervision and safety in building construction. *Safety Science*, 17, 257–68.

Mazur, A. (1990). Nuclear power, chemical hazards, and the quantity of reporting. *Minerva*, 28, 294–323.

Mearns, K., Whitaker, S. M. and Flin, R. (2001). Benchmarking safety climate in hazardous environments: a longitudinal, interorganizational approach. *Risk Analysis*, 21, 771–86.

Mechitov, A. I. and Rebrick, S. B. (1990). Studies of risk and safety perception in the USSR. In D. I. Borcherding, D. I. Larichev and D. M. Messick (eds), *Contemporary Issues in Decision Making* (pp. 261–70). Amsterdam: Elsevier.

Mehta, M. D. and Simpson-Housley, P. (1994). Perception of potential nuclear disaster: the relation of likelihood and consequence estimates of risk. *Perception and Motor Skills*, 79, 1119–22.

Middleton, W., Harris, P. and Surman, M. (1996). Give 'em enough rope: perception of health and safety risks in bungee jumpers. *Journal of Social and Clinical Psychology*, 15, 68–79.

Miles, S. and Frewer, L. J. (2001). Investigating specific concerns about different food hazards – higher and lower order attributes. *Food Quality and Preference*, 12, 47–61.

Miles, S. and Rowe, G. (2004). The laddering technique. In G. M. Breakwell (ed.), *Doing Social Psychology Research* (pp. 305–43). Oxford: Blackwell.

Millar, M. G. and Millar, K. U. (1996). The effects of direct and indirect experience on affective and cognitive responses and the attitude–behaviour relation. *Journal of Experimental Social Psychology*, 32, 561–79.

Miller, J. D., Lynam, D., Zimmerman, R. S., Logan, T. K., Leukefeld, C. and Clayton, R. (2004). The utility of the Five Factor Model in understanding risky sexual behaviour. *Personality and Individual Differences*, 36, 1611–26.

Miller, R. L. and Mulligan, R. D. (2002). Terror management: the effects of mortality salience and locus of control on risk-taking behaviours. *Personality and Individual Differences*, 33, 1203–14.

Minsky, H. P. (1975). *John Maynard Keynes*. New York: Columbia Press.

Mok, S. C. and Savage, I. (2005). Why has safety improved at rail–highway grade crossings. *Risk Analysis*, 25, 4, 867–81.

Moliner, P. and Tafani, E. (1997). Attitudes and social representations: a theoretical and experimental approach. *European Journal of Social Psychology*, 27, 687–702.

Moore, S. M. and Rosenthal, D. A. (1993). Venturesomeness, impulsiveness, and risky behaviour among older adolescents. *Perceptual and Motor Skills*, 76, 76–98.

Moray, N. (1994). Human factors in waste management. *Radwaste Magazine*, October, 58–63.

Morgan, K. M., DeKay, M. L., Fischbeck, P. S., Granger Morgan, M., Fischhoff, B. and Florig, H. K. (2001). A deliberative method for ranking risks (II): evaluation of validity and agreement among risk managers. *Risk Analysis*, 21, 923–37.

Morgan, M. G., Fischhoff, B., Bostrom, A. and Atman, C. J. (2002). *Risk Communication: A Mental Models Approach*. New York: Cambridge University Press.

Moscovici, S. (1976). *Social Influence and Social Change*. London: Academic Press.

   (1988). Notes towards a description of social representations. *Journal of Social Psychology*, 18, 211–50.

Moscovici, S. and Farr, R. (eds) (1984). *Social Representations*. Cambridge University Press.

Moscovici, S. and Zavalloni, M. (1969). The group as a polarizer of attitudes. *Journal of Personality and Social Psychology*, 12, 125–35.

Moscovici, S., Mugny, G. and van Avermaet, E. (1985). *Perspectives on Minority Influence*. Cambridge University Press.

Motoyoshi, T., Takao, K. and Ikeda, S. (2004). Determinant factors of residents' acceptance of flood risk. *Japanese Journal of Experimental Social Psychology*.

Muller, S. and Johnson, B. T. (1990). Fear and persuasion: a linear relationship? Paper presented to the Eastern Psychological Assocation Convention, New York.

Musch, J. (2003). Personality differences in hindsight bias. *Memory*, 11, 473–89.

Myers, D. G. and Lamm, H. (1976). The group polarization phenomenon. *Psychological Bulletin*, 83, 602–27.

Myers, J. R., Henderson-King, D. H. and Henderson-King, E. I. (1997). Facing technological risks: the importance of individual differences. *Journal of Research in Personality*, 31, 1–20.

Nagy, S. and Nix, C. L. (1989). Relations between preventative health behaviour and hardiness. *Psychological Reports*, 65, 339–45.

Navas, E. (2002). Problems associated with potential massive use of antimicrobial agents as prophylaxis or therapy of a bioterrorist attack. *Clinical Microbiology and Infection*, 8, 534–39.

Nevid, J. S. and Maria, N. L. S. (1999). Multicultural issues in qualitative research. *Psychology & Marketing*, 16, 305–25.

Nisbett, R. and Ross, L. (1980). *Human Inference: Strategies and Shortcomings of Social Judgment*. Englewood Cliffs, NJ: Prentice-Hall.

Nordhøy, F. (1962). *Group Interaction in Decision-Making Under Risk*. School of Industrial Management, MIT.

Nyland, L. G. (1993). Risk perception in Brazil and Sweden. RHIZIKON: Risk Research Report 15.

O'Connor, R. E., Yarnal, B., Dow, K., Jocoy, C. L. and Carbone, G. J. (2005). Feeling at risk matters: water managers and the decision to use forecasts. *Risk Analysis*, 25, 5, 1265–75.

Ostrom, L., Wilhelmsen, C. and Kaplan, B. (1993). Assessing safety culture. *Nuclear Safety*, 34, 163–72.

Otten, W. and van der Pligt, J. (1996). Context effect in the measurement of comparative optimism in probablity judgements. *Journal of Social and Clinical Psychology*, 15, 80–101.

Otway, H., Haastrup, P., Cannell, W., Gianitsopoulos, G. and Paruccini, M. (1988). Risk communication in Europe after Chernobyl: a media analysis of seven countries. *Industrial Crisis Quarterly*, 2, 3–15.

Parry, S. M., Miles, S., Tridente, A. and Palmer, S. R. (2004). Differences in perception of risk between people who have and have not experienced Salmonella food poisoning. *Risk Analysis*, 24, 289–99.

Pastel, R. H. (2001). Collective behaviours: mass panic and outbreaks of multiple unexplained symptoms. *Miliary Medicine*, 166, 44–6.

Pease, M. E., McCabe, A. E., Brannon, L. A. and Tagler, M. J. (2003). Memory distortions for pre Y2K expectancies: a demonstration of the hindsight bias. *Journal of Psychology: Interdisciplinary and Applied*, 137, 397–9.

Pereira-Henriques, A. M. and Lima, M. L. (2003). Estados afectivos, percepcao do risco e do suporte social: a familiaridade e a relevancia como moderadores nas respostas de congruencia com o estado de espirito. *Analise Psicologica*, 21, 375–92 (Affective states, perception of risk and of social support: familiarity and relevance as moderators in responses of congruency with mood states).

Perloff, L. S. and Fetzer, B. K. (1986). Self–other judgements and perceived vulnerability to victimisation. *Journal of Personality and Social Psychology*, 50, 502–10.

Peters, E. and Slovic, P. (1996). The role of affect and worldviews as orienting dispositions in the perception and acceptance of nuclear power. *Journal of Applied Social Psychology*, 26, 1427–53.

Peters, E. M., Burraston, B. and Mertz, C. K. (2004). An emotion based model of risk perception and stigma susceptibility: cognitive appraisals of emotion, affective reactivity, worldviews, and risk perceptions in the generation of technological stigma. *Risk Analysis*, 24, 1349–67.

Peters, E., Slovic, P., Hibbard, J. H. and Tusler, M. (2006a). Why worry? Worry, risk perceptions, and willingness to act to reduce medical errors. *Health Psychology*, 25, 144–52.

Peters, E., Vastfjall, D., Garling, T. and Slovic, P. (2006b). Affect and decision making: a 'hot' topic. *Journal of Behavioural Decision Making*, 19, 79–85.

Peters, R. G., Covello, V. T. and McCallum, D. B. (1997). The determinants of trust and credibility in environmental risk communication: an empirical study. *Risk Analysis*, 17, 43–54.

Peterson, D. (1993). Establishing good 'Safety Culture' helps mitigate workplace dangers. *Occupational Health & Safety*, 62, 20–4.

Peterson, M. (2006). The precautionary principle is incoherent. *Risk Analysis*, 26, 3, 595–601.

Petty, R. E. and Cacioppo, J. T. (1986). *Communications and Persuasion: Central and Peripheral Routes to Attitude Change*. New York: Springer-Verlag.

Pezzo, M. V. (2003). What removes hindsight bias? *Memory*, 11, 421–41.

Phimister, J. R., Oktem, U., Kleindorfer, P. R. and Kunreuther, H. (2003). Near-miss incident management in the chemical process industry. *Risk Analysis*, 23, 445–59.

PHLS (2000). *AIDS/HIV Quarterly Surveillance Tables: UK Data to End September 1999*. Report 44:99/3. PHLS.

Piaget, J. (1936). *La Construction du réel chez l'enfant*. Neuchâtel: Delachanx et Niestlé.

Pidgeon, N. F. (1991). Safety culture and risk management in organizations. *Journal of Cross-Cultural Psychology*, special issue: Risk and Culture, 22, 129–40.

Pidgeon, N. F. and Turner, B. A. (1997). *Man-Made Disasters*. Oxford: Butterworth-Heinemann.

Pidgeon, N., Hood, C., Jones, D., Turner, B. and Gibson, R. (1992). Risk perception. In Royal Society (ed.), *Risk: Analysis, Perception and Management* (pp. 56–72). London: Royal Society.

Pillisuk, M. and Acredolo, C. (1988). Fear of technological hazards: one concern or many? *Social Behaviour*, 3, 17–24.

Pillisuk, M., Parks, S. H. and Hawkes, G. (1987). Public perception of techno-logical risk. *Social Science Journal*, 24, 4, 403.

Pohl, R. F., Bender, M. and Lachmann, G. (2002). Hindsight bias around the world. *Experimental Psychology*, 49, 270–82.

Pohl, R. F., Eisenhauer, M. and Hardt, O. (2003). SARA: a cognitive process model to stimulate the anchoring effect and hindsight bias. *Memory*, 11, 337–56.

Poortinga, W. and Pidgeon, N. F. (2003). Exploring the dimensionality of trust in risk regulation. *Risk Analysis*, 23, 961–72.

(2004). Trust, the asymmetry principle, and the role of prior beliefs. *Risk Analysis*, 24, 1475–86.

(2005). Trust in risk regulation: cause or consequence of the acceptability of GM food? *Risk Analysis*, 25, 199–209.

Poumadère, M., Mays, C., Le Mer, S. and Blong, R. (2005). The 2003 heat wave in France: dangerous climate change here and now. *Risk Analysis*, 25, 6, 148–94.

Raats, M., Sparks, P., Geekie, M. A. and Shepherd, R. (1999). The effects of providing personalized dietary feedback: a semi-computerized approach. *Patient Education and Counseling*, 37, 177–89.

Rayner, S. (1988). Muddling through metaphors to maturity: a commentary on Kasperson *et al. The Social Amplification of Risk. Risk Analysis*, 8, 201–4.

Rayner, S. and Cantor, R. (1987). How fair is safe enough? The cultural approach to societal technology choice. *Risk Analysis*, 7, 3–9.

Read, D. and Morgan, M. (1998). The efficacy of different methods for informing the public about the range dependency of magnetic fields from high voltage power lines. *Risk Analysis*, 18, 603–10.

Reason, J. (1987). The Chernobyl errors. *Bulletin of the British Psychological Society*, 40, 201–6.

(1990). *Human Error*. New York: Cambridge University Press.

(1995). A system approach to organizational error. *Ergonomics*, 38, 1708–21.

(1998). How necessary steps in a task get omitted: reviving old ideas to combat a persistent problem. *International Journal of Cognitive Technology*, 3, 24–32.

(2000a). A cognitive engineering perspective on maintenance errors. In R. Amalberti and N. Sarter (eds), *Cognitive Engineering in the Aviation Domain* (pp. 309–25). Mahweh, NJ: Lawrence Erlbaum Associates.

(2000b). The Freudian slip revisited. *Psychologist*, 13, 610–11.

Reason, J., Parker, D. and Free, R. (1994). *Bending the Rules: The Varieties, Origins and Management of Safety Violations*. Leiden: Rijks Universiteit Leiden.

Redmond, E. C. and Griffith, C. J. (2004). Consumer perceptions of food safety risk, control and responsibility. *Appetite*, 43, 309–13.

Renn, O. (1990). Public responses to the Chernobyl accident. *Journal of Environmental Psychology*, 10, 151–67.

(1991). Risk communication and the social amplification of risk. In J. Kasperson and P.-J. M. Stallen (eds), *Communicating Risks to the Public: International Perspectives* (pp. 287–324). Dordrecht: Kluwer Academic Press.

Renn, O. and Levine, D. (1991). Credibility and trust in risk communication. In J. Kasperson and P.-J. M. Stallen (eds), *Communicating Risks to the Public: International Perspectives* (pp. 157–218). Dordrecht: Kluwer Academic Press.

Renn, O., Webler, T. and Johnson, B. (1991). Public participation in hazard management: the use of citizen panels in the US. *Risk: Health, Safety & Environment*, 2, 197.

Renner, B. (2003). Hindsight bias after receiving self-relevant health risk information: a motivational perspective. *Memory*, 11, 455–72.

Richard, D. E. and Peterson, S. J. (1998). Perception of environmental risk related to gender, community socioeconomic setting, age and locus of control. *Journal of Environmental Education*, 30, 1, 11–16.

Richard, R., van der Pligt, J. and De Vries, N. (1996). Anticipated regret and time perspective: changing sexual risk-taking behaviour. *Journal of Behavioural Decision Making*, 9, 185–99.

Richardson, B., Sorenson, J. and Soderstrom, E. J. (1987). Explaining the social and psychological impacts of a nuclear power plant accident. *Journal of Applied Social Psychology*, 17, 16–36.

Richardson, K. (2001). Risk news in the world of internet newsgroups. *Journal of Sociolinguistics*, 5, 50–72.

Ridley, D., Young, P. D. and Johnson, D. E. (1981). Salience as a dimension of individual and group risk taking. *Journal of Psychology: Interdisciplinary and Applied*, 109, 283–91.

Rimal, R. N. and Real, K. (2003). Perceived risk and efficacy beliefs as motivators of change. *Human Communication Research*, 29, 3, 370–99.

Rip, A. (1988). Should social amplification of risk be counteracted? *Risk Analysis*, 8, 193–7.

Rodgers, J. (1999). Trying to get it right: undertaking research involving people with learning difficulties. *Disability and Society*, 14, 421–34.

Rogers, R. W. (1975). a protection motivation theory of fear appeals and attitude change. *Journal of Psychology: Interdisciplinary and Applied*, 91, 93–114.

Rohrmann, B. (1991). A survey of social-scientific research on risk perception. *Studies on Risk Communication*, 26, 1–56.

Romer, D., Jamieson, K. H. and Aday, S. (2003). Television news and the cultivation of fear of crime. *Journal of Communication*, 53, 88–104.

Rosa, E. A. (1998). Metatheoretical foundations for post-normal risk. *Journal of Risk Research*, 1, 15–44.

    (2003). The logical structure of the social amplification of risk framework: metatheoretical foundations and policy implications. In Royal Society (ed.), *Risk: Analysis, Perception and Management*. London: Royal Society.

Rosenbloom, T. (2003). Sensation seeking and risk taking in mortality salience. *Personality and Individual Differences*, 35, 1809–19.

Rothman, A. J., Klein, W. M. and Weinstein, N. D. (1996). Absolute and relative biases in estimations of personal risk. *Journal of Applied Social Psychology*, 26, 1213–36.

Rottenstreich, Y. H. and Hsee, C. K. (2001). Money, kisses and electric shocks: on the affective psychology of risk. *Psychological Science*, 12, 185–90.

Rotter, J. (1966). Generalised expectancies for internal versus external control of reinforcement. *Psychological Monographs*, 80.

Rowe, G. and Frewer, L. J. (2000). Public participation methods: a framework for evaluation. *Science Technology & Human Value*, 25, 3–29.

Rowe, G. and Wright, G. (2001). Differences in expert and lay judgments of risk: myth or reality?. *Risk Analysis*, 21, 341–56.

Royal Society (1992). *Risk: Analysis, Perception and Management*. London: Royal Society.

    (2006). *Pandemic Influenza: Science to Policy*. London: Royal Society.

Rundmo, T. (1994). Associations between organisational factors and safety and contingency measures on offshore petroleum platforms. *Scandinavian Journal of Work, Environment and Health*, 20, 122–7.

    (2002). Associations between affect and risk perception. *Journal of Risk Research*, 5, 119–35.

Salmon, C. T., Park, H. S. and Wrigley, B. J. (2003). Optimistic bias and perceptions of bioterrorism in Michigan corporate spokespersons. *Journal of Health Communication*, 8, 130–43.

Sandin, P. (1999). Dimensions of the precautionary principle. *Human and Ecological Risk Assessment*, 5, 889–907.

Sandin, P., Peterson, M., Hanson, S. O., Ruden, C. and Juthe, A. (2002). Science and the Precautionary Principle. *Journal of Risk Research*, 5, 4, 53–62.

Sandman, P. (1989). Hazard versus outrage in the public perception of risk. In V. T. Covello, D. B. McCallum and M. T. Pavlova (eds), *Effective Risk Communication* (pp. 45–9). New York: Plenum Press.

Satterfield, T. A., Mertz, C. K. and Slovic, P. (2004). Discrimination, vulnerability, and justice in the face of risk. *Risk Analysis*, 24, 115–29.

Saucier, G., Tsaousis, I., Georgiades, S. and Goldberg, L. R. (2005). The factor structure of Greek personality adjectives. *Journal of Personality and Social Psychology*, 88, 856–75.

Savage, I. (1993). Demographic influences on risk perceptions. *Risk Analysis*, 13, 4, 413.

Schank, R. C. and Abelson, R. P. (1977). *Scripts, Plans, Goals and Understanding*. Chichester: Wiley (Halsted Press).

Schapira, M. M., Nattinger, A. B. and McHorney, C. A. (2001). Frequency or probability? A qualitative study of risk communications formats used in healthcare. *Medical Decision Making*, 21, 459–67.

Schmidt, M. R. and Wei, W. (2006). Loss of agro-biodiversity: uncertainty, and perceived control: a comparative risk perception study in Austria and China. *Risk Analysis*, 26, 2, 455–70.

Schmidt, F. N. and Gifford, R. (1989). A dispositional approach to hazard perception: preliminary development of the environmental appraisal inventory. *Journal of Environmental Psychology*, 9, 1, 57.

Schmitz, P. G. (2004). On the alternative five-factor model: structure and correlates. In R. M. Stelmack (ed.), *On the Psychobiology of Personality: Essays in Honor of Marvin Zuckerman* (pp. 65–87). New York: Elsevier.

Schumacher, J. and Roth, M. (2004). Sensation seeking, gesundheitsbezogene Kognitionen und Partizipation am Risikosport. *Zeitschrift für Gesundheitspsychologie*, 12, 148–58 (Sensation seeking, health-related cognitions and participation in high-risk sports).

Schutz, H. and Wiedermann, P. M. (2000). Hazardous incident information for the public: is it useful? *Australasian Journal of Disaster and Trauma Studies*, 4.

Schwarz, M. and Thompson, M. (1990). *Divided We Stand: Redefining Politics, Technology and Social Choice*. London: Harvester Wheatsheaf.

Schwarzer, R. (1994). Optimism, vulnerability, and self-beliefs as health-related cognitions. *Psychology and Health*, 9, 161–80.

Scottish Poverty Information Unit. (1999). *Poverty in Scotland 1999*. Glasgow Caledonian University.

Shaw, D. L., McCombs, M., Weaver, D. H. and Hamm, B. J. (1999). Individuals, groups and agenda melding: a theory of social dissonance. *International Journal of Public Opinion Research*, 11, 2–24.

Shrader-Frechette, K. and Cooke, R. (2004). Ethics and choosing appropriate means to an end: problems with coal mine and nuclear workplace safety. *Risk Analysis*, 24, 147–56.

Siegrist, M. and Cvetkovich, G. (2000). Perception of hazards: the role of social trust and knowledge. *Risk Analysis*, 20, 713–19.

Siegrist, M. and Gutscher, H. (2006). Flooding risks: a comparison of lay people's perceptions and expert's assessments in Switzerland. *Risk Analysis*, 26, 971–9.

Siegrist, M., Earle, T. C. and Gutscher, H. (2003). Test of a trust and confidence model in the applied context of electromagnetic field (EMF) risks. *Risk Analysis*, 23, 705–16.

Siegrist, M., Keller, C. and Kiers, H. (2005a). A new look at the psychometric paradigm of perception of hazards. *Risk Analysis*, 25, 209–20.

Siegrist, M., Earle, T. C., Gutscher, H. and Keller, C. (2005b). Perception of mobile phone and base station risks. *Risk Analysis*, 25, 5, 1253–64.

Siero, F. W., van Diem, M. T., Voorrips, R. and Willemsen, M. C. (2004). Perconceptional smoking: an exploratory study of determinants of change in smoking behaviour among women in the fertile age range. *Health Education Research*, 19, 418–29.

Silver, N. and Braun, C. C. (1999). Behaviour. In M. S. E. Wogalter, D. M. Dejoy and K. R. Langhery (eds), *Warnings and Risk Communication* (pp. 245–62). Philadelphia, PA: Taylor and Francis.

Simarra, J., de Paul, J. and San Juan, C. (2002). Malos tratos infantiles: representaciones sociales de la población general y de los profesionales del ambito de la infancía en el caribe colombiano. *Child Abuse and Neglect*, 26, 815–31 (Child abuse: social representations from the general public and from professionals working with children in the Caribbean area of Colombia).

Simpson-Housley, P., de Man, A. F. and Yachnin, R. (1986). Trait-anxiety and appraisal of flood hazard: a brief comment. *Psychological Reports*, 58, 2, 509–10.

Sjöberg, L. (1995). *Explaining Risk Perception: An Empirical and Quantitative Evaluation of Cultural Theory*. RHIZIKON: Risk Research Report 22.

(1997). Explaining risk perception: an empirical evaluation of cultural theory. *Risk Decision and Policy*, 2, 113–30.

(1999a). Consequences of perceive risk: demand for mitigation. *Journal of Risk Research*, 2, 129–49.

(1999b). Risk perception in western Europe. *Ambio*, 28, 555–68.

(2001). Limits of knowledge and the limited importance of trust. *Risk Analysis*, 21, 189–98.

(2002). Are received risk perception models alive and well? *Risk Analysis*, 22, 665–9.

Sjöberg, L. and Drottz-Sjöberg, B. M. (1993). *Attitudes Toward Nuclear Waste*. RHIZIKON: Risk Research Report 12. Sweden: Stockholm School of Economics, Center for Risk Research.

Sjöberg, L. and Wåhlberg, A. (2002). Risk perception and new age beliefs. *Risk Analysis*, 22, 751–64.

Slovic, P. (1993). Perceived risk, trust, and democracy. *Risk Analysis*, 13, 675–82.

(1996). Perception of risk from radiation. *Radiation Protection Dosimetry*, 68, 165–80.

(1997). Trust, emotion, sex, politics, and science: surveying the risk-assessment battlefield. In M. H. Bazerman, D. M. Messick, A. E. Tenbrunsel and K. A. Wade-Benzoni (eds), *Environment, Ethics and Behaviour* (pp. 277–313). San Francisco: New Lexington.

(1999). Perceived risk, trust and democracy. In G. Cvetkovich and R. E. Löfstedt (eds) *Social Trust and the Management of Risk* (pp. 42–52) London: Earthscan.

(2000). *The Perception of Risk.* London: Earthscan.

(2001). Cigarette smokers: rational actors or rational fools? In P. Slovic (ed.), *Smoking: Risk, Perception and Policy* (pp. 97–124). Thousand Oaks, CA: Sage Publications.

Slovic, P., Fischhoff, B. & Lichtenstein, S. (1979). Rating the risks. *Environment,* 21, 14–20, 36–9.

(1980). Societal risk assessment: how safe is safe enough? In J. E. R. C. Schwing and W. A. Alberts (eds), *Facts and Fears: Understanding Perceived Risk* (pp. 137–44). New York: Plenum Press.

(1982). Why study risk perception? *Risk Analysis,* 2, 283–93.

(1985). Characterising perceived risk. R. W. Kates, C. Hohenemser and J. X. Kasperson (eds), *Perilous Progress: Managing the Hazards of Technology* (pp. 156–71). Boulder, CO: Westview.

Slovic, P., Lichtenstein, S. and Edwards, W. (1965). Boredom-induced changes in preferences among bets. *American Journal of Psychology,* 78, 208–17.

Slovic, P., Flynn, J., Mertz, C. K. and Mullican, L. (1993). *Health Risk Perception in Canada.* Ottawa: Department of National Health and Welfare.

Slovic, P., Finucane, M. L., Peters, E. and MacGregor, D. (2004). Risk as analysis and risk as feelings: some thoughts about affect, reason, risk and rationality. *Risk Analysis,* 24, 311–22.

Slovic, P., Flynn, J., Mertz, C. K., Mays, C. and Poumadère, M. (1996). *Nuclear Power and the Public: A Comparative Study of Risk Perception in France and the United States.* Report 96–6. Eugene, OR: Decision Research.

Slovic, P., Peters, E., Finucane, M. L. and MacGregor, D. G. (2005). Affect, risk and decision making. *Health Psychology,* 24, S35–S40.

Slovic, P., Kraus, N., Lappe, H., Letzel, H. and Malmfors, T. (1989). Risk perception of prescription drugs: report on a survey in Sweden. *Pharmaceutical Medicine,* 4, 43–65.

Slovic, P., Layman, M., Kraus, N., Flynn, J., Chalmers, J. and Gesell, G. (1991). Perceived risk, stigma, and potential economic impacts of a high-level nuclear waste repository in Nevada. *Risk Analysis,* 11, 683–96.

Slovic, P., Malmfors, T., Krewski, D., Mertz, C. K., Neil, N. and Bartlett, S. (1995). Intuitive toxicology II: expert and lay judgments of chemical risks in Canada. *Risk Analysis,* 15, 661–75.

Smith, J. (2005). Dangerous news: media decision making about climate change risk. *Risk Analysis,* 25, 6, 1471–82.

Sparks, P., Shepherd, R. and Frewer, L. J. (1994). Gene technology, food production and public opinion: a UK study. *Agriculture and Human Values,* 11, 19–28.

Spencer, L., Ritchie, J., Lewis, J. and Dillon, L. (2003). *Quality in Qualitative Evaluation: Framework for Assessing Research Evidence.* London: Sage.

Spigner, C., Hawkins, W. and Loren, W. (1993). Gender differences in perception of risk associated with alcohol and drug use among college students. *Women and Health*, 20, 87–97.

Spitzenstetter, F. (2003). Biais d'optimisme et biais de mesure: l'évaluation relative ou absolue du risque personnel. *Cahiers Internationaux de Psychologie Sociale*, 58, 19–27 (Optimistic bias and measurement bias: relative or absolute valuation of the personal risk).

Stacy, A. W., Newcomb, M. D. and Bentler, P. M. (1991). Personality, problem drinking and drunk driving: mediating, moderating and direct-effect models. *Journal of Personality and Social Psychology*, 60, 795–811.

Stahlberg, D. and Maass, A. (1998). Hindsight bias: impaired memory or biased reconstruction? *European Review of Social Psychology*, 8, 105–32.

Starr, C. (1969). Social benefits versus technological risk. *Science*, 165, 1232–8.

  (2003). The precautionary principle versus risk analysis. *Risk Analysis*, 23, 1–3.

Steger, M. A. and Witte, S. L. (1989). Gender differences in environmental orientations: a comparison of publics and activists in Canada and the US. *Western Political Quarterly*, 42, 627–49.

Stein, J. G. (1988). International negotiation: a multidisciplinary perspective. *Negotiation Journal*, 4, 221–31.

Steptoe, A., Doherty, S., Kerry, S. and Rink, E. S. (2000). Sociodemographic and psychological predictors of changes in dietary fat consumption in adults with high blood cholesterol following counselling in primary care. *Health Psychology*, 19, 411–19.

Stern, P. C., Dietz, T. and Kalof, L. (1993). Value orientations, gender, and environmental concern. *Environment and Behaviour*, 25, 322–48.

Stevens, S. S. (1936). A scale for the measurement of a psychological magnitude: loudness. *Psychological Review*, 43, 405–16.

  (1961). To honor Fechner and repeal his law. *Science*, 133, 80–6.

  (1962). The surprising simplicity of sensory metrics. *American Psychologists* 17, 29–39.

Stoner, J. A. F. (1961). A comparison of individual and group decisions including risk. Thesis quoted in R. Brown (1965) *Social Psychology*. New York: Free Press.

Summers, C. and Hine, D. W. (1997). Nuclear waste goes on the road: risk perceptions and compensatory tradeoffs in single-industry communities. *Canadian Journal of Behavioural Science*, 29, 3, 211–23.

Svenson, O. (1988). Mental models of risk communication and action: reflections on social amplification of risk. *Risk Analysis*, 8, 199–200.

Swanson, E. R. and Fosnocht, D. E. (2000). Anthrax threats: a report of two incidents from Salt Lake City. *Journal of Emergency Medicine*, 18, 229–32.

't Hart, P. and Pijnenburg, B. (1989). The Heizel Stadium tragedy. In M. T. Charles and U. Rosenthal (eds), *Coping with Crisis: The Management of Disasters, Riots and Terrorism* (pp. 197–224). Springfield, IL: Charles C. Thomas.

Tait, J. (2001). More Faust than Frankenstein: the European debate about the precautionary principle and risk regulation for genetically modified crops. *Journal of Risk Research*, 4, 175–89.

Takano, K. I. and Reason, J. (1997). Modelling of human errors in cognitive processes observed in dynamic environments. In J. Reason (ed.), *Managing the Risks of Organisational Accidents* (pp. 63–70). Burlington, VT: Ashgate Publishing Co.

Tanaka, Y. (2004). Major psychological factors affecting acceptance of gene-recombination technology. *Risk Analysis*, 24, 1575–83.

Taylor, S. E. and Brown, J. (1988). Illusion and well being: a social psychological perspective on mental health. *Psychological Bulletin*, 103, 193–210.

Teigen, K. H., Brun, W. and Slovic, P. (1988). Societal risks as seen by a Norwegian public. *Journal of Behavioural Decision Making*, 1, 111–30.

Tesser, A., Martin, L. and Mendolia, M. (1995). The impact of thought on attitude extremity and attitude–behaviour consistency. In R. E. Petty and J. A. Krosnick (eds), *Attitude Strength: Antecedents and Consequences* (pp. 73–92). Mahweh, NJ: LEA.

Thompson, K. M. (2002). Variability and uncertainty meet risk management and risk communication. *Risk Analysis*, 22, 647–54.

Thompson, M., Ellis, R. and Wildavsky, A. (1990). *Cultural Theory*. Boulder, CO: Westview.

Thomson, M. E., Önkal, D., Avcioğlu, A. and Goodwin, P. (2004). Aviation risk perception: a comparison between experts and novices, *Risk Analysis*, 24, 6, 1585–95.

Tickner, J. and Gouveia-Vigeant, T. (2005). The 1991 cholera epidemic in Peru: not a case of precaution gone awry. *Risk Analysis*, 25, 3, 495–502.

Townsend, E., Clarke, D. D. and Travis, B. (2004). Effects of context and feelings on perceptions of genetically modified food. *Risk Analysis*, 24, 1369–84.

Trumbo, C. W. (1999). Heuristic-systematic information processing and risk judgment. *Risk Analysis*, 19, 391–400.

Tullar, W. L. and Johnson, D. F. (1973). Group decision making and the risky shift: a trans-national perspective. *International Journal of Psychology*, 8, 117–23.

Tulloch, J. (1999). Fear of crime and the media: sociocultural theories of risk. In D. Lupton (ed.), *Risk and Sociocultural Theory: New Directions and Perspectives* (pp. 34–58). New York: Cambridge University Press.

Turner, B. A. (1991). The development of a safety culture. *Chemistry & Industry*, 241–3.

Turner, J. C. (1985). Social categorization and the self-concept: a social cognitive theory of group behaviour. In E. J. Lawler (ed.), *Advances in Group Processes: Theory and Research* (vol. II, pp. 77–122). Greenwich, CT: JAI Press.

(1991). *Social Influence*. Buckingham: Oxford University Press.

Turner, J. C. and Giles, H. (1981). *Intergroup Behaviour*. Oxford: Blackwell.

Turner, J. C., Wetherell, and Hogg, M. A. (1989). Referent informational influence and group polarisation. *British Journal of Social Psychology*, 28, 22, 135–47.

Turner, J. C., Hogg, M. A., Oakes, P. J., Reicher, S. D. and Wetherell, M. S. (1987). *Rediscovering the Social Group: A Self-Categorization Theory*. Oxford: Blackwell.

Tversky, A. and Kahneman, D. (1974). Judgement under uncertainty: heuristics and biases. *Science*, 185, 1124–31.

(1981). The framing of decisions and the psychology of choice. *Science*, 211, 453–8.

(1991). Loss aversion in riskless choice: a reference-dependent model. *Quarterly Journal of Economics*, 106, 1039–61.

Twigger-Ross, C. L. and Breakwell, G. M. (1999). Relating risk experience, venturesomeness and risk perception. *Journal of Risk Research*, 2, 73–83.

Tykocinski, O. E., Pick, D. and Kedmi, D. (2002). Retroactive pessimism: a different kind of hindsight bias. *European Journal of Social Psychology*, 32, 577–88.

Ulleberg, P. and Rundmo, T. (2003). Personality, attitudes and risk perception as predictors of risky driving behaviour among young drivers. *Safety Science*, 41, 427–43.

van der Pligt, J. (1992). *Nuclear Energy and the Public*. Oxford: Blackwell.

van der Pligt, J. and Richard, R. (1994). Changing adolescents' sexual behaviour: perceived risk, self-efficacy and anticipated regret. *Patient Education and Counseling*, 23, 187–96.

van der Velde, F. W., Hooykaas, C. and van der Pligt, J. (1992). Risk perception and behavior: pessimism, realism, and optimism about AIDS-related health behaviors. *Psychology and Health*, 6, 23–38.

Vaughan, E. and Seifert, M. (1992). Variability in the framing of risk issues. *Journal of Social Issues*, 48, 119–35.

Verplanken, B. (1989). Beliefs, attitudes, and intentions toward nuclear energy before and after Chernobyl in a longitudinal within-subjects design. *Environment and Behaviour*, 21, 371–92.

Vidmar, B. and Burdeny, T. C. (1971). Effects of group size and item type in the 'group shift' effect. *Canadian Journal of Behavioural Science*, 3, 393–407.

Viklund, M. J. (2003). Trust and risk perception in western Europe: a cross-national study. *Risk Analysis*, 23, 727–38.

Villejoubert, G. (2005). Could they have known better? *Applied Cognitive Psychology*, 19, 140–3.

Wåhlberg, A. (2001). The theoretical features of some current approaches to risk perception. *Journal of Risk Research*, 4, 237–50.

Walker, G., Simmons, P., Wynne, B. and Irwin, A. (1998). *Public Perception of Risks Associated with Major Accident Hazards*. Sudbury: Health and Safety Executive Books.

Wallach, M. A., Kogan, N. and Bem, D. J. (1962). Group influence on individual risk-taking. *Journal of Abnormal Social Psychology*, 65, 75–86.

(1964). Diffusion of responsbility and level of risk-taking in groups. *Journal of Abnormal Social Psychology*, 68, 263–74.

Walls, J., Pidgeon, N. F., Weyman, A. and Horlick-Jones, T. (2003). Critical trust: understanding lay perceptions of health and safety risk regulation. *Journal of Risk Research* (Report). Norwich: Centre for Environmental Risk. Published in *Health Risk and Society*, 6, 133–50.

Wallston, K. A. (2005). Overview of special issue on research with the multi-dimensional health locus of control scales. *Journal of Health Psychology*, 10, 619–21.

Weimann, G. (1991). The influentials – back to the concept of opinion leaders. *Public Opinion Quarterly*, 55, 267–79.

Weimann, G. and Brosius, H. B. (1994). Is there a two-step flow of agenda-setting. *International Journal of Public Opinion Research*, 6, 323–41.

Weinstein, N. D. (1980). Unrealistic optimism about future life events. *Journal of Personality and Social Psychology*, 39, 806–20.

(1982). Unrealistic optimism about susceptibility to health problems. *Journal of Behavioural Medicine*, 5, 4, 441–60.

(1984). 'Why it won't happen to me': perceptions of risk factors and suscept-ibility. *Health Psychology*, 3, 431–57.

(1987a). *Understanding and Encouraging Self-Protective Behaviour*. New York: Cambridge University Press.

(1987b). Unrealistic optimism about susceptibility to health problems: con-clusions from a community-wide sample. *Journal of Behavioural Medicine*, 10, 481–500.

(1989). Optimistic biases about personal risks. *Science*, 246, 1232–3.

Weinstein, N. D. and Lyon, J. (1999). Mindset, optimistic bias about personal risk and health-protective behavior. *Bristish Journal of Health Psychology*, 4, 289–300.

Weinstein, N. D., Sandman, P. M. and Roberts, N. E. (1991). Perceived suscept-ibility and self-protective behaviour. *Health Psychology*, 10, 25–33.

Weinstein, N. D., Rothman, A. J. and Nicholich, K. (1998). Use of correlational data to examine the effects of risk perceptions on precautionary behaviour. *Psychology and Health*, 13, 3, 479–86.

Weinstein, N. D., Lyon, J. E., Rothman, A. J. and Cuite, C. L. (2000). Preoccupation and affect as predictors of protective action following natural disaster. *British Journal of Health Psychology*, 5, 351–63.

Wernstedt, K. and Hersh, R. (1998). Through a lens darkly: Superfund specta-cles on public participation at brownfields sites. *Risk: Health, Safety & Environment*, 9, 153–73.

Wessely, S. (2002). The Gulf War and its aftermath. In J. G. Cwikel and J. M. Havenaar (eds), *Toxic Turmoil: Psychological and Societal Consequences of Ecological Disasters* (pp. 101–27)). New York: Kluwer Academic/Pleanum Publishers.

Wetherell, M. S. (1987). Social identity and group polarization. In J. C. Turner, M. A. Hogg, P. J. Oakes, S. D. Reicher and M. S. Wetherell (eds), *Rediscovering the Social Group: A Self-Categorization Theory* (pp. 142–70). Oxford: Blackwell.

Whalen, C. K., Henker, B., King, P. S., Jamner, L. D. and Levine, L. (2004). Adolescents react to the events of September 11, 2001: focused versus ambient impact. *Journal of Abnormal Child Psychology*, 32, 1–11.

Whalen, C. K., Henker, B., O'Neil, R., Hollingshead, J., Holman, A. and Moore, B. (1994). Optimism in children's judgment of health and environmental risks. *Health Psychology*, 13, 319–25.

White, M. P. and Eiser, J. R. (2005). Information specificity and hazard risk potential as moderators of trust asymmetry. *Risk Analysis*, 25, 5, 1187–98.

White, M. P., Eiser, J. R. and Harris, P. R. (2004). Risk perceptions of mobile phone use while driving. *Risk Analysis*, 24, 323–34.

Wiegman, O. and Gutteling, J. M. (1995). Risk appraisal and risk communication: some empirical data from the Netherlands reviewed. *Basic and Applied Social Psychology*, 16, 227–49.

Wiener, J. B. and Rogers, M. D. (2002). Comparing precaution in the United States and Europe. *Journal of Risk Research*, 5, 317–49.

Wildavsky, A. (1993). The comparative study of risk perception: a beginning. In Bayerisohe Rnck (ed.), *Risk is a Construct* (pp. 89–94). Munich: Knesebeck.

Williams, J. C. (1988). A data-based method for assessing and reducing human error to improve operational performance. Paper presented to the Institute of Electrical and Electronic Engineers Fourth Conference on Human Factors and Power Plants, New York, pp. 436–50.

Williams, P. R. D. and Hammitt, J. K. (2001). Perceived risks of conventional and organic produce: pesticides, pathogens, and natural toxins. *Risk Analysis*, 21, 319–30.

Williams, S., Zainuba, M. and Jackson, R. (2003). Affective influences on risk perceptions and risk intention. *Journal of Managerial Psychology*, 18, 126–37.

Willis, H. H., DeKay, M. L., Granger Morgan, M., Florig, H. K. and Fischbeck, P. S. (2004). Ecological risk ranking: development and evaluation of a method for improving public participation in environmental decision making. *Risk Analysis*, 24, 363–78.

Wilson, D. K., Kaplan, R. M. and Schneiderman, L. J. (1987). Framing of decisions and selections of alternatives in healthcare. *Social Behaviour*, 2, 51–9.

Wilson, D. K., Purdon, S. E. and Wallston, K. A. (1988). Compliance to health recommendations: a theoretical overview of message framing. *Health Education Research*, 3, 161–71.

Wilson, K., Leonard, B., Wright, R., Graham, I., Moffet, J., Pluscauskas, M. *et al.* (2006). Application of the precautionary principle by senior policy officials: results of a Canadian survey. *Risk Analysis*, 26, 981–8.

Witte, K. (1992). Putting the fear back into fear appeals: the extended parallel process model. *Communication Monographs*, 59, 329–49.

Wong, N. D. and Reading, A. E. (1989). Personality correlates of type a behaviour. *Personality and Individual Differences*, 10, 991–6.

Wright, G., Bolger, F. and Rowe, G. (2002). An empirical test of the relative validity of expert and lay judgments of risk. *Risk Analysis*, 22, 1107–22.

Wright, G., Pearman, A. and Yardley, K. (2000). Risk perception in the UK oil and gas production industry: are expert loss-prevention managers' perceptions different from those of members of the public. *Risk Analysis*, 20, 681–90.

Wynne, B. (1989). Sheepfarming after Chernobyl. *Environment*, 31, 11–39.

Xie, X., Wang, M. and Xu, L. (2003). What risks are Chinese people concerned about? *Risk Analysis*, 23, 685–95.

Yamamoto, A. (2004). The effects of mass media reports on risk perception and images of victims: an explorative study. *Japanese Journal of Experimental Social Psychology*, 20, 152–64.

Yin, J. (1999). Elite opinion and media diffusion – exploring environmental attitudes. *Harvard International Journal of Press-Politics*, 4, 62–86.

Zajonc, R. B. (1980). Feeling and thinking: preferences need no inferences. *American Psychologist*, 35, 151–75.

Zeelenberg, M. (1999). Anticipated regret, expected feedback and behavioural decision making. *Journal of Behavioural Decision Making*, 12, 93–106.

Zeelenberg, M. and Beattie, J. (1997). Consequences of regret aversion 2: additional evidence for effects of feedback on decision making. *Organizational Behaviour and Human Decision Processes*, 72, 63–78.

Zhu, J. H., Watt, J. H., Snyder, L. B., Yan, J. T. and Jiang, Y. S. (1993). Public issue priority formation – media agenda-setting and social-interaction. *Journal of Communication*, 43, 8–29.

Zohar, D. (1980). Safety climate in industrial organizations: theoretical and applied implications. *Journal of Applied Psychology*, 65, 96–102.

Zuckerman, M. (1979). *Sensation Seeking: Beyond the Optimal Level of Arousal.* Hillsdale, NJ: Lawrence Erlbaum.

(1987). Is sensation seeking a predisposing trait for alcoholism? In E. Gotheil, K. A. Druley, S. Pashkey and S. P. Weinstein (eds), *Stress and Addiction* (pp. 283–301). New York: Brunder/Mazel.

(1992). What is a basic factor and which factors are basic? Turtles all the way down. *Personality and Individual Factors*, 13, 675–81.

(1996). The psychobiological model for impulsive unsocialized sensation seeking: a comparative approach. *Neuropsychobiology*, 34, 125–9.

(2002). Zuckerman Kuhlman personality questionnaire (ZKPQ): an alternative five-factorial model. In B. de Read and M. Perugini (eds), *Big Five Assessment*, (pp. 376–92). Göhingen: Hogrefe Verlagsgruppe.

(2003). Biological bases of personality. *Handbook of Psychology: Personality and Social Psychology*, 5, 85–116.

(2004). The shaping of personality: genes, environments, and chance encounters. *Journal of Personality Assessment*, 82, 11–22.

(2005a). *Psychobiology of Personality.* New York: Cambridge University Press, 2nd edition.

(2005b). Faites vos jeux à nouveau: still another look at sensation seeking and pathological gambling. *Personality and Individual Differences*, 39, 361–5.

Zuckerman, M. and Kuhlman, D. M. (2000). Personality and risk-taking: common biosocial factors. *Journal of Personality*, 65, 96–102.

Zuckerman, M., Ball, S. and Black, J. (1990). Influences of sensation seeking, gender, risk appraisal and situational motivation on smoking. *Addictive Behaviours*, 15, 209–20.

Zuckerman, M., Tushup, R. and Finner, S. (1976). Sexual attitudes and experience: attitude and personality correlates and changes produced by a course in sexuality. *Journal of Consulting and Clinical Psychology*, 44, 7–19.

Zuckerman, M., Khulman, D. M., Thornquist, M. and Kiers, H. (1991). Five (or three) robust questionnaire scale factors of personality without culture. *Personality and Individual Differences*, 12, 929–41.

Index

Abric, J. C. 256
absentmindedness 175
acceptability
    and benefit 35–6, 37, 207
    comparison of risks 37–40
    and emotional gain 114, 115
    and hazard characteristics 29, 37
    measures of 25
    personal and societal 140
    and risk perception 35–41
    and trust 140, 143, 144, 220
accidents
    data processing difficulties in low-
        probability 183
    industry plants with low rates 208,
        209 (Box 8.2)
    and passive hazards 181
    and safety culture 208
    waiting to happen 174, 215
accidents (major) 184–90
    and emergencies 190
    global effects 4
    local effects 185–7
    model of aetiology of 176–9
    'near misses' 217
    nuclear industry 176, 177–9 (Box 7.1),
        184–90, 239
    psychological consequencies of 185, 192,
        193, 195, 271
    public inquiries after 207
    ripple effects 205
    and social representation of hazard types
        189, 195
accountability, in risk society 4
activity (personality factor) 49 (Box 3.2)
adjustment see anchoring heuristic
affect
    and cognition in psychology 128,
        269, 273
    in decision-making 111, 128
    manipulation of impact of 113
    and risk 109–18, 266

in risk communication 172
in risk-taking 51
affect heuristic 109–15, 220
affectivity, positive and negative 116
age, and risk perception 66
agency, and self-efficacy beliefs 54 (Box 3.3)
aggression-hostility 49 (Box 3.2)
agreeableness 49 (Box 3.2)
Ahern, J. 193
Ahmed, E. 102
Albery, I. P. 85
alcohol 29, 30, 51
Alhakami, A. S. 36, 112
anchoring 254, 255, 259, 263, 272
anchoring heuristic 28 (Box 2.5), 81, 82, 268
Anderson, C. 77
anger
    and fear 123–4, 188
    and optimism 123
    and outrage 125
Ansell, J. 18, 21
anti-social behaviour, in emergency
    situations 193
anticipated regret 121–3
anxiety 48, 49 (Box 3.2)
    enduring and transitional 52
    in risk communication 132 (Box 6.1),
        155 (Box 6.3), 188
    and risk evaluation 52, 114, 116
    and risk perception 52, 77
    self-efficacy and locus of control 53
apathy 5
Arkes, H. R. 91
Aronson, E. 139
assimilation, of social representations 259
assumptions
    in assessing paradigms 42
    based on death as worst possible
        consequence 24
    expert as applied to a new hazard 98
    simplifying in complex system analysis 19
at risk populations, cultural value systems 126

314